"A thorough and detailed guide to using Final C. those boring textbook-style manuals that puts you to sleep. With everything from basic editing to color correction for film, this comprehensive and user-friendly guide for digital editors/filmmakers of all levels covers every aspect of the editing process from beginning to end, and will inform and please both advanced 'geeks' and newbies."

— Marie Jones, AbsoluteWrite.com book reviewer

"*Digital Editing* wisely combines a base of practical FCP usage with a dash of aesthetics and project management tips. Finished off with a pinch of humor, this book makes for an easy read of a topic that can easily be made tedious and over-complicated. Kudos to the authors for coming up with a highly useful guide suitable for a novice, yet still containing new tidbits for the experts."

— Vicki Parks, Film Ireland

"An excellent guidebook to the functions and features of Final Cut Pro 4, and a perfect primer for anyone who's ever been intimidated by the complexity and power of Apple's superb digital editing suite. I give it a strong "buy" recommendation."

— Patrick Beltran, www.absolutewrite.com

"This new book covers the complexities of video editing far better than any of the other books out there! His explanations do not assume that the reader is fully versed in editing; he covers the BASICS as well as the advanced aspects of FCP. It's refreshing to find a textbook that does not require a second textbook to explain itself!"

— Fred Ginsburg, Equipment Emporium Inc

"It is nice to see a book about Final Cut Pro that was written through the editor's point of view. It teaches the software within the framework of the editing process. The writing is clear and conversational and the examples address important issues in editing. The book is a great tool for the classroom environment."

— Enie Vaisburd, Faculty, Northwest Film Center, Portland, Oregon

Digital Editing

with FINAL CUT PRO 4

Professional Post-Production Technique

BRUCE MAMER

WITH

JASON WALLACE

COMPATIBLE WITH FINAL CUT PRO HD

Published by Michael Wiese Productions,
11288 Ventura Boulevard,
Suite #621
Studio City, CA 91604
(818) 379-8799, (818) 986-3408 (FAX).
mw@mwp.com
www.mwp.com

Cover design: Objects of Design
Interior design: William Morosi
Printed by: McNaughton & Gunn
Manufactured in the United States of America

Library of Congress Cataloging-in-Publication Data

Mamer, Bruce.
    Digital editing with Final Cut Pro 4.0 : professional post-production
technique / Bruce Mamer and Jason Wallace.
        p. cm.
    Includes bibliographical references.
    ISBN 0-941188-91-4
    1. Motion pictures--Editing--Data processing. 2. Digital
video--Editing--Data processing. 3. Video tapes--Editing--Data
processing. 4. Final cut (Electronic resource) I. Wallace, Jason,
1969- II. Title.
    TR899.M264 2004
    778.59'3'0285536--dc22

                                                    2004004447

To my parents, Donna and Stuart Mamer, and all the great students with whom I have had the pleasure of sharing a classroom over the last twenty years.

Bruce

To my mother Georgie, my first teacher and the person who provided me with everything I needed to succeed: creativity.

Jason

SYSTEM REQUIREMENTS

The DVD included in this package contains both visual tutorials based on written material and rough footage of a scene for the reader to follow along and edit.

— Playing the three visual tutorials on either Mac or PC requires Quicktime 6 or above and a DVD drive. Access to all written documentation on the DVD will require either Adobe Reader (Version 6 or above) or Apple's Preview software, the latter provided with all Macs with OS X.

— If your computer does not have Quicktime or Reader, you can get a free download of the most recent version of Quicktime at www.apple.com and Reader at www.Adobe.com.

— System requirements for importing and cutting tutorial materials: Macintosh G4 or G5 processor, Final Cut Pro 4, OS X, 5 gigabytes hard drive space.

— All questions about installing or using tutorials and materials can be answered at **www.digitaleditingFCP.com**.

The information in this book is compatible with Apple's recent upgrade to Final Cut Pro HD. See page 316 for a note on FCP HD and the website for further updates.

CONTENTS

SYSTEM REQUIREMENTS vi

ACKNOWLEDGMENTS xii

INTRODUCTION xv

CHAPTER I — GETTING STARTED 1

HISTORY 2
THE PROCESS 4
    The Digital Interface 9
    Launching the Program 10
    Copying the Tutorial 13
SOME MAC THINGS 14
ISSUES, CONCEPTS, AND DISTINCTIONS 17
    Mini TOC 17
    General Issues You Need to Understand (G) 18
    Reference Issues (R) 28
    Final Cut Pro–Specific Issues (FCP) 31
THE SOFTWARE MENUS 32

CHAPTER II — THE PROCESS 39

STAGES 39
    Rough Cut 40
    Working Methods 42
    Fine Cut 44
THE EDITOR 45
    The Video Editor 46
THE TUTORIAL 48
    How to Use the DVD Tutorial 48
    Read the Script 50
    The Rough Footage 51
    Notes on the Tutorial 52

PAPERWORK   **53**
   The Lined Script   **54**
   Camera Reports   **56**

CHAPTER III — THE DESKTOP   **59**

THREE (OR FOUR) WAYS TO DO EVERYTHING   **59**
THE WINDOWS   **62**
   Scrubber Bars and the Playhead   **63**
   The Browser   **64**
   The Viewer   **66**
   The Canvas   **74**
   The Timeline   **78**

CHAPTER IV — THE DESKTOP: TOOLS AND TRICKS   **85**

THE TOOL PALETTE   **85**
THE AUDIO METERS   **90**
TRICKS   **92**
   Moving Around in the Timeline and Clips   **92**
   Trimming Clips   **93**
   Drawing Clips Up   **96**
   Fixing Sync   **97**
   Creating New Tracks   **98**
   Keyboard   **99**
   Reconnecting Media   **100**
   Fit to Window, Wireframe, and Missing Tools **102**
   Remember...   **102**

CHAPTER V — EDITING   **103**

STRAIGHT CUTS   **104**
MOS INSERTS   **112**
A (NOT SO) RADICAL APPROACH TO AUDIO   **114**
BOUNCING TRACKS   **118**
SAVING   **120**

CHAPTER VI — ADVANCED CUTTING   **121**

OVERLAPPING CUTS   **121**
TRACK CONFIGURATIONS   **123**

CHAPTER VII — TITLING, COMMON EFFECTS, AND RENDERING   **129**

CREATING TITLES   **129**

RENDERING **139**
COMMON EFFECTS **141**
  Drag, Drop, and Render **142**
SUPERIMPOSITION/LAYERING VIDEO **147**
  Composite Mode **149**
  Supering Titles **150**

CHAPTER VIII — AUDIO DESIGN **153**

BUILDING AUDIO IN FINAL CUT PRO **154**
  Adding Sound Effects **155**
  Repositioning Sound Effects **157**
  Volume Control **160**
  Replacing Dialogue **162**
  Completing AB Rolling **164**
  Effects and Music **165**

CHAPTER IX — STARTING YOUR OWN PROJECT **167**

FORMATS **167**
  Analog Formats **170**
  Digital Formats **172**
HARDWARE AND SOFTWARE **175**
PRESETS AND PREFERENCES **176**
  Easy Setup **178**
  Audio/Video Settings **179**
  User Preferences **182**
  System Settings **186**
  Sequence>Settings **188**
  Menu Preferences **190**

CHAPTER X — THE CAPTURE PROCESS **193**

LOG AND CAPTURE **194**
  Logging **200**
  Capturing **202**
AUDIO CAPTURE **204**
  Subclips **206**
SYNCING UP **207**
LINKING **209**

CHAPTER XI — WORKFLOW **211**

FILE MANAGEMENT **212**
STORAGE AND RUNTIME LIMITATIONS **212**

EDIT DECISION LISTS **213**
THE BIG FOUR **214**
Shoot on Video, Edit on Video, Finish on Video **214**
Shoot on Film, Edit on Video, Finish on Video **215**
Shoot on Film, Edit on Video, Finish on Film **219**
Shoot on Video, Edit on Video, Finish on Film **220**
FRAME RATE BLESSINGS OR BLUES **221**
BACKUP **222**
GRAPHICS AND COMPOSITING WORKFLOW **223**
Titles/Overlays **224**
CGI **225**
Compositing **226**

CHAPTER XII — SPECIAL EFFECTS **227**
IMAGE MANIPULATION **228**
The Video Filters Menu **228**
The Wireframe **229**
Crop/Distort Tools **232**
Slow Motion/Fast Motion **232**
Freeze Frames **234**
THE MOTION TAB **234**
COMPOSITING **238**

CHAPTER XIII — FINISHING IN FINAL CUT PRO **243**
AUDIO **243**
The Mixer **243**
Using Handles **245**
Filling Ambience Holes **245**
Signal Processing **246**
Final Mix **249**
THE COLORIST **249**
The Video Scopes **252**
COLOR CORRECTION **254**
Black and White **255**
PRINT TO VIDEO **258**

CHAPTER XIV — FILM MATCHBACK **259**
WHY FILM? **262**
THE MATCHBACK PROCESS **265**
THE FILM PROCESS **266**
Formats **268**

Cutting Sound and Image   **269**
FINISHING   **271**
   Mix   **272**
   Negative Cutting   **273**
   The Answer Print   **275**
   Critical Concerns   **276**
THE VIDEOTAPE   **278**
THE TRANSFER INTERFACE   **278**
   3:2 Pulldown   **279**
   Pullup and Pulldown   **281**
   Reverse Telecine   **282**
   How the Feature World Is Doing Matchback   **283**
   Our Approach with *WT*   **285**

CHAPTER XV — CINEMA TOOLS   287

FLEX FILES   **288**
THE PROCESS   **289**
   Using Cinema Tools Without a Flex File   **294**
   Reverse Telecine   **297**
   To 23.98 or to 24   **297**

CHAPTER XVI — FINISHING/ BEYOND FCP   299

OPEN MEDIA FRAMEWORK   **300**
   Making Start Marks   **302**
   Creating the OMF File   **303**
   The Session   **304**
   Effects   **307**
CUTTING THE WORKPRINT AND NEGATIVE   **308**
THE ONLINE EDIT   **313**

CONCLUSION   315

A NOTE ON FINAL CUT PRO HD   **316**

GLOSSARY   317

INDEX   323

ACKNOWLEDGMENTS

By its nature, a book like this has to include the talents of many different people. Like the process of editing itself, understanding and working effectively in Final Cut Pro, particularly when interfacing with film, requires a network of people to trade knowledge and tips about the program, as well as a battery of professionals to do all the work that must be out-sourced.

The authors would particularly like to thank the cast and crew of *Waiting Tables* for their generous participation. Credits are found on the DVD, but special appreciation goes to Freya Rae Schirmacher for script and performance and to cinematographer Matt Ehling and gaffer Ramy Selim for their extensive visual contributions. Sound person C. Andrew Mayer and jack-of-all-everything Chaucey Dunn also brought their inestimable skills to the venture.

The authors are also indebted to all the people who made technical contributions to the tutorial in postproduction. We would like to thank the folks at Hi-Wire Tech and particularly the telecine crew — Oscar Oboza, senior colorist, and Andrew Carranza. I would also like to thank Heidi Stokes and Phil Aaron of Aaron-Stokes Music & Sound for allowing us to do the audio finish at their facilities. Particular thanks go to Darin Heinis of Aaron-Stokes both for his mixing skills and for sharing his knowledge of the current situation in postproduction audio. Darin's assistant, Jason Almendinger, was also a great help . In terms of audio, Dennis O'Rourke of CineSound II provided most of the audio elements of the conventional film interface for the tutorial, besides being an invaluable and essential resource for information for many, many years.

Our particular thanks go to the people at Michael Wiese Productions — to Ken Lee for his enthusiasm, and Michael himself for seeing the need in the marketplace for just such a book. Thanks for your commitment. And for Michael, our fathers approve. Thanks also go to copyeditor Paul Norlen for his fine work and unflagging attention to detail, as well as to Bill Morosi for his excellent design.

FROM JASON

First and foremost I would like to thank Bruce Mamer. Bruce is the only film production instructor I have ever had or needed. The biggest lesson he taught is that while planning is important, never let it keep you from sitting down and actually accomplishing the project itself. Thank you for your trust and belief in me and for pushing me to get it done.

Thanks also to the folks who helped make the DVD content possible. To producer Sonya Tormoen for the hours invested in sitting through the first drafts of the tutorials and making usability suggestions…trust me, your frustration paid off. A number of other people have read parts of the manuscript and test-driven the DVD and we are particularly thankful to Robert Seabold, Matt Giovinetti, and Alex Murrill for the insights, comments, and catches. To compositing guru Andrew Hill, thanks for the all-night compression tests and audio checks. You truly are a man of many talents. To Shari Singerhouse at HDMG Post, thanks for teaching me the importance of communication in the postproduction process. Your input has been invaluable.

Thanks to Victoria Lauing at MCTC Continuing Ed for encouraging me to develop an editing course of study that tutored students with the widest range of skill levels. You showed me what fun teaching can be. And to all of the students I've had over the last four years, thanks for editing yourself into seemingly impossible corners; you pushed me to understand Final Cut Pro far beyond what I ever thought possible.

And on a personal note, thanks to my family for giving their unconditional love and support. To my dad, Vernon, for giving me an unstoppable work ethic. To my grandmother Viola for passing on her love of the written word, my sister Billie for demonstrating that you actually can be anything you want in life, my brother Rory for showing me that if you love it, work is its own reward, and my sister Erin for showing me there is no problem a little creativity cannot solve.

And finally to Courteney for supporting how important this work is to me, and for making me celebrate the little accomplishments along the way. You've added years to my life.

FROM BRUCE

First, and foremost, I would like to thank my partner in crime, Jason Wallace, for his many months of steadfastness in the face of relentless questioning. As with all true collaborations, this book would not have been possible without his participation. Collaborations can frequently be very stressful, but we have had a lot of fun along the way.

A lot of people have helped along the way. Dan Geiger has been a huge resource in walking through the wilderness of film matchback for the independent. Systems are in place in the industry to make this process easier, but for the independent it is often like re-inventing the wheel. Dan has been a big help.

This project was initiated during a one-year sabbatical from my teaching responsibilities at Minneapolis College. My thanks to the faculty and staff in the Film/Video department and Dean Mike McGee and President Phil Davis for their support of this project. It would not have been possible without this much-needed time.

In Los Angeles, a number of people have given valuable information and support. I give the warmest thanks to Anna and Blake Rizk for their generous hospitality and their insights into the industry. Chris Weaver has been a great source and friend in helping with contacts in the industry and many aspects of this project. Brian Crewe has also kept me abreast of many trends in the editing and production world. Benno Nelson has also been an invaluable resource and a great supporter as a daily user of Final Cut Pro.

I would particularly like to thank the producers and editorial staff of *NYPD Blue* (Steven Bochco Productions) for very graciously allowing me to be a fly on the wall during postproduction of a number of episodes. I am especially appreciative of the time and attention given to me by to Han Van Doornewaard, Etienne DesLaurier, and Supervising Editor Farrell Levy. Particular thanks go to Travis Sittard for walking me through the steps and making it all happen.

And, of course, to my family, nuclear and otherwise, all of whom put up with that guy who sits in the corner and taps on a Powerbook all day long.

INTRODUCTION

After the lengthy evolution of very expensive nonlinear video editing (NLE) systems in the 1980s and '90s, Final Cut Pro (FCP) has been a breakthrough product in allowing the average individual access to high-quality editing solutions. In 1994, Sony, Panasonic, and a bunch of other companies got together to devise standards and blueprint equipment for new **Digital Video (DV)** systems — systems for which FCP would eventually play a role. These are in all respects truly extraordinary technologies, albeit based on existing high-end technology already in use in the professional world. The creation of the **Mini-DV** format, and its brethren, is one of the marvels of the computer age. It was virtually unthinkable only 25 years ago that an individual would (1) have a small sync sound camera for shooting; (2) interface that camera with a computer; (3) transfer all the media onto that computer; (4) edit footage to one's heart's content; and (5) send a finished product back out to tape in the camera. And the few who did envision it are now probably deservedly rich. The rest of us ordinary folks just get the pleasure of working with it.

So, we have to start with the hype. The power to make and distribute movies is now within the grasp of almost any individual. With revolutionary new low-price cameras and editing systems like Final Cut Pro, anyone with a few thousand dollars or some type of access can create a movie. Wrenched from the hands of the rich and powerful, the medium will now truly become the democratic art form for which it has always, although in a flawed way, been hailed.

Okay, the hype has started to pale a little. Final Cut Pro is not a panacea. It is an excellent product that will allow you to do a very important job at an incredible price. FCP was an almost immediate success with independent and student filmmakers. That promise remains. However, the way movies are distributed and shown has changed little over the last ten years, and while a few breakthrough independent movies have made the grade, it remains enormously difficult for an independent artist to reach a mass audience. More troubling, the Digital Revolution, as it was so loudly touted, generated a lot of new work that, frankly, ranged from vaguely engaging to downright bad — with the majority tending toward the latter.

It is not enough just to have a camera and go shoot something. First, you need to know how to craft a quality script. Robert McKee, the great screenwriting instructor, has wisely observed that because there is so much empty space on a page — because you do not have to fill the page up with so many words — screenwriting looks easy to the outsider. It isn't. It requires understanding how a script is structured, how to make a film a visual experience rather than a written one, how to craft scenes so they accomplish specific goals, and a host of other things. Beyond the script, novice directors need to learn how to choose all resources wisely, shape scenes with pace and clarity, work with actors to get exceptional performances, and deal with the many, many issues that make film shoots appear to be only marginally controlled events. While aspiring young makers will come down on all sides of the spectrum on the subject of big-budget filmmaking, Hollywood's ability to craft efficient and appealing stories is unparalleled and the independent world needs to understand the fundamentals — the rules of the road as it were. While people may want to work outside of the Hollywood tradition, there are lessons to be learned.

The question now is whether this new accessibility is a good thing. The answer, of course, has to be yes. But just because people have access does not mean that they are making great movies. What people outside of the industry are finding out is what people on the inside have been saying all along. Making movies is hard work and making great movies is damn near impossibly hard work.

Final Cut Pro is truly a marvel, but it is only as good as you are. When Final Cut Pro was introduced, it was justly hailed as *the* piece of software that would allow independent filmmakers to produce quality projects on miniscule budgets. What is clearly called for now is for film and video makers to create work that is held to progressively higher standards. With the increasing sophistication of upgrades as well as the inclusion of Cinema Tools in version 4.0, Final Cut Pro has further positioned itself for extensive use in the professional world as well. Its acceptance within the pro world is increasing although its main competitor, Avid, still holds dominance. As FCP is used more, independent and student contact with the pro world will increasingly raise the bar for the quality of work.

I come to this endeavor with a background in motion picture film. For those of us trained in the old film days. it is absolutely stunning what FCP is capable of doing. I remember walking into my first professional audio mixing studio in the early '80s and being intimidated by the bank of playback machines, the massive mixing board, and the complex hardware to interlock the film projector. And this was a reasonably small, regional studio — not the facilities at LucasFilms or GlenGlen Sound. Now that entire studio almost fits in my laptop. But just because FCP has the capabilities to do so much does not mean that you have all the proficiencies to execute projects at the highest quality. Just because you *can* do it, does not mean you can do it, as it were. A major premise — a thread — that will run throughout this text is that film/video is a specialists' field, and involving creative and experienced professionals will bring your project to a higher level. For so many of the tasks you will face, there are many proprietary professionals who do that specific task for a living. Learning how to find the right people and work with them intelligently is the goal of every person who wants to produce better and better work, whether as a living-on-a-shoestring independent or as a flush commercial producer.

I still love film and hope (and firmly believe) that it will stay with us for a long time. FCP and its software brethren are wonderful things. People who never had access to the complexities of film editing, could not breach the expense of early NLE systems, or put up with the clumsiness of analog video editing can now practice the editing craft at will. And practice — experience — is critical to becoming thoughtful and resourceful editors. Students who are computer savvy will look at film editing compared with NLE editing and wonder why anyone would ever choose the prehistoric monster that is the conventional film edit. FCP is reasonably easy, reasonably fast, and immensely gratifying in the creation of what can be accepted by many as a final product. But, at the end of the day, what you have is a video. Your final product is on videotape or DVD. As such, there are limits to what you can do with it. Film is still the medium of choice for many applications, particularly exhibition, and its inclusion may stretch your budget as well as the concepts and technologies you need to know.

As a teacher, I still teach conventional film editing. I think it is an excellent discipline for beginners to touch and manipulate those little strips of celluloid, to struggle to maintain synchronization with sound, and to walk through the demanding finishing processes. But in the professional world, the need to know film editing has been reduced to the occasional noble holdout and the specialized, but very important, world of film matchback. This book will take two paths. We will teach you FCP as a cutting system exclusive of these other concerns, but also talk in later chapters about potential interface with film. There is nothing about the inclusion of film in the mix that guarantees a higher quality product, but it certainly raises the ante. Be aware that matchback is very complicated and requires careful scrutiny by all postproduction personnel. If you are the type who likes to jump in feet first and solve problems as you go, be prepared to part with a lot of money to correct your many mistakes.

As suggested, there is nothing inherent in film that guarantees better results. And there is certainly nothing in video that guarantees lesser results. Film may be beyond the budgetary limitations of many readers, so video will be the starting point for many. (Low-budget video to boot.) So we will work from twin realities. We want you to execute everything at as high a level as possible — involving professionals and postproduction facilities as much as possible — but we realize that you may be doing a lot of the hard job of editing on your own.

A couple of general notes about our approach:

— It is not the goal of this text to go through absolutely every one of FCP's features. Even Apple's three-volume manual does not do this. We will be going through the salient features needed to cut a complex project. We will talk about issues like how to trim shots, but FCP has so many ways to do everything that you can even cut just by using the time code numbers. We will not go that far, but will cover all of the features that you are liable to use.

— With the inclusion of a film component, this text necessarily has a bias toward film-style cutting — the old-fashioned stacking of shots end to end to build scenes and sequences. A text more biased toward the music video and commercial worlds may use extensive layers of video, with numerous examples of compositing and Computer Generated Images (CGI). We will give general information on these, but trying to do too many things would water down the main thrust of this book. In a certain way, FCP is designed with the music video editor in mind. However, as it becomes increasingly versatile and gains wider acceptance, it will be used for more and more varied projects.

— At times we will sound like scolds. At a certain level, FCP is very simple. But the more ambitious the project, the more you need to have complete control over everything you are doing. The old system of film was cumbersome but virtually bulletproof. The digital world and computers are far from bulletproof and you need to fully understand all options before embarking on editing a project. Whatever your approach, it takes scrupulous preparation and execution — it takes following a point-by-point process — to accomplish complex goals. In certain ways it is a harder world, but it is in many ways a better world for the lonely editor.

— I am not a computer guru. I do not have the extensive computer savvy that many practitioners do. My colleague in this endeavor, Jason Wallace, does and he is largely responsible for that element. However, neither he nor I really consider this to be a computer book. It is a film and video editing book, with the computer being the means to that end. There will be plenty on the ins and outs of the program, but hopefully within the larger notion of creating a media project as opposed to just operating computer software.

— The video tradition has grown up in the shadow, and sometimes a bitter shadow, of the film world, creating traditions and approaches of its own. Sometimes the language is different just to create a different identity from the sometimes oppressive film presence. For example, film editors call what they are editing shots, while NLE editors call them clips. We will try to be consistent in usage, but a few odd film terms may pop in.

— All the references in the popular media to "digital film" and "digital filmmaking" have made it necessary to define terms. When we use the term film in this text, we mean motion picture film, with the image on a celluloid medium that can be projected on a screen. When we say video, we mean an electronically recorded signal, be it analog or digital, which can be shown on a monitor. Do not confuse the two. I will have parents proudly tell me that their little geniuses made a film in high school (or junior high). I will comment on what an amazing thing that is: an actual movie created in K-12. Well, not exactly, of course. They actually made a video. That can be a great thing and I have seen some wonderful projects, but a movie is a movie is a movie. At a certain level, the technology to create a video is so simple that any idiot can produce one. Maybe not a good one, but.... To produce video at a high level, however, does require extensive knowledge. Film, even at a basic level, is a much more demanding medium. Nothing is automatic and it takes some learning and thinking and planning to make even a bad movie.

The introduction of Final Cut Pro and other low-cost nonlinear editing systems has indeed changed many things. It has brought the experience of high-level editing, which had only just recently made it out of the back-rooms of Hollywood for use by the intrepid voyagers into the worlds of independent film/video and cable access, to a wider group of people than ever imagined. As a teacher, my students frequently come in with a level of experience unimagined even ten years ago. This, however, can be a double-edged sword. Demonstrating the talent and experience it takes to be an excellent editor requires a depth and richness of understanding of how moving images combine. The hard-won ability to manipulate clips and timelines effortlessly is important, but only a starting point.

GETTING STARTED

I t is the express goal of this text to get the reader into Final Cut Pro and actually cutting as quickly as possible. Too many books on this subject spend inordinate time on throat-clearing — presets, protocols, digitizing, and the like. Apple's own FCP manuals devote the entire first 500-page volume to setup, with actual software description coming in the second 600-page volume (there are three altogether). That we start with editing is not to suggest that setup is not important. Once you start to work on your own complex projects, you will see that initial decisions are so important that failure to address critical issues may derail all your work somewhere down the line. But getting some editing under the belt informs your understanding of what has to happen in the early stages.

We want, therefore, to get you into the process and to the practical goal of editing — getting shots into the timeline and trimming them down (not necessarily in that order). Editing, of course, is much more than putting shots together. It is giving shape and pace to the scenes. It is discovering the center and the purpose of a scene and cutting to get to the heart of it. Editing is an art, and to create a project that has vitality and is engaging, what you (the editor) do must be "artful." While the aesthetic dimension will be part of the discussion, there needs to be a basic starting point — like how do things work — before you can get to the weightier issues of what it is we are really trying to accomplish when we are editing a piece.

All this does not mean, however, that we can jump right into FCP head first without checking the depth of the water. FCP is a complicated program and requires that you understand how things can be accomplished and the pitfalls to be avoided. At a certain level, FCP is very simple. But the more ambitious the project, the more you need to have complete control over what you are doing. We will thus provide systematic coverage of the basics of the program, but be aware that it is a challenging program to master. Many people are attracted to computer editing because it looks, and has been sold by some as being, easy. It is not easy. To a certain extent, it is just that there are so many steps to remember, so many different things that have to be done in just the right order. Until you get a handle on it, it can be very frustrating. And that goes for the whole process of making a film or video project. It takes talent and drive and a willingness to not accept easy answers. Mediamaking is many things, but easy is not one of them.

So, after saying we are going to get right to it, we are going to put four meaty chapters in your way. It is stuff we just need to go through before you have a meaningful starting point. A little background first.

HISTORY

The path to this bright new shiny world started in the late 1960s. The development of portable video gear and the later introduction of reasonably accessible analog editing systems brought video, which had previously been only a studio- and broadcast-based medium, to the mid-level production company, the cable access junkie, and the reasonably savvy independent.

But the editing was cumbersome. There are arguments about whether to call motion picture editing nonlinear or just nonlinear-like, but analog video editing was as analog as analog could be. You stacked shots up one after another on the tape and, while you could go in and substitute other material of the same length, you could not go back and shorten or lengthen shots. The ability to trim shots is at the heart of effective editing, at least in narratives and projects of any complexity. Then there were questions of how to build complex audio tracks. Analog editing was fine for TV stations (who are just going to throw stuff up on their news broadcast), industrials (who seem not to mind boring their often captive viewers to death anyway), and commercials (with spots short enough that they could easily be re-edited). But for more ambitious projects, the shortcomings were almost insurmountable.

In the mid-1980s, a real alternative started its lengthy evolution. Around 1983, George Lucas started his historic work with the EditDroid, an early prototype of nonlinear editing (NLE). The concept was picked up by a number of developers who started fine-tuning what was at that time a cumbersome and difficult system. CMX weighed in with important advances in an eventually abandoned system that employed interfaced optical discs. The eventual winner was Avid Technologies, at least in terms of widespread industry acceptance. Predominantly Macintosh-based in the early years, they remain the big gun in commercial production practice. They had viable systems by the late '80s, with their earliest system costing over $150,000. They have slowly but surely come down, but their highest-end systems still cost around $30,000.

NLE quickly dominated the short-form commercial world and music television, projects that would by their nature be finished on video anyway. The old timers who had stuck with film editing for this kind of work because of its flexibility were quickly won over. The problem in the feature world, however, was how to interface NLE with motion picture film. The huge storage required for the hours of footage that a feature shoots was also a major issue. Feature films were, and still are, projected on motion picture film on a screen. You could do all your editing in the computer, but how did one translate all those decisions back to a piece of film? The basic problems had to do with fundamentally incompatible speed and frame rates. We will lay it all out in later chapters. The first features started to be edited in NLE in the late '80s. Prince's *Graffiti Bridge* (1990) was one of the more notorious early stabs at it, with post-production horror stories still reverberating in the rumor mills.

Meanwhile, many competitors kept up their pressure on Avid. Media 100, D Vision, and a host of others have had varying impact. Adobe Systems was probably the first to offer truly low-cost NLE software with its introduction of Premiere. For a variety of reasons, it never quite caught on as much as those looking for low-cost NLE alternatives would have hoped. Apple thus was perfectly positioned when it acquired FCP from Macromedia, which had spent some time developing the software but decided to recommit its focus to web-based products. Apple was able to take an already reasonably well-developed program, fine-tune it, and make it a product that because of its low cost and relatively bulletproof perfomance, had an immediate appeal. Apple has been refining and improving FCP ever since.

THE PROCESS

The obvious starting point is to shoot your project. Even with that there are a myriad of options you need to consider. Formats, cameras, and the like all need careful consideration. It is clearly beyond the scope of a book like this to address many of these considerations, although a number of things will be clarified along the way. Then there is the whole aesthetic dimension — the art of filmmaking. This, too, is beyond our fairly specific goals, although we are hopeful some valuable ideas will emerge along the way. On both topics — technology and art — there are lots of good books out there (I have written a pretty good one and this publisher has many excellent titles) that provide good background both on how-to about gear and how to think about shooting a project. Simply be aware that the way you shoot your project, both technically and aesthetically, has a huge impact on the post-production process. What medium you want your project to end up on (film, standard video, HDTV) will dictate many technical considerations — but often in a rather ambiguous fashion. And a clear vision of how you want your scenes to look, what is referred to as "shooting for the edit," should inform every shooting choice you make on location or in the studio.

Once a project is shot, the first step for initiating the editing is **capture**. Capture is the process of transferring your footage, whether it is on analog video or digital video, into your computer. If you shot on film, which we did with the *Waiting Tables* tutorial, you must transfer to a video format before you capture. You can capture picture, picture linked with audio, or audio by itself. Footage that is already in a file form can also be brought in at File>Import — more on both later.

Many books start out with the many steps that lead up to capture, but since the included DVD provides you with footage with which to start experimenting, we can delay discussion of this time-consuming initial step. Because we would have to go through so much information about logging, formats, settings, submenus and the like (exactly what we are trying to avoid), this will be saved for Chapter IX. We strongly recommend that you spend some time with the tutorial before you start whacking away at your own footage. What you are after in the capture process all starts to make sense once you understand what a clip is, how sync works, and at least more than a few of the other myriad complexities

(continued on pg. 9)

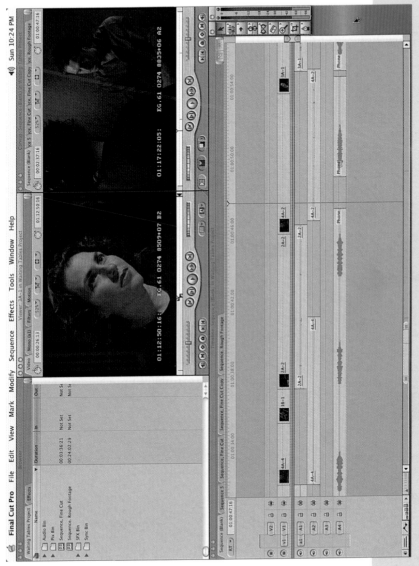

FIG. 1.6

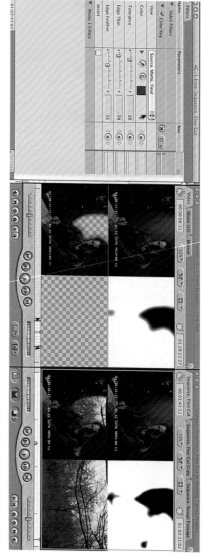

FIG. 12.25

FIG. 3.22

FIG. 13.15

FIG. 13.16

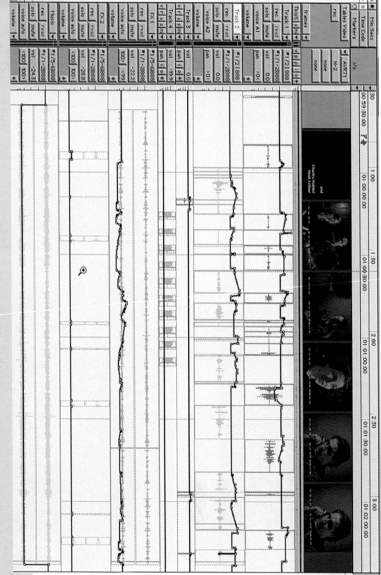

FIG. 16.13

8

(continued from pg. 4)

of the digital world. In any project, however, capture is obviously the first step before anything else can happen. If you cannot bear to wait, you will have to read around a little bit.

THE DIGITAL INTERFACE

Capture and the whole digital interface depends on establishing a connection between a camera or deck and a computer. The standard is called IEEE 1394, but the actual setup is referred to as a **FireWire** connection. A FireWire cord connects your CPU with the playback unit, either a **digital camera** or a **digital VTR** designed specifically for the purpose. FireWire is a not-so-simple cord — it is an interface protocol of which the cord is just a part — that can transmit not only a huge amount of visual information in real time but also operational instructions between computer and camera and vice versa. This is referred to as **deck control**, in which the computer is controlling everything the playback unit does. The camera or VTR essentially becomes a computer peripheral with all the playback functions (Play, Pause, Rewind, et cetera) taken over in the appropriate windows in the software. In Final Cut Pro, the camera or deck that you use is referred to as an **external video device (EVD)**.

Following is a standard setup for FCP editing with a DVCAM deck that runs both DVCAM and Mini-DV tapes (see Figure 1.1). FCP does not work solely with Mini-DV, but that is certainly the most common format used in the independent world. FCP can be set up to use pretty much any standard, although some need third party hardware and/or software, many of which will be discussed in Chapter IX. Illustrations in this

FIG. 1.1

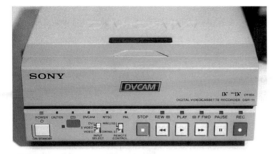

FIG. 1.2

chapter will use a Sony DSR-11 DVCAM deck (see Figure 1.2), set up with a Macintosh G4 computer. For maximum efficiency, a typical home desktop situation will employ the camera as the external video device — eliminating the need to buy both a

camera and an expensive VTR. FireWire is attached from the "DV In/Out" port on the deck or the camera to the FireWire connection in the back of the computer. There is both a four-pin (small) and six-pin (large) FireWire connection (see Figure 1.3). Cameras and decks frequently employ the small pin and CPUs the large.

FIG. 1.3

LAUNCHING THE PROGRAM

With OS X, all the applications can be put on what is called the **Dock**, a bar at the bottom of the screen (see Figure 1.4). This is a rather useful new feature, allowing easy access to desired applications. You generally

FIG. 1.4

want to use the hide function for the Dock (the menu with the Apple symbol>Dock>Turn Hiding On) so it only appears when you draw the cursor down to the bottom of the screen — it will take up valuable real estate needed by the FCP windows if you do not.

Double-click on the FCP program icon. Unless you have a deck or camera connected, a dialogue box — titled "External A/V" — will appear

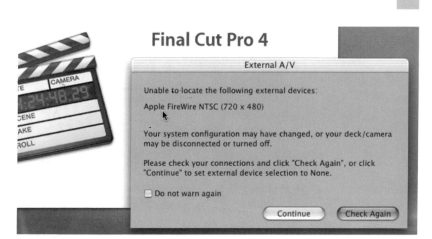

FIG. 1.5

when you open the program indicating that FCP cannot locate an External Video Device (see Figure 1.5). Although there can be reasons to have one connected, an EVD is generally only necessary when capturing, outputting, or sometimes when using an NTSC or PAL monitor. Just click "continue" and the program will open. You can check the "Do not warn again" box if you want to skip this Dialogue Box, there being other ways to check connection to an EVD. The ability to bypass this warning is new to FCP 4 and it is quite nice not having to address this formerly ever-present obstacle between you and opening the program. It can be turned on again in the Final Cut Pro menu>Audio/Video Settings ... >A/V Devices tab. This dialogue box is called "External Video" in earlier versions of FCP.

When the program opens, you will be confronted with four windows: the Browser, the Viewer, the Timeline, and the Canvas (see Figure 1.6). In addition, FCP has two vertical bars on the lower right side: the Tool Palette and the Audio Meters. The Viewer and the Canvas are for viewing media and are very similar windows with many of the same controls.

The Browser is used to store information and the Timeline is where you build your show. Each individual piece of audio and/or video is stored and brought into the Timeline as a **clip**, essentially the NLE term for what filmmakers refer to as a **shot**, that piece that is defined as the material from the point you turn the camera on to the point you turn it off. Clips differ slightly from shots because you can capture a lot of different shots as a single clip and audio pieces are defined as clips as well. In the case

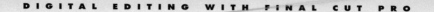

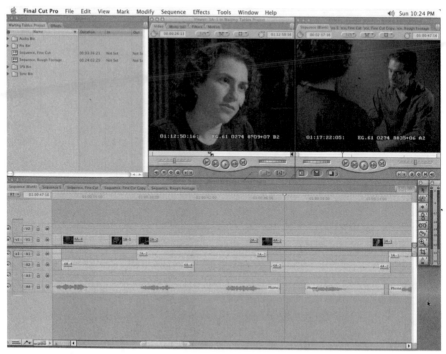

FIG. 1.6 (see Folio page 5)

of the former, most editors like to bring in every shot as an individual clip — organization can be messy otherwise.

Media brought into the Timeline is represented as a horizontal block (see Figure 1.7), with the audio and video represented on separate tracks. At the beginning of the video clip, there will be the written name and/or number of the clip as well as a thumbnail of the first frame of picture — these are defaults that can be changed. Audio will just have the written

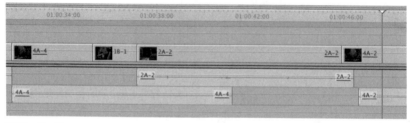

FIG. 1.7

clip name. In Figure 1.6, you see several clips cut into a sequence of picture with its attendant audio. These windows will be covered in depth in Chapter III.

COPYING THE TUTORIAL

We will not be cutting for a while, but you may want to start following along with a few examples. First, be aware that you will need 5 gigs of disc space to handle all the media. Put the DVD in your computer's drive. A DVD Icon will appear on your desktop, labeled Waiting Tables DVD. Open this by double-clicking on it and you will see one folder. Copy this onto your computer by simply dragging it to your desktop. Be sure to drag it to the desktop, not the hard drive or another folder, because we will be navigating to it later. The tutorials require Quicktime to run and the PDF files require Preview or Adobe Reader to open. All either come with your computer, whether Mac or PC, or are easily downloadable.

Once transferred, EJECT THE DVD, as it may cause problems if you don't. Double-click on this new folder and you will see three folders: Waiting Tables Media; Waiting Tables Documents; and Tutorials. Open each folder by clicking on the right-facing triangle by each one. The directory (see Figure 1.8) has all the contents of the DVD. There are three tutorials.

FIG. 1.8

One of the tutorials covers installation so you can follow along with it or follow the ensuing directions. The second folder contains documents relating to the project: a Camera Report — the shooting logs for the actual production; crew credits; and a negative cut list. There are also two versions of the script, each of which will be discussed in Chapter II. The Waiting Tables Media folder has the folders that FCP creates for all projects (Capture Scratch, Audio Render, and Render Files) two project files — one for you to work on and a finished version (this latter may require some rendering, see page 136), and two files relating to Cinema Tools. The Waiting Tables Project file will be the most-used item. Double-click on it to open. The Waiting Tables Project file will be the most-used item. Double-click on it to open.

IMPORTANT/RECONNECTING MEDIA: Moving files from the DVD to your hard drive will have a tendency to disconnect the link between the Final Cut Pro project and its associated media. If this happens, a warning box called Offline Files will appear telling you that certain files are not connected. Click the Reconnect button and FCP will find them if they are on any connected drive (again, be sure the DVD is ejected). A window will come up that points to the file. Be sure "Reconnect All Files in Relative Path" is checked, then click Choose as many times as necessary. You should be set to go. Again, consult the installation tutorial if questions arise; details of Reconnect Media are covered at the end of Chapter IV.

- Playing the three visual tutorials on either Mac or PC requires Quicktime 6 or above and a DVD drive. Access to all written documentation on the DVD will require either Adobe Reader (Version 6 or above) or Apple's Viewer software, the latter provided with all Macs with OS X.

- If your computer does not have Quicktime or Reader, you can get a free download of the most recent version of Quicktime at www.apple.com and Reader at www.Adobe.com.

- System requirements for importing and cutting tutorial materials: Macintosh G4 or G5 processor, Final Cut Pro 4, OS X, 5 gigabytes hard drive space.

- All questions about installing or using tutorials and materials can be answered at www.digitaleditingFCP.com.

SOME MAC THINGS

This book presumes some general Macintosh experience. For those who have only used PCs, PC and Mac have evolved to the point where their functions are not all that different. Windows was an attempt to capitalize on the user-friendly features of the Mac while OS X, Mac's new completely redesigned operating system, was an attempt to capitalize on some of the more logical structures of Windows. If you are familiar with the PC platform, Mac is very intuitive and it should not take you long to get up to speed.

A few things on the Mac keyboard bear discussion. Keyboard shortcuts are familiar to everyone and learning them in FCP can maximize your efficiency. Most everything is accessible through menus as well, but learning to use the keyboard can make the flow of your efforts highly instinctual. Many of the commonly used tools can be accessed by a simple tap on the appropriate key, but many of the executable functions (saving, quitting, et cetera) require a combination of keys.

On the lower left side, and echoed on the right, are the Control (ctrl or ^), Option (alt), and Command (open apple) keys (see Figure 1.9). In conjunction with other keys, these three keys provide access to many of the functions of the operating system and any software. The ubiquitous Shift key is also combined with other keys for access.

FIG. 1.9

The Command key, with its squiggly line design, is the central player in many Mac functions (see Figure 1.10). All Saving, Quitting, Copying, Pasting, New anything, Selecting, Preference access, et cetera can go through here. The Control key is generally saved for less commonly used functions and the Option key will get separate treatment later.

FIG. 1.10

1.11

Across the top are all the Function keys (F1-15). These are also access keys, some heavily used in FCP. F9 through F12 are used particularly heavily, representing critical editing functions (see Figure 1.11). For those with

FIG. 1.12

higher-level computer skills, you can customize your keyboard and assign frequently used actions to these keys (see page 100). There is also an Escape key on the top left, which is not used as extensively as on a PC.

On the numeric keypad, several keys are heavily used. The arrow keys on the lower right get considerable use (see Figure 1.12), with left/right being a single frame function and up/down jumping through the program.

Just above that, Home and End jumps you to the beginning and end of the program respectively (see Figure 1.13). The Ripple Delete key is heavily used (see Figure

FIG. 1.13

FIG. 1.14

1.14). It is for deleting media in the Timeline, while drawing the program up behind. More on this later. The top of the numeric has volume controls for the computer's speakers and a mute control. On the very lower right is an Enter function that again is not as heavily used as the one on a PC.

FIG. 1.15

On Powerbook G4s and iBooks, the lack of a numeric part of the keyboard requires alternatives for some functions. The **fn** (see Figure 1.15) key on the lower left gives you access to some numeric keypad functions. Used in conjunction with the left/right arrows, you

get the home and end jumps (see Figure 1.16). The Control and Command keys are only on the left, although an alternative Option key can also be found on the right side of the space bar next to an Enter key.

FIG. 1.16

This will all be repeated elsewhere, but there are a couple of keys that are used constantly. The A key gives you immediate access to the computer's cursor, variously called the selector, arrow, or pointer. We will refer to it as the arrow throughout this text. In FCP, one is frequently calling up specific tools and an easy quick return to the arrow is a must. The B key calls up the razor blade, a frequently used trimming tool. The JKL keys control Play and Fast Forward/Reverse modes. N controls a function called snapping, a critical function that will be turned on and off frequently and will be discussed in the next section. Become well-versed in their use!

ISSUES, CONCEPTS, AND DISTINCTIONS

Following are a number of concepts you need to understand in order to follow any discussion of any NLE software — an almost "pre-" glossary. Things that are more pertinent to individual topics will be addressed in sidebars. We will break them down into three categories:

General issues (**G**)

Reference issues (**R**)

Issues specific to Final Cut Pro (**FCP**)

One of the challenges of a text like this is to keep the reader familiar with concepts and yet not repeat lengthy explanations every time something is used. When, in the general flow of the text, we refer to a concept like

GENERAL ISSUES (G)

Time Code 18
NTSC 19
Frames and Fields 19
Formats 20
Files 21
Telecine 21
Synchronous Sound 22
Linking 23
Rendering 24
Window burns 26
Dropframe/Nondropframe 26
Compositing 27
Commercial/Independent 27
Film and Video 28

REFERENCE ISSUES (R)

MOS 28
EDLs 28
Resolution 28
Offline/Online 29
Heads/Tails 29
In/Out 29
Incoming/Outgoing 29
Non-destructive Editing 30
RGB 30
Final Audio Mixdown 30
Color Correction 30

FCP-SPECIFIC ISSUES (FCP)

Active Windows 31
Snapping 31
Undo 31
Transitions 32
The Show 32

"synchronous sound" or "linking," it would bog the proceedings down to launch into a lengthy explanation. When you see something marked with a letter, you can refer back to the appropriate following section. How much time you want to spend here on the first pass is up to you. For easy reference we will also provide a Mini TOC so you can look back and get questions answered easily.

GENERAL ISSUES YOU NEED TO UNDERSTAND (G)

• **Time code** — This is the big one. Time code is the driving force of all things video. It provides what is referred to as a "permanent address" for all video frames, with sequential numbers assigned to every frame in both the raw footage and the program. It is a rolling clock that is encoded in a control track on both digital and analog tapes as well as presented in a number of boxes in the program windows in FCP. It reads in hours: minutes: seconds: and video frames (Icon **A**) . All your clips will have time code and independent audio will have it as well. The Timeline — the show itself — will also have **program time code**, creating an important resource for tracking and locating things in your show.

Time code can be generated at a number of stages of a project's creation, but is usually introduced either in the camera on location or in initial transfer. Because *Waiting Tables (WT)* was shot on film, we had the time code laid down when the original film was transferred to video. The telecine studio — in this case, Hi-Wire of Minneapolis — chooses this first frame for time code. They usually pick the first frame on a roll that has a legible film edge number and put a hole punch in it (edge numbers will be covered in Chapter XIV). Hours — being the starting point — are assigned at your request with most producers tending to start the first tape, as we have here with *WT*, at one hour (using zero hours leads to some confusion). If we open a random clip in *WT*, say Scene 1B-1 from the Sync Bin, the time code on the first frame is 01:02:59:11. That means this shot is two minutes, fifty-nine seconds, and eleven frames into what we shot on location — at least from the start point established at telecine. There are colons between each two-digit set of numbers. The only exception is if you are cutting footage that uses **dropframe** time code, which uses a semi-colon between seconds and frames. This is to distinguish it from **nondropframe** footage (see page 26 for a discussion of these two important choices).

While someone just starting out can edit a simple project without ever noticing the time code, it becomes a major force in organizing and moving through the footage, locating and executing cuts, and communicating edits to other post-production professionals. Start to pay attention to it.

• **NTSC** — Another big one. NTSC stands for National Television Systems Committee, the organization that analyzes and sets standards for all broadcast and video signal issues. However, you will recognize NTSC as the umbrella term used to describe the broadcast video standard for the United States, Japan, Canada, and many other countries (particularly in the Western Hemisphere). Most video devices in these countries — broadcast, VHS, DVDs, camcorders — record and play the NTSC signal. Be aware that a new standard is starting to press — progressive video, the most common example of which is a computer screen. More on that later. The other popular international standard is PAL (Phase Alternating Line) which is used in the United Kingdom, many continental European countries, and quite a few other nations around the world. SECAM is another important standard, slightly less used than NTSC or PAL. It has been adopted in France, Iraq, and a number of other countries.

NTSC quantifies the way a signal is captured and recorded. It has been the standard since the beginning of the broadcast industry and, while it has a number of inherent problems, it has been a hardy system that has served its users well. FCP can be set up to a number of standards, but we will be concerned with NTSC. PAL, however, became more of a force in the US. Steven Soderbergh shot *Full Frontal* in PAL, because of its general higher quality and because it is more easily transferred to other formats, particularly to film for release.

• **Frames and Fields** — Technical descriptions of NTSC will be saved for later (see pages 278-81), but suffice it to say that the standard runs at a nominal thirty **frames per second (fps)** — actually 29.97, a distinction that takes on some importance later. The standard running rate for motion picture film is 24 frames per second, that is 24 individual still photographs are shot per second. Arranged vertically on the film, the still photographs blur into movement when presented sequentially. Film is a very tactile medium — you can handle it, hold it up to the light, and look at the image, albeit a small one, with the naked eye. The video frame is not as discrete and certainly not viewable as an entity.

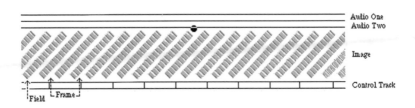

FIG. 1.17

Each video frame is composed of two pieces of magnetic information called fields, each arranged diagonally on the videotape (see Figure 1.17; some formats configure tracks differently). NTSC is composed of 525 vertical lines of information and each field has alternating lines of information, that is, one field has all the odd-numbered lines and the next field has all the even-numbered lines. NTSC is called an interlaced signal because when the two fields are presented sequentially, they interlace and are seen as a single image. Thus every image is made of two pieces of interlaced information. The interlace standard has served the industry well but its compatibility with other standards poses problems.

The difference between NTSC and the standard computer screen should be noted as it can cause complications. All computer screens are progressive, meaning that you cannot automatically play standard video on them. A conversion is needed to input from the interlaced video of an NTSC source to the progressive scan of the computer. For many years, you had to have a special video card installed in your CPU to play any NTSC signal through your monitor. Most modern computers, particularly any Apple product, come with this feature factory-installed because the demand has been so extensive. Again, the progressive scan of a computer monitor is the same as that of HDTV and other progressive formats.

• **Formats — Mini-DV** is the format that has captured the public imagination. It is great for home and semi-professional use. However, the Mini-DV format requires quite a bit of compression of the image and may not be robust enough for a number of applications. **Compression** is where duplicate visual information is thrown away in order to be able to store and retrieve an already complex image. The blue sky example is often cited, with Mini-DV discarding repeating blue information to function as well as possible. There are digital formats that are a step up from Mini-DV: DigiBeta, DVCPRO, DVCAM, D series formats. They either compress less or not at all. They will be discussed in detail in Chapter IX, but be aware that there are steps up from Mini-DV.

• **Files** — When you capture a clip, a Quicktime file is created that stores its digital information. These "source" files can range from big to very big, depending on the length of the clip. The general rule of thumb is that you need one gigabyte of storage for every four-and-one-half minutes of video footage (see Resolution in the next section for some variations on this).

The information in a Timeline is actually very small file stuff. A Timeline is just a couple hundred kilobytes, because it simply provides the reference information needed to access the actual files. The same is true of the icons in your Browser. In essence, a clip is not truly in your Browser, but the data that refers to the clip is there — an icon represents a good-sized file. It is your choice where the actual clip is stored and this important issue will be discussed in Chapter X. In the tutorial folder, you will see a folder titled "Capture Scratch" that has all the video files for *WT.*

• **Telecine** — Telecines are high-end transfer machines that are used to convert the motion picture film image to video. The film image must be transferred to video before it can be captured into an NLE program. Obviously, many reader's projects will be originating on video so a transfer is not needed. However, whenever a project originates on film, as *WT* did, a telecine session is required. There are a number of manufacturers out there, but Rank Cintel, Bosch, and Kodak have commonly-found units in telecine suites. There are a number of types of telecines, but the high-end ones generally have a **flying spot scanner** that pans multiple times horizontally at incredibly high speed across every image. The image is often transferred to a high-end tape format (often DigiBeta, a high-end digital format) and then clones (Mini-DV or a similar format) are made for capture into FCP. This approach usually assumes a return to the DigiBeta tape for a high-end finish (see Online/Offline in the next section for more).

Telecine is big business, with substantial material still originating on motion picture film and going to video for post-production. The telecine process employs complex technologies, representing substantial investments for any post-production facility. Most major urban centers will have one or more professional facilities, with Los Angeles having hundreds. The mom-and-pop transfer houses — places to get your home movies transferred — have much more humble transfer setups and would never be used for anything remotely approaching professional standards.

At a telecine session, there are extensive opportunities for manipulating the image. The **colorist**, the person running the telecine, has a full palette at his or her disposal. They have full control of color and brightness, and can address either the full frame or portions of the frame. Many telecine studios have extensive sideboard software programs that can address every image from an almost Adobe Photoshop-style graphics approach.

• **Synchronous Sound** — For beginners and people with limited experience in video editing, you tend to see a shot with audio as a single entity. You had a microphone on the camera when you shot and you have that shot and the sound is just with it. **Synchronization** of sound and image appears to be a fact of life — it just kind of exists. However, as you advance in your cutting abilities and as your projects become more complex, you will come to see sound and image as very separate entities — each having a highly defined life of its own.

In film, sound and image have always been handled as separate entities and are not "married" together on the same medium (a final film print) until the very end of the editing process. They are recorded separately on the set and are handled as such throughout post-production (many high-end video projects take this route as well). The issues of sync — that is, keeping shots in sync — have always been present with film. As you gain more experience as a video editor, you will more and more perceive sound and image in this same separate way. As we will see, sound is almost always manipulated at different points than picture in the Timeline.

When we start handling audio and picture separately, the potential for slippage between the two becomes an issue. If you do not give sync careful attention, you can be cutting in one place in FCP and throwing the audio off entirely in another section of the Timeline. Having people's mouths moving locked with their attendant audio counterparts becomes something that requires a substantial amount of considerations. You are building this beautiful, rich sound track. But it has to be thought of and handled as a separate entity. And it must wind up back in sync with your show.

With picture and sound being recorded separately on a film shoot, the two must be matched up. This is called **syncing up** and must be done whether you go NLE or with a conventional film edit. The folks in the telecine suites can do this for you or you can do it yourself. Each approach has advantages and disadvantages. If you have the telecine folks do it, sound and picture can be captured as a single file and are then forever linked. The disadvantage here is that you have to pay out the nose for something you can easily do yourself. The disadvantage of doing it yourself is that sound and picture will always exist as separate files and linking can become a problem (see next topic).

• **Linking** — Linking is a critical concept that is related to synchronous sound. Linking has to do with the way FCP, and almost all NLE programs, allows you to connect and disconnect audio and video. When you capture shots into FCP, you can bring them in as audio only, picture only, or, probably most commonly, picture with the audio that was recorded with it. When you bring things in this last way, the picture and audio pieces visible in the Timeline are called a **linked clip**. The visual indication that clips are linked is that the written names of the clips are underlined. If you click in any part of a linked clip — video or any audio — all linked pieces will highlight.

The idea of highlighting is important in FCP, as it is in any software. Clips are a light shade of green (video darker than audio) when sitting in the Timeline. When you click on a clip, it darkens — highlights — with the video becoming brown and the audio purple. The clips must be highlighted in order to trim them or apply any effect. If we want to move on to something else, we must click outside the clip to remove the highlight.

As suggested, we frequently want to work on only one track of a linked clip, a key both to creative editing and to producing consistent sound tracks. More on this last part later. To work on tracks separately, we must unlink the clip and then make the cut. Then we need to relink. There are a number of ways to do this. The easiest way is to use the Option key. As you use any tool, keep the Option key depressed and the effect will only apply to the track that you have the tool over (technically speaking, the tracks are never unlinked here). The linked track will not be affected.

The second way is to highlight the clip and then hit Command: L, also found at Modify: Link in the menus. The underline disappears and the clip is no longer linked. The tracks, however, are sill highlighted together so in order to work on an individual track you must click outside the clip and then click on the piece on which you want to work. To re-link, you click on one of the tracks and then Command click on the other (or others). They will then be highlighted together and hit Command: L (or menu Modify: Link) again. The underlines will reappear. Do not forget to re-link. In addition, Link will be checked in the Modify menu if the selected pieces are linked and unchecked if not. Given the male gender's propensity for just wading in and floundering about, I used this quite a bit when I first started working with FCP. I eventually discovered the Option key's connection to a more direct route.

The Timeline also has a linking control. There are two buttons on the upper right side, The button on the left turns linking on and off (**B**) — Shift>L on the keyboard toggles back and forth as well. . . . When the linking control is highlighted (on), all clips that have somehow been linked maintain that link. When you click on the Link button, you turn linking off and all bets are off — all the clips in the entire Timeline are no longer linked. The underlines remain in the clips, to indicate what is what, but all audio and video can now be moved separately. Of all the ways to turn linking off, this to my mind has some inherent dangers. With the underlines remaining, you can forget you have turned things off. If you are not careful, you can make a real mess of things. Use this cautiously. One good thing is that if you move a clip, a small box appears indicating precisely how many frames you have moved out of sync. You can always put things back — remember undo as well — but it can get messy if a lot gets moved.

One thing that FCP does in this regard is when you have linked audio and video in a clip or subclip (see page 206), that relationship is forever forged in FCP's metadata. If you take a clip out of sync in the Timeline, or if it somehow falls out of sync, a small box appears in the clip that tells you exactly how many frames the shot is out of sync. This box will stay there for the life of the program.

• **Rendering/Real-time** — **Rendering** refers to any NLE program's need to "finalize" or "complete" any changes you have made to a clip or sequence of clips. **Real-time** refers to FCP's way of indicating whether a change in a clip or clips can be previewed immediately. There are a number of factors involved in this (power of your computer, tape format, image quality), but some changes can be played without rendering.

Rendering is an irritating necessity in all NLE programs and is particularly bothersome in FCP, although it is getting better with successive versions. Several other NLE programs have a slightly better approach (but you pay for it). I have heard some very experienced editors state that FCP's only drawback is that it is slow and the rendering part is the main culprit. This may be the one and only trade-off for FCP's great price.

As stated, a clip exists as a file. That file just *is*, it essentially cannot be changed or altered in any way (with limited exceptions). But if you make a change to a clip in the Timeline (add an effect, add titles, do color correction, et cetera), the clip with that change does not really exist anywhere. Also, if you just create something — a title is the best example — it exists on your screen but there is no attendant file. When you apply a change or put anything with a change in it in the Timeline, a colored line will show up in the Render Bar, the strip just below the Ruler in the top of the Timeline. In earlier versions of FCP, the render bar would almost always be red, indicating that the material must then be rendered. That is, a file must be created that is this new entity — the old clip with the new effect. If you tried to play a clip without rendering, the "Unrendered" title would appear in the Canvas. However, if you moved into the clip with the playhead, FCP should be able to show still frames of the effect or title.

FCP 4 has improved on its real-time performance but significant issues remain. The program now comes with the ability to analyze the power of your computer (the processor, et cetera) and can indicate the computer's ability to play unrendered effects. The render bar now comes in different colors that indicate how viewable the clip is. If the bar is green, you can preview without rendering: if it is red, you have to render; and so on. If your computer is screamin', you may be able to play quite a few things without rendering. If you are limping along on a small, early G4, you may not be able to look at much without rendering first. For the first part of working with the tutorial, rendering will not be an issue. But once we start messing around with fades and titles and the like, the process and the color coding will be covered in depth and other complications will be discussed as well.

In short, to render we highlight or put the playhead in the clip and go to Sequence>Render All, or Option: R on the keyboard. Rendering can take anywhere from five to ten seconds to many minutes depending on the length and complexity of the clip.

• **Window burns** — A window burn is created at a transfer house when you are making dubs of your original tape or in telecine. It is simply a burn in — a visual overlay — of the rolling clock numbers of time code right on the frame, in the bottom area of the video frame (see Figure 1.18). In this way, we can always easily identify any frame we want.

```
01:12:50:16:        EG.61 0274 8509+07 B2
```

FIG. 1.18

These numbers are extremely handy for general organization. Though not completely necessary for cutting video material, their presence will make your life much easier. For film matchback, their use is even more strongly advised. In the case of *WT*, we also had the film's permanent address system burned in on the right side of the frame — for example, 61 0274 8509+07 B2 (see pages 260-1 for full details) across the bottom. Having the numbers easily visible will help us catch any mistakes. Window burns are not an absolute necessity for matchback, but their absence can make difficult questions unanswerable.

• **Dropframe/Nondropframe (DF/NDF)** — This is actually not an issue that needs to be addressed this early on, but because it will be a peripheral part of the discussion in places, it will be given a brief intro here. DF/NDF is about creating accurate timings of shows, a must in any broadcast applications. If 29.97 frames is an exact second in NTSC, then thirty frames is a little more than a second. But the time code clocks count thirty frames as a second. This leads to a small discrepancy between the actual time of the show and the time code time. Dropframe time code is designed to make up for these timing discrepancies. It drops a frame every minute except for the tenth minute, making the number count match up with real time. FCP defaults to dropframe, which may require change for many projects. Again, this is not very meaningful to the independent, but it causes messiness in the necessarily exact timings of broadcast programs.

• **Compositing** — Compositing functions are available in many NLE programs. In its simplest form, compositing is the layering of images to create superimposed effects. In its most complex application, it can be the blending of images to create complex special effects.

• **Commercial/Independent** — Throughout this text, we will make a distinction between big budget, commercial productions — what we will refer to as "high-end" commercial production — and independents, what can be referred to as low budge/no budge (LBNB) productions. In the latter there is virtually no budget and no room for movement from that figure. We want to emphasize that there is a gap between the way you will do things, at least the novices among you, and the way the rest of the world does things. The two approaches, dictated more by necessity than desire, simply have a different set of operating circumstances. When we refer to something as high-end we are not suggesting it is better, we are simply saying that the project is being produced under a certain set of assumptions — that it will be produced at a certain level. This means that it will be shot on top-notch equipment with reasonably high production values (a term denoting the resources devoted to the image), and it will be professionally mixed, color corrected, and onlined (color correction is part of the online process). In this world, a project is embarked upon with the understanding that it will be created and finished at a certain level. This includes virtually anything on television — commercials, music videos, episodic television, pretty much everything. Live sports and news are not finished per se, but their production values are usually far from humble. High-end also includes most motion pictures — the mix of course being critical, color correction occurring in a process called timing, and then the creation of a final print. LBNBs are produced frugally, and professional mixing and color correction may be beyond their reach. An online finish is often out of the question. LBNBs frequently creep upward and stretch their limits, but there is a clear distinction between stuff shot and finished on the cheap and stuff that is for popular consumption.

We will be constantly encouraging you to think big — to execute at as high a level as possible. It is not so much that success is not possible at an indie level, it is that the more legible and audible your work is, the greater chance it will have to appeal to an audience. In every project you want to take things to the next step and, while not saying that Hollywood quality is the last step on the ladder, to deny audience standards is to tempt artistic suicide. Plus, every good professional experience you gain is fodder for creating richer and more varied work.

- **Film and Video** — Keep in mind that when we say film we mean motion picture film and when we say video, we mean video.

REFERENCE ISSUES (R)

- **MOS** — MOS stands for "Mit Out Sound" which Hollywood lore has it that a German director uttered in the early days of sound when he wanted to do a shot without sound (picture and sound are recorded separately on motion picture film shoots). When there is no dialogue or significant movement, shots can be executed without the sound recorder rolling. Rolling sound on takes complicates life (finding boom position, watching for shadows, staying out of the shot) and was avoided when unnecessary. That said, the modern trend is to just roll sound on everything, keeping the mics safely out of the picture. It makes life easier for the editors. We did a few MOS shots on *WT* just to show you how they operate.

- **EDLs** — EDL is short for **edit decision list**. An EDL is simply a data list, a list of the starting and ending time code numbers of every shot along with their placement in the show. An EDL also will have information on effects as well. EDLs can be imported and exported and can recreate edits done on one computer on other computers. You can copy and paste Timelines between computers with FCP as well. These lists are extremely important for moving the project out of your computer so other post-production professionals can work on it. FCP and all high-end NLE programs can create these lists in their export functions or there is simply a command for it. More on these later.

- **Resolution — High Res/Low Res** — Resolution refers to the number of pixels devoted to the video image. A high resolution image (high res) has many pixels and a low res image has a smaller number. Obviously, the high-res image is a much sharper and detailed one and the low-res will be softer and poorer quality. Unless going for a stylized effect, you obviously want your final product to be as high quality as possible. However, working with a high-res image could (note the past tense) tax both the functioning of FCP and create storage issues. For a long time, people would do all the hard work of editing with a low-res image and then, with the use of EDLs, return to high-res footage for a high-quality end product. This is much less of an issue now than it was in the '90s because of the rapid advance in storage technologies. In 1995, an individual having access to a gigabyte of storage was a rare thing.

Even large projects frequently worked with what we would now consider very minimal storage. Obviously, this has all changed. Still, working with low-res footage or footage transferred or captured from less robust formats is common.

• **Offline/Online** — Offline and online are also slightly less compelling issues than they used to be, but are still things that come into play with some frequency, particularly in high-end commercial practice. Related to resolution as well as other issues, an offline edit is simply an edit done on less powerful, less sophisticated equipment. It is doing the time-intensive work of making painstaking editorial decisions in a low-cost environment. All the decisions are thus already made and are easily duplicated when you go into the expensive, sophisticated finishing environment — the online edit. Again, EDLs are the key with low-res footage usually used in the offline edit. Professional online facilities can be very expensive, with costs typically ranging from $700 an hour and up. Onlining is standard operating procedure in commercial — that is large budget — production. In this day and age, you can finish a project in FCP with Mini-DV and have a good-looking product. Still, you can achieve higher quality when going to an online facility, often employing a better format.

• **Heads/Tails** — The head of a shot is the beginning; the tail the end. The beginning of the whole show (the left of the Timeline) is called the head; the end the tail (the right of the Timeline). These are useful terms simply for orienting yourself to which way we are talking about going.

• **In/Out** — In and Out points are central to FCP and, of course, all editing, whether NLE, film, or analog video. They are simply the points where we are going to enter and exit individual clips in our edited program. We analyze the tail of a shot and determine where we want to leave it — our Out point. Then we analyze the head of the next shot and determine where we want to enter it — our In point. Great effort is extended to make this transition from one shot to the next as fluid and/or dynamic as possible.

• **Incoming/Outgoing** — This is a way we talk about clips we are editing in the Timeline and the Viewer. The incoming shot is simply the next shot you are going to put into the program — the shots for which we are finding our In points. The outgoing shot is the shot we are leaving — the shot for which we are determining an Out point.

- **Non-destructive Editing** — This is one of the great joys of nonlinear editing. It is not specific to FCP and will be found in all high-end NLE programs. After you trim a shot, whether in the Viewer or in the Timeline, it is represented as a specific length in the Timeline. Non-destructive editing simply means that the original capture scratch file has not been changed and either end of the shot can be restored to its original (or anything in-between) length. That is, the shot can be lengthened at the head or the tail. If you decide that a shot is too short, you can simply drag it to a longer length in the Timeline without taking it back into the viewer, resetting points, and recutting. This is a great time-saver and provides a very efficient way of trying different cutting options.

- **RGB** — RGB is short for Red/Green/Blue. Red, green, and blue are the primary colors of light, also called the additive colors. All color changes in video and film are controlled in RGB and their employment in finishing a project will be a later topic.

- **Final Audio Mixdown** — This is one of the major finishing stages of any project. When all the tracks of audio have been built and layered to your satisfaction, they must be mixed down to two (assuming stereo) tracks of audio. This is a very major undertaking done at a post-production audio facility designed for the purpose. Several members of the editorial staff are in attendance and the mix is run by a studio employee — the **rerecording mixer** (both this person's role and title have evolved over the years). In a film finish, a mix is virtually inescapable (not that one would want to avoid it). It should be, and generally is, a big proposition for a video piece as well. However, with FCP and other NLE programs, you can shortcut (I would say shortchange) this hugely important stage by mixing within the program yourself. Recognizing the shallow pockets of many independents, this may be unavoidable. However, professional mixes will be in the future of anyone wanting to execute at a high level.

- **Color Correction** — This is also a major finishing process. Color correction can be done in FCP, but in standard commercial practice the tape is taken to a post-production facility where the color of every individual shot is analyzed and corrected if necessary. As suggested, extensive correction can be done and this is the opportunity to create a great-looking and visually consistent product.

FINAL CUT PRO-SPECIFIC ISSUES (FCP)

Some of these are specific to FCP, while others show up in competing NLE programs in some other form or name. Whichever, they will come up in the context of actual use of the program.

• **Active Windows** — One irritation of working with any NLE program is that you always have to think about which window is active. The last window you clicked on is active. If you ever hit a function, say something as simple as Play, and nothing happens or the wrong thing happens, make sure the window that you want to function is active. Many times I have been sitting in front of a class wanting to look at a cut I have just demonstrated. I hit play and nothing happens. While the idiots in the class giggle, I have to demonstrate active windows.

• **Snapping** — This function means that the arrow or any media you are moving will snap (jump) to the playhead or the nearest edit or marker when you come close to it. It is great for making sure you do not leave gaps between shots or accidentally cover up anything by moving a clip too far.

• **Undo** — There are equally important times when we will want it turned off. Undo is present in almost all software, from simple word processing to graphics. It does not take on any added significance here except that it is its usual wonderful thing. Editing is all about trying something and if it does not work, trying something else (different cuts). In the old film days, that meant cutting two pieces of film down to the desired length and splicing them together. If you did not like it, you had to tear the splice apart, trim down one or both shots (or even messier, restore frames), and re-splice it back together. In some basic way, this may be the most attractive feature of NLE over film editing — the ability to just try and re-try things at will.

In most software, Undo is something you use when you have made a mistake. In NLE, Undo is a way of trying endless, and you have to be careful they are not too endless, variations. Many people have suggested that this is also the major weakness of NLE editing, that the opportunity to try so many things makes one indecisive about cutting — constantly second-guessing the cuts with endless sessions of trying different things. However, if you can build enough confidence to not be tentative, looking at and evaluating different options can be extremely valuable. Undo is also great for saving your rear end when things get confusing or completely out of hand — a not uncommon occurrence when you are first starting out.

FCP defaults to ten levels of Undo. You can program in more through the Preferences window. Obviously, there is a Redo as well.

• **Transitions** — This is a loose term for almost any kind of effect. Most people are familiar with fade-ins and -outs (where the picture goes to or from black), dissolves (where one shot fades out as the next fades up), and a number of other effects. FCP has a number of different types of transitions and effects.

• **The Show** — We will usually refer to your sequence as the "show." I went to an art school so, having the prerequisite art school haughtiness, I was mortified the first time I went to a post-production facility and someone referred to my project as a show. "This isn't a show, this is cinema, a film, a work, a… a…" In the final analysis, they are all shows. So show it is.

THE SOFTWARE MENUS

The menus, of course, contain or provide access to almost all the functions of FCP. All the mechanical functions of editing — the moving-things-around functions — are also available on the windows or through the keyboard, but a lot of deep structure stuff is only available through the menus. Oddly enough, the only major thing not available in the menus is titling.

While it would be too cumbersome to go through every item on the menus at this point, you should be aware of some of the elements. So we apologize if we are frequently saying that we will talk about it later but we do not want to get bogged down. At this point, we just want to talk about the general things that can be found there and specifics will, for most things, come later.

The menu items are listed and then are always followed, if applicable, by the keyboard shortcuts that will get you the same function. All menu items with an arrow (**C**) to the right of them have submenus that provide further options. Shaded items are "not available."

FINAL CUT PRO

While this text will focus exclusively on OS X, a couple of distinctions between FCP in System 9 and FCP in X are in order. Things are pretty much the same between the systems menu-wise except OS X has a new software menu that is to the left of the old OS 9 File menu (see Figure 1.19). It takes over a few of the functions of the old File, including the Quit command and a few other things. The major items of interest here are **User Preferences, System Preferences**, and **Audio/Video Settings**. For now, we will use the program defaults, but herein are many of the settings and choices for how you are going to run the program. These will be detailed in Chapter IX. **Services** includes a number of things you can set up through Apple or within FCP and the others are simple desktop functions.

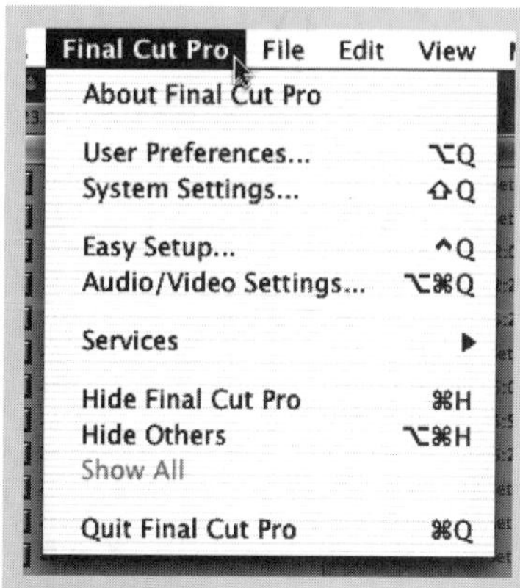

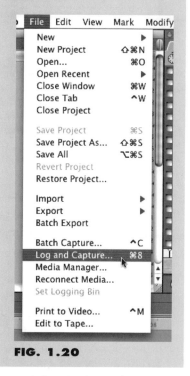

FIG. 1.19

FILE

Most of the elements for getting projects started, organized, saved, and out of the computer are found in the File menu (see Figure 1.20). They will all be discussed as we move through the tutorial. Toward the middle of the menu, both the **Import** and **Export** functions will become exceptionally important later on when we start manipulating the sound outside of FCP and particularly when we start collecting film matchback information.

Log and Capture is also quite important. As stated, we will not start talking about bringing media into FCP until Chapter X, but this is the doorway to that whole process and thus is obviously critical. **Reconnect Media** is an important function because occasionally, for

FIG. 1.20

a number of reasons, clips can become disconnected from their Capture Scratch files. Reasons for this range from renaming clips, to upgrading to new versions, to moving projects from one computer to another, to a host of other things. **Print to Video** and **Edit to Tape** are both finishing processes, followed by recently opened items.

EDIT

Edit menu has many of the functions associated with word processing, particularly Microsoft Word (see Figure 1.21). You will find **Cut**, **Copy**, **Paste**, **Duplicate**, et cetera. While I find myself using these occasionally, they are somewhat counterintuitive to the way a visual media program works. The clips exist as files that you can draw from and the need to copy and paste them seems redundant. In addition, some clips are so large, they will not fit on a clipboard. However, these functions occasionally come in handy.

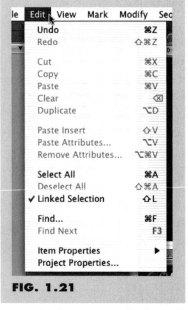

FIG. 1.21

The ever-present **Undo** and **Redo** are located here, plus means of selecting large bodies of material. The only somewhat foreign presences here are **Item** and **Project Properties**, both of which seem oddly placed. They contain essentially Preference-style choices and information, all of which will be discussed in Chapter IX. They are both important for tracking the stability of your clips.

VIEW

View, as its name suggests, lists the choices in the manner you look at things or the way they are displayed (see Figure 1.22). These resources can be found in many different places. The items range anywhere from simple zooming in and out (see page 82) to complex image manipulation and compositing tools. The top five items are rarely used, while the next three have to do with image manipulation and will be covered in the appropriate discussions. The set starting with **Show**

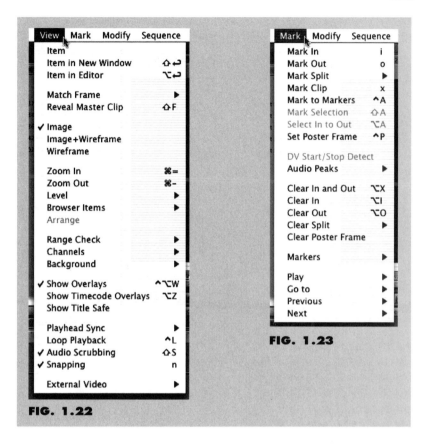

FIG. 1.22

FIG. 1.23

Overlays has to do with information you can display within the Viewer or Canvas. **External Video** monitors whether you have an External Video Device connected. If no device is connected, no changes can be made here.

MARK

The Mark menu (see Figure 1.23) is used to identify all individual frames and editing functions. Marking is covered in the section on the Viewer in the next chapter. It makes sense to have marking functions somewhere in the menus, although this is not the most efficient route to any of them.

MODIFY

Most of these items have to do with changing the properties of the clips (see Figure 1.24). Here you can link clips, change speeds, make freeze frames, and a host of other issues. **Timecode...** allows you to address time code discrepancies. The bottom items have to do with compositing and give a variety of possibilities for layering image.

SEQUENCE

This menu gives access to choices and procedures specifically related to the Timeline (see Figure 1.25). **Settings...** gives access to many preference tabs. Unlike the ones in the software menus, these allow changes during the editing process. Rendering, adding a favorite transition, creating new audio and video tracks, and some specific procedures (**Ripple Delete**, **Close Gap**, and so on) can all be done here.

FIG. 1.24

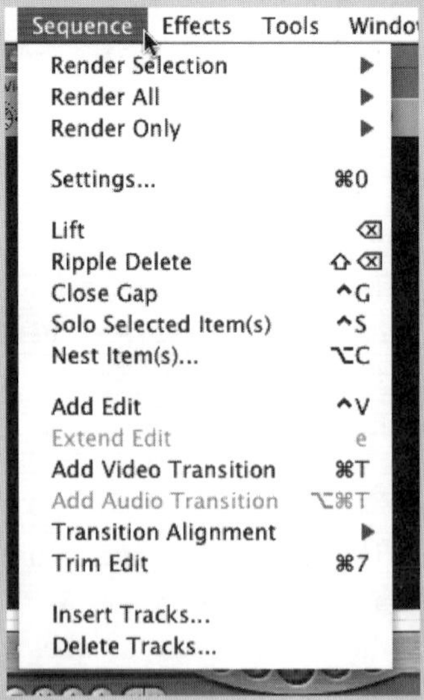

FIG. 1.25

EFFECTS

As the name suggests, here-in are all the manipulations that can be made to audio and video. (see Figure 1.26). Dissolves, Fades, and all simple filters — for both picture and audio — can be found here. Favorites can only be set in the Effects tab in the Browser but, once set, can be accessed here.

TOOLS

This has a lot of rather arcane high-end monitoring and manipulation items — mostly for the techs (Figure 1.27). There are other ways to access and do these things, but here are video scopes (waveform monitor, vectorscope, et cetera), the mixer, a voiceover function, and the like. The **Keyboard Layout** option is great as a reference as well as to customize the short-cuts.

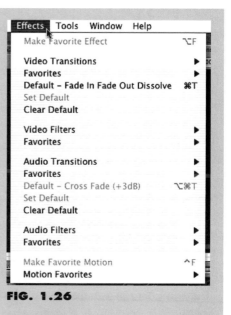

FIG. 1.26

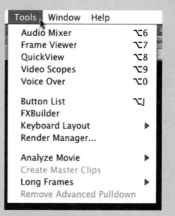

FIG. 1.27

WINDOW

This just gives you quick access to any individual window, tab, or tool in the program (see Figure 1.28). If a window has disappeared off your desktop (and things can vanish), look for it here. The **Arrange** function allows you to go to default setups and thus is particularly good for finding windows if they disappear.

HELP

... is help — obviously a lot of good things are available here (see Figure 1.29). Only the person who uses FCP every day can remember all the paths, routes, and shortcuts, and here is a quick answer desk for many different things. Online access is integral to effectively using a number of the features available.

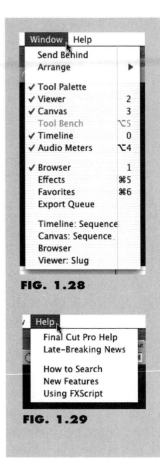

FIG. 1.28

FIG. 1.29

THE PROCESS

Where do you start when cutting a scene? This needs both practical and philosophical answers.

First, some modest philosophy.

We will start by repeating a notion suggested in the first chapter that, while this is a horrible simplification, the fundamental basis of nonlinear editing (and all editing) consists of two actions: getting your clips into the Timeline and trimming them down to the desired length. The clips need to be analyzed and trimmed down to meet the needs of the scene or segment being cut and the project as a whole. The clips can either be trimmed in the Viewer or in the Timeline itself, or, as is most people's approach, some mixture of both. At this point, we are obviously leaving out the enormous job of building and layering additional audio tracks. Just keeping sound and image in sync is another challenge.

A third highly pragmatic goal is to draw up the rest of the show behind the section where you are working — a necessity when trimming clips in the Timeline. Keeping all the later sound in sync is the issue and the more complex the overall design, the greater the challenge this will be. More on this later.

Of course editing is much more than placing and trimming. Editing is about creating relationships, dramatic tension, pace, kinetic energy, complex and suggestive sound, and a host of other things. But to get started and at its fundamental core, editing is about getting the shots into position and trimming them to their appropriate lengths.

STAGES

A project goes through a number of stages in its editing — an evolution as it were. There are options as to how to address the work and how to proceed, but there are a number of necessary phases in the development of a work from the chrysalis of the rough footage to the beautiful butterfly of a dynamic and engaging finished piece.

ROUGH CUT

The first stage of editing a project of any size is creating what is called a **rough cut**. The main focus in the rough cut is to make basic decisions in terms of shot choice and coverage, and to make every cut — that is, transition from one shot to the next — work. While the word "rough" suggests an unpolished stone, the rough cut is a very advanced work. You have done your very best job and made all the micro decisions of how to make each cut work at its highest and most efficient level. You have eliminated as much excess as appears logical and should have a reasonably streamlined and viewable work. At this point, you step back and take a more global view and create the **fine cut**. With the rough cut, you can win the battle of cuts but still lose — at least for the moment — the show (the overall structure of the scenes), because of poor pacing, bad shot selection, or missing the dramatic center of the scene. In the fine cut, we fine-tune all the inner workings of the scene. This is where you are shaving off frames to streamline the work, but are also making sure that every scene works as a whole.

In creating the rough cut, there are fundamentally three decision-making processes. These are all completely interrelated, but here goes:

1. Choose from what angle you want to show each part of the action, that is, how you want to cover the action.

2. Choose the take.

3. Make the cut — the transition — work.

By "cover," we simply mean that we have to choose what camera angle, or combination of angles, we are going to use to show any given action. This appears simple, but is one of the fundamental challenges of editing. As with everything, you are faced with a choice. Who or what do you want to be on the screen as the action is unfolding? If you have two people arguing, which person do you show? There is no fundamental rule, but clearly there should be some logic as to who is on-camera at any given time — what character's delivery or response is most important. Stanly Kubrick's

Full Metal Jacket (1987) yields a classic example of this. Toward the end of the first part of the film, there is a scene where the Drill Instructor is in the dysfunctional private's face, letting him have it verbally. The DI is doing all the talking, but who does the viewer want to see? We want to see both of them, but we are equally or more interested in seeing the private's response. The dramatic logic of seeing stimuli and response is inescapable.

The second item means that we need to choose which take to use, having usually done a number from every setup. You must evaluate the quality of each take, gauging the performance and technical quality of each shot, and choose the "keeper" — the one you want to use. In the old-fashioned world of film editing, these are called **selects**. The editor, actually the apprentice editor, would then pull these selects from the larger rolls of film that have all the takes — the rushes or dailies — and cut them together in order on a single roll, called the **string out** or the **first assembly**. There is nothing completely analogous in video editing, although in NLE, making a string out is a viable option (see page 43).

"To make the cut work" is a little trickier. What works and what does not work can appear to be quite subjective. But on closer analysis, we find that there are principles that have been applied for many years that make a scene coherent visually. Now, making a scene "coherent visually" is based on some fundamental assumptions. It is based on the dominant tradition of filmmaking, what we could call the "Classical Hollywood Style" or the "American Model." This simply asserts that the editing — the transitions from shot to shot — should be as unnoticeable as possible. That is, the scenes should "flow" and be efficient and the construction should not call attention to itself. This operates around a number of basic concepts — the match cut and cutting on action being most notable — and is most descriptively called "Invisible Cutting" by the theory folks.

Simply stated, the theory puts forward that the cutting should not call attention to itself because that would distract the viewer from involvement with story and character — what people have called "the willing suspension of disbelief." American films are great at many things but their hyper-efficient storytelling qualities are possibly their greatest attribute. And anything that distracts from this fundamental forward movement is bad — at least in this approach. If you as a viewer are sitting there saying, "Boy this is great cutting (or my isn't that a great shot)," your involvement is being disrupted. These are the underlying principles behind a substantial percentage of films and clearly the traditional and conventional approach. Whether one hates or loves those two concepts — traditional and conventional — they are both forces to be reckoned with. A number of critics have postulated that one of the problems with the focus on newness and unconventionality at many film schools is that students fail to learn the not-so-simple basics of how to tell stories visually. Whether one agrees or not, engaging and connecting with an audience is a fundamental part of making successful films, whether you are going for the mass audience or the art house demanding and discerning few.

So, make the cut work. Do you go with the old fluid, a-cut-should-flow approach or do you attempt a more in-your-face style? The argument, of course, will never be resolved. As it shouldn't be. There is not one right place to cut. That said, it must be strongly noted, and I am perhaps too fond of telling students this, that while there may not be one right place to cut, there are a myriad of wrong places to cut. There are places where the pacing simply is wrong or the matching of action is wrong. Moreover, the dramatics simply do not support showing a specific part of the action. Where you cut matters terribly in the grand shape of your project.

WORKING METHODS

There are essentially two ways you can proceed with an NLE edit. One is based on the system developed for cutting analog (linear) video and the other analogous with the old film style of cutting. Film and analog video editing — the former we will cover in depth later and the latter, thankfully, will be left to the overflowing junk heaps of video technology history. The old analog video way is, however, a model for many NLE functions and does have an impact on the way we work.

In the analog video approach, there was a source deck and a program deck — a not-so-loose model for the Viewer and the Canvas. The source deck was where you played back the tapes you shot on location or in the studio. The program deck was where you built your new show straight onto a new tape. Between the two was an Edit Control Unit (ECU), with controls not unlike the Viewer in any NLE program. By necessity, the show is built from the beginning and this central fact dominated the entire process. We had to consider everything that was going to happen at the beginning (titles, et cetera), because we could not go back and "make room" for other shots.

On the source deck, we would find where we wanted to start the first shot — the "In" point. It would then be punched in on the ECU. Then you needed to set an "Out" point for the shot. This did not need to be quite so exact because we would decide where we wanted to end this first shot when we next were deciding the outgoing/incoming transition with the following shot. So we wanted to set our Out point just somewhere past where we knew we were no longer going to use this first shot — what I like to call "sloppy outs." You would then set both points (or just stop recording when we want our Out point) on the ECU. There were two types of edits — Assemble and Insert. Assemble edit just stacked the shots one shot after another from the beginning — with the irritating by-product of pushing an erased portion of the tape in front of it (assemble editing in the middle of an already-edited tape was disastrous for this reason). Insert edit was used to go back in and rearrange and replace already-edited material with shots of equal length.

So you would drop this first shot over to the program deck with an assemble edit. On the program tape, we would find where we want to exit this first shot and mark an In point. We would find our second shot on the source deck, and then mark our In and a sloppy out. The one saving grace of analog was that you could then preview this edit to your heart's content before executing. And you needed to, because once you committed, going back could prove either very difficult or you had to compromise your visuals. Analog video forced you to be decisive but, while you want to be decisive and NLE can encourage indecision, you ultimately do want and need the ability to change your work.

Because of its roots in analog video, the general NLE workflow takes essentially the same approach, without the messy erasure and with the ability to change lengths and timings at will. This is, of course, huge. We find the In points, drop the shot in with sloppy outs, and then work on the next shot. And we can change anything anytime.

The major difference with film is that you create the previously mentioned string out — all the selects in order with all the slates and a lot of extra material. This string out is a viewable entity that has a productive role in a film's construction. As you look at the string out, you can start to devise a strategy that serves the needs of the whole scene. In the -build-from-beginning approach, you can get so focused on making individual cuts that the more global issues get short shrift. There is plenty of time to address these issues but, if you are not careful, some of the project's potential can get swept under the carpet.

In terms of actual cutting, you have the outgoing shot followed immediately by the incoming shot. You would analyze the end of the outgoing and the beginning of the incoming. Once determined, you would mark your In and Out points with a grease pencil, cut out the intervening footage, and splice the new ends together. While this is a time-consuming process, it allows for a truly consecutive viewing of outgoing/incoming while analyzing choices.

I suppose because I am so used to it, I like this latter approach. A film style string out can be created in the Timeline. The Viewer is just used to rough things into position and then all the trimming would be done in the Timeline and Canvas. Again, you can watch a scene in its proposed order and create a strategy for the whole scene. Most NLE editors work in the first method, and that is what we will do with the tutorial, but think about trying the film-style approach some day.

FINE CUT

Once you have a rough cut, you will then proceed to the fine-tuning stage. Again, while what you have is called a rough cut, be aware that it is a very advanced cut. Things are not just "roughed in," as it were. Very advanced decisions have been made and, although there may be some elements missing such as music and sound effects, it should be something that you could show to colleagues and people with informed opinions.

Still, at the rough cut stage, you may notice that the film can still feel somewhat unwieldy and slow in spots — that the scenes do not quite have the energy for which you originally saw potential. You have all the cuts working, but sometimes the pacing and shape of a given scene may feel slightly off. The scenes have their general form, but the most efficient and thoughtful presentation is just a shade away. You have been focusing on the micro view, and your charge now is to maintain and refine that micro view while moving toward a more global perspective.

Now we want to go and make the few frame cuts that give the scene the pace and vitality needed. We also, and maybe more importantly, want to go in and look at the "logic of the camera." Are we showing the right parts of the action (what subject or object) in the right shots (close, far, above, below, and the endless list of aesthetic choices)? Have we made the right decision to have this character on screen during this important action, or might this other character be more pertinent to the drama? Would a close-up be better here or can we stay with the medium shot we originally chose?

This is where NLE shines. It completely blasts analog/linear video out of the game in that the close-up we decide is a better choice dramatically may be shorter or longer than the medium shot. NLE allows us to change lengths. NLE is moderately brighter than conventional film editing in the ease and speed of finding and inserting the shot — and the ability to change back if you decide your original decision was correct. The fine cut is the process of the editor going in and finding the full and final potential of every sequence in the project.

THE EDITOR

What is an editor's responsibility? This is only brought up because as we go through the tutorial, we will be attributing more freedom of choice to the editor than perhaps he or she actually has. As with every crew member, the editor's role is to give form to another person's vision. Since the late 1950s and the introduction of what has been called the "auteur theory," that vision has generally been ascribed to the director. This is for the most part correct although the director in many cases is the hired gun of a producer. There are many producers, and this has been coming back into fashion recently, who are every bit or more a driving force in fashioning the general feel and tone of a film. The editor is there to understand the way the director or producer saw the scene, and give it its fullest expression.

Still, this begs a key issue. You never fully understand this until you are there working in the field, but the old cliché is exceedingly true: Film is a collaborative art. It must be. To say that a crew member is there to execute another person's vision only tells half a story. Within that context, there is tremendous opportunity for creative contribution. A director of photography, for instance, is doing the shots that the director requested but is bringing — must bring — a new dimension, a vitality to their work.

The editor is the same. The director should have a clear notion of what he or she expects every scene to look like. Within that, the editor can provide different options and bring new ideas to the task. Problems will be found that the director did not, could not, anticipate. Solutions can bring new possibilities.

In discussing the editing approach to the tutorial, we will make the assumption that the editor is working free, unfettered by the expectations of a producer or director. This, of course, is not natural. The editor may have very clear verbal or written instructions as to how a scene should work. At least one (or more) little voice will — should — always be behind the movement of hands and eyes in the editing room. Still, those hands must perform at their optimal level.

THE VIDEO EDITOR

With the flourishing of portable video 25 years ago, the notion of what an editor is and what an editor does changed significantly. When more companies and individuals started doing their own video editing (circa 1978), they frequently found an employee or friend who could master the hardware and deemed them "the editor." This editor was then expected to take the raw footage and carry the project from beginning to end. They were expected to produce titles, find music, gather sound effects, design visual effects, sweeten audio, and a host of other things.

But that is not the way films were, or are still, made. All these are very specialized tasks and while you might find a person who is pretty good at some of these things, to find a whole package who can execute everything at the highest level is a rarity, if not an impossibility. In professional filmmaking, each one of the tasks would be farmed out to a person skilled in the craft. Indeed, people devote their entire professional lives to mastering any one of the many ancillary skills — location sound, audio mixing, graphic design, post-production color control, and on and on. The poor guy or gal that got called "the editor" was overwhelmed by needing a host of abilities that they did not necessarily have and to which other people brought years of experience. So people were completing projects bringing little or no skill to many important aspects. An even greater downside has been that the people who really knew what they were doing received less work and started to disappear, while the people who understood just a little were proliferating. Why bring in an expensive technician when my buddy Jack knows the equipment and can probably do it just as well? He can do it "just as well" if you are willing to accept mediocrity.

The "DV Revolution," such as it was, with its emphasis on a single person producing an entire project, exacerbated the problem. One person trying to do everything is one of the reasons, if not the main reason, that so many of these videos were so bad. It is simply impossible for any one individual to have all the skills necessary to execute a feature film at a high level. People seem to understand that they need to bring pros in for certain things, music being a great example. Why isn't it understood that collaborators are useful in almost everything — people who bring every bit as much talent and vision to a project as its creator does?

The most illustrative story I have on this subject involved a young video maker who was making a DV feature, doing his finish in FCP. He showed me a rough cut of his video and I looked at and listened to it and said, whatever you do, take this to a professional audio mixing studio to have the sound finished. He gave me the standard answers: He understood how to do all the volume controls and stuff in FCP, it sounded pretty good on his computer, and, of course the clincher, he could not possibly afford it. Against my better judgment, I attended the premiere. He had rented a large movie theater and had his little video projector, with his little speaker hookups, set up in the middle of it. Of course, the sound was all over the map. Things came in too loud. Things came in too soft. Things could not be understood. Background sound was uneven. It was a disaster. At the very least, a skilled audio technician has an understanding of how the dynamics of sound play out in a large theater. In retrospect, I was actually probably wrong in my assessment. The video was not good enough that it made any sense to spend more money on it, but the notion of creating quality sound remains intact. For this guy, it was time to chalk it up to experience and move on. But moving on is not valuable if some central lessons have not been learned.

Happily, the definition of the role of the editor, and all it entails, has started to return to its original meaning. The mythology of the lone genius creating all this electrifying work, which gained heightened popularity in the '60s and '70s, maybe at last is cooling off. Maybe the proliferation of bad product made people step back and consider this possibility: maybe I need to involve other talented voices in this project. And that is true everywhere from the cinematographer to the guy or gal who designs your titles. We tend to think: cinematographer, wow, creative person; title designer, umm, mousy, boring person who works with a ruler in a small, dark room. Everyone contributes at a high level to a successful project.

Part of the reason the designation "editor" is returning to its original meaning is that Hollywood never lost sight of how things should really work. And that is finally, after many false starts, beginning to seep down into all aspects of production. On projects of any size, they still farm out all the necessary work. The person who is credited as the editor on a feature film or episodic television, say a show like *NYPD Blue*, only takes the film to a certain point. They will primarily cut picture and the sound done on location, and that is all. They may have a few effects, like the telephone in WT, and some scratch music, but their primary work is with the picture and those audio tracks that were recorded in the studio or on location. Once they have finished their part (and even before), the project is turned over to a host of other technicians who add to and streamline their work. The film will go to sound effects and music editors, as well as people who make the dialogue sound perfect. Pros will be brought in even before picture lock to design title sequences and plan out and execute special effects. The person that we call the editor is the head of an extensive, and expensive, team of individuals who bring their experience and creativity to bear. All the skill positions are farmed out to professionals who know their tasks inside and out and bring tremendous craft ability to everything they do.

THE TUTORIAL

It needs to be emphasized that the shooting of the tutorial material was purposely very straightforward. We shot this in the classical Hollywood approach of starting with an establishing shot and then breaking the scene down into a series of medium shots and close-ups. The body of the scene is done in what is called "shot/reverse shot" style (see Figure 2.1), the bread-and-butter approach to handling dialogue scenes. This is just the back-and-forth camera angles — intercutting cameras A and B — that is so common that some people dismiss it as old hat. Be aware that it is much harder

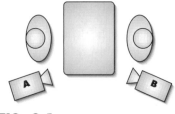

FIG. 2.1

for the novice to do well than it looks at first and, when a scene calls for it, it has a clearness and simplicity that more adventurous styles often overcomplicate. So, our approach is very conventional. A different director, given a different set of circumstances and goals, may have shot the scene entirely differently. But for a tutorial, if the style gets too informal or experimental, then an "anything goes" mentality can start taking hold among beginning editors. It shouldn't, though, because experimental forms require equally tight editorial control.

You might get an animated argument from editors on both sides of the questions, but we probably over-covered the material in the tutorial. This was done to give users a number of options of how to play around with the material. We also designed in a number of continuity errors (yeah, right) to give you a few problem points where you need to find a solution. Coverage is one of the great flashpoints between directors and editors. If the director does not give the editor enough material, or enough choices, scenes can prove very difficult to cut. You always need some options in case something does not work. Particularly in student or novice filmmaking, I could tell you a myriad of stories about conceptions on the set that simply did not work in the editing room. No one knows better what material you need to cut a scene effectively than an editor.

The flipside is the director who shoots everything from every conceivable angle, then hands it over to the editorial staff with a cheerful "Good luck." Editors hate this. They then have to redo the work of the director. The editor has to redirect the scene. This approach is mostly taken by insecure directors who are not assertive about the visual approach of the movie and have not made simple decisions about character and motivation.

How can shot choice reflect a lack of decisiveness about character, you might ask. One of the most striking things that I found when I first started teaching is that whenever I demonstrated editing to a class by taking on a scene, the discussions always moved very quickly from the mechanics of editing to character and motivation. Why are we cutting to this reaction shot now? Don't we want to see the response of this character when a critical question is asked? Editing quickly takes on the task of communicating key aspects of the character's inner lives.

Every aspect can become subject to critical discussion. Sound becomes critically important. I was sitting in on a sound mix where the off-camera sound of a handbag being dropped on a table turned into an intense discussion of the character's life circumstances. The character was a street person and all her life was in that bag. The sound had to reflect that. It isn't just putting shots together.

READ THE SCRIPT

So, how do we approach this scene? The starting point is to read the script (provided on pages 54-55) and ask yourself some very basic questions. The first one goes back to a central film directing question. That is: Who is this scene about? It is somewhat difficult to answer this question without the rest of the script, but pretty obviously Judy is the main character. Fritz is what we might call an "action" character. He serves to provoke Judy's actions and reactions. He seems to have no discernable inner life and it is Judy's character who seems to have some inner conflict and some issues with where she is in her life.

The second and third questions are critical and harken back to some basic screenwriting questions: Who is Judy as a character? And what does she want? She seems to be coasting in life, in a go-nowhere relationship, with some major family (sisterly) issues. What is this business about the sister? This is clearly laid out as one of the major issues that will be fleshed out in future scenes. This is one of those things in a script that just jumps up and down waving a big red flag indicating that this is clearly something we are going to hear about again.

Editors will always ask these questions but, as suggested, it may be someone else who supplies answers. Why does an editor have to ask these questions? How can the way a scene is cut suggest anything about a character? Judy only has six lines and most are exceptionally brief. Fritz does all the heavy lifting. (An actor's complaint: Ahh, man, I got to memorize all this dialogue.)

The way a scene is designed and cut can subtly influence our perceptions of character and motivation. Theorists love to wax philosophical about "visual subtext" — visual information that has symbolic references to character or action. But there is also editorial subtext. And it is maybe the hardest thing for even the most sophisticated viewer to see and the most difficult thing to discuss. One of the best learning experiences of my life was watching a noted academic break down the first scene from John Huston's *The Maltese Falcon* (1941). He very clearly laid out all the tenets of classical style, scene establishment, visual shorthand, and the profound visual efficiency of films of that period (and all periods). But he missed how the patterns — the specific points of the edits and recurrent cutting motifs — in the editing subtly established character relationships and answered all those directing and screenwriting questions we asked earlier.

THE ROUGH FOOTAGE

In terms of actual cutting, the starting point is a basic one. Get familiar with the footage. There are just over sixteen minutes of film (some takes were eliminated for space considerations). After reading and rereading the script, you should get familiar with every second of it. The rough footage in the order shot is provided in Sequence, Rough Footage. Watch it once just to get a sense of what is there. One of the problems with NLE is that all the shots, if allowed, just exist as individual clips. The great editor Walter Murch (*Apocalypse Now*, et cetera) has noted that one of the great things about conventional film editing is that to find things, you have to run through entire rolls of picture to get to what you want. As you watch that picture rush in fast forward past the gate, you often see the footage in new ways and get ideas that can significantly improve the final product. With NLE, the clips and files can hide in the netherworld of ones and zeros. That one magical shot that did not look so magical the first time around, can sit never to be seen again in the bin or sub-bin in a hidden corner of the virtual hard drive galaxy. Your footage is all there, but if you never see it again, it does not do you much good. For your own projects, make a timeline of the raw footage with sound and watch it several times.

Read the script again. In classes, I occasionally get the cretinous guy, and it is usually a guy, who looks at you funny when you start talking about dramatic centers of scenes and the like. For me, it is simply an announcement of not "getting it." "What is this @#$&, just cut the shots together," is the attitude. If you are looking at some unedited footage and thinking it is just a matter of stitching it together, you are probably better off doing something else. Even in the most routine project as a director or editor, your scenes will be flat and listless until you understand some basic principles of dramatic construction.

Read the script again.

NOTES ON THE TUTORIAL

The script for the tutorial is a scene from an unfinished script by film-maker Freya Rae. She also appears in the film along with Jeff Gilson, Charles Hubbell, and Heidi Fellner. The film was shot on 16mm film by cinematographer Matt Ehling, with gaffer Ramy Selim executing his light-ing plan. The sound was recorded by C. Andrew Mayer on a time code DAT, although audio time code was not necessary for the approach we are taking. Further credits can be found on the DVD.

The shots were composed for academy aperture (1.33:1) to yield the approximate frame size of standard video. If we truly were going to take this to a 35mm print, which is what matchback is frequently about, we should have composed for 1.85:1 which is the standard widescreen frame in which feature films are projected. In retrospect, part of me says we should have composed widescreen but the matchback component of this text is an add-on and the focus is rightly left on video framing.

The 16mm negative was transferred to Digital Betacam videotape (DigiBeta) by Oscar Oboza Jr. and Andrew Carranza at Hi-Wire Tech in Minneapolis. We shot on film because of the text's major matchback com-ponent, information found in the last three chapters. To provide the information for matchback, it is an exceedingly good idea — though it must be stated not an absolute necessity — to have window burns (G). For editing for a video finish, they are not completely necessary although they can also be extremely useful. At the telecine studio, we made both a window burn copy and a clean copy (one without a window burn), anticipating having a videotape available. We are using the window burn copy in the tutorial because having the time code numbers always avail-able makes identifying frames much easier for the reader. Again, window burns are not absolutely necessary for material originating on video but they make life a whole lot easier.

After telecine (G), each shot from the camera rolls was captured indi-vidually into FCP with the help of a flex file (see pages 288-93). The audio, which is recorded separately on a film shoot, was brought in uncut as an entire file — **WaitingTables48KL.aif**. This clip name is of our design but the 48K refers to the digital sampling rate with 48 kilo-bytes being the standard. The L means that the location recording was on the left channel. "aif" is short for Audio Interchange File Format (they sometimes drop the second f), one of the many audio file formats that can be imported into FCP.

One option is to drop this entire audio file into a Timeline, sync up picture against the uncut audio, and then just pull shots as needed from this Timeline to the rough cut. Working out of a Timeline, however, can have some confusing elements, so we made all the individual sound takes into subclips and put them in an Audio Bin in the Browser. From there, we synced all shots individually and then brought them back into their own bin called the Sync Bin in the Browser. While not technically accurate, we threw the MOS shots (R) into this bin so everything would be together. You should, unless you are going at it cowboy-style, be working exclusively out of the Sync Bin.

PAPERWORK

The script we have included here is a **lined script** (see Figure 2.2) A color version of this is also provided on the DVD as well as a standard (unlined) version. A lined script is created by the **script supervisor**, the person responsible for continuity, among many other things, during shooting. The lined script simply has vertical lines down the page, indicating what action is covered from what camera angle. Red is for master shots, green is for medium shots, and blue is for close-ups. The length of the line indicates how much material is covered. The squiggly line indicates that that line is being said off-camera. When it says Scene 4A-4, it indicates the setup number and the number of the take done from that camera position. We are also including the **camera report** (see Figure 2.3), the log of what was shot, so you can find where shots are in the Rough Footage Timeline, if necessary.

WAITING TABLES

by Freya Rae

INT. AN EMPTY, COZY RESTAURANT - AFTERNOON

FRITZ, a disengaged young man, sits behind the host station
concentrating on a crossword puzzle. A COUPLE walks in and
waits to be seated. Fritz continues to work on his crossword.

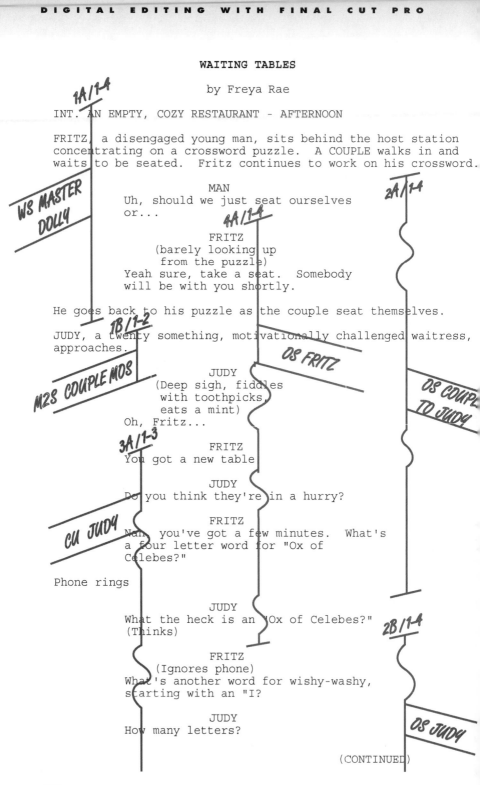

                    MAN
          Uh, should we just seat ourselves
          or...

                    FRITZ
               (barely looking up
                from the puzzle)
          Yeah sure, take a seat. Somebody
          will be with you shortly.

He goes back to his puzzle as the couple seat themselves.
JUDY, a twenty something, motivationally challenged waitress,
approaches.

                    JUDY
               (Deep sigh, fiddles
                with toothpicks,
                eats a mint)
          Oh, Fritz...

                    FRITZ
          You got a new table

                    JUDY
          Do you think they're in a hurry?

                    FRITZ
          Nah, you've got a few minutes. What's
          a four letter word for "Ox of
          Celebes?"

Phone rings

                    JUDY
          What the heck is an "Ox of Celebes?"
               (Thinks)

                    FRITZ
               (Ignores phone)
          What's another word for wishy-washy,
          starting with an "I?

                    JUDY
          How many letters?

                                        (CONTINUED)

1A/1-4

WS MASTER DOLLY

2A/1-4

4A/1-4

1B/1-2

OS FRITZ

OS COUPLE TO JUDY

M2S COUPLE MOS

3A/1-3

CU JUDY

2B/1-4

OS JUDY

FIG. 2.2

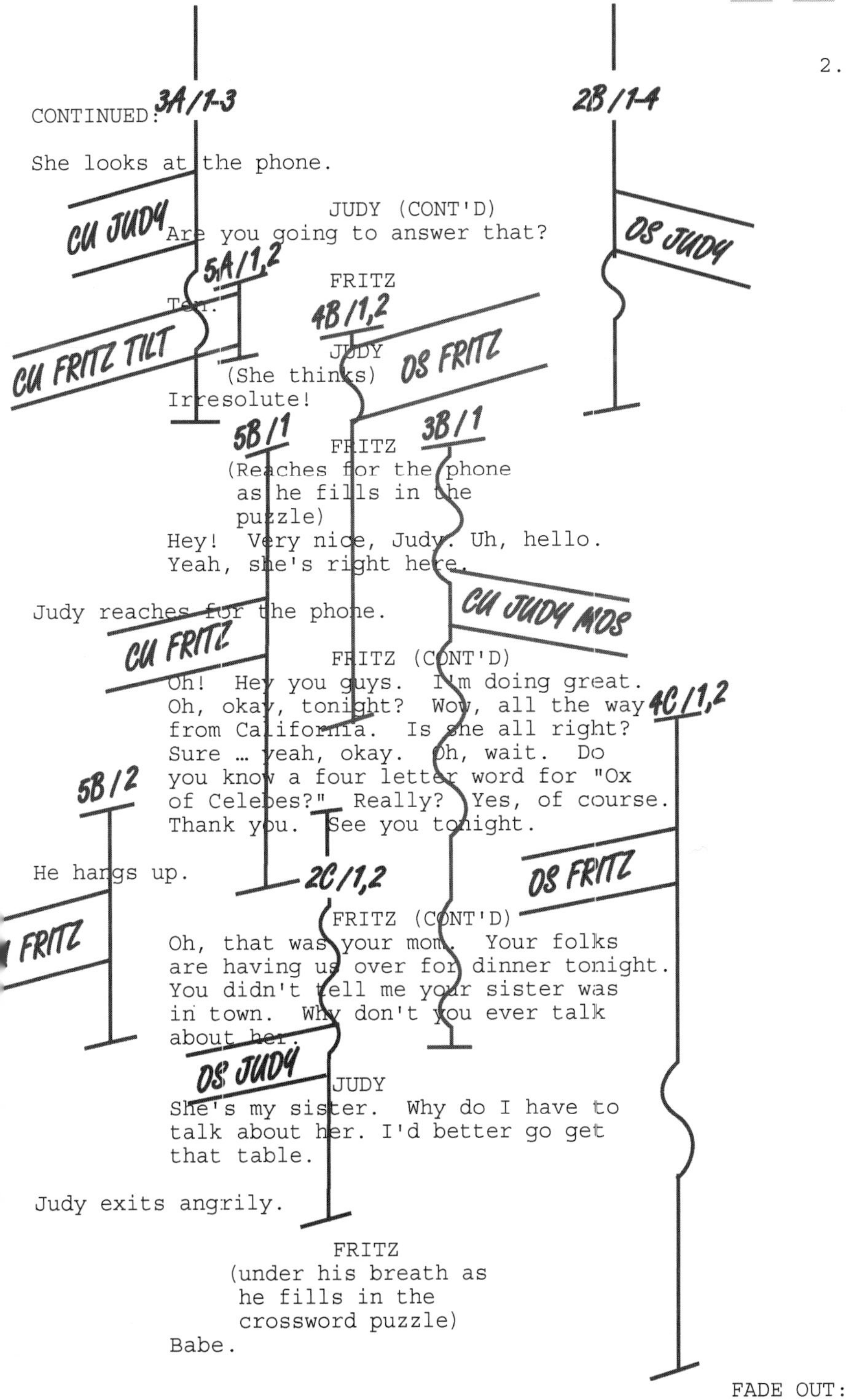

CONTINUED: *3A/1-3* *2B/1-4*

She looks at the phone.

CU JUDY *OS JUDY*

                JUDY (CONT'D)
    Are you going to answer that?

5A/1,2
                FRITZ
    Ten.

CU FRITZ TILT *4B/1,2*
                JUDY *OS FRITZ*
        (She thinks)
    Irresolute!

5B/1 *3B/1*
                FRITZ
        (Reaches for the phone
        as he fills in the
        puzzle)
    Hey! Very nice, Judy. Uh, hello.
    Yeah, she's right here.

Judy reaches for the phone. *CU JUDY MOS*

CU FRITZ
                FRITZ (CONT'D)
    Oh! Hey you guys. I'm doing great.
    Oh, okay, tonight? Wow, all the way *4C/1,2*
    from California. Is she all right?
    Sure … yeah, okay. Oh, wait. Do
5B/2   you know a four letter word for "Ox
    of Celebes?" Really? Yes, of course.
    Thank you. See you tonight.

He hangs up. *2C/1,2* *OS FRITZ*

FRITZ   FRITZ (CONT'D)
    Oh, that was your mom. Your folks
    are having us over for dinner tonight.
    You didn't tell me your sister was
    in town. Why don't you ever talk
    about her.

OS JUDY   JUDY
    She's my sister. Why do I have to
    talk about her. I'd better go get
    that table.

Judy exits angrily.

                FRITZ
        (under his breath as
        he fills in the
        crossword puzzle)
    Babe.

                        FADE OUT:

FIG. 2.3

WAITING TABLES	CAMERA REPORT DIRECTOR: Bruce Mamer PRODUCER: Jason Wallace	PAGE # 1

SCRIPT SUPERVISOR: _KATI MARCUS_ _____ DATE: _3-30-03_

CR/SR	Scene	Take	Lens	F-Stop	Filter	Sound	Description/Action	Comments
1/1	1A	1	10mm	2.8	NONE	GOOD		BUMP AT TOP OF DOLLY
		2				CAMERA NOISE		CAMERA/DOLL GOOD
		3				VOICES IN HALL		HAND JERK ON CAMERA MOVE
		4	↓	↓		GOOD		GOOD
	1B	1	50mm	2.8		M.O.S.		GOOD
		2	↓	↓		M.O.S.		GOOD
	2A	1	9mm	2.8		OUTSIDE SOUND		?
		2				OUTSIDE SOUND		MAY SEE C-STAND
		3				FALSE START		FALSE START (NOT SLATED)
		4	↓	↓		GOOD		HAS CHAIR GOOD
	2B	1	14mm	4 (Oops)		GOOD		BRUCE CUT TOO SOON
		2		2.8		GOOD		ACTOR MISTAKE
		3				GOOD		GOOD
↓		4				GOOD		GOOD
2/1	2C	1				GOOD		GREAT!
↓		2	↓	↓	↓	GOOD		GOOD

WAITING TABLES		CAMERA REPORT DIRECTOR: Bruce Mamer PRODUCER: Jason Wallace					PAGE # 2	

SCRIPT SUPERVISOR: *KATI MARCUS* DATE: *3-30-03*

CR/SR	Scene	Take	Lens	F-Stop	Filter	Sound	Description/Action	Comments
2/1	3A	1	30mm	4 (OFF STOP)	NONE	GOOD		GOOD
		2		2.8		NO GOOD		GOOD
		3				GOOD		GOOD
	3B	1	24mm	2.8		M.O.S.		GOOD
	4A	1				STEP ON LINES		CAN SEE KATI'S SHOULDER
		2				GOOD		FREYA ENTERS TOO EARLY
		3				GOOD		SEE KATI'S HAIR CUT EARLY
		4				GOOD		GOOD
	4B	1	12mm	2.8		GOOD AMBIENCE		GOOD
		2				GOOD		GOOD
	4C	1		2.8		GOOD		GOOD
		2				GOOD		GOOD
	5B	1		2.8		GOOD		CAMERA ROLL-OUT
SWAP	OUT	MAG	TWO	WITH	MAG	ONE TO	COMPLETE SCENES	
1/1		2				GOOD		MESSED LINES STARTED OVER
	5A	1		2.8		GOOD		TAIL SLATE
		2				GOOD		ROLL-OUT PRE TAIL SLATE

THE
DESKTOP

N ow for some practical answers to the question posed at the beginning of the last chapter.

Again we start with two apparently simple things. 1) Get the shot into the Timeline. This can be a challenge for someone completely unfamiliar with the software or perhaps not particularly computer savvy, but it is clearly the easier of the two. 2) Trim it down. This is eventually easy as well, but here we are faced with a vastly greater number of options and potential problems. And here you get into the great creative choices that make the old editing room cliché true: This is where the magic really happens.

THREE (OR FOUR) WAYS TO DO EVERYTHING

What may initially be a source of some frustration is one of FCP's greatest features — albeit one that is shared with other NLE programs. There are literally three or four ways (and sometimes more) to do any of the editing functions in FCP. At first, this may seem immensely confusing. Given too many choices, we sometimes fumble around. But over time, FCP allows you to find the best working method for your own approach.

In essence, the options for all functions boil down to four standard ways of working on a computer. They are:

- Using click buttons on the software's windows.
- Using the menus (and contextual menus).
- Using the keyboard.
- Clicking and dragging.

All these are standard ways of operating and you simply have to find which way is right for you. You have undoubtedly found approaches that you like in other software (word processing, graphics, et cetera) and this will direct the path you take. Having started with a Macintosh 512 in 1983, some folks find me a little old-fashioned in the ways I work. When I first started to teach FCP, my background as an old "menu and click" guy produced some humorous moments with cutting-edge technology students. They would find the keyboard shortcuts quickly while making it clear that touching the mouse was just short of beneath them. "You'll go crazy with all that mouse stuff," as one particular keyboard-addicted phenom made the "get away from me" motion to the infernal rodent.

It is the difference between what my colleague calls a "mouse editor" (boy does that dredge up an interesting image) and I suppose what we might call a "keyboard editor." When I started with FCP, I was definitely a mouse editor. This is somewhat natural for those of us who have not sucked the inner workings of the computer into our interior beings, producing the ability to fly through even the most complex configurations of ones and zeros. All the buttons and menus are there in front of you and there is not a level of memorization to wade through to get where you want. But as you become more adept at FCP, you find yourself wanting more — speed-wise at least. Why find your mouse, find where the cursor is, and move it to click on a tool, when you can tap on a key and you are there. Obviously, you have to use the mouse for some things, but you start finding the keyboard very attractive. I have not memorized everything on the keyboard, but I have many commonly used functions down to where I would not think of using the mouse. A specialized keyboard is available as well as stick-on key caps to identify everything. They are extremely handy if you can have a computer dedicated to FCP, a great idea if you can swing it. My computer is a multi-tasking dragon awaiting conflicting-software doom.

Again, working style should become intuitive. However you can operate most efficiently should be the goal. Certainly in professional work, it is a question of speed. You must work quickly and efficiently. Not only are you always working on deadline, but time on expensive equipment, and with expensive people, may be limited — access being divided between many pressing projects. Back when a system like FCP cost $120,000, you had better believe that there was intense pressure to make every minute count in the editing room.

Speed also affects storage issues. While storage options and capacity have improved tremendously over the last few years, projects have to be moved out of the system fairly rapidly for new projects to come in. For an episodic TV show, *NYPD Blue* for example, the editor is given an average of thirty days for forty-two minutes of a show. That does not include all the out-sourced finishing stages. When the show is done, they have to get it out of the computer and make room for the next show.

Working on a home system, the idle dabbler or unpressured independent may not need to worry too much about how fast he or she is working. However, even in the amateur world, speed is important simply because editing takes a huge amount of time. If you go about it slowly, you will drag the process out to unbearable lengths. One of the hardest things about editing is having the patience and temerity to see edits of the project over and over and over. If you are not efficient, you can literally exhaust yourself with your footage. I used to work in a production office where we could overhear the activities of several editing rooms (a space design that should be avoided at all costs). There are pieces of music and lines of dialogue that will be burned indelibly into my memory, and not in a good way. You simply need to run your cuts and your sequences and scenes many, many times until you have found the optimum cut. And if you are not being efficient, that multiplies the number of times you have to look at already well-viewed footage. More projects die from spiritual exhaustion than any other cause except, of course, lack of money. Sometimes they are interrelated.

In addition, the more time you take, the more time there is for media to get funky. Software and hardware producers might argue this vehemently, but the longer files hang around and the more upgrades and crashes they suffer through, the more problems occur. FCP files become disconnected from their names with some ease and the longer it all hangs around, the shakier the whole edifice can become. One time I was just idly tapping on some keys to wake the computer up and I accidentally renamed a folder, thus disconnecting the files for an entire project. It took me some time to reconnect everything.

So, every operation you want to do has a number of routes to get to the end. We will indicate all means to get to a goal and let you go from there. When we get to actual cutting (Chapter V), we will indicate all the options the first time we mention something and then proceed with our preferred way after that.

THE WINDOWS

There are three "access" routes with FCP: the windows, the Tool Palette, and the menus — all with keyboard shortcuts. We have briefly addressed the menus and as we cover the first two, we will pull things back out of the menus for further discussion.

As we go, be aware that in addition to the regular menus, there are also **pop-up menus** and **contextual menus**. The pop-up menus are available through the windows whenever you see a button with a downward arrow on it (see Figure 3.1). The contextual menus contain functions which are more unique and are available by pressing the control key and clicking on certain areas

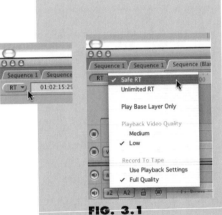

FIG. 3.1

of the windows. Both pop-up and contextual menus will be covered in discussions of windows or of specific functions.

Final Cut Pro is composed, as most NLE programs are, of the four previously identified individual windows: the Browser, the Viewer, the Timeline, and the Canvas. The first item on this list might be called a passive window because essentially nothing occurs to the clips here other than storage (there are other things stored here as well). The last three are active with the manipulation of the media occurring in and between these windows. All the windows have some of their functions divided into tabs, folders which are hidden in the background. The program opens to either the most used tab or, in the case of the Timeline and the Canvas, the most recently saved sequence.

All four windows can be moved and re-sized, arranged in any way you desire. To resize, click in the small thumb set in the bottom right corner. To move, click in the top bar and drag to the desired position. Tabs can be moved as well by clicking on them and dragging them to a new spot.

This is done quite a bit when we actually start working on effects and the like. The default arrangement of windows that comes up when you launch FCP 4 is different from previous versions with the Browser, Viewer, and Canvas arrayed across the top, and the Timeline taking up the entire bottom. The Timeline requires a lot of real estate once you start cutting so this is probably a good thing, although there are many steps to go through before you can actually start cutting. Those who have worked with earlier versions of FCP are probably familiar with the old arrangement, which had the Browser on the lower left. If desired, the older arrangement can be laid out automatically at Window>Arrange>Two Up in the menus. The new FCP 4 Standard arrangement is right above it (Option>U). Right below Two Up, you can also save arrangements that you have created that have worked well and you want for further use. I find that there are different arrangements that work particularly well for different stages of editing.

SCRUBBER BARS AND THE PLAYHEAD

Controlled movement through a clip is called scrubbing. Underneath the viewing areas of the Viewer and the Canvas there is what is called a **Scrubber Bar**. The Timeline has a more complex scrubber bar as well, found above where the show is built. Here it is called the "Ruler," but its function is essentially the same. All three of them are a narrow horizontal bar that represents the duration of the clip or the show (see Figure 3.2). This is where movement through the video, either the show or a

IG. 3.2

clip, is indicated. You can move through the video in about any fashion you desire — movement can be normal speed (forward or reverse), one frame at a time, a small number of frames at a time, and fast or slow — either forward or reverse. The Ruler is a little more sophisticated, with the elapsed time of the show displayed along the way (see Figure 3.3).

| 01:00:34:00 | 01:00:38:00 | 01:00:42:00 | 01:00:46:00 | 01:00:50:00 | 01:00:54:00 |

FIG. 3.3

As you play a clip or the show, you will notice the **playhead** (see Figure 3.4) moving left to right through the scrubber bar. Everything revolves around the playhead. Well, there are actually three playheads (you will find even more in specialized windows). They are found, and are centrally used,

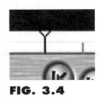

FIG. 3.4

in the three active windows. They represent the temporal movement through a clip or program. The playhead is the cursor, as it were, that indicates where in the clip or the show you are at any given time. As a clip or the show is playing, the playhead travels frame-by-frame indicating the forward movement of the media. If you use the arrow keys to single-frame, the playhead will move one frame at a time for the number of times you tap it.

There are ways of jumping the playhead around that allow you to travel within clips or within the program. You can click on the playhead and drag it through the clip or show. This is a great way to move quickly or slowly — **scrub** — through any media. Also if you click anywhere in a scrubber bar, the playhead will immediately jump to that spot.

The three playheads are the critical indicator of where you are and how you are moving. The playhead in the Timeline probably gets the most use, with the one in the Viewer being of almost equal importance. The playhead in the Viewer is used to analyze the shot, to stop and move frame by frame, to scrub through the action, and find In and Out points. In the Timeline, we are constantly going over the cuts and the sequences.

THE BROWSER

The Browser is where you store all your video and audio clips as well as individual sequences (see Figure 3.5). As such, it is the starting point for pretty much everything you do. As stated, the clips are the individual

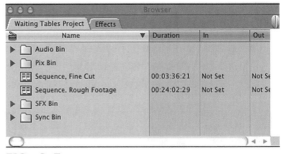

FIG. 3.5

takes, whether audio or picture. Picture, whether with audio or without, is represented by (**A**) and audio alone by (**B**). A **Sequence** is just an individual Timeline and is represented by the icon (**C**). You can make as many Sequence/Timelines as you want, depending on how you want to be able to access material and how many alternative cuts and backups you want. We have supplied three sequences in the Waiting Tables Project file: one for you to view the unedited footage; the second for you to make your own cut; and the third a finished rough cut to demonstrate some principles. The (**D**) symbol represents a subclip, which will be covered in Chapter X.

WT aside, when you first create a new project (File>New Project), the Browser will open empty except for a single sequence designated as Sequence 1. To make another new sequence, go to File>New>Sequence. The new one will appear as Sequence 2, with the name highlighted for immediate renaming. If later you want to rename a sequence (or anything else), click in the name area, wait a second, and single-click again. The name will be highlighted and you can just type in what you want. If you double-click on a clip, it will open in the Viewer and if you double-click on a sequence, it will open a Timeline.

When you create a new project, it will be assigned a tab called "Untitled Project" that can be seen at the top of the Browser. You will notice that in the background there is another folder called "Effects." This is where FCP stores all its video and audio effects, such as fades, dissolves, and a host of other useful to useless transitional effects. These will be covered in Chapter VII.

As you capture your footage, the Browser will start to fill with the individual clips that you log and name as you go. This can range from a small number of clips for a short show to a very substantial number for a larger project. For a feature film or any long-form piece, it is very typical to create individual Bins (see below) for scenes or short sequence of scenes. To try to put an entire feature film, with thousands of clips, into one unorganized Browser invites disaster.

Keeping your project organized in the Browser is critical. To that end, the material in the Browser can be divided into individual **Bins** (File>New>Bin) to give less cluttered access to the sometimes-unmanageable number of clips. The Bin symbol is (**E**) and a new one will appear in the Browser as Bin 1. Clips can be dragged individually into the bins or they can be boxed and dragged as groups — click outside the desired clips and drag a box around them.

Click on the triangle to the left of a bin and it alternates between showing the contents of the bin (pointing down) and hiding it (pointing right). Double-click on the bin and it opens in a separate window. Bins can be renamed just like sequences.

When opened in the standard arrangement, the Browser is relatively narrow, with just the contents and then columns displaying, duration, and in and out points. However, the window actually provides quite a bit more info, maybe more than you could ever possibly use. You can access it either by using the blue slider button on the bottom of the window or by dragging the lower right corner horizontally. The Browser is actually several times wider than your screen and displays many of the properties of the clips. This information can also be accessed in "Item Properties" which can be found either in the Edit menu or by Control clicking on the clip itself and going to the contextual menu.

With short projects, there may not be great significance in keeping the Browser orderly, but the larger the project, the greater the importance.

You may pay a steep price for a messy Browser. Other organizational issues will be addressed in Chapter XI.

THE VIEWER

The Viewer (see Figure 3.6) is where you look at and analyze your video and audio clips for use in the Timeline. Eventually, it will be used for many other things — titling, effects, compositing, and a host of others. When you open FCP for the first time, the Viewer will open with four tabs (see

FIG. 3.6

Figure 3.7). The Video tab — where the picture is played — will be in the foreground. The Audio tab — in this instance labeled Stereo a1a2 — and the Filters and Motion tabs will be in the background. The Audio tab will be covered forthwith. The Filters tab controls the application of chosen effects and Motion the animation of images and image elements (see Chapter XII for these).

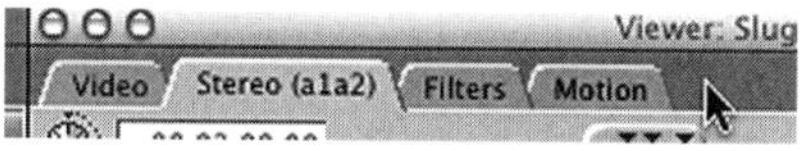

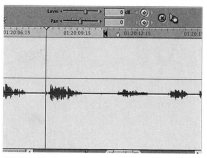

FIG. 3.7

Again, to work on a clip from the Browser, you double-click on the clip and it will open in the Viewer. You can also just drag the clip to the Viewer, or Timeline for that matter, although to no particular benefit. Video clips are obviously represented as picture in the Viewer and the audio clips are represented as a **waveform** — the visual representation of an audio signal (see Figure 3.8). If a video clip has linked audio, the clip will open to the picture and you can simply hear the audio as the picture is played. To get access to the clip's audio waveform, click on the Audio tab in the background. There will be a tab for every individual channel of audio. If the video has four tracks, four tabs will appear. WT was recorded mono, as many film shoots are, so there is only one tab — identified as Mono (a1).

FIG. 3.8

You can also "re-open," as it were, clips from the Timeline and re-work them in the Viewer. Double click on the video in the Timeline and it will open in the Viewer. If you double-click on the audio's representation in the Timeline, it will open as a waveform.

The controls in the Viewer are also found, often in a different arrangement, in the Canvas as well. All the explanations will be found here and referred to in the section on the Canvas.

Unless you have done something to the clip already, the clip will open to the first frame of the shot after you double-click on it in the Browser. The crucial functions that you want immediately are, of course, play and stop. There are, as usual, a number of ways of doing this. The primary ones are

1) the symbol **F** in the Transport Controls, the middle set of controls in the center bottom of the Viewer; 2) the space bar; and 3) the J, K, L keys.

1. The Play button is alternately play and stop, depending on what mode you are in. It is yellow when playing and blue when stopped.

2. The space bar is alternately play and stop.

3. The L key is play at normal speed. The K is a universal stop. Tapping the J key runs backwards at 30 fps. Tapping more than once on either the J or L key will create accelerated speeds in their respective directions. Every tap doubles the speed, with a cap of four taps to create eight times normal speed.

Personally, I find the space bar very efficient. Not being Tetris-addicted, I did not gravitate naturally toward JKL. I am, however, starting to effectively use them more and the games crowd will no doubt find them natural extensions of their keypad fingers. Clicking the Play button is for the birds. To play, you can also go to the menus and Mark>Play>Forward, but that is really for the birds.

So, play the clip you are considering. The next logical step is to find the section of the clip you want to use in the Timeline, that is, find and mark the clip's In and Out points. Editorial functions — how and in what way to get things into the Timeline — will be covered in the section on the Canvas, but marking the In and Out point defines the section of the clip that you will send to the Timeline.

There are variations on ways to mark Ins and Outs that we will expand on later, but analyze the clip, going forwards, backwards, a single frame at a time, scrubbing, whatever it takes to decide what part you want to use. Once you decide what frame you want to start the clip on, go to the Mark In function. The first way to do this is to click the In symbol (**G**) just to the left of the **Transport Controls**, second is to go to the menus and Mark>Mark In; third is to just tap kybd = I. For some reason, I do not mind clicking the Mark In button nearly as much as I mind hitting Play (probably because one does not do Mark Ins quite as often as one hits Play), but the i key is obviously the most efficient. The Mark Out button (**H**) is just to the right of Mark In, and thus Mark> Mark Out in the menus and O on the keyboard. When you set ins and outs, sideways triangle symbols appear in the Viewer's scrubber bar (see Figure 3.9). This is a

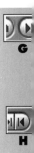

FIG. 3.9

very handy reference to double-check your work and in case you need to return to it later. A triangle with a line (see Figure 3.10) also appears in the upper-left corner of the chosen frame in the Viewer. It will show up when you stop on the chosen frame, but not in Play mode. An oppositely directed Out symbol appears in the upper right corner. Again, marking Ins is a very frame-specific process — you should spend the time to choose a frame that is correct — and marking Outs is generally a matter of finding something beyond where we know we are going to use the shot — a sloppy out (see page 43).

FIG. 3.10

While found only in the Menus and not on the Viewer, the Mark Split function should be noted here. A major theme of later discussions is that you may frequently want to cut the audio and video of a clip in different places. In fact, eventually you will find that audio and video are rarely cut in the same place, although this style of cutting may happen deeper in the post-production process (see page 116). With a Mark Split you can separate in points for video and audio — outs as well. Dropping picture over the end of another character's dialogue is very common. If we want to see a character before their line of dialogue, we can find the first frame

FIG. 3.11

that we want to see them, go to Mark>Mark Split> Video In (kybd: Control>I). Find where they start speaking and Mark>Mark Split> Audio In (kybd: Option>Command>I). Note the keyboard shortcuts in both cases. This will be represented as separate Ins in the scrubber bar (see Figure 3.11). I suspect most editors do not use this that much, choosing instead to trim with the razor blade or use the roll tool, but I find it very handy for getting stuff into the Timeline without requiring a whole lot of further manipulation.

Most of these operations can also be found in the contextual menus: Control click on the appropriate place in a window.

Marking Ins and Outs, and all that entails, are the two critical operations in the Viewer. Past those simple things, there are many other functions that you eventually will want to have at your fingertips — things that

FIG. 3.12

will make the editing job much more streamlined and efficient. Again, we will be breezing past some things, saving them for future discussions. Starting in no particular order, the group of buttons to the left of Mark In/Out are the **Marking Controls** panel (see Figure 3.12). It is highly helpful to be able to mark or otherwise identify or cue certain frames so you can either return to them, match other media to them, or plot media movement.

(**I**) — The button on the right — the **Marker** function — is the most used. When clicked, it simply leaves a symbol (**J**) at the playhead on the frame in the scrubber bar or media of the active window. The keyboard stroke is M or in the menu, Mark>Markers> Add. This is handy if you find a frame that might be a good starting or ending point for the clip, but you first want to check it against other things or have another possible point that you do not want to lose. You will find this function even more useful in the Timeline and, by extension, the Canvas.

FIG. 3.13

When you set a Marker, or return to one, a light overlay will appear in the viewer that identifies the Marker by number (see Figure 3.13). The same is true of the Canvas/ Timeline if you set a marker there. Markers are very handy but they can also clutter up your life. To remove them, go to Mark>Marker>Delete.

FIG. 3.14

Clips that you have put markers in will be identified by a right-facing triangle in the Browser. As with the bins, if you click on the triangle it will open the contents, in this case markers, in the clip (see Figure 3.14). If you double-click on one of these marker symbols, the clip will open in the Viewer at that marker.

(**K**) is to the left of the Marker function. **Keyframes** are similar to markers except they have a more active life in the process — Control K on the keyboard. They can be used to mark specific signposts in effects, transitions, or movement. An easy example is in audio, where they can be used to plot out changes in volume levels. They can be used on the video as well, in particular for motion effects and compositing. They tend to be used more in the Timeline and in clips opened from the Timeline. More on this later.

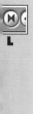

(**L**) Again to the left, **Mark Clip** simply marks the beginning and end of the clip as the in and out points — X on the keyboard. It is for just moving the entire clip into the Timeline. This is not something you do a lot because you are always trimming. You might do it if you are doing a film-style string out or doing all your trimming in the Timeline. Still, there are easier ways of getting the clip in whole, so this does not get a lot of use.

(**M**) **Match Frame** is at the end of the line. This is an odd feature that is probably there for the music video producers — F on the keyboard. If you have the same clip open in the Viewer as you have selected in the Timeline, when you click Match Frame the playhead in the Timeline will jump to the same frame selected in the Viewer. Go figure.

Back to the **Transport Controls** panel (see Figure 3.15). The buttons other than Play are as follows:

FIG. 3.15

The buttons on the far left and right are jump-to-the-next-edit buttons. In the Viewer, these allow you to jump from the beginning of a clip to the in point, to the out point, to the end and back. (**N**) is jump to previous edit — going backward toward the head of the show. (**O**) is jump to next edit — going to the tail. They do not stop at markers. If you have a really long take — as in a documentary — this can be handy, but otherwise this function finds much more employment in the Canvas. Even there, this operation is much more easily handled by the up/down arrow keys. "Jump to" functions, however accessed, can be very handy for moving through a program.

(**P**) is Play In to Out and does just that, plays from your selected In point to your selected Out point (kybd: Shift>l). Once you have set points, it can be useful to just look at your chosen section to make sure it is right before you move it into the Timeline. I usually just take it into the Timeline where it operates next to its intended neighbors. Undo if you don't like it.

(**Q**) is Play Around Current (kybd: \). In the Viewer, this plays a seven-second stretch around where you have the playhead parked. When you hit it, the playhead will jump back five seconds and then play the clip until two seconds after the original playhead point. The playhead then jumps back to the original point. The value of this may not sink in for a while, but this is very handy for analyzing the action at any point, particularly clips that you are thinking of for ins and, to a lesser extent, outs. Again, its value in the Canvas is even greater.

In the lower right hand corner, you will see two pop-up menus.

(**R**) is called Recent Clips and lists as well as gives you instant access to the most recent clips you have opened — up to ten (changeable in Preferences). Slide down the menu to the clip you want, let go of the mouse and it will open in the Viewer. Very nice when you have to sort through a lot of material in the Browser.

(**S**) is the Generator menu and is a much more complex beast, with access to a number of critical post-production operations, most notably titling. Many of these will be discussed in their appropriate chapters.

Across the top of the Viewer, you will notice two time code (G) windows. The time code box on the left (**T**) lists the elapsed time from your In to Out point, that is, the length of the section of the clip you are intending to use in the Timeline. This is very useful in terms of pacing, for monitoring the length of the pieces you are putting into the Timeline. The more experience you get, the more you will be able to sense the general pace of your project through the length of the pieces. Pace is equally dependent on the content of the clip, but length can be monitored to good effect.

The second time code window lists the time code of the frame displayed in the Viewer, the frame where the playhead is parked — (**U**). This allows you to monitor the accuracy of your time code. This is where window burns are so handy. You can look at the time code in the window burn and compare it with this window. Time code can get off, particularly if you are syncing up sound and picture manually. FCP has a bad habit of defaulting to different time codes and if your audio has its own time code, things can get messy. This actually happened in rough edits of *WT* and fortunately FCP's creators provided a solution (see page 36). Having incorrect time code can mess up EDLs something fierce and should be closely monitored.

The small clocks next to the time code boxes (**V**) are used for highlighting time code numbers. Once highlighted, you can type in new numbers and the clip or program will jump to the time code typed. This function is used to move around in the clips and, more effectively, in the show itself in the Canvas. Mercifully, you do not need to type in all the colons and semicolons. If you put in a number, FCP will supply the punctuation. In fact, FCP will supply anything you do not put in. If we open Scene 1A-3, the clip opens to time code (TC/)01:01:32:11. If we click the right hand clock and type 22, hit return, it jumps to TC/01:01:32:22. If we type in 4200, hit return, it jumps to TC/01:01:42:00. And so on. Obviously, the parameters of the clip are the limits. If you enter an invalid number, it will jump back to the original. Again, this gets more play in the Canvas.

Using time code in the left-side Duration box may be useful to some editors. If you have not yet set Ins or Outs, the box defaults to the duration of the entire clip. If you set an in, the box will display the time from the in to the end of the clip. If you want to quickly and easily set a sloppy out, you could type in 1500 (you know you are not going to move more than that), hit return, and you are ready to move 15 seconds of the clip starting with your in point into the Timeline. Not my style, but there are some possible applications.

Between the two time code windows, there are three pop-up menus — earlier versions of FCP just had two. The Zoom menu on the left (see Figure 3.16) pertains to how the clip is displayed in the Viewer and the way the image is cropped or magnified. FCP defaults to Fit to Window and this is where we want to be 99% of the time in standard cutting. If the image is ever displayed oddly, and there are a number of things that can happen that will reset it, go back to Fit to Window.

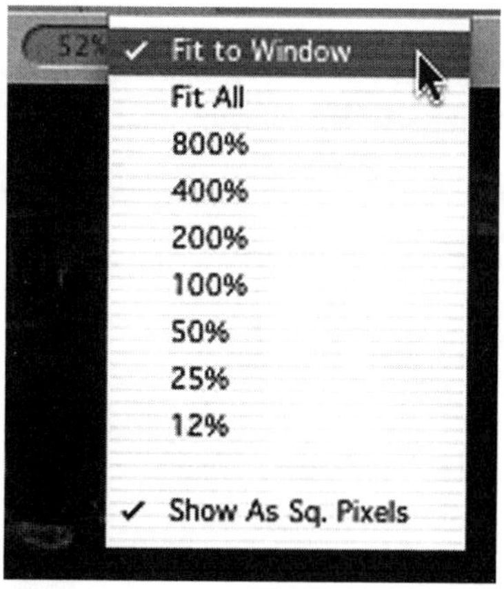

FIG. 3.16

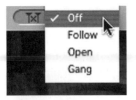

FIG. 3.17

The Playhead Sync pop-up menu — the one in the middle — is new to FCP 4 (see Figure 3.17). It works when the clip is opened from the Timeline and is used to lock the playheads in the Canvas and Viewer together. Any movement on either window is duplicated in its companion. The choices are Off, Follow, Open, and Gang. Follow locks the playheads for the single clip you have opened from the Timeline; Open for the entire show; and Gang consistently duplicates whatever displacement of the two playheads was present when you opened the clip.

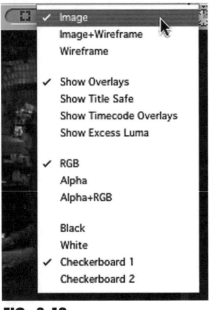

FIG. 3.18

The View pop-up menu on the right (see Figure 3.18) is a heavy hitter, giving access to a number of the functions also found in the main View menu. It is used for image manipulation, compositing, color monitoring, backgrounds, and a variety of other things. More on this later.

So the Viewer is where you look at and make all decisions about individual clips. Eventually, you will be using it to create new material and apply many effects to the clips.

THE CANVAS

The Canvas is where you view your edited program (see Figure 3.19). In that, it is the last place you go. It does, however, have some editorial functions and is as good a place to start discussing how to get things into the Timeline as any. Many writers on the program tend to describe the workflow in FCP as a clockwise movement, starting in the Browser, moving to the Viewer, then Canvas, then on to the Timeline. Going back to the Browser for the next shot completes the circular movement. My workflow is different. In the old Two Up desktop arrangement, I tended to think of movement as more of an "N" shape, starting in the Browser, moving to the Viewer, to the Timeline, and playing the final result in the Canvas. Now, I guess it is a "cardiac monitor" movement — it is straight line, then it dips and returns. The clockwise movement gets play because you can use functions on the Canvas to get the clips into the Timeline, but there are other ways and it seems a minor function that could be anywhere.

FIG. 3.19

The Canvas, of course, looks very similar to the Viewer. Some of the controls are in reverse order and on opposite sides, but otherwise most of the functions are the same. The Zoom, the Playhead Sync, and View pop-up menus are exactly the same. The other pop-up menus are gone, but the presence of the edit buttons (see Figure 3.20) is the significant addition. If you click on the small arrow on the right, more options appear (see Figure 3.21).

FIG. 3.20

FIG. 3.21

The Mark In and Out functions bear some discussion. When you bring a shot from the Viewer, you theoretically use Mark In for the point you want to put the shot in the Timeline. If you have marked an In and Out in the Viewer, you only need to mark an In in the Canvas/Timeline because the length of the clip being inserted will determine the end. However, the playhead in the Timeline also serves as an In point. If you have not set an In on the Canvas, FCP will automatically place the In at the point where you have parked the playhead. Since the last thing you probably did was determine where in the Timeline you wanted to put the new clip, the playhead is all you need. Occasionally, the Mark In/Out functions in the Canvas prove useful and occasionally you do set an Out in the Timeline/Canvas, particularly when you want to replace a specific part of a clip in the Timeline. However, an awful lot of the work can be done with the playhead. Choosing an In overrides the playhead.

There are five potential editing operations found on the Canvas — seven if you count the ones that add a transition with the edit. The options are **Insert, Overwrite, Replace, Fit to Fill**, and **Superimpose**. Overwrite and Insert are by far the most commonly used. If you are doing simple assemble edit, you can use either one. Both Insert and Overwrite can also be executed with a transition, making the total seven.

Insert (kybd: F9): Inserts the chosen clip at the playhead or In point, pushing any existing material toward the tail end of the show.

Overwrite (kybd: F10): The most used editing operation, this inserts the clip at the point of the playhead, covering any existing material for the length of the inserted clip.

Replace (kybd: F11): This simply replaces a selected clip in the Timeline with a clip you have chosen from the Viewer at the playhead. Unlike Overwrite, the playhead and the boundaries of the existing clip are the determining factors.

Fit to Fill (kybd: F12): This is kind of a neat idea. It inserts a clip into an existing Timeline, but will change the length, that is, speed, of the clip to match. If you have a two-second clip but need to fill a two-and-a-half-second hole, this is perfect. The action is slowed down to last the extra length. Obviously there are limits before the motion will start to look unnatural. For us guys from the film editing world, we just stand back and shake our heads.

Superimpose (kybd: Shift: F11): Puts the chosen shot at the playhead on a second or new video track. This makes it ready to be superimposed — what was called a double exposure in the photographic world — with material already in the Timeline.

Bottom line is that Overwrite covers up existing material and Insert pushes existing material back to make room for the edit. If there is nothing in the Timeline, you are "assemble" editing and, as suggested, you can use either. The last three are specialized edits that are used only in certain circumstances. Insert with transition and Overwrite with transition (kybd: Shift>F9 and F10, respectively) simply add a chosen transition at the In point. Choosing effects will be covered in Chapter VII.

In essence there are four ways to get a shot into the Timeline.

1. The simplest, although most inelegant, way is to just drag the clip straight from the Browser into the Timeline. Click on the shot you want (don't double click or it will open in the Viewer) and simply drag it over. The entire clip will show up in the Timeline and can then be trimmed to your heart's content. Be aware, however, that while you can still open the clip in the Viewer from the Timeline, there are some functions that can only be applied when the clip is opened from the Browser (Mark Splits, et cetera).

2. When you click anywhere in the image in the Viewer, the displayed frame shows up as a thumbnail. Drag this thumbnail over to the Canvas and the five editorial choices will appear (see Figure 3.22, Folio page 6) in an embedded layer. This is very sexy but not particularly intuitive. You can also just drag this thumbnail straight into the Timeline, which I suppose you could count as another way.

G. 3.22

3. Click on one of the edit buttons on the Canvas shown in Figure 3.21. The Canvas only shows three edit functions, the first two being the most used: Insert (**W**) and Overwrite (**X**). The third button defaults to the last used of the other five functions. Again, you can get access to the other functions by clicking on the little arrow on the right and sliding to the desired function. Whatever function you choose now defaults as the third option.

4. My preferred way is to use the F9 through F12 keys on the upper right side of the keyboard. Each key — sometimes in conjunction with the shift key — represents a specific editing function. Keyboard functions are as follows: **Insert** (kybd: F9); **Overwrite** (kybd: F10); **Replace** (kybd: F11); **Fit to Fill** (kybd: F12); **Superimpose** (kybd: Shift: F11). Combine the Shift key with F9 and F10 and the edit will execute with a transition.

Again, the Canvas is where you play your show, whether just roughed in or finely tuned. Depending on your working method, it can either be a very active part of your workflow or, at least initially, a place simply to view what you have done. Once we factor in compositing, titles, and a few other things, it will get more play.

THE TIMELINE

The Timeline is where the lion's share of the action occurs (see Figure 3.23). It is where your program is built and all the cuts are represented. After initial actions in the Viewer, it is where you will do much of your trimming, most of your re-arranging, most of your layering of sound, all effects, and a host of other things. For the good, old-fashioned straight line cutting of the film world, you can do 100% of your editing here if you want.

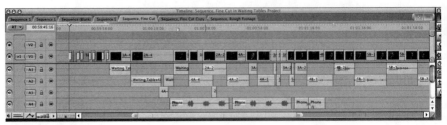

FIG. 3.23

In the film-style editing approach that we are focusing on in this text, we are just cutting one "track" of picture and cutting and layering a number of audio tracks to create a rich and consistent sound design. To boil it down is impossible, but the goal is to stack your trimmed clips up end to end, making sure to keep the audio in sync, as well as planning out any visual transitions and the like. When we are done with *WT* we are going to have our one video track and an as-yet-to be-determined number of audio tracks. Other approaches would have other designs. A music video might have ten video tracks and one audio.

The Timeline opens to one track of video and four tracks of audio — what Apple calls the **Base Tracks**. FCP is really designed for the high-end video guys, the music (or similar) video projects where there is a whole lot going on visually. To that end, there is a lot of real estate devoted to the potential for more video tracks for layering and effects. We will talk about adding tracks later. We are going to artificially remove that area in our graphics to streamline the presentation.

When you bring a clip into the Timeline, the playhead comes in parked at the end. Obviously, you can bring in clips that are MOS picture, audio by itself, or picture and audio together — linked clips (G).

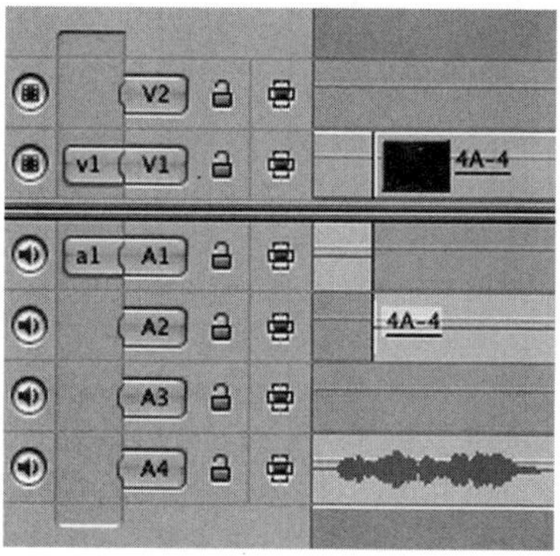

The left center side (see Figure 3.24) of the Timeline — where the base tracks are — is devoted to three things: 1) selecting the destination for clips; 2) selecting what we want to see and hear at any given moment; and 3) maintaining the viability of the video and audio tracks.

FIG. 3.24

The green buttons on the left are called **Track Visibility** controls (**Y**) and are used for disabling and enabling tracks. If we want to not hear or see any tracks, we simply click the desired buttons to turn off what we do not want. This is particularly good for isolating unwanted sounds and the like. It is also nice not to have to listen to sounds over and over again. Once we have positioned some sounds, we do not have to listen to them every time we check edits or sequences. Working at home, my family got tired of constantly jumping up for the phone whenever I played *Waiting Tables*. Turning off certain sounds can save wear and tear on the nerves of both you and anyone else who might have the misfortune to be within hearing distance. FCP opens with everything enabled.

FIG. 3.25

The next column of track **Destination Control** buttons is constantly used (see Figure 3.25). These simply select what is going where. The destination of audio will consume most of our attention in our approach. Once you start building and layering dialogue and effects and music, where you place things will take on critical importance. Even apparently simple cutting of sync sound can start to become more complicated as you take more issues, particularly consistency, into consideration. Remember, however, that all this applies to video as well. Other approaches may require quite a few layers of picture, and some people like to bounce image back and forth to different video tracks so they can maintain certain clips and sequences in certain places. We will be working with only one video track for the bulk of the demonstrations, but be aware that other applications may be more complex.

Both the design and the function of the destination control buttons, which used to be called targets in earlier versions of FCP, has changed in FCP 4. They used to be the little dainty butterfly/bowtie-looking things, but now they are good solid-looking toggle type buttons. The buttons are separated into two parts — the **Source Control** (SC) on the left side and the **Destination Control** (DC) on the right.

The number of DC buttons is just your number of tracks — four audio in this case when you open FCP. They are labeled A1 through A4 and will simply go up numerically as you add tracks, unless you alter the order. The SC buttons are slightly more complicated. When you open an audio or video clip in the Viewer, FCP senses how many tracks of audio the clip has and provides that number of SC buttons. If there is only one track of audio, as there is in all of *WT*, only one SC button will appear, labeled A1. Digital video cameras frequently have stereo mics — two tracks, two SC buttons — labeled A1 and A2, and so on. If picture was shot MOS, nothing will appear.

If we open Scene 1A-3 in the Viewer, one SC button will appear on track A1 in the Timeline. If we want to assign it to a different track, we simply click the DC side on that track and SC button jumps to the new track. We can also drag it, which is unnecessary in this case, but this may come in handy if you have more source tracks. If we click on either side, the SC and DC sides separate (**Z**). In this instance, no audio will be sent to that track. This is mostly used when you have a video clip with sound, but do not want to use the sound — a not at all uncommon occurrence. Bottom line is click them together if you want the track to go there.

To the right of these are the **Track Locks** (**AA**), which simply locks the tracks so nothing can be done to them. If you are fiddling with audio and are afraid you might be affecting the picture, simply lock it and no changes can be made to the video. A cross-hatched design covers locked tracks. These can make certain operations more efficient, but more importantly can save you an awful lot of pain. The last button in this area is the **Auto Select** (**BB**) control, which is new to FCP 4. It allows you to highlight areas of a track by using the In/Out functions on the Canvas. This one has not yet entered my workflow vocabulary.

Across the bottom of the Timeline are a number of critical options. Starting from the left, the **Audio Controls** (**CC**) button is new to FCP 4. It opens two options for all audio tracks, appearing to the left of the visibility button (see Figure 3.26). This allows you to either mute (again the speaker symbol) the track or run it **solo** — the headphone symbol. The latter is a quick way to turn off all other tracks so you can just listen to and analyze one at a time. When you start building multiple tracks, it is nice not to have to turn everything off to hear a single track. You can click the solo button on more than one track to hear any combination you want.

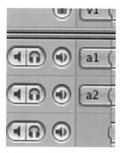

The next is **Clip Keyframes** control (**DD**), which opens a narrow band below both video and audio tracks that display the positioning of and actions associated with keyframes. This is used mostly for motion and compositing effects. See Chapter XII.

FIG. 3.26

The next is **Clip Overlays** (**EE**), which drops a narrow line on all tracks — black for video, red for audio. The black line controls a clip's "visibility" (see page 143 for more on this). Red lines are used for audio and are a standard way of manipulating volume. When you place the pointer on top of a red or black line in the clip it will change into the vertical drag symbol (**FF**). You can then click and drag the volume level up or down. A small box will appear (**GG**), indicating the change in volume in decibels. Thus, you can change the volume for the entire clip. In conjunction with either keyframes or the pen tool, you can also shift to different volumes within individual clips (see pages 160-62).

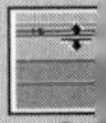

The next is **Track Height** which simply changes the vertical size of all tracks in the Timeline. Second from left is default. Among other things, this is very handy if you are using the just-described volume change and need to do very fine discriminations. In default height, you can only move in increments of 3 or 4 db. Next is **Zoom Control (II)**. This lengthens the Timeline horizontally, making each clip longer and devoting more space to it. This is a much-used function to get alternately micro or more global views of the Timeline, allowing tighter discriminations on cuts and a host of other things. FCP gives you more ways to zoom than you could shake a stick at — there are at least five ways to do this — and there are probably more efficient ways to execute. The zoom mechanism only changes size horizontally — vertical change can only be done with the Track Height control.

Moving to the right is the **Zoom Slider** (see Figure 3.27). The arrows on

FIG. 3.27

FIG. 3.28

either end allow you to scroll through the Timeline. It is okay, but a little slow. The slider itself is much faster. If you click in the center of the slider (**JJ**) and drag either way, you can move quite quickly through the show. If you click on the **thumb tabs (KK)** on either end of the slider, you can also zoom into or out of the Timeline (second way). Click and drag on these — and the slider itself — will get smaller of bigger.

Along the right side of the Timeline are sliders to scroll vertically through the height of both the audio and video sections of the Timeline (see Figure 3.28). You can either click on the blue slider and drag or click on the up/down arrows beneath the sliders. Obviously, when you wind up with a substantial number of audio tracks, or video tracks for that matter, they cannot all be visible in the Timeline at the same time. These sliders give access as desired. There is also a Divider line between the audio and video that can be repositioned with the little thumb tabs between the sliders.

Right above these sliders are the link (left) and snapping (right) buttons (see Figure 3.29) that were covered in Issues. These are both critical functions although they can be easily accessed elsewhere.

FIG. 3.29

As stated, the scrubber bar across the top is called the Ruler (see Figure 3.30). The numbers across are the time code of the show. Above the

FIG. 3.30

Ruler, every sequence you create for a project has a tab. You can quickly move to different sequences here. Between the Ruler and the tabs, is the already mentioned Render Bar (R) — two slim lines, the upper one representing video and the bottom representing audio. With all of its color-coding, this is useful for more than keeping track of render status (see Chapter IX). The render bar will be gray if the media does not need rendering and steel gray if it is something that has already been rendered. If there is a gap in a render bar, it indicates there is a point where there is no media in the Timeline. This is not necessarily a bad thing, but should be monitored to make sure you are not leaving any holes, particularly in the audio. To the left is the Real-Time pop-up menu (see Figure 3.31), which allows you to set the quality of playback which gives you options

FIG. 3.31

as to whether effects can be played with or without rendering (see pages 139-141 for a complete discussion).

On the top right of the Timeline is a standard box displaying the program time code at the present position of the playhead. This is important for double-checking positioning of cuts and effects. You can also type numbers into it to move around in the show. The time code box on the upper left indicates the entire length of the show.

There are a few more functions that will be covered in due time, but that is pretty much it. The Timeline is where the rubber meets the road, where the real action occurs. This is where your project either happens or doesn't, depending on your creativity and your vision.

THE DESKTOP—
TOOLS & TRICKS

THE TOOL PALETTE

FCP's Tool Palette (see Figure 4.1), which many people call the toolbar, is used constantly. Certainly most of its functions can be accessed through the keyboard or accomplished other ways, but an integrated conception of what can be accomplished here is important to the process of editing. Here you will find most of the tools for trimming, controlling, changing, and grouping all your visual and audio material.

In the standard arrangement, the toolbar is found in the lower right corner of the desktop, although it can be positioned wherever you find most convenient. It is accompanied by the Audio Meters, a useful bar for monitoring sound. The most commonly used tools appear by default in the toolbar and a simple mouse-click puts them into use.

All the selections, except the first one, have a number of options. To access them, one simply clicks on the default tool and holds on it. The options will appear, and one simply slides over and lets go of the mouse on the desired tool. The keyboard commands for the default selections are usually a single letter, with options being multiple letters.

FIG. 4.1

Starting from the top, the first function is simply the computer's selector (**A**) (kybd: A). Called the **Selection Tool**, this simply toggles between the mouse/trackball functions of the computer and the other tools on the toolbar or functions of the computer. This is one time you really want to know and use the keyboard function. You will forever be pushing the mouse around to get back to this if you do not. Get used to the **a** key. More than anything else, knowing the keyboard command for this can save time as well as wear and tear on the carpal tunnels.

Initially, the second tool — **Edit Select** — is one of the least-used functions on the toolbar (see Figure 4.2). It is used in a similar fashion to how a boxing tool is used in Adobe Photoshop or similar graphics programs. It is for selecting individual or groups of edit points

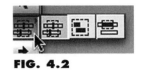

FIG. 4.2

to apply trims or effects. I generally do not use it much when doing the rough cut and have found limited use for it in advance cutting. When you start to get a large number of audio tracks, it can be very handy. The options allow you to group edits differently.

The third tool — **Track Select** — is much more useful and controls how you apply effects to or move tracks (see Figure 4.3). I use this last function extensively, to move tracks individually

FIG. 4.3

or, most frequently, in tandem. It is very useful for shifting whole segments of the show and keeping them all in sync. Very frequently, when I am micro-managing a clip — shaving off a frame of audio or video here or there — gaps will be created in the Timeline. If you just grab the next shot and move it up, you simply cause a different gap down the road or, worst of all, pull things out of sync. This function allows you to move all the desired tracks together while maintaining their relationship with each other. There is another menu/keyboard function called Close Gap (Sequence> Close Gap or Control> G) that does this, but it only works on straight cuts (where audio and video are cut in the same place). While this is the main function of this tool set, the individual options allow you to be much more discretionary in your movements.

The fourth and fifth tool sets — **Roll/Ripple** and **Slip/Slide/Timemap** — are related and will receive varying testimonials to their credibility depending on the editor to whom you are speaking (see Figure 4.4). Some people probably use them constantly and others may never touch them at all. Their application is so specific that it is pretty much a matter of what working style one finds most comfortable. I find them minimally useful, but do occasionally find their capabilities come in very handy. I do not use them much during the rough edit but, used in conjunction with the ever-useful "Undo" function, they can be a great way of seeing if you can find a slightly better edit point. These tools may also represent a couple of the fundamental problems with nonlinear editing: a bewildering number of choices that renders some people indecisive, as well as causing them to focus on micro-management rather than the big picture.

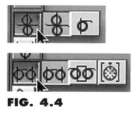

FIG. 4.4

As with all the tools, these two tool sets are used exclusively for working on edits in the Timeline. The first of the two defaults to the roll edit and the option is the ripple edit. The second defaults to the slip edit with the option being slide. When tracks are linked, the effect will be applied to both picture and audio. Frequently you want to change just one, in which case the previously described Option key should be employed in conjunction with the tool.

To use a tool, move it into the desired clip. Slip and Slide can be used anywhere in a clip. Roll and Ripple can only be used toward the beginning or end of clips — a small x on the lower right side of the tool indicates it is not in position to be used. When the tool is in position to be used, the x will disappear. With all four, click on the spot and dark borders will appear around the edges of the affected clip or clips. Drag the edit point or the clip to the desired spot. In all instances, a small box in the clip will indicate the number of frames moved and affected clips will be represented in the Canvas.

ROLL — (**B**) allows you to move the edit point between two shots without affecting the duration of the sequence. You can simply jog the edit point back and forth and see if you can find the best edit point. The duration of each shot changes but the overall length of the two shots in the Timeline remains the same. It is great for when you have the timing between two shots, say the pause between two lines of dialogue, just the way you want it but want to check other edit points.

RIPPLE — (**C**) is, for someone with a film editing background, the tool that is initially most attractive. It most embodies what the nonlinear edit is all about and its absence in analog video editing is why it was so hated. It allows you to trim frames, while bringing the rest of the show up behind. Unfortunately it is somewhat limited in what it can do and, at least for my working style, cannot execute the function I do most often.

Slip and slide edits are even more specific, but again can be useful.

SLIP — (**D**) is where the content of the clip you have clicked on changes. The clip remains exactly the same length and the shots on either side also remain the same, but the content shifts one way or the other, depending on which way you drag. The in and out points move forward as you drag right and backward as you drag left.

SLIDE — (**E**) is where you move the clip in the Timeline vis a vis the surrounding clips. Here, the content remains exactly the same but the relationship to the preceding and succeeding clips changes. If you slide the clip toward the head of the show, you subtract content (frames) from the tail of the first shot and add an equal amount of content at the head of the third shot.

TIME REMAP — (**F**) is new to FCP 4. It does not quite seem to fit with this set of tools, but allows you to change the speed for the whole clip or in the middle of the clip.

These are particularly good for analyzing the insertion of shots and in a music video context are great for pushing material around. If you want to line up the sound of a cymbal being hit with a drumstick, they can be great. The best example of slip and slide editing in our approach is the manipulation of an MOS shot that has been inserted into a longer piece. Inserting MOS shots of Judy into Fritz's long phone conversation or reaction shots of the couple will provide some good examples of both slip and slide edits.

On all four of these, a double window opens in the Canvas that gives a visual representation of both the outgoing (left) and incoming (right) clips (see Figure 4.5). As you shift the cut, the new last and first frames are displayed. While I think this is a great idea and fully support its inclusion, I find these dual images somewhat hard to follow and a little inexact. It is hard to conceptualize what you have done and you need to stop and play the sequence (which, of course, you need to do either way). The crux of narrative editing is to look at shots in real time, get a sense of what might

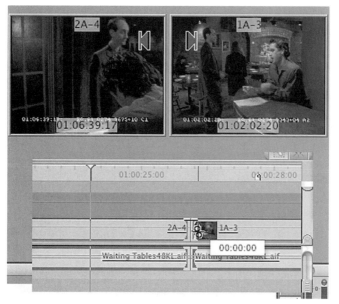

FIG. 4.5

work, and then single-frame to find the right frame. Displaying the last and first frames does not give you a sense of how the cut will flow. While some editors would disagree, editing should be the process of analyzing your shots and cutting to accomplish a kinetic or dramatic goal rather than randomly trying something and deciding if it works or not. I find trimming frames with the razor blade and then looking at the cut to be far more precise. These tools are simply not very exact.

The sixth function (see Figure 4.6) is used constantly. The **Razor Blade** (kybd: B to select) is used to cut and trim the shots in the Timeline. If you hit Control V, it will cut on the selected track at the point of the playhead. If two or more tracks are

FIG. 4.6

linked, the Razor Blade will cut all of them. If tracks are linked and you only want to cut one of them, depress the Option key while clicking with the blade. The Razor Blade's option is the double razor blade, which simply cuts all parallel tracks in the Timeline.

The **Zoom** tool (kybd: Z) is also quite handy although there are many other ways to accomplish its function (see Figure 4.7).

FIG. 4.7

Click on the tool and the cursor will turn into a magnifying glass. Click on the Timeline and the clips expand horizontally, which allows you to make tighter discriminations and thus accurately trim frames or sequences of frames. In the size that FCP defaults to it is sometimes difficult to drag in increments of individual frames. Zooming in allows you to have more pinpoint access to the clips. The tool defaults to the magnifying glass with the plus (zoom in on the Timeline). Its options are the magnifying glass with the minus (kybd: ZZ), which will make each shot smaller, thus giving you a more global view of the Timeline.

These tools get used with great frequency, although there is easier access. Command + and Command – duplicate the function, as does clicking and dragging on either end of the slider on the bottom. The Zoom tools also work on the Canvas and the Viewer if you want, for example, to examine small areas of a particular frame. The **Hand** (kybd: H) tool allows you drag the Timeline around, either vertically or horizontally. The next tool, **Scrub Video** (kybd: HH), allows you to change the thumbnail image — click in the thumbnail with the tool and drag in either direction. Neither of these tools seems particularly germane.

FIG. 4.8

Below this is the **Crop** tool (kybd: C) and its option, the **Distort** tool (kybd: D) (see Figure 4.8). These are for relatively advanced image manipulation functions that will be covered in Chapter XII.

FIG. 4.9

The last tool is the **Pen** tool (kybd: P), which lays keyframes where you click in the Timeline (see Figure 4.9). When employed here, it is most commonly used for setting the beginning and end of audio level changes in the Timeline. All audio issues will be covered in Chapter VIII, but you use it to mark points where you want volume shifts to start and stop. The options are **Pen Delete** (kybd: PP), which deletes pen marks, and **Pen Smooth** (kybd: PPP).

THE AUDIO METERS

The audio meters (see Figure 4.10) are more for monitoring your sound at this point, rather than for doing anything specific to it. However, any problem they indicate should be addressed. They are a constant reminder of whether the levels are within tolerances for good sound reproduction. In digital recording, the biggest thing to watch for is when the sound is over-recorded.

For those familiar with the old-fashioned VU (Volume Unit) meters, a note on digital recording is in order. Everyone has seen 0 VU on the old analog meters and they have undoubtedly been warned that going over that level will create distortion. This is only partially true. VU meters are built with substantial **head-room**, room over 0 VU where you can still get a quality recording. So, many sounds can exceed 0VU and not only not have problems but profit from the experience. Certainly, the occasional swings above O are rarely an issue. In fact, under-recording is almost more of a problem in analog than over. If the recording is too low, then volume levels need to be increased, thus amplifying the general ambience and, more importantly, system noise. This latter can be thought of as **hiss** but more accurately is called the **noise floor**. Jacking volumes causes immediate problems with excess noise, as well as long-term ones as the audio moves through the transferring and rerecording process.

FIG. 4.10

On a digital meter, as are the meters in FCP, zero is zero. Past that point, you will get absolute distortion. All care should be taken in location recording to not go over zero. If it is going over zero while in the Timeline, you should backtrack and find out where the problem was introduced. Under-recording does not present quite the same problem, because digital essentially does not have a noise floor. Zero VU on an analog meter translates to –12dB on any digital meter. Above that is a VU meter's headroom — from there it heads eventually to the threshold. FCP's meters will go yellow between –9 and –3, indicating an approaching problem (see Figure 4.11). The meters go red above –3. If the sound goes above zero, the small red dot at the top, on either left or right, will light indicating a significant distortion event. Keep an eye on this.

Final Cut Pro captures audio at the level at which it was recorded or digitized. Changing the volume of sound prior to or during capture requires either a third-party audio card or manipulating volume while transferring recorded audio to

FIG. 4.11

another medium. This latter is not uncommon, with creating files of audio a useful way of getting your sound into a project (see pages 205-6).

TRICKS

Final Cut Pro's workflow consists of a number of commonly executed actions, in terms of viewing, analyzing, and moving media. All of these have been discussed in some form already. However, there are also a few ways of doing things that have not been covered in the course of describing the features of the windows. Here is a quick overview.

MOVING AROUND IN THE TIMELINE AND CLIPS

There are lots of ways to move around in the program and the clips. There are of course the jog and shuttle controls in the Viewer and Canvas. You will have to determine the value of these for yourself. Then there are the multiplied speeds of the J and L keys, although fast forward and reverse are not the most efficient ways to travel long distances. I find the Jump to Next, or Previous, Edit functions, found on either side of the Transport Controls or at the up/down arrows, to be a great and heavily used resource for moving around in a section I am editing, but again not efficient for long distance travel. All the arrow keys can cover a lot of real estate. It is fairly quick to just move frame by frame with the left/right arrows and it also gives you a good sense of the qualities of the clip. Again, obviously not good for long distances. All arrow functions can also be found in the menus at Mark>Previous or Next, although why you would use them there is beyond me.

Just scrubbing in the scrubber bar (we are including the Ruler here) with the playhead is reasonably efficient for long and short distances. Click on the playhead and simply drag it — you can travel near or far quite quickly. The slider on the bottom is probably the favored way for long distances — click in the center and drag. Remember, however, that the playhead does not travel with you when you do this. You have to click in the scrubber bar when you get to your destination and the playhead will jump to that spot. Many times I have traveled some place, hit play, and then found myself back where I started because the playhead got left behind. The Home and End keys are obviously great for full-show moves.

One way not yet discussed is traveling with time code. If you highlight the upper left time code box in the Canvas, either by clicking in the clock or the normal way, you can type in a number, hit return, and the playhead will jump to that point in the scrubber bar. This can be done in the Timeline as well as with clips in the Viewer. This can be very good if you are the kind who likes numbers and is fastidiously prepared with the logs and reports that make time code readings quickly available. Not quite my style, but the production notes and the people to read them are always available in a highly prepared professional editing room.

Using the zoom out function is probably the last way to move efficiently. If you zoom out to where the entire show is visible in the Timeline (see Figure 4.12), it is easy to click in the Ruler to drag or jump the playhead to the desired areas.

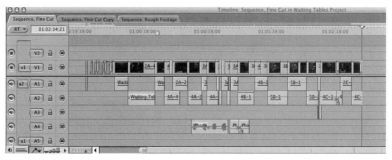

FIG. 4.12

TRIMMING CLIPS

You can trim or get access to trimming clips either in the Viewer or in the Timeline. Three of the key ways have been covered: 1) setting in and out points in the Viewer; 2) using the Razor Blade in the Timeline; and 3) using one of the trimming tools (Roll, Ripple, Slip, Slide). The Viewer is clearly a valuable place to make decisions. However, I tend to use it to rough things in. I will get a clip the way I think it ought to be, bring it into the Timeline and then have at it with the Razor Blade until I get it the way it really ought to be. I find Roll, Ripple, Slip, Slide to be useful for specialty cuts and looking at slightly different options for edit points. In this last regard, however, keep in mind that when we say "slightly" in the every-frame-makes-a-difference world of editing, it can make a world of difference. Roll, Ripple, Slip, and Slide can be useful.

There are two ways to trim shots that have not yet been addressed: simply dragging the shot longer or shorter and the **Trim Edit** window. This former is obviously huge and returns to the concept of non-destructive editing. The selection tool is always represented as the arrow when you place it on a clip in the Timeline. However, as you drag it toward the head or the tail of the clip, it will change into the drag symbol, two vertical lines with arrows on either side (see Figure 4.13). Click and you can now drag the clip longer or shorter. It will only allow you to drag to the limits of the clip and it will only drag something longer if there is open real estate in the direction you are dragging. If there is another clip there, dragging goes nowhere. When you drag, a box will appear telling you both how much you are adding or subtracting — in seconds and frames — and the clip's new duration, again in seconds and frames. Snapping can be a hindrance to this process. Having to toggle it on and off is a common workflow thing in FCP and you can simply hit n on the keyboard. The icon in the upper right of the Timeline allows you to keep track of whether snapping is on or off. If the clip has linked audio, it will change the same amount as the picture whether the two are cut in the same place or not. Again, and very significantly, clicking in conjunction with the option key allows you to work on linked audio and video pieces separately.

FIG. 4.13

The Trim Edit window is a great idea and at first looks like a tremendous resource. For me, it is great in theory but winds up being slightly problematic in application. It again will be loved by some and left alone by many. If you place the pointer right on a cut in the Timeline, it will again change into the drag symbol. Double-click and the Trim Edit window will appear over the Viewer and Canvas (see Figure 4.14). It will show the last

frame of the outgoing clip on the left and the first frame of the incoming clip on the right. There are a number of ways you can affect the cut, but most typical is to hit the plus and minus frame buttons right in the center-bottom. FCP defaults to one frame and five frame changes, with the latter number resettable at User Preference>General (see page 183). If you hit –1, it will subtract one frame from the outgoing and add one frame to the incoming — a roll edit. Plus numbers add to the outgoing and subtract from the incoming. You will see the new beginning and ending frames displayed in Trim Edit and you will see the cut jump in the

FIG. 4.14

Timeline if you are looking at it. You can also drag the in and out points in the scrubber bars to affect changes.

Very significantly, the Trim Edit window can also be opened with the Ripple tool in which case it executes a Ripple edit. This, to me, increases its value significantly. The Ripple tool will just select one side of the cut or the other — either incoming or outgoing, with the window's tools just affecting the selected side. Obviously, if you trim frames from the outgoing, it will pull up the rest of the show behind. Same with incoming. The window can be opened with the roll tool as well, but is just the same as double-clicking the drag symbol.

As always, remember the option key to use Trim Edit for one part of a linked clip — Option double-click on the chosen track. Picture can be trimmed separate of audio and vice versa. Two speaker symbols come up if you choose audio and the result of trimming can both be heard and seen in the clips in the Timeline.

It may be my film background, but I like to analyze the clip and trim where I think it will be right. Trim Edit is of the try-something-and-see-if-you-like-it approach, so it boils down to working methods again. In its defense, the Trim Edit allows a quick route when I know I want to just trim or add a frame or two. It is a great idea and should be there, but I do not use it that frequently.

Again, the central question is whether to do the bulk of the work in the Viewer or the Timeline. There are advantages and disadvantages to both.

At first, it appears as if NLE software is designed for you to do all this work in the Viewer and that is how the workflow is often presented and, to a certain extent, is presented in this chapter. However, depending on working style, a great amount, if not all, trimming can be done in the Timeline if desired.

DRAWING CLIPS UP

While we have stated that the two primary practical goals are to get things into the Timeline with trimming occurring either there or in the Viewer, there was also a third important goal mentioned briefly: closing any gaps created by trimming while keeping the audio in sync. That is, drawing the show up while keeping the sound correct.

The need to close gaps occurs particularly when using the Razor Blade. We create a trim, select it, and then delete it. If we simply hit delete, the trim will disappear, but a gap in the show will remain. Obviously we have to draw up the show behind. The Ripple tool will do this but is somewhat inexact and can knock things out of sync. There are a number of other ways of doing this, but three main ways suggest themselves. The first two, however, can only be used when sound and picture are cut in the same place, a shortcoming that will complicate our efforts.

Ripple delete — Briefly described in Chapter I, the Ripple Delete key (**G**) key is found between the numeric keypad and the main keyboard. If you have cut a trim, select it and hit the Ripple Delete key. The trim is gone and the show pulls up. A PowerBook does not have this key but this operation can be done at Shift>Delete on the keyboard. This works on a standard keyboard as well.

Close Gap — is found in the menus at Sequence>Close Gap (kybd: Control G). If the playhead is placed at the beginning of a gap, this function will close any gap whatsoever. If audio and video are cut in different places at the point of the gap, the Close Gap function may not perform.

Select Track, particularly (**H**) (All Tracks Forward — an option in the Select Track tool set), allows you to select and thus move all tracks from a certain point onwards. In my approach, if I want to lengthen a clip, I like to drag it so it is longer than I know I want to use, analyze it in real time and frame by frame, and "re-trim" it with the razor blade. To do this, I need to create some empty real estate in the direction I am trimming.

I can select everything with All Tracks Forward and move it down the road, make my cut, then re-select the end of the show again and move it back into place.

As your audio tracks get more complex, be aware that this tool may have more difficulty isolating which clip fragments are desired. While occasionally it seems like FCP has a mind of its own in instances like this, trying to get it to interpolate things that are in our heads is not possible. You may have to finesse it.

Nesting — is a function that allows you to group clips and segments together on a permanent basis so they cannot be changed at all (except deleted). Select the desired section with the standard boxing tool and choose Sequence>Nest Items in the menus. It will ask you to name the nest and after clicking OK, the section will be represented as one clip of that name. Nesting creates a new sequence in the Browser that can still be modified.

FIXING SYNC

If you either purposefully move audio and video out of sync or accidentally knock them out, there are simple ways to reestablish sync. If the clip is linked in FCP's database, a small red box will appear as the audio and video are moved out of sync, indicating exactly how far they are out (see Figure 4.15).

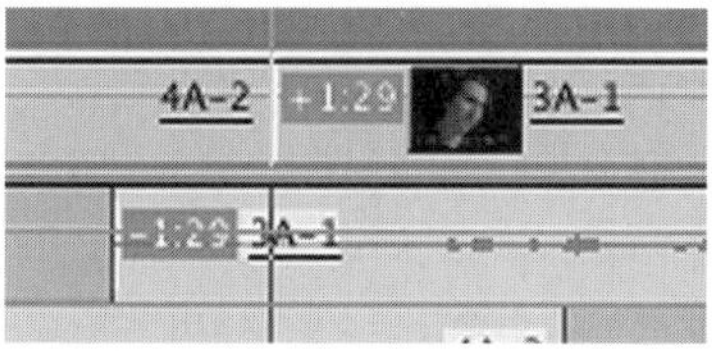

FIG. 4.15

The re-syncing function is only found in the contextual menus. Control-click on the red box in the audio and a two-item menu will appear (see Figure 4.16). Choosing "Move into Sync" will simply move the audio piece back into sync. "Slip into Sync" will also move

FIG. 4.16

things back into sync, but it keeps the audio's new location in the Timeline while shifting the audio within. Clicking on the red box in the picture will give the additional option of moving or slipping adjacent clips.

While "Move into Sync" is probably most efficient, another way can be used that is useful for many applications. Clips can be shifted a frame at a time with either the comma key — toward the head of the show — or the period key — toward the tail of the show. First, unlink the audio and video that is out of sync—highlight the clip and hit Command>L or go to Modify>Link in the menus. Both audio and video are still highlighted together so click outside to un-highlight. Click on the audio and press comma or period the number of frames out of sync. The small box will count down until it hits zero and disappears. Relink the clips (G).

Using the comma and period can be useful for many other applications, but particularly in testing different relationships between picture and sound. Lining up visuals with music is particularly easy with this function. If you had a drummer hitting a cymbal, you can move the visual against the audio, testing different positioning until you get the perfect relationship. Once established, markers are very useful in creating reference points should you ever knock the shot out of sync. To move picture or audio, you have to have real estate on either side of the clip in the Timeline. You can create this either by pulling back the other clips on either side or, more efficiently, by moving the clip to another track. See the next section for this.

Knocking things out of sync can be particularly trying. This can happen if you try an editorial function that is going to affect different tracks differently. FCP has a warning dialogue box that alerts you if this is going to occur. The more complex your project, the more synchronization will require careful management. As suggested, you can be working somewhere in the beginning of a Timeline and be wholly unaware that you are creating problems later in the show. This should not happen if you are linking everything properly and laying out your sound well, but things can fall through the cracks. Monitor this carefully.

CREATING NEW TRACKS

Obviously, a complex project will require more audio tracks but you will find that moving video to other tracks is also very helpful in facilitating many of the things you are trying to accomplish in FCP.

Final Cut Pro 4 opens with four audio tracks and those four will be all we need for the basic edit of *WT*. However, if you want to experiment with more audio, additional tracks will be necessary. As with everything, there are a number of ways to create additional audio tracks. The easiest is to just grab any old piece of audio and drag it toward the bottom of the Timeline. To make room for the piece of audio, FCP automatically creates new tracks. Do this with the Shift key depressed, so you do not pull whatever it is you are dragging out of sync. If you are dragging linked audio, the picture may also want to move to a new video track. Lock it at the locking symbol on the left if it is being troublesome.

It is equally easy to go to Sequence>Insert Tracks. The Insert Tracks window will appear (see Figure 4.17). Select the box between Insert and Audio Tracks and type in 1. The selection for positioning defaults to After Last Tracks and this is usually where you want new tracks to go. Hit OK. The other choice is in front of the first track. Once the track is inserted, click the target desti-nation buttons to send audio there. For picture, the same pro-

FIG. 4.17

cedures apply. The only extra thing here is the Superimpose edit. It will automatically create a new video track if used (see pages 143-5 for more).

KEYBOARD

As suggested, the keyboard provides great shortcuts to many FCP func-tions. New to FCP 4, complete keyboard diagrams can be accessed in the menus at Tools>Keyboard (see Figure 4.18). The tab in front, No Modifiers, is the simple individual key taps. In the background are tabs for combinations for all the critical keys (Command, Option, Control, Shift, et cetera), plus all the three-key combinations. The keyboard can also be customized. On the bottom left, there is a button to unlock the keyboard and you can then drag symbols to new keys or drag items from the list on the right. You can really streamline things here. I get very irritated with constantly having to click on windows to make them active. Although this does not really work with the Browser, I assigned the other three windows to a key on the numeric keypad and now just tap to move around.

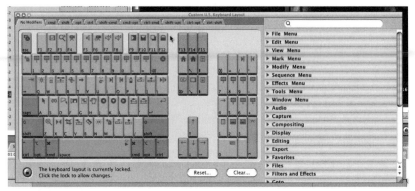

FIG. 4.18

RECONNECTING MEDIA

This refers to an ugly part of the process that could well drive strong men and women to find solace in the bottle. The clips in your Browser occasionally get disconnected from their Quicktime files in Capture Scratch. Without that relationship, the Timeline cannot play. Usually it is something you have done — you have somehow changed the path of the media from its original location when the project was created. Examples would be moving audio or video files or renaming something, but occasionally it just seems to be FCP cussedness. If files have become disconnected, it generally needs to be addressed immediately.

If clips have become disconnected, a warning box (see Figure 4.19, box is shortened) will appear when you launch the program. In the background the red line will appear through the affected clips in the Browser and the render bar will be red in the Timeline. Click on Reconnect at the bottom. The Reconnect Options will appear (see Figure 4.20) and should

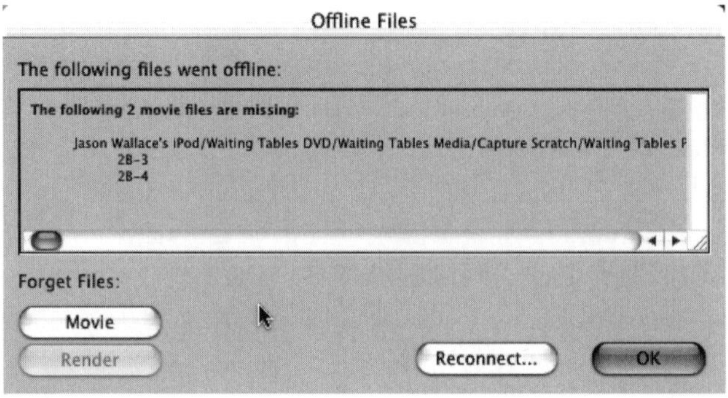

FIG. 4.19

have Offline checked. Click OK. FCP will search your hard drive and any other local drives for the missing file. If FCP finds it, it will bring up the Reconnect window (see Figure 4.21) and all you have to do is make sure the path is correct and click Choose. Make sure "Reconnect All Files in Relative Path" is checked.

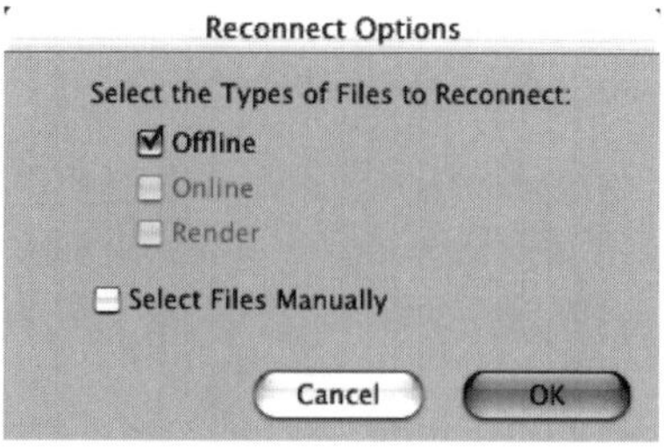

FIG. 4.20

If FCP does not find it, you will have to manually go through files in the Connect window and track it down yourself. Making sure that there is a clear path to all media is of paramount importance. If you are unsure where something is, then you may be unsure what you named it. Finding it again could be next to impossible. If you have organized correctly, it should be easy to find.

Things can become disconnected. Be ready to find things quickly. Occasionally, FCP will lose render files that are no longer pertinent. If FCP comes up missing a render file, check to see if it is still being used before spending time tracking it down. If you just click OK on the Offline Files window, FCP will open without the missing piece.

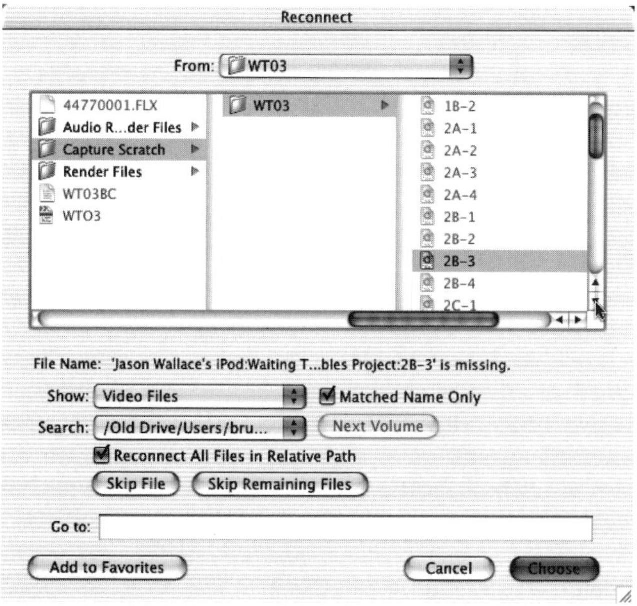

FIG. 4.21

FIT TO WINDOW, WIREFRAME, AND MISSING TOOLS

Several of these have already been discussed, but here is a quick recap. Occasionally, odd things will happen to your image, usually in the Canvas or sometimes in the Viewer. Either the image will suddenly be larger or smaller and not play well, or the X-shaped lines of the Wireframe will appear. This is always based on something you have done, usually accidentally, although FCP will sometimes appear to have a mind of its own. In the former case, you have usually had the Viewer or Canvas active while you thought you were using the zoom tool on the Timeline. You wind up zoomed in on an image and you not only are not seeing the whole thing, but playback is often affected. The solution is simple: Go to the Zoom Pop-up Menu and select Fit to Window. I have not figured out what makes the Wireframe appear, but it will occasionally just make an appearance as if by magic (see pages 229-232 for a discussion of its function). If it shows up, go to the View menu. You will see that Wireframe is checked. Scroll down to Image and let go of the mouse. The Wireframe will disappear and Image will now be checked.

Occasionally tools or windows will just go missing. There is always a reason, but.... In the menus, go to Window>Arrange>Standard and everything will reappear. This is also good if you have resized everything and want to get back to the default quickly. If a Timeline disappears, re-open the sequence from the Browser.

REMEMBER...

The option key — for working on tracks separately.

Locking — for making tracks so they cannot be changed while you are manipulating other elements.

Linking — and all the ways to link and unlink audio and video.

Active Windows — can drive you crazy. If something is not working it may be because you do not have the window selected. Check the window first. This happens mostly when using keyboard shortcuts, but if you click on something and nothing happens it is because the first click makes the window active and the second click will execute the operation.

Save — all the time.

It is a complicated program — be patient.

EDITING

I f you are anything like me, you would never read a book like this sequentially. My problem is that I start to read sequentially but then I say, I want to know how to do this or that, or I want to find out what something does. Then I go off to the index, find the topic elsewhere in the book, and start wandering around looking for whatever.

The Chapter 5.mov tutorial on the DVD follows along with the information in this chapter. The tutorial is designed to stand alone, but be aware that mastering the terminology from the previous two chapters is a necessity for complete comprehension.

First off, I recommend that you do read this book sequentially. Every effort has been made to anticipate questions and provide what you need to know in an orderly fashion. Okay, now that that's out of the way, let's say you start here. You should be all right but be aware of a couple things. If there are terms that you do not recognize or menu functions you are curious about, odds are that they are covered in the Issues section of Chapter I — G, R, or FCP in parenthesis guides you to the definition (see the Mini TOC on page 17). If you have questions about how the tutorial is set up, answers can be found in Chapter II. If there are Timeline functions, or tools that you do not remember, look in Chapter III and IV for their description.

First, open Sequence (Blank) from the Browser. Make sure the playhead is parked at 01:00:00:00 in the Timeline. Check it in the time code window in the upper left of the Canvas.

So, how do we get started?

There are, in essence, two kinds of picture cuts when working with dialogue scenes (we will identify a third later — the MOS Insert). The first is called a straight cut and, like its name, it is the most straightforward. It is, however, the least pleasing and the least used. The second type of cut is called an overlapping cut — in the video world also variously called J cuts and L cuts. These are the bread and butter of dialogue cutting. We will give them extended coverage after a few straight cut examples.

STRAIGHT CUTS

In a straight cut, the editor simply cuts from one character to another character at the end of a line of dialogue or during an action. A conversation between two people is the most common example. Judy says: "Do you think they are in a hurry?" The picture cuts to Fritz and he says: "No, you've got a few minutes." This kind of cut can be effective in certain instances, but when used consistently, the scene starts to look like a tennis match with the viewer following the ball from one line of dialogue to the next. Dialogue-cut. Dialogue-cut. And on and on. The scene will feel very choppy and will not have the kind of flow that we associate with any dialogue scene. Try it with some of the *WT* footage and you will get a graphic example.

If you are just cutting visuals, free of any dialogue considerations, you are for the most part using straight cuts, although the approach to audio presented later will complicate this. What is being discussed here really only pertains to scenes that are very dialogue heavy.

> Be aware that when you set an out point, the frame you are looking at in the Viewer or the Canvas gets cut off. This may not have much of an impact on cutting your own project, but is important to understand to follow examples in this chapter.

There are many ways to cut our tutorial scene. As an unfettered editor, you are faced with many, many options as to where to play the action from. As you look at the script — at pages of dialogue and action — you formulate a strategy for cutting the piece. Obviously, the entire action from the beginning to Judy's entrance could be played in one shot — the master shot. But masters very quickly become uninteresting. They are there for a purpose, but once that purpose is accomplished, we — the

The lingo of shots is reasonably well known. But we should just clarify the terminology at this point.

— **Master Scene Technique** is a theory term for a common and efficient, some would say boring, way of approaching the shooting of a scene. A scene starts with a wide view, a **Master** or establishing shot, of a scene that establishes the space, characters present, and any other salient features of the scene. Then the scene is broken down into a series of...

— **Medium Shots (MS)**, a person from roughly waist up, and **Close-Ups (CU)**, a tighter shot roughly from the top shirt button up. This approach was the bread and butter of American film of the great studio years (circa 1920-65). To a large extent, it still is. Masters are also frequently called **Long Shots (LS)** or **Full Body Shots (FBS)**.

— An **Over-the-Shoulder Shot** (OTS) is essentially a medium shot that picks up a little bit of the reverse character's shoulder.

— A **Match Cut** is when the action of a character or thing is matched from one shot to the next. If a person starts to sit down in one shot, they complete the action in the next shot.

— **Cutting on Action** is a term that suggests that the best, i.e. least noticeable, place to cut is on some kind of character or object action.

Anticipating cut points is a major aspect of a concept that directors need to clearly understand called "shooting for the edit." Shooting for the edit is generally presented as a much broader concept than this, mostly as a director's need to have a clear vision of how a scene is going to be cut to give the scene dramatic logic and coherence. This is usually spoken of in more general terms of shot selection, but can also be extended to understanding what makes good cut points between shots. This is a director (and DP) thing, not an actor thing. Actors should never be asking themselves if they are creating good edit points. The director should be thinking about every element, from whether a close up is appropriate to when an actor should take off his or her glasses.

viewers — have a natural curiosity to see something closer. Again, the choices are many and we recommend that you eventually try different options than what we recommend here. Here is what we have done.

Our first decision is where to start the scene (we will deal with titles and the like later). The couple opens the door and enters. In the Sync Bin in the Browser, double click on the takes of Scene 1A. Take a look at each one and decide which one you want to use (Takes 1 and 2 were not included on the DVD for space reasons).

Open each clip, hit Play — Space bar, click on (**A**) , hit L key — and take a look.

In this instance we chose scene 1A, Take 4. Double-click on it and the clip opens in the Viewer. If it does not open at the beginning, hit the up arrow key until the playhead goes to the beginning. The first decision is relatively simple. What exact point do we want to be the first frame of the scene? Hit play. The director calls "action." As the door starts to open, stop the video. Use the single frame backward (left arrow key) to find the exact starting point. The start point of the clip is up to you, but let's move to a point 20 to 30 frames ahead of the door starting to open — TC/01:02:24:05 (see Figure 5.1). Do not go back into the word "action." If you do, we will hear it in the audio, although there is a very simple remedy for this if we wanted to use more of the shot.

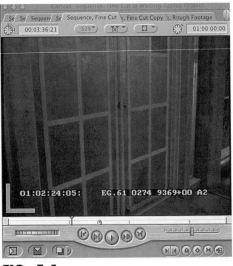

FIG. 5.1

Mark your In point—click on (**B**) in the Viewer; hit the I key on the keyboard; go to Mark>Mark In in the menu). We will not mark an out point because we will determine that when we put in the next shot. Again, the In is marked by (**C**) in the shot's scrubber bar in the Viewer. If we know we are not going to use a shot past a certain point, we might want to mark an Out just to reduce clutter in the Timeline.

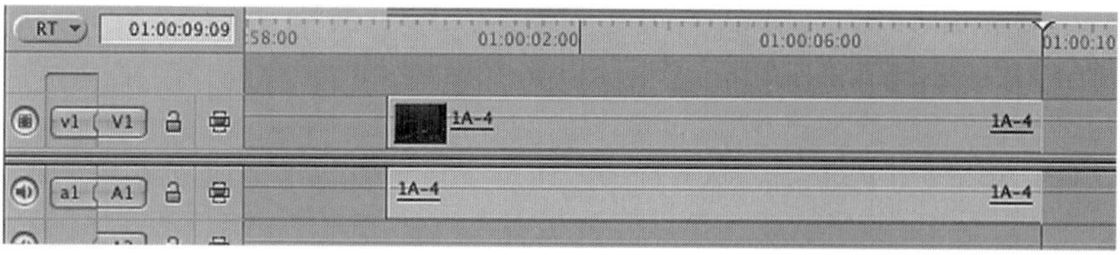

FIG. 5.2

Move the shot into the Timeline (see Figure 5.2) using the Overwrite function (kybd: F10), (**D**) on the Canvas, click on the picture and drag it to the embedded function in the Canvas, or simply click on the picture in the Viewer and drag it straight to the Timeline). The playhead automatically lands on the last frame of the moved shot, so hit the up arrow key to return it to the head of the shot. The Canvas is up as the active window, so hit Play (Space bar, (**A**), kybd: L). The shot starts, there is a moment's pause, and the couple enters. Now this would be a perfect place for a fade-in, but we will show you how to do that later (see page 140). For aesthetic as well as technical reasons, it is often good to execute all fades, dissolves, and the like later in the editorial process.

The next two cuts in this piece are not based on dialogue. So we will base them on action. Our decision is to cut to Fritz's OTS to see the couple's discomfort. Another option would be to cut to Fritz's MS as he delivers his lines of dialogue, but the cut from the master to Fritz's medium is a slightly awkward cut because its view is somewhat similar to the master shot's. We could throw some of Fritz's OTS in there to get us to his MS, but the whole thing might become too complicated. When you have a lot of short lines of dialogue, beginning editors can be tempted to try to cut to everything. However, if you try to throw in too much, the scene may look too "cutty" — that is, there are so many edits that the scene jumps around too much and the cutting starts to call attention to itself. It will start to look like a music video, but this scene, at least as this editor has defined it, does not require that look. Some would argue with great validity that we need an earlier and better introduction to Fritz, but you will find that you sometimes cannot accomplish every goal when editing a scene.

Moreover, we do not necessarily want to establish him as too strong a presence. Dramatic necessity should usually overshadow considerations of mechanics. So we go to the OTS. There is a perfect match on them approaching the counter, but that would leave the master awfully short and could give the scene a choppy feel. So we are just going to find as nice a place as we can to cut from the master to the OTS. My goal here is to draw the pause out a little longer than the actors did it for comic effect. So we double-click on scene 2A — this time we have chosen Take 4 — in the Browser and it opens in the Viewer. In this instance we want to work between the Timeline and the Viewer to choose the best out point for Scene 1A (Timeline) and the best in point for 2A (Viewer).

As suggested, we generally want to find some action to cut on. I decided to use the movement of the man taking off his glasses to make the cut. The continuity is not quite right on the female customer, but this is something most people will not notice. I was nervous that this did not give us enough of the master, but it looks fine and the decision has been, in pre-conceptualizing the editing, that we are going to return to the master later anyway. So we are doing a match cut on this action, as the actor duplicates the movement very nicely in both master and OTS.

In the Timeline, we analyzed the movement and decided to cut fairly shortly into the movement, but enough that we definitely see the movement. I like TC/02:33:13 (see Figure 5.3). We could hit the In button on the Canvas but with the playhead now parked there, that is where the next shot will come in anyway. Now use the Viewer to analyze 2A-4. We find a place where it looks like the action is going to match (TC/06:22:23) and hit I on the keyboard. Perform Overwrite. Click Play Around Current Edit (**E**), or kybd: \. This looks good.

We want to base the next cut solely on action again. We are going to cut from the OTS back to the master as the couple takes their seats. There will be a number of good places to cut, but we like the look the actor gives Fritz so we are going to let him give the look and then cut as he steps off toward the table. So we find a frame after he has stepped off in the outgoing shot in the Timeline — TC/06:39:17 — and park the playhead there. Open the master shot in the Viewer; in this case we are going to use Take 3 (1A-3) in anticipation of an upcoming continuity problem. We find a point where we think the action is going to match — TC/02:01:22 (see Figure 5.4). Hit kybd: I. Perform Overwrite. Hit Play Around Current Edit (kybd: \). This does not look so good.

We realize that we have a few too many frames — there is a duplication of action (okay, so we did this on purpose). What tools are pertinent to

FIG. 5.3

FIG. 5.4

trimming down one or both shots? Obviously we could just go back into the Viewer and redo the cut. The razor blade is a good choice to perform this task. Which of the trim tools would work? We need to shorten the piece here and the Ripple tool is the only one that shortens. The Trim Edit window opened with the Ripple tool would also work.

I like the exit point on the outgoing shot so we will make all adjustments to the incoming shot. To perform the trim with the Razor Blade, we analyze 1A-3 in the Timeline. We use the left/right arrow keys to move until we find a more suitable frame. The actor does the look and then there is a better match on TC/02:02:20. Select the razor blade—

click on (**F**) or B on the keyboard—and, with the help of snapping, position the blade at TC/02:02:20 and click. Get the selection tool by hitting kybd: a on the keyboard, click on the piece to be trimmed, and hit (**G**) or Shift>Delete on the keyboard and you have your cut (see Figure 5.5). Hit kybd: \. This seems to be a reasonable cut, but try some other options if you don't like it.

Just for comparison, how would we do the same adjustment with the Ripple tool? First, turn Snapping off — (**H**) click on in the Timeline or N on the keyboard. Select the Ripple tool by single-clicking on Roll in the Tools and sliding to the (**I**) symbol or kybd: RR. Click on the front of 1A-3 in the Timeline and drag to the right. Both the outgoing and incoming shots show up in the canvas and you can drag until you see a frame that looks good (see Figure 5.6). In this case, we will go to TC/02:02:20 again. The representation of the shots is very small and control over movement frame-by-frame in the shot is not as fluid as with the left/right arrow keys. While these tools have their role and there are undoubtedly some editors who use them constantly, for me they somehow lack the precision of the razor blade trim. On the plus side, it does pull the whole show up behind very easily.

Now we run into our first potential continuity problem. We want to get from the Master (1A-3) to the shot in which Judy enters (4A). At the end of the master, Fritz has his right hand up by the side of his face and in all takes of 4A he has his hand on the crossword puzzle. Now we could choose other shots or we could cut earlier in the master, but I like what we have going and that would make the second use of the master too short for the general shape of the scene. However, as we look through all the takes, we notice one hopeful detail. Fritz does a little flourish with the pen that is going to provide just what we need. In scene 4A-4, he does it just before Judy enters and this will be perfect (The director had Judy enter too early in the first three takes and did not catch and correct the mistake until the fourth take).

So we are going to match on his hand movement. In the Timeline, find a good point to exit the master — TC/02:08:09 (see Figure 5.7). Move to TC/02:08:10 and Mark In. Open 4A-4 in the viewer and find a close match — TC/18:23:26 (see Figure 5.8). You will notice that the match is not perfect but, when cut together, no one is going to notice. The phrase in the

FIG. 5.5

FIG. 5.6

FIG. 5.7

FIG. 5.8

industry is, "If they are looking at that, we are doing something wrong." Mark In and perform Overwrite. Hit kybd: \. Perfect.

Continuity problems are not uncommon. If you look at the logs, you will notice that the master shot was done first and Scene 4A was done much later in the day, after all of Judy's side was shot. In that interim, it is easy to forget details as small as exact body positions. This is a crew thing, not an actor thing. However, many highly experienced actors get the smallest details of their performance down and do it exactly the same every time. This is the script supervisor's responsibility and even the best of them can miss something as nuanced as this.

MOS INSERTS

Now we want to throw in a shot of the couple noticing Judy's entrance (1B-2 takes). Some editors might argue this is unnecessary. The couple perform a function at the beginning of the scene and then are not really needed. But using them here may add some comic tone and the presence of the clip may make the next cut more fluid. The shot of them at the table was not in the storyboard. It was a grab shot, something we decided to do on the spot because we liked what the actors who played the couple were doing, we had the area lit (a very big consideration), and the camera was basically in position.

The shot was done without sound — MOS (R) — and we simply have to drop it in over the existing sound of shot 4A. We noted earlier that the trend on most current film sets is to just roll sound on something like this. If there were sound we would simply eliminate it (unlink, select, and delete) and handle the shot exactly as described below.

This is the first time we are going to insert a shot into material already in the Timeline, bringing up a concept called three-point editing — a procedure that applies to both MOS and sync shots. This gets a lot of play in many editing books because of its extensive history in analog video editing, but is somewhat of a minor concept. To insert a shot into existing material, there are four points involved — the in/out of the shot you want to insert and the in/out of the location in which it is going to be inserted in the Timeline. To do this, however, the editor only needs to establish three of those points because the fourth will be supplied automatically. If we establish the in and out points of the couple's shot and the in point on the Timeline, the out point in the Timeline will simply be where 1B ends. Duh. We can establish any of the three points and the edit will execute.

First we want to find where we are going to exit 4A. We want Judy to enter from behind Fritz and then we want to cut to the couple. Many novice editors are under the impression that you should let a character completely exit a frame before you cut, but any experienced editor will

tell you to cut a few frames before the character exits. It will give forward movement into the next shot and avoid the pause that an empty frame can create. So we will choose a point in 4A in the Timeline right before Judy exits frame left. TC/18:27:09 looks good (see Figure 5.9). Mark In on the Canvas on TC/18:27:10 or just park the playhead there.

FIG. 5.9

Now for the MOS shot. Open 1B in the Viewer; in this case we chose take 2—takes 1 and 2 were captured together. We want Judy a little bit in the frame at the beginning — -TC/03:26:23. Mark In. However, at the end we do want Judy to exit because we want to catch the woman's look. It would be lovely to include the man turning — he gives a marvelous deadpan — but too much time would elapse before Judy's arrival at the counter. We may use this later. So Mark Out at TC/03:28:19. Perform Overwrite (see Figure 5.10). Hit \.

FIG. 5.10

In this instance, everything looks great except that we just reenter 4A with an uninteresting OTS of Judy. We will fix that next. All we need to do is get Judy in and speaking her first lines in Scene 2A — an over-Fritz's-shoulder MS of Judy. Again we do not want to cut before she enters the frame — that would create a dead spot. We want a little bit of her shoulder to be coming into view just past Fritz. We choose Take 2 — the better performances in takes 3 and 4 were unfortunately spoiled by movement reflected in the window. You can "steal" the audio from the preferred take and replace it in the used take, but eventually we decided against it. We find TC/05:08:22 is a reasonable entrance point.

First we need to get rid of that extra piece of scene 4A-4. Click on it and hit delete on the keyboard (see Figure 5.11). This is fine but the sound remains. Now the sound is perfectly fine and there is no particular reason to get rid of it. In fact, its presence will help cushion any differences

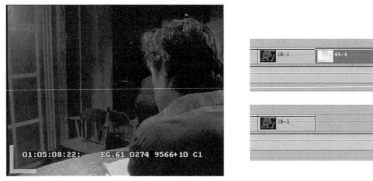

01:05:08:22:   EG.61 0274 9566+10 C1

FIG. 5.11

between the audio in the takes. We will find that one of our main goals is to maintain as much extra audio as we can in order to make seamless sound transitions from take to take. This leads us to an important issue.

A (NOT SO) RADICAL APPROACH TO AUDIO

If you have decent speakers hooked up to your computer, you may notice that in the cut from the audio of 4A-4 to the audio of 2A-2 there is a significant change in the background sound. This "little problem" illustrates one of the central issues in how to cut quality audio tracks. If you cut in what we will call the **single strand** process, where all sync audio

— the **production sound**, the audio recorded while shooting — is on one track, you will notice that there will frequently be audible changes at the cuts. All places have some level of ambient sound, variously called **ambience**, **presence**, or **room tone**, and every place is different. Ambience is simply the general sound character of any given space. What we think of as silence is not the absence of sound. The actual complete absence of sound can be unnerving. Every space has its own distinct character, and that is a significant part of your recorded sound.

The audio crew is generally made up of two people. The head of the crew is the **sound mixer** — the person who runs the recorder (or the mixer if you are recording onto the camera's audio track). He or she supervises and is responsible for quality of the audio. The second person is the **boom operator**, the person who, at the direction of the sound mixer, handles the microphone, usually held above the scene on a fishpole. Bigger productions may have a **cable puller** to help with the organizational and practical aspects of recording.

The main goal of the sound mixer is to record the audio at optimal levels and to eliminate as much extraneous noise as possible — refrigerators, air conditioners, and the like. The first part of this statement means that, when shooting a conversation between two people, if one actor's voice is quieter than the other's, the mixer has to set the record level higher to get a good recording. The second part of the statement means that if there is something you cannot get rid of, and this is particularly an issue with location shooting, both its presence and shifting audio record levels are going to create problems for the editors. Sound mixers have many tricks for minimizing these issues, but even the best-recorded tracks require attention in post-production.

Occasionally people will think that the sound mixer has done their job incorrectly when there are shifts in ambience. On the contrary, if there are no shifts in ambience, it is proof that the mixer has done his or her job wrong. If the ambience is even, they are not doing the necessary shifts to respond to shifts in volume level. All evening out of the levels should occur in the editing room and, eventually, at the final mix.

To help in this, the sound mixer will record several minutes of room tone at every location in which a film is shot. There is always an awkward moment, wonderfully parodied in an excellent indie called *Living in Oblivion*, where the whole crew simply has to stop and be quiet while the sound mixer records this.

When the record level is higher, the ambient sound will be higher. Maybe one actor's voice was quieter and the sound person had to crank the volume, thus amplifying not only the actor's voice but also the ambience (see sidebar). Maybe the mic was picking up a little more distant ambience, a cooler or air ducts or something. When we cut this shot in, there will be an audible shift in ambience. There can also be problems with more defined ambient sound. If there are things going on in the background, say loud cars passing by or airplanes overhead, this may complicate things in the editing room. So, as there are variations in recording, there are variations in ambience and background sound.

What is going to be put forward here is an approach to your audio tracks that is only radical in that it contradicts the way most manuals and other books like this one demonstrate building the audio. Their approach is to show the reader how to cut your sound as you cut your picture, all on to one track of audio in the Timeline. Just as we have suggested so far, when you set cut points, both the audio and video are cut at that spot and the shots with video are dropped consecutively into the Timeline.

We are going to suggest that you build the production audio into two tracks. That is, bounce or alternate the sync sound — generally the dialogue — from one set of tracks to another set. This is generally called A and B rolling or checkerboarding. Rather than being stacked consecutively on the one track, the audio for each track alternates between tracks 1 and 2. Doing this is really only pertinent to scenes with a lot of speech, whether fictional or documentary. This approach does not have much application in music videos or most commercials, although it follows a fundamental principle of audio building that has far-reaching implications for the way you approach sound.

Why should you do this? By alternating the audio, you can save ambience before and after lines of dialogue (called creating **handles**) and extend offending sounds so they can be covered, blended in, or faded out. In essence, you can overlap the sound of each clip to create a softer audio impact at the cut. At the final mixdown, this allows the rerecording mixer (G) to "finesse" the sound between two shots with all the onboard and sideboard mixing and equalization strength they can muster.

This is standard industry practice. However, the big question is when to do it. To understand this we need to go a little bit into the workflow of how a commercial project is cut. If you were to walk into the editing room of any episodic television program or feature film, you will probably see the editor cutting single strand. The person who is credited as the editor — and they deserve that credit — on a feature film or episodic television will pretty much just work with the production sound — the sound done during filming. And, again, they will probably cut it single strand. They may have a few effects, like the telephone in *WT,* and some scratch music, but their primary work is with those tracks that were recorded in the studio or on location. Once they have finished the cut — have everything exactly the way they want it — they declare **picture lock**, a term indicating that there will be no more changes in the picture. The not-quite-finished product is then turned over to a host of other editorial technicians who add to and streamline the audio tracks. Most pertinent to this discussion is the **dialogue editor**. The dialogue editor's main task is to make the dialogue flow naturally. They need to address any differences in the ambient quality of the dialogue, make sure any ADR (Automatic Dialogue Replacement) material blends in appropriately, and, most of all, make sure there are no "blemishes" that will be noticeable and detract from audience involvement in the show. These blemishes can include the aforementioned ambience shifts and awkward background sounds, as well as drop-out and a host of other audio troublemakers.

The dialogue editor will take the single strand edit from the editor and, all alone in a dark little room, will AB the dialogue themselves. Then, through the pleasures of non-destructive editing, they can extend the sound to create overlapping audio to cushion or finesse the rough spots. They will create the handles mentioned earlier. They will use the room tone recorded by the sound mixer to patch in holes. They will add in effects to cover or extend problematic background sounds. They do not actually execute the transitions; they create the material that the rerecording mixer uses to finesse the sound at the final mix. The dialogue editor and the sound effects editor are in attendance at the mix in order to explain their work and potentially modify their work if necessary. Under supervision, they may actually run the dialogue aspect of the mix.

The dialogue editor will not be the only one involved in the process, with sound effects editors, Foley editors, music editors, and a number of others adding their creative input. Picture lock is a critical concept which requires understanding how the synchronization of picture and audio works. The audio tracks are exported out of FCP in a cross platform/cross software function called **Open Media Framework (OMF)**, which will be covered in detail later. The audio tracks can then be opened in other audio-specific software, such as Pro Tools, and all the adding and layering of the sound is done there.

Using two tracks lays the groundwork for evening out the inevitable inconsistencies of production sound. A good location mixer should be able to provide relatively evenly balanced tracks. Even then, the dialogue editor will have to address many issues. But you may not be working with a pro sound guy and, worse yet, you may even be working with the automatic record levels in a DV camera. In both cases, the best case scenario is minor shifts in the ambience. The worst-case scenario, which is achieved frequently in low budge/no budge production, is big shifts and gaping holes.

So, what we are recommending here is that, because you are not handing it over to a deservedly well-paid dialogue editor, start working on the AB rolling now. There are reasons not to do extensive AB rolling at this stage (see sidebar), but you need to be aware of it and have it as a tool on your tool belt (as it were).

It is important to note that A & B rolling sound can play havoc on some of the common functions of FCP, so it should be done judiciously. Close Gap, Shift Delete, All Track Select and a number of other things may not function or may operate oddly. There are always work-arounds on all of these but you have to be sure sync is being maintained throughout the Timeline.

This is only radical in that most texts on NLE software present sound edited single strand. Going to two tracks clearly complicates your task but, once mastered, the benefits will show up in better sound. It is also radical in that tracks are not generally done this way professionally, at least during the cutting process. As stated, the tracks will eventually be set up this way in a commercial cutting setup. It is a question of when, not if.

BOUNCING TRACKS

So we are going to bounce the sound for Scene 2A-2 over to the second track (A2). Click on the A2 destination button and the A1 source button will jump to it (see Figure 5.12). While we are at this, we might as well save as

FIG. 5.12

FIG. 5.13

much audio at the head of 2A-2 — our incoming shot — as possible. We will do this with a Mark Split. With 2A-2 still open in the Viewer go to the frame we originally picked, TC/05:08:22. Go to Mark>Mark Split>Video In. Now move back in the shot — toward the head — listening to the sound. You can hear the couple's footsteps as they walk off. After that — beautiful silence. Find the earliest point in the silence possible, roughly TC/05:04:28, go to Mark>Mark Split>Audio In. The Mark split symbol will appear in the Viewer's scrubber bar (see Figure 5.13).

Park the playhead at the end of 1B. Perform Overwrite. Being ahead of video, the audio will come in at the playhead (see Figure 5.14), leaving a gap in the video.

G. 5.14

With snapping on, simply drag the video up and close the gap (see Figure 5.15). Take a look at everything you have done so far.

While there has been dialogue in this first part, it has not been the

G. 5.15

driving force in the cutting. At this point, however, maintaining pace in the conversation becomes a dominant factor and the potential subtlety of dialogue cutting becomes a primary consideration. On to the overlap.

SAVING

One of the beauties of FCP, and a tremendous selling point, is that it is relatively crash-free. This was the Achilles heel of many of the other NLEs and there is nothing more crushing than having a project fade into the great digital graveyard. But any program can freeze up and the computer itself can come unraveled. FCP works best when you can have a dedicated machine for it. But that's not the real world for many people. A sequence in FCP is like any other document you would create. You want to save constantly and make back-ups. People would never think of not backing up some document (a term paper, an important business letter) and yet I will constantly have people saying, I lost my cut (Yeah, right Smokey).

Project files can be duplicated. Project files can be saved to other drives. Project files can be e-mailed. At the end of the day, be sure all work is duplicated somewhere else. Editing a complex project takes nothing but brutal, unavoidable time. Feature films typically take six months to edit. A lot of this editing happens as the project is passed from hand to hand, but it still takes putting in the hours. Losing those hours can be a crushing experience. You should not even have to lose your work once — but sometimes it takes that — to realize how crucial this information is to the ongoing effort.

It can be difficult to back-up the Quicktime files because they are so huge. Still, there are large hard drives that can handle a huge amount of media. 100 to 200 gig drives have come down in price to the extent that having one or more on hand not only makes sense, but becomes a no-brainer.

ADVANCED EDITING

OVERLAPPING CUTS

Now we can move into overlapping dialogue cuts. Basically this means that rather than cutting at the end of a line of dialogue, we cut during the line of dialogue. You can cut away from the character as they are still speaking to the character who is going to respond (in the video world called a J cut) or you can hold on the speaker while the second character starts to speak (in the video world called an L cut). The first variation (J cut) is more common than the second. This is perfectly natural. Everything that we say, particularly in movie speak, is designed to provoke a reaction — to accomplish some communicative goal. Thus we are naturally curious about the reaction being provoked (and we do not confine the use of the word "provoke" solely to negative connotations). We want to see how the second character is responding. Plus, our speech has trigger words — things that, whether by design or not, provoke a reaction in the listener(s). We want to see that. When Fritz goes into the bit about the "Ox of Celebes" while he is on the phone, this undoubtedly is going to get some kind of rise out of Judy. We are naturally curious about her reaction.

It has been stated too many times that movies are not the art of action but the art of reaction. The drill instructor castigating the goof-off private in Stanley Kubick's *Full Metal Jacket* provides an excellent example of this. Neal La Bute's tremendous new play, *The Shape of Things*, is a great example of shifting perspective (it has been filmed as well). One of the concluding scenes of the play has a long speech by one of the main characters designed to have a powerful impact on the play's three other characters. Attending a play, every audience member's point of attention is different. Who does each individual audience member watch? As I look at the speaker, the person next to me may be looking somewhere else altogether. One person may be craning to focus in on an expression, while another audience member is trying to take in a much wider perspective. It would be an intriguing study to track the gaze of audience members during a play. The movies are different in that they more aggressively direct viewer attention, with there being a great theoretical debate about just how aggressive that direction should be. There is one point in *The Shape of Things* where the speaker asks if there are any questions and one of the more volatile characters raises his hand. He is ignored but how many audience members noticed him? It is highly interesting to ponder what his question might have been. Those who did not notice his subtle movement may never ponder this small, but potentially intriguing, action. A film editor can make sure that we see this one significant detail — given the footage is there to do it.

When you watch a film for the second time (and anyone interested in making them should watch films they have a high regard for several times), watch where the editor has chosen to cut vis-à-vis the dialogue. The first observation will be what we have just asserted; the edits are very rarely at the end of a character's line. Beyond that, why did the editor choose to edit at this point and why did they cut to the shot that they did? You will slowly work out a conscious pattern of decision-making — the editor is trying to accomplish certain things in the way he or she is showing things.

The great rule of editing, potentially the only unbreakable one, is this: THERE HAS TO BE A REASON FOR A CUT. There has to be a positive reason that you want to move from one view to another. In a narrative, the rationale is often dramatic necessity. In other forms, like music video, it can be for visual energy. But there has to be some underlying reason why you are making a cut — what are you trying to accomplish?

Overlapping cuts are the route to the flow and pace that we associate with any reasonably well-cut scene. They will, however, require some fancy footwork in the timeline. Many manuals and texts on NLE would appear at first glance to maintain that you can just stack the shots with their sync audio up end-to-end. However, the crux of editing when working with any dialogue, whether it is voice over or lines from a character, is to cut picture away from pauses. It is all right to stack shots end to end for a while, but you will eventually have to alter either your approach or the material you have already cut.

TRACK CONFIGURATIONS

At this point in our rough cut, we have Judy up to the counter. We will play Fritz's "You have a new table" in OTS, then Judy says: "Think they're in a hurry?" What I want to do is leave Judy's shot during the end of her question, somewhere in the words "in a hurry." Almost exclusively, Judy's response will be more important than Fritz's, but our choice will suggest a few things here, most notably Fritz's detachment.

Now there are, of course, a number of ways of doing this. One would be to straight cut it into the Timeline and then use the Roll Edit tool (83) to move the picture cut to where you want it. When you do this, the audio cut needs to remain the same and only the picture cut needs to change. Thus you use the option key (or lock the audio) when you use the Roll Edit function. You can also unlink pix and audio for both shots and cut the picture separately, although this has some inherent dangers (like forgetting to relink).

Let's try this the Roll Edit way. Our last sound is on the second track so we will send the next audio there as well. While you will eventually internalize this process, you literally need to determine how long a pause there should be between Judy's line and Fritz's line. In scene 4A, Judy feeds her line so that will give us some guidance, but I would actually like the pause to be a little longer. So step one is determining the pause we want between the two lines.

> "Do you think they are in a hurry?"
> "Nah, you've got a few minutes."

A second? Two seconds? Pauses are tricky things in movie time. A second can be lengthy and two seconds can be an eternity. We will call the pause 20 frames (two/thirds of a second) to cut to the chase. Find the end of Judy's line in 2A-3, use the right arrow to move down the road 10 frames, and park the playhead there (TC/05:18:01). Open 4A in the Viewer (here we chose take 2), find the beginning of Fritz's line, and use the left arrow key to back up about 10 frames ahead of "Nah..." toward the head of the show (TC/17:21:04). Mark In, perform Overwrite, and hit kybd: \ (see Figure 6.1).

This is a pretty awful-looking cut, but we clearly never intended to keep it. It is blocky and does not feel very fluid. We want to create an overlap.

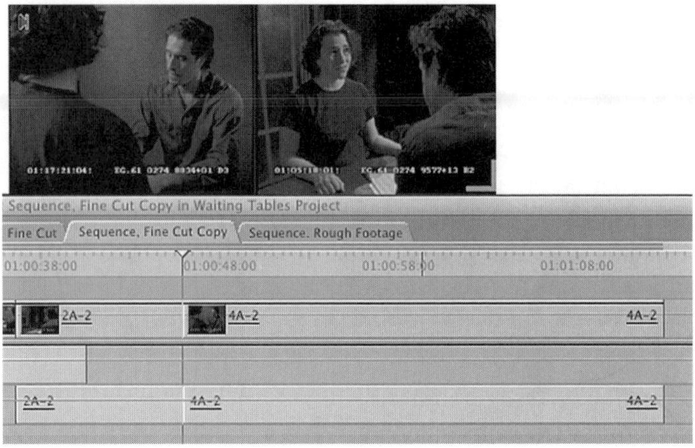

FIG. 6.1

Turn off snapping and select the Roll Edit tool. Another problem with this group of tools is that you cannot hear the sound while you are performing the cut. So we will use a marker. We want to cut away just before the word "hurry" so find a likely frame; TC/5:17:10 is a good choice. Click on the shot in the Timeline and set the marker — click on (**A**) in the Canvas, kybd: m, or Mark>Set Marker>Add in the menus (see Figure 6.2).

FIG. 6.2

Hit Command + to zoom in once so you can have better control. With the option key depressed, click on the front of 4A-2 and hold it. It takes a second for the outline to appear and then drag to the left (see Figure 6.3). The two shots appear side-by-side in the Canvas. Drag 4A-2 back to TC/5:17:10, release the mouse (see Figure 6.4). Hit kybd: \. This is good.

There is a slight mismatch in Judy's head movement, but the saying, again, is "if they are looking at that, we're doing something wrong." One of the reasons we chose TC/05:17:10 is because cutting any earlier would aggravate this problem.

FIG. 6.3

FIG. 6.4

But the Roll Edit is too inexact for me and using the marker is cumbersome. Plus, I want to do the bouncing tracks and create the handles described in the last chapter. My preferred way is to bring the shot into the Timeline and then use the razor blade to trim all pieces as desired. We can also work the Mark Split function into this. Again, I suspect not many editors use this function, but I find it very handy. Mark Splits allow you to choose separate in and out points for picture and audio. And this is exactly what we are trying to accomplish with an overlapping cut. Undo the Roll edit if you want to try this.

Mark Splits can only be applied to clips in the Viewer, opened from the Browser. The outgoing shot (2A-3) is already in the Timeline, and unless we had the great foresight to set our in and outs at the same time, we need to trim it with the razor blade. Again, we are going to cut audio and video in separate places. So where do we want to leave Judy's picture? We want to keep the entire sound of her question. If we were to try to supply it from another take, it would not match — actually, a rather preposterous notion.

So we again want to leave her visually right before the word "hurry." We will use the same numbers as in the roll edit example. Select the razor blade and make sure snapping is on. Find TC/05:17:10 and remember that to maintain this frame we want to cut at TC/05:17:11. Park the playhead there. While pressing the option key, put the blade by the playhead line in the video track and click (see Figure 6.5). The picture will cut at the playhead (see Figure 6.6). Delete the picture trim (see Figure 6.7). Remembering the previous discussion, we want to save as much ambience as possible. Using single frame, we find the sound is usable until just before the director says "cut." Park the playhead there, press the option key, and click in the audio by the playhead line (see Figure 6.8). Click on the trim and hit the delete key (see Figure 6.9).

Before we edit in the next shot, we are going to want to send Fritz's sound back to track 1. This is done, again, with the destination buttons

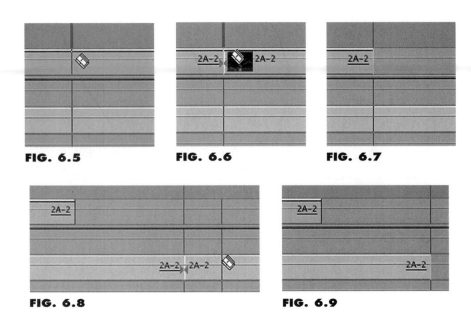

FIG. 6.5   **FIG. 6.6**   **FIG. 6.7**

FIG. 6.8   **FIG. 6.9**

just to the left of the tracks (see Figure 6.10). Click on DC A1 and SC A1 will jump to it.

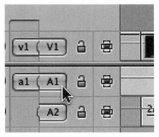

FIG. 6.10

FIG. 6.11

Open 4A (we have selected the third take) from the Browser. Again we want to save all the audio we can, so listen to the end of Judy's over-the-shoulder line and find clean audio — TC/17:21:03. Go to Mark>Mark Split> Audio In. We want to enter Fritz's shot somewhere in Judy's question, but I want to draw it out a little. We can always adjust in the Timeline, so we will select TC/17:20:13. Go to Mark>Mark Split> Video In. The split edit symbol will appear in the scrubber bar (see Figure 6.11). Make sure the playhead is parked at the end of 2A-3 in the Timeline, perform Overwrite, and hit \ (see Figure 6.12). The audio for 4A-2 actually starts after the picture, but such is life in the editing room. We still have a nice overlap. Again, if the cut is not quite to your taste, try other options. This could also be done

FIG. 6.12

FIG. 6.13

in the Trim Window, but using the razor blade, at least for this editor, affords more control.

Let's do one more. Now we want to bounce our audio tracks back so we target Track 1. In destination, click on Track 1. The next dialogue transition is:

"What's a four letter word for 'Ox of Celebes?' "
"What the heck is an Ox of Celebes?"

I want to cut away from Fritz right before he says "Celebes."

In 4A-2 in the Timeline, I find a good place right before the word — TC/17:28:07. Park the playhead on TC/17:28:08. Select the Razor Blade, then option-click the picture at the playhead (see Figure 6.13). Keeping as much sound as possible, I find the audio frame right before Judy feeds her line — TC/17:29:20.

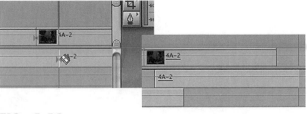

FIG. 6.14

Option key, razor blade at playhead on audio, click. Delete both trims (see Figure 6.14).

FIG. 6.15

Open 3A, in this case Take 1, in the Viewer. Where do we want to cut in to Judy's shot? Again you have to think about the pause and you also want to catch Judy's reaction. Without going too much into rationales, I like TC/12:50:16 as a starting point. Mark>Mark Split>Video In (see Figure 6.15). Fritz's line is over at TC/12:51:16 — exactly one second later. Mark>Mark Split>Audio In.

Make sure the playhead is parked at the end of picture on 4A-2 in the Timeline (see Figure 6.15). Perform Overwrite and Hit kybd: \.

An editor will not worry too much about ambience shifts. It's somebody else's job to fix that. If they are wildly disparate, then that signals a problem that will probably have to be repaired by the dialogue editor.

Okay, we have you started now so for the rest of the piece, have at it. Finish the piece with all the creativity and thoughtful choices you can bring to bear — there are lots of questions to be answered. Do you use the couple at the table again? Their impatience at not being served can add a comic tone to the piece. But it is somewhat of a red herring. Does it divert us from the forward movement of the narrative? Be aware that the more complicated you try to be, the more advanced knowledge of FCP you will need to have.

TITLING, COMMON EFFECTS, & RENDERING

T itles and effects are similar in that they are things that you are creating in FCP and there is no attendant file that contains their content. This is where rendering comes into play and all three will be our subject. The initial goal as we create titles and effects is to either see what we have done immediately or preview some form of it. FCP has a number of different possibilities for this.

Not to beat the drum too many times, but again we emphasize the proprietary nature of the greater enterprise, at least regarding the titling part of this chapter. You can create some marvelous and/or highly functional titles in FCP. But again let us suggest that there may be talented professionals who can bring a new dimension to your work. This is a polite way of saying that you may not be the most qualified graphic designer in the world. Many things can be imported into FCP and a creative designer can work marvels. Titles distinguish a work. Think about options before crunching a lot of bland letters. That said, here is how to do them yourself.

CREATING TITLES

Titles created in FCP can be done many different ways. There can be the vertical crawl that you see at the end of most feature films, you can lay titles over picture, you can animate titles or create animated graphics around the text, and a host of other things. The most common type of title is the white or colored title on a black background and we will make that our starting point. The standard desire is to get a title into the Timeline, tweak it a little bit, and then move the text into the desired position in the frame. This is relatively simple but for some reason, the FCP manuals and most other sources are not particularly straightforward in their approach. Here goes.

Step number one is to go to the Generator popup menu on the Viewer. Click on it and go to Text>Text (see Figure 7.1). Text can also be accessed through the Effects tab in the Browser (see next section). A text window will appear in the Viewer (Viewer: Text) with the words "SAMPLE TEXT" on top of a background. Standard choices for backgrounds can be found at View> Background submenu choices. The Checkerboard option is for a number of different things, but particularly for laying picture over picture (see pages 150-152). When the text screen comes up, a new "Controls" tab will also appear in the background of the Viewer. Click on it. The Controls tab has a large text box on the top (see Figure 7.2). Below that is a list that starts with all the essentially word processing options like fonts, size, et cetera. Below these are all the graphics options like positioning, color, et cetera. To the right of all this, there is a tall section with a reduced scrubber bar at the top. This is used to animate titles and any other elements in FCP. Some of the key basics for compositing (G) are found within the design of this box. Animating titles and general compositing will be discussed in Chapter XII.

FIG. 7.1

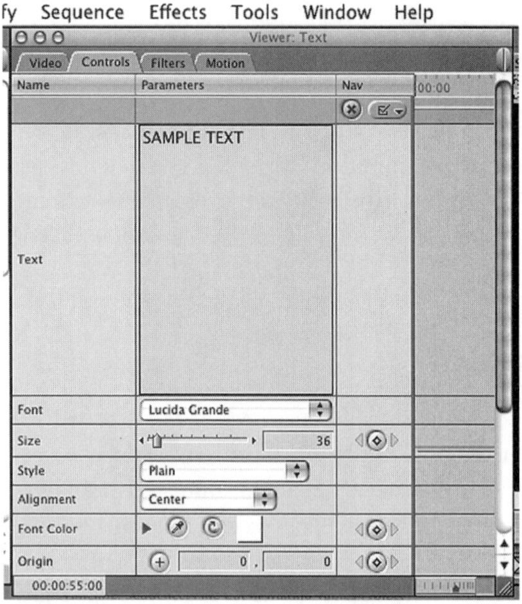

FIG. 7.2

General choices for the color of backgrounds can be accessed at View>Background: with the choices themselves in the submenu.

Click on the words SAMPLE TEXT in the text box of this new window and they will highlight. Determine what you want to type. Let's start simple with the main title card, so type in "WAITING TABLES." There are essentially two philosophies as to what to do next. The first is to pick all the options here and then just create your title. This takes some experience to know what is going to happen. We will start with the other way, which is to take the title into the Timeline and work on the particulars from there.

Once you have the text typed in, the next step is thus to bring it into the Timeline. Let's put these titles at the head of your edited version of *WT.* Open Sequence (Blank) from the Browser. Hit the home key. Choose Insert Edit (kybd: F9, et cetera). The title will appear in the Timeline, pushing the entire show back. FCP defaults to creating ten seconds of any still image you produce, with the amount being changeable in the menus at Final Cut Pro: Preferences> General tab (which Preferences opens to)>Still/Freeze Duration — type in the new time.

Whether you can play this new title or not without rendering depends on the power of your processor. If the render line at the top of the Timeline is red, the title must be rendered in order to be played — "Unrendered" will appear in the Canvas if you try. If the render bar is light green, it can be played and never needs to be rendered, although there are reasons you may want to anyway (see "Rendering" later in this chapter for a discussion of this and to interpret other colors). No matter what the color, an individual frame of the title can be seen in the Canvas when the playhead is stopped — still-framed — in the new clip in the Timeline. Remember that FCP drops the playhead on the first frame of the next shot when you drop anything into the middle of the Timeline. The playhead will drop onto a black frame in this instance so be sure to scrub back into the title or single-frame backwards before proceeding. Be aware, and this is a critical point, that if your machine is not powerful enough to play things without rendering, you will still be able to single-frame, and sometimes even slowly scrub, through the title and see the image. This can be extremely valuable for analyzing spacing and movement without investing precious time in rendering.

Double-click inside the new clip and it will open in the Canvas. We can work on it there. A purple border around the frame in the Canvas indicates that you can now fine-tune. If we have misspelled anything or otherwise want to change the content or line spacing of the text, re-type in the text box. Be careful, the entire body of text highlights when you click in it to retype. If you just start typing, you will delete the whole thing. Make sure the cursor is in the right place and type in the changes. Click in the Canvas and the changes will apply.

In the lines below the text box, we can make all the graphics changes to the text that we want (see Figure 7.3). There are over one hundred fonts in FCP (which uses Mac system fonts), so choose a font that you deem suitable. For even more options, FCP 4 comes bundled with Live Type — a 3-D text animation program. Size is clear-cut as well. FCP defaults to 36 point, but you can either highlight and type in a new number or use the slider to change it. I would not go too much smaller than 36, or it may be too small to be easily read by the average viewer. Remember, you know what your titles say, so check typeface and length with viewers unfamiliar with the project. Style choices are the usual suspects: Plain, Bold, Italic, and Bold/Italic. Alignment defaults to Center, with the other two options to align all the text lines on the right or the left. The main title is frequently centered and that is where we will go with *WT*. These all can pretty clearly be decided upon before you bring the title into the Timeline, but things work either way.

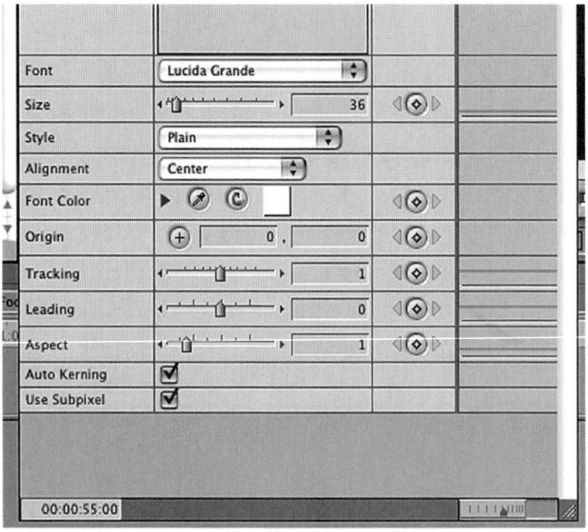

FIG. 7.3

The next choices are best made in the Canvas, at least for now. Font color can be changed a number of different ways. If we click the right triangle on the left of the Color panel, sliders for Hue, Saturation, and Black (HSB)

FIG. 7.4

will appear (see Figure 7.4). Not coming from the print world, I find these a little hard to use although many will find them valuable. The eyedropper can sample a color from an image, presumably in the Canvas. Get the clip you want up in the Canvas, click on the eyedropper and drag it to the color you want in the image in the Canvas. Let go of the mouse and then click at the desired point. The color will appear in the small box two items to the right of the eyedropper. The next item — the circular arrow — is rather esoteric and controls the direction color travels if you animate it.

The last item on the right is probably the most useful. If you click on the square, the "Colors" window will appear (see Figure 7.5). This is our first view of a **Color Wheel** — a standard approach to color selection for many years — and there are a number of important ones in FCP. The color wheel represents the three primary or additive colors of light — red, green, blue (**RGB**) in equidistant areas of the circle. Between each primary color are the subtractive colors of light —cyan, yellow, magenta (**CYM**). Unlike pigments, when you add all the spectrum of colors, you get white, which is at the center of the wheel.

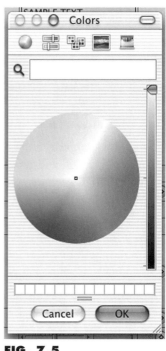

FIG. 7.5

A small square in the center of the color wheel is used to select the desired color. You can click on the square and drag it to other parts of the circle or simply click in the other parts of the circle. A larger representation of the color you have clicked on will appear in the bar across the top next to the magnifying glass. This latter can be clicked on to get a closer view of the color wheel. There are also five icons across the top of this box that provide other color choice options. To create deeper colors you can use the slider to the right of the color wheel — a saturation control. As you slide it down, the whole color wheel becomes darker until at the bottom it is black.

There are lots of options here, so you can manipulate to your heart's content. When you are done, click OK in this window and the text in the Canvas will change to the color chosen. This color will also appear in the small square in the color panel.

Right below the Color panel is one of the key options: **Origin**. It allows you to move the text to the desired position in the frame. It also gives you the required positioning information to create consistent placement between sequential titles, not always a worthwhile goal. Click on the little + marker on the left of the panel (see Figure 7.6). A + (crosshairs)

FIG. 7.6

symbol will appear in the center of the title in the Canvas. You may now click on the title and drag it to the desired position. The positioning of the *WT* title is probably OK, but it is your choice. We will want to reposition other titles anyway. Every time you want to move the text, you have to click the +. The movements you make are given numerical values from center, shown in the boxes to the right of the + . You may want to write these down to create similar positions for other titles, although the numerical value will be displayed anytime you re-open the clip.

Before we get too far along in the discussion of positioning your titles, you should be aware of "Title Safe" issues. Title Safe, found in the menu at View>Title Safe, is a reference overlay that indicates how to place information within a frame so it will show on all the various video screens. There can be a substantial difference in how much image is cropped off the edges between the different formats and manufacturers of television sets. Standard video crops differently than HDTV, Sony crops differently than Panasonic, et cetera. When you select Title Safe, two borders will appear in the frame showing in the Canvas (see Figure 7.7). The outside one is called the **Action Safe Frame** and the inside one is called the **Title Safe Frame**. Action Safe goes beyond mere titles and suggests that all-important action occur with this first frame, if you want to be reasonably sure that it will show on all screens. Some sets can crop even past Action Safe, so all titles should be placed within Title Safe Frame to ensure their visibility. I pay modest attention to the first frame, with action around the edges of the frame often being suggestive of things off-

FIG. 7.7

screen. Plus, what are you going to do anyway? What's shot is shot. Okay, there are some cropping tools, but their application can be problematic (see page 232). The Title Safe Frame is much more critical, as lettering hanging off the edge of the frame looks highly unprofessional.

The last five on the list get less employment but all have their uses. **Tracking** spreads or squashes the title horizontally; going the squash direction eventually inverts the title so the letters read backwards. **Leading** (pronounced ledding) only applies when you have multiple lines of text. It spreads out or condenses the space between lines. It can only do so uniformly. If you want different spacing between different lines, that will have to figured out between leading and hard return in the text box. **Aspect** uniformly controls the height of the text. **Auto Kerning** controls how close the letters are to each other based on their shape — it should be checked and unchecked to see what difference is created. **Use Subpixels** should generally remain checked as it provides sharper quality. Again, uncheck to see the difference.

> Be aware that on less powerful machines, titles can look slightly indistinct in the Canvas. Check all your titles on an External Video Device before you panic.

So you have the *WT* title in the Timeline. First we need to decide length — how long do you want the title on screen? The length varies with the purpose. End credits are frequently presented faster than the ordinary person can read because those really interested in an individual credit will find it from a different source and because the presentation will go on forever if we give time to everyone. End credits on television shows are mercilessly rapid. The general rule for titles that you want the audience to read is: time it while you read the credit twice slowly. Not terribly slowly but just slow. That will give even the slowest reader in the audience a chance to get it. Waiting Tables...Waiting Tables...about three seconds. You will save render time if you trim before you render. Even if you cannot view the clip in Real Time you can time it with the Ruler, typing the desired number into the duration time code box, or simply counting from the beginning of the clip. With the Razor Blade, trim off what you do not need, select and Shift/delete the trim, and render the remaining clip if necessary. Save.

To create another new title, you must go to Generator>Text>Text again. If you just clear the text box and start to work again, the changes will be applied to the previous title — an irritating result. Save and start Text over every time (there are workarounds on this. Before typing, let's select Left in the Align panel on the controls tab — we anticipate dragging it to the left edge of the frame. Type in: **with** (hit return twice) **Freya Rae** (hit return once) **Jeff Gilson**. With the playhead parked at the end of the first title, do an Insert edit. The title comes in left aligned but in the center of the frame — an odd effect (see Figure 7.8). Double click the new text to open it in the Canvas. Go to Origin and hit +. Click on the text in the Canvas and drag it wherever you want — the lower left in our example (see Figure 7.9). Does that look good? Try all the Tracking, Leading, and Aspect you want. When you like it — time and render.

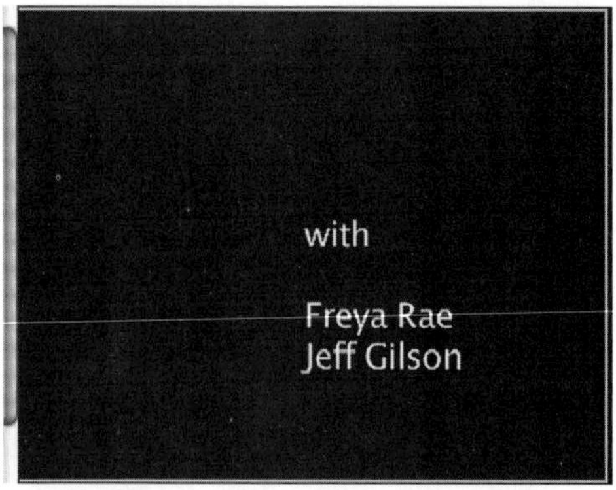

FIG. 7.8

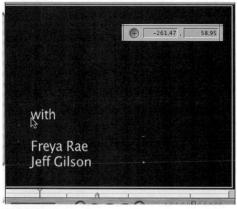

FIG. 7.9

Do one more with Align: Right. Start fresh: Go to Text: Text and then the Controls tab. Type in: **and** (hit return twice) **Charles Hubbell** (hit return once) **Heidi Fellner**. Insert edit. Double-click on this new text in the Timeline. Go to Origin and hit +. Click on the text in the Canvas and drag it — the lower right in our example (see Figure 7.10). When you like the title — time and render. When you play this new sequence, the cuts may look abrupt but we can work in fades later.

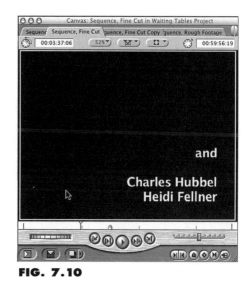

FIG. 7.10

That is the good old-fash-ioned, plain title on a black background. Within the Text menu of the Generator pop-up, there are a number of other valuable options as well. Just like the Viewer: Text window, selecting any one of the options from the menu brings up the effect's own window. Each menu has the already-seen panels for font, color, et cetera, and then will have controls for its own effect.

Crawl, and here the terminology is different from the film world, scrolls the text horizontally across the bottom of the frame. The seventh panel lets you determine the direction of travel, right or left, with titles traveling from right to left being the norm. That is the direction we read and traveling the other direction can be quite disconcerting. There is a default rate of travel and the inserted title will simply be as long as it takes the text to travel its entire distance.

Lower 3rd places the titles within that particular area of the frame. This can be done for a number of purposes, but is mostly useful for subtitles. The window defaults to two lines of text (see Figure 7.11) and has

Name	Parameters	
Text 1	Sample Text 1	
Font	Lucida Grande	
Style	Plain	
Size		36
Tracking		1
Font Color		
Text 2	Sample Text 2	
Font	Lucida Grande	
Style	Plain	

FIG. 7.11

separate panels (Text 1 and Text 2) for each line. If you were creating subtitles you would usually delete Text 1 and just use Text 2.

Outline allows you to put borders and/or shadows on the text, a common way of making titles more distinct and more distinctive. Again you have to type in the text. Change the color of the text if desired at Text Color. You then need to determine a color for the outline area at Line Color — it defaults to black which will not show if you have a black background. Once colors are chosen, the two heavy lifters for the outlining are Line Width and Line Softness. Each approach has its own set

FIG. 7.12

of parameters and here is an example of at least one (see Figure 7.12). Play around with them and see what they will do. The Background Settings area below is for creating a highlight box — of any color — that can be behind all or part of your titles.

Scrolling Text is what many filmmakers call a crawl, and is a very typical way of handling a large number of credits. In film, scrolling credits can be expensive and time-consuming to produce. In NLE, of course, they are disgustingly simple, although it will take you some time to get it right. Again, the title sequence you insert will be as long as it takes to scroll through what you have created at the default speed. To create each new line, you simply put a hard return in between each line of text. Be aware that these almost surely need to be rendered and with such complex data, rendering will take a long time.

Below Text is **Typewriter** which simply allows you to have titles appear as if being typed in by a typewriter.

As suggested, titles can be animated, the motion element casting this discussion in a much different light. Some animation suggestions will be offered in the section on compositing.

RENDERING

Rendering is the creation of new elements in FCP. If you create a title, layer image, or apply any effect, it does not actually exist in any of the original Capture Scratch or imported files — the Quicktime files always being the source from which FCP draws. If you make changes to a clip or clips in the Timeline, what you have done does not exist in those files. Rendering is the process of creating a new file — creating the image — for the changed material. FCP calculates the changes you have made to every frame in the chosen area of the Timeline and then builds a new render file.

The previously mentioned Render Bar in the top of the Timeline indicates what kind of rendering is required. The upper bar is video and the lower bar audio. If the bar is any shade of gray, the scene does not need rendering or has already been rendered. If the bar is a color, it indicates the clip's **render status** with different colors indicating different status. This expanded, color-coded handling is mostly new to FCP 4. The software now comes with the ability to analyze the power of your computer and decide whether an effect has to be rendered to be viewed, can be previewed before rendering, can maybe be previewed before rendering, and a number of other options. The issue is how playable the changed clip is in real time. FCP has to "re-draw" the changed frames and whether it can do it in real time is dependent on the processing power of your computer.

In earlier versions of FCP, the basic choice was to render or not to render (...unto Caesar. That is the question.). It was either the red bar or the high-way. Again, if your machine is screamin' you may be able to look at a lot of things without having to render. If not, you will be seeing a lot of red. The more complex the effect, the more likely it will need to be rendered.

The Real-Time pop-up (RT) menu on the left side of the Timeline plays a significant role in the playability of render clips (see Figure 7.13). The RT menu controls the quality of the playback image — the resolution (R). At lower resolutions, the processor does not

FIG. 7.13

have to work as hard and more things can be previewed. But they often look crummy. But you can see what is going to happen in a general way before devoting large amounts of render time.

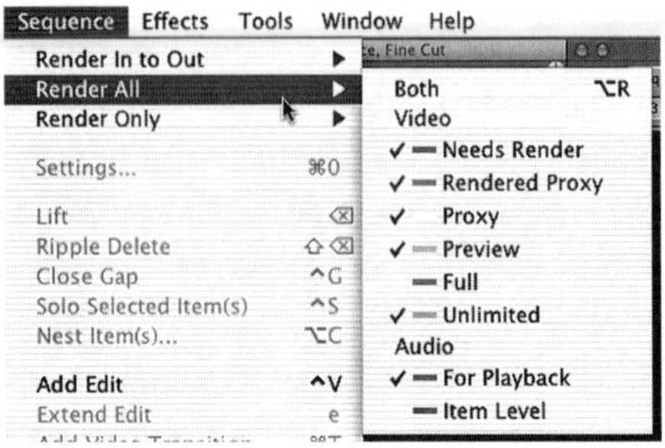

FIG. 7.14

All render information can be found in the first three menu items under Sequence. All three menu items open submenus that show all the color-coded render possibilities (see Figure 7.14). Render colors are as follows:

Dark Gray — the clip does not require rendering.

Steel Gray — the clip has already been rendered.

Red — needs rendering.

Green — means it can preview in real time without rendering, although there may be some playback issues down the road.

Dark Green — will playback in real time in full resolution.

Yellow — Proxy — means that FCP can approximate the effect in playback; in essence, it will do its best, but playback may be a little ragged.

Dark Yellow — means that you have used the Render Control tab in Sequence>Settings or FCP menu>User Preferences to set playback or resolution at lower rates than the rest of the sequence.

Orange — means that you have selected a lower resolution from the Real-Time Effects pop-up menu, either the pop-up menu on the Timeline or at Sequence>Render. Changing playback resolution puts less stress on your processor so it can do more things. FCP will do the best it can here but again some raggedness may occur.

The same ideas apply to audio. Red means it needs to be rendered. Green means that a sample rate conversion is required. The complexity of your audio — equalization, other signal processing, extensive layering — and the power of your processor are the determining factors again, although audio files are generally not as complicated and do not require rendering as frequently.

Last, yet very important, everything that you render is sent to the Render Files folder that FCP creates for every new project. There is also an Audio Render Files folder. Both can be found in the same place as the Capture Scratch and all are probably best kept in a Project file like the one we created for the *Waiting Tables* DVD.

Rendering, and the time it takes, is a major part of your activity once you start creating and adding effects to your clips. One added issue is that when you move rendered clips, move whole sections, or make even minor positioning changes, clips may require re-rendering. This is one reason why it may be a good idea to save applying many effects until very late stages in the editorial process.

COMMON EFFECTS

Final Cut Pro, like most NLE programs, has a wide range of simple transitional devices that can be used to get us from one time and/or place to another. By common effects, we simply mean the myriad of transitional devices — fades, dissolves, wipes — that are commonly, and sometimes uncommonly, used. For old film guys, they can be applied with shocking ease. In film (16mm at least), dissolves and fades (see sidebar) are executed in the final stage of the editing process — created in the final print. They are planned during the editing process, but you do not get to see them until the very end. If you don't like them, it's tough. At not-insubstantial expense, you can go back and reprint them. Fades and dissolves are the easy ones. Wipes, irises, and the like must be generated in an expensive animation-style process on an optical printer. That is part of the reason you do not see a huge number of them in films. The other reason is that effects can be easily overused and frequently are used to repair mistakes. The old saying is "if you can't solve it, dissolve it." FCP, and its NLE brethren, make it wonderfully simple to throw a lot of stuff in, but watch out for overdoing. That said, well-timed and thoughtful effects are an

— A **fade** is where the image either fades out to black or up from black. It can be done to colors or white as well.

— A **dissolve** is a fade-out of a shot layered on top of a fade-in of another. The second shot replaces the first as the first "dissolves" out.

integral part of many projects. This will be covered in Chapter XIV, but be aware that if you are matching back to film, the complications of recreating your digitally-produced effects on film must be carefully considered.

With the exception of fades, all effects depend on having overlapping footage in your edit. When we make a cut to which we know we want to apply a dissolve (or any effect), we need to cut it so there is extra footage at the end of the outgoing shot and at the beginning of the incoming shot. That is, there must be more frames than represented in the Timeline. And these frames must be good and ones we want to see, because many will be very visible in the dissolve. One second is FCP's default effects rate, so you need at least 15 good frames to the tail and head of the respective shots. If you have fewer frames, it will simply make a shorter dissolve. If you have no frames, the effect will not apply.

DRAG, DROP, AND RENDER

All effects can be found in the "Effects" tab in the background of the Browser, as well as in the menus. They can be accessed and applied simply, it being merely a matter of drag, drop, and render. The only mild irritation is the time required to render, although times vary from machine to machine. The typical effects discussed here are not the only things stored in the Effects tab. There are quite a few other options, many of which will be discussed elsewhere.

When you click on the effects tab, it will open to six options (see Figure 7.15). Opening each one of these bins, we will find a bewildering number of options that take a fair amount of time to sort out. You will probably never use many of these options, but they add to the incredible functional strength of FCP. Favorites is where you can put things that you use on a regular basis. The Effects tab is the only place where you can physically put things in a favorites folder, but then they will show in all other standard and pop-up menus. Video Transitions is where we will find most of the items discussed here — all also found in the menus at

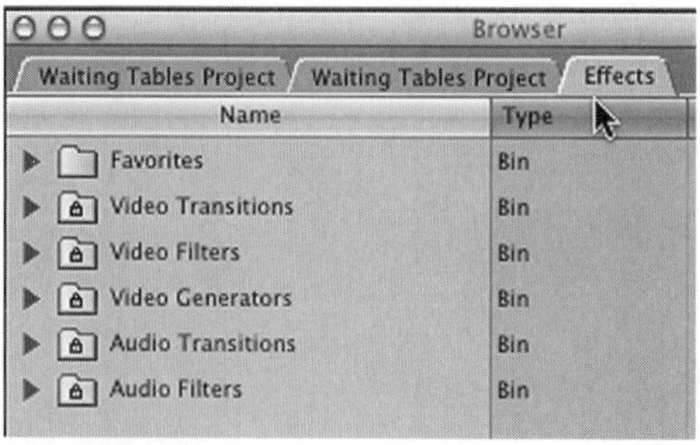

FIG. 7.15

Effects: Video Transitions. Video Filters is for manipulating image quality (Sharpen, Distort, Color Correction, et cetera) — menus found at Effects: Video Filters. Video Generators is another route for accessing the same items as in the Generator Pop-up menu on the Viewer. The last two are obviously for audio effects options.

When you click on the arrow by Video Transitions (or double-click on the icon to open its own window) all the categories of options appear (see Figure 7.16). Within each of these "sub" bins are the myriad choices that you can apply to your edits. They range from the hardy stalwarts used in movies for years and years (like fades and dissolves), to those less used but good for many situations (like wipes), to the esoteric if not downright silly (like the Center Split Slide). There seems to be a

FIG. 7.16

tradition in video transition generators, dating back to the first generation of digital studio switchers, to throw a couple of goofy numbers up there like dollar bill shapes replacing one image with another. FCP has a couple of odd ones — but that's the fun.

When you open all these bins, you will find there are over sixty possibilities available to you. Within that, you should be able to find something, but these are *the* options. All these transitions are explained somewhere (that is why the FCP manual is three volumes), but you are better off finding some time when you have nothing better to do and then just throw a couple of shots together and try them all out.

Many of these options are useful but the Dissolve bin has the standard options that the industry has been using since time immemorial — well, at least from the early twentieth century. Double-click on (**A**) and the dissolve options appear (see Figure 7.17). There are a number of different types of dissolves, but the Cross Dissolve is the standard with which most people are familiar. This is what film folks just call a plain old dissolve and it is one of the most commonly used effects, along with the standard fade from or to black. In keyboard shortcuts and menus, FCP defaults to the Cross Dissolve. The (**B**) icon represents the effect, and all effects, and

FIG. 7.17

is simply dragged to the desired position in the Timeline. FCP automatically defaults to a one-second effect. The render bar will indicate how playable the effect is.

The only effects in *WT* that actually make any sense to use are fades — there are no time transitions in the middle. FCP calls a fade a **Fade In Fade Out Dissolve**, and in a sense you are dissolving to or from black. Because of this last thing, fades unfortunately are the only effects that have a mild complication (see sidebar).

The tutorial scene could very effectively start with a fade-up from black. With your cut of *WT* still open, drag the fade symbol to the very beginning of the first non-title visual (Scene 1A-4). It will drop in as an effects

FIG. 7.18

symbol (see Figure 7.18). Render it if necessary and take a look at it. This is reasonably satisfactory. The scene could end with a fade as well, but we will do something else in the chapter on compositing.

While the scene really cannot support any dissolves, you should try one to see what it looks like. We can always undo it or not save changes. Pick the cut between 1A-3 and 4A-4; any old cut will do but this is the only one where a dissolve comes anywhere close to making some sense. Click on **Cross Dissolve** in the Browser and drag the icon to the cut in the Timeline. The effect symbol will appear on the cut. Many machines will require that this be rendered. Go ahead if necessary or, again, you can single-frame through to get an idea of what it will look like. You have a typical dissolve. This does not really make any sense dramatically, but you get the idea. Undo (twice if you rendered).

What if you want the effect shorter or longer? This is quite simple. Double click on the desired effect in the Browser — in this case, let's just make a

The complication with fades is that they are designed to go on an edit and then fade-out/fade-up from outgoing to incoming. When the icon is placed on an edit, the effect symbol should straddle the edit and then, when doing a 30-frame fade, the outgoing shot does a 15-frame fade out followed immediately by a 15-frame fade-up on the next shot. The screen is only black for a split second, creating a somewhat odd effect. So, a true fade should come or go to some black — black being the absence of a clip in the Timeline. Therefore, the effect symbol should just be put on the front of a clip when there is no clip preceding it — then you will theoretically have a 30-frame fade-up. However, if placed on an image coming from black, the fade-out part will stay black at the beginning and the fade-up will not actually start until halfway through the icon. The solution is to use the Threshold slider in the Fade In Fade Out Dissolve tab to change when everything starts (see the next paragraph for access paths and Figure 7.20 for what this slider looks like). Set it to 0 for a fade-up and 100 for a fade-out.

longer dissolve at the same cut. The Viewer will open with a **Cross Dissolve** tab (see Figure 7.19). This is where you see a vivid representation of how the outgoing and incoming shots overlap, with ramps between them indicating how they fade up and down. A one-second effect starts 15 frames before the end of the outgoing shot and ends 15 seconds after the beginning of the incoming shot. To change duration of the effect, there is the usual

FIG. 7.19

clock and time window in the upper left corner of the tab. The default time is displayed — one second. Highlight and type in 200. Hit return and it will list as 2 seconds and zero frames. On the upper right is a dragging symbol (**C**) . Click on it and drag the effect to the appropriate place in the Timeline. This will create your longer dissolve. Double-clicking on an effect already in the Timeline will bring up this same window for changes.

C

The three-button panel in the top center controls (**D**) which is the dominant shot. The window opens to the standard triangle, meaning each shot is equal with the ramps meeting in the center of the dissolve. If you click the left triangle, the ramp goes downwards, right triangle upwards. Sometimes it is difficult to tell the difference between these three choices, but the equal gives equal balance and the other two lightly favor the chosen shot.

The other dissolves all have some other distinguishing features. The **Additive Dissolve** is very poorly described, partially because it is pretty tough to figure out what it does. It appears to match shot densities, the result being that the two shots kind of "blossom" in the middle for a somewhat odd effect. The **Dip to Color Dissolve** may be the most useful of the bunch with a color effect added in the middle for accent. If you apply it, the color panel will appear with access to the color wheel. The dissolve will go the the chosen color and then to the incoming shot. **Dither Dissolves** have kind of a pixelly shimmering quality. **Non-Additive** sequentially replaces the lighter pixels of the outgoing with the darker of the incoming, creating a kind of staggered effect. **Ripple** distorts the outgoing clip in a drop-in-water-rippling-out fashion as it exits to a similarly distorted incoming clip.

I would go through and put fade-ups and fade-outs on all your titles. Again, remember the Threshold business (see Figure 7.20).

All the other effects have a varying degree of usefulness. Wipes are reasonably common, although they can feel artificial along with having their

FIG. 7.20

'60s *Batman* show associations. Depending on the style of your show, you may find the perfect effect that everyone else thinks is odd in any other application. Again, there are some pretty silly ones (I just had to find out what the Jaws Wipe was). But just for argument's sake, try a couple of effects of choice throughout. You can always undo or not save changes.

Again, for any kind of transitional effect except a fade, you have to have material to overlap. What you cut into the Timeline must have at least 15 more frames available to the tail for the outgoing shot and another 15 frames to the head in the incoming shot, at least for a one-second effect. And they must be frames we want to see. If you cut the last frame of a clip to the first frame of the next one, you will not be able to design in your effect. The longer the effect, the more overlap you need.

To get rid of an effect after it has been rendered and/or saved, simply click on the effect and hit Delete. The clip or clips will restore to original length.

SUPERIMPOSITION/ LAYERING VIDEO

Final Cut Pro, like many NLE programs, offers the opportunity to easily create many layers of video. In the film world, this is called superimpositon or, when done in the camera, double exposure.

Superimposition and compositing are closely related and many of the procedures are similar. Both require adding more tracks of video and then putting the clips you want to combine on these new tracks, layered above the other clips you want to combine. It is not enough to simply drop the shot to another layer, you must alter the clip's "visibility' so that other clips can be seen "through" it — that is, layered on top. The clip that is on the uppermost — the highest — track is the default, meaning it is always the one that is visible. FCP calls this "vertical editing." If we made the Timeline 3-D and pulled it out so we could look down on it from above, the top layer 'blocks out" lower layers. So, we must reduce the visibility of the top layer so we can see the lower levels through it. This is done with the Clip Overlays bar. It can be done with as many clips as you want.

Waiting Tables does not really lend itself to superimposition as it is pretty much a stacking up shots, film-style edit. We will throw one super in just for demonstration purposes. We can always get rid of it. We will super a shot of the couple wondering what is going on over the phone conversation. Let's do this in Sequence, Fine Cut.

Step #1 is to determine what part of the clip to be supered we want to use — the MOS shot 1B-1. In this case, we will choose TC/03:29:04 as our In point and TC/03:35:04 as our Out.

Step #2 is to determine where we want it in the Timeline. At this point, we want to start referencing a number of the operations we are doing in terms of the time code of the show instead of the time code of the clip that we have used so far. This is called **program time code** (G). We will refer to it as TL-TC (Timeline time code) and it is found in the upper-right-hand time code box on the Canvas. Run the cut of the scene in the Timeline and find a good place to start the clip we are going to superimpose. We are being somewhat random about this, but we will choose TL-TC/01:45:09 as our In point. Click the In symbol in the Canvas. For this operation, it is important to set your In point, because the playhead is referring to the other video track. The clip will come in at the wrong place if you do not choose an In point, although it is easy enough to move.

Step #3 is to bring it into the Timeline. Here, we need to create another video track in order to accommodate layered picture. The easiest way to do this is to use the Superimpose Edit function in the Canvas. When you do that, FCP automatically creates the new track. So, click in the Viewer and drag the thumbnail over to Superimpose — kybd:F12 or the (**E**) icon. The clip appears above the picture you have been editing (see Figure 7.21).

Again, FCP always plays the higher track. If we play

FIG. 7.21

this, it will just do a straight cut to the couple where we inserted the shot. Be sure this new video track is enabled at the farthest left green button.

Step #4 is to create the layering. Go to Clip Overlays on the bottom left of the Timeline. When you click on it, red lines will appear through the middle of all the audio clips, eventually used for volume control, and a black line will appear in all the video clips. The latter controls clip visibility.

Step #5 — When you put the arrow on the black line, it will change into the horizontal drag symbol. Simply drag the bar down and a small box will indi-

FIG. 7.22

cate percentage of visibility (see Figure 7.22). Obviously, if you want an equal amount of each, you want to drag to 50%. If it will not drag to exactly 50–50, use the Track Height tool on the lower left of the Timeline

to get increased discrimination. This will probably need to be rendered, but wait for the last step to do so. If you park the playhead in the middle of the layered area, you will see the superimposed frames in the Canvas (see Figure 7.23).

Step #6 — It is going to look kind of odd to just have the clip appear. So we recom-

FIG. 7.23

mend that you put a fade-up at the beginning of the supered shot and fade out at the end. Go into the Effects Tab in the Browser and drag a

standard fade to both ends of the clip (see Figure 7.24).

Step #7 — Render and play.

FIG. 7.24

COMPOSITE MODE

Compositing can also be used to layer, although it always creates a more complex effect than a straightforward 50–50 superimpose (more complex compositing is covered in Chapter XII). The different compositing options

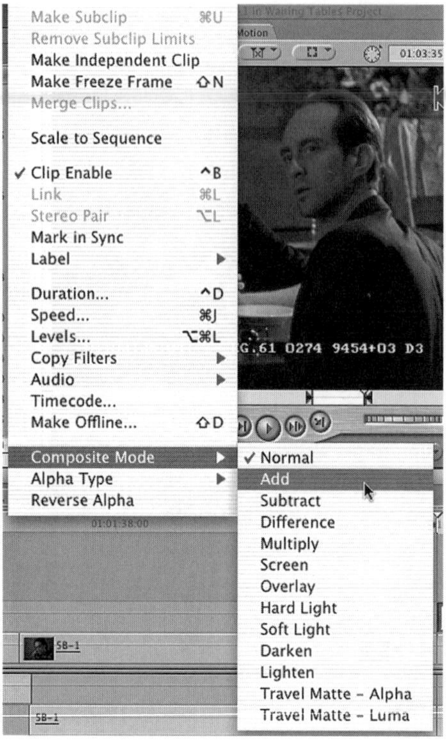

FIG. 7.25

are found at Modify>Composite Mode in the top menus or contextual menu (see Figure 7.25). Again, the options are bewildering, and in some cases silly, but the most typical one for a simple layering is the Add option. This simply adds the two images and, while it basically looks like a standard super, it will be a little brighter because there has been no exposure compensation. To do this you go through steps one through three in the previous process.

Step #4 is to open the newly positioned clip in the Viewer from the Timeline. Go to Modify>Composite Mode>Add. The clip will appear in the Viewer with a faint layer of the checkerboard visible in the background. The checkerboard again gives a visual representation of a layer's or clip's transparency. The layered result should be visible in the Canvas.

Do Steps #6 and #7 from the previous example.

Other choices provide a wide variety of results. Experiment. Remember you can see what a superimposed or composited frame looks like in stop and single frame mode.

SUPERING TITLES

Supering titles is very straightforward. Simply go through all the steps in the first section on titles, except use the checkerboard as the background. The checkerboard again indicates visibility; everything in the lower image will show through where the checkerboard is visible. The higher track is still dominant so you will not see any picture through the title.

For a quick example, let's super a title over the first shot. The scene could use a quick establishment of time of day, so we will just identify this with a quick super of "3 pm."

Step #1: Go to the first shot and decide where you want the title to come up. Let's say we want it a few frames after the first fully visible frame. Find the appropriate starting point TL-TC and Mark In on the Canvas.

Step #2: Go to View>Text>Text. If the Sample Text title comes up with any other background than the checkerboard, go to View>Background> Checkerboard 1 (it will actually work with a black background as well).

Step #3: Open the Controls tab in the Viewer, highlight Sample Text and type in "3" space "pm."

Step #4: Click on the Video tab to bring the title back up in the Viewer.

It will not edit into the show unless you do. Then hit Superimpose Edit. The title, usually requiring rendering, will appear in Video 2 track (see Figure 7.26).

Step #5: Move the playhead into the new clip and double-click on it. The title overlaying image will appear in the Canvas. Re-open the Controls tab in the viewer, click on the + in Origin, go back to the Canvas and move the title to where you want it — the lower left in our example.

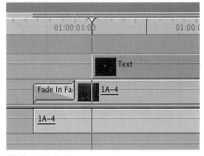

FIG. 7.26

FIG. 7.27

Step #6: It would be too abrupt to just have the title appear, so we will again work in a fade-in and a fade-out. From the Browser's Effects tab, drag a fade to the beginning. How long do we want to see this title? A couple of seconds, then fade-out? Count off three

FIG. 7.28

seconds to include the fade. Get the razor blade, cut, and delete the excess. Drag over another fade (see Figure 7.27).

Step #7: Render and play (see Figure 7.28).

AUDIO DESIGN

A full and rich sound track can be built entirely in Final Cut Pro. That said, however, the professional world exports basic audio tracks to an OMF (Open Media Framework) file format, building sound in an even more robust audio environment. Pro Tools is a commonly used program, with a number of other significant players as well. Here, an experienced editorial sound crew would build and refine your audio. A professionally mixed final product would be the standard destination. The case has already been made for a professional mix (see page 43). You may choose to disregard this advice, but keep in mind one central fact: acknowledging the random high-end reader, you do not know beans about sound. With a little common sense we can do lots of things in FCP, but the pros bring the ability to both add to and get the best out of your tracks.

However, understanding the financially challenged independent maker that may be reading this book, we will talk about building tracks in FCP. We will take you through and show you how to lay out the tracks and what kind of things you can accomplish in FCP (which is a lot). With the bundling of a limited version of Peak software, the ability to fashion sound becomes even greater. In Chapter XVI, we will talk about how OMF operates and a little bit about final mixdown in a professional studio.

Before doing any audio editing, it is very useful to access a commonly used FCP option — having the waveform of each clip displayed in the Timeline. This can be selected in the User Preferences menus, but this only works when chosen before you initiate a project. To change in

FIG. 8.1

mid-edit, we go to Sequence> Settings in the menus. Choose the Timeline Options tab and check "Show Audio Waveforms," second from the bottom on the list (see Figure 8.1). With the waveforms open we can both see and hear audio events.

BUILDING AUDIO IN FINAL CUT PRO

To go through some examples, we will use "Sequence, Fine Cut" which you can find and then open in the tutorial's Browser. This is a fine cut of the full piece. You might want to take a look at it. We have left some of the tracks single strand except where we needed to work a couple of things out. The sound editing is pretty straightforward except at the end where I wanted to speed up the phone conversation a little bit. We dropped some of Fritz's lines to the second track and pushed them forward a little. This is extremely common. The only problem was that it made his "OK" a little close to his "Bye." As it is off-camera, I took the razor blade and clipped on either side of "OK" in 5B-2 and dropped it down to the third track — A3 — and moved it ahead to where I liked it (see Figure 8.2). While the resulting hole in the ambience would usually be addressed further down the road, ambience from another shot effectively covered it.

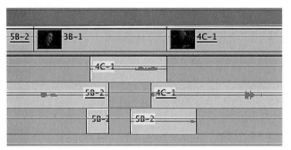

FIG. 8.2

While this gets into small details, once I have put Fritz's "OK" on this third track, we should call it a dialogue track and leave it free of any effects or music. While this may have limited application for indie editors who know their tracks and are going to mix themselves, in the pro world audio is laid out to very specific norms. Effects are never put on dialogue tracks. Music is never put on effects tracks. And so on. Once we have designated a track as a "dialogue track" nothing else will go on it other than dialogue — even if this one piece is the only thing on the track.

Configuring your tracks to these standards simply makes the final mix more organized for the rerecording mixers. Their time is very expensive and if they have to search to find your audio, the cash register keeps ringing and, moreover, they get frustrated. You want the best sound possible and a distracted or irritated mixer is not going to give you his or her most dedicated effort. Anyway, we will find other dialogue uses for this third track somewhere down the road as we create our handles, et cetera.

ADDING SOUND EFFECTS

The next obvious step with *Waiting Tables* is to put in the phone sound. Final Cut Pro 4 opens to four sound tracks, so we do not need to add tracks yet (see pages 98-99 for this). We will put the phone on the fourth track. In the Browser, open the SFX bin and you will see an audio clip labeled "Phone." Open and play it. There are only four rings on the audio (it was too much trouble to find a phone that was not interrupted by an answering machine). This is fine. We will just re-use the clip again or do a word processing thing — copy and paste it.

In the Viewer, find the first frame of the first ring — TC/17:42:10 (see Figure 8.3). Hit Mark In. Next we need to decide where we want the rings to start. The script calls for them to start after Fritz's "What's a four-letter word for Ox of Celebes?" No disrespect to the screenwriter, but the editor finds that if we

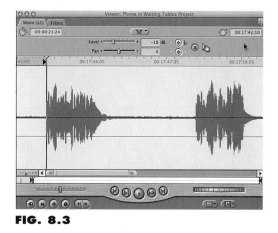

FIG. 8.3

start the phone here, it only rings three times before Judy gets itchy about it. Not enough buildup. So, we are going to start it earlier. Where? We want to find a placement where it will not cover dialogue and it can be clearly focused on by the viewer. Some disinterested observers have suggested the ringing should start before or during the titles. An interesting idea, but we will start it all later. Exact positioning is, of course, up to editorial discretion, but as the couple is heading toward the table seems to

155

FIG. 8.4

be a particularly good spot. Having tried a few options, we decide we want the rings to start at TC/06:38:27 in scene 2A-4. We want to continue our focus on the Timeline so we are again going to identify all placement by the Timeline time code (TL-TC) found in the upper right hand corner of the Canvas. It is TL-TC/00:25:13 in this case and we park the playhead here. In the Timeline, make sure the destination toggle is on the fourth track. Overwrite edit. Play. Listen to the sequence with all four rings — obviously too loud, but we will deal with that momentarily. The positioning seems to work pretty well on everything so far (see Figure 8.4). We got lucky.

Now we can be very systematic about putting in the second set of rings. We can plot out the exact distance between rings and make them 100% consistent. With the phone audio open in the viewer, find the very end of the ring — we will go for the actual end of the waveform and disregard the reverberation. As long as we are consistent, it does not make any difference and the end of the ring is easier to identify on the waveform. Note the time code in the upper right hand corner (TC/17:45:00). Play until you find the beginning of the next ring (see Figure 8.5). Use the left/right arrows to land on the very first frame of the ring. Note this time code — TC17: 48:10 — exactly 100 frames. Remembering that video is 30 fps, do the simple math 30 + 30 + 30 + 10 = 100. Just a hair over three seconds.

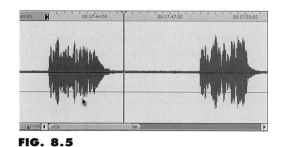

FIG. 8.5

Single-click on the phone clip in the Timeline and hit Command C (Copy) — we will do this word processor-style just for a change of pace. Find the end of the fourth ring (TL-TC/00:46:04) and go 100 frames down the road (TL-TC/00:49:14). To do this we just add three seconds, 10 frames. Remember you can just type 4914 into the upper right hand time code window in the Canvas and it will reposition you at the number — adding colons and semi-colons as necessary. Park the playhead here and hit Overwrite. Go through the same process four rings down the road — the last ring ends at TL-TC/01:10:04 and thus paste at TL-TC/00:55:14. This is all we need except there are too many rings now. Fritz picks up the phone after the second ring in this last set.

Take the razor blade and cut somewhere between the second and third ring (approximately TL-TC/01:23:27). We do not have to be too exact here. The rings are all in place with exact timing (see Figure 8.6).

FIG. 8.6

REPOSITIONING SOUND EFFECTS

With the phone evenly spaced, we are covering a few key pieces of dialogue (it is still too loud as well). You might get an argument on this in some editing quarters, but we want to very subtly move a few rings so they are not quite so intrusive. When we do this, we risk disrupting some natural rhythms. When confronted with a repetitive sound, we come to expect them to continue at regular intervals. A phone ringing is as good an example of this as anything and our anticipation is pretty specific. There is, however, a little room for play. Things can be moved within reason and almost no one will be the wiser. As we create these effects, we sometimes over-scrutinize them and in our knowledge of them, we can see how artificial the changes are. However, always keep in mind that a generalized viewer is not sitting there with a stopwatch holding your feet to the proverbial temporal flames. You have to make a very large shift for people to buy out. It is that old willing suspension of disbelief. Unless you willfully flaunt that great concept, nobody is going to squawk. Again it is a variation on the ever-present concern, "if they are listening to that, we are doing something wrong."

The second ring of the second set does not come in well with the line "What the heck is an Ox of Celebes?" It comes in at TL-TC/00:55:14, which is a little early, covering up the beginning of Judy's line. To move the ring, we need to create empty space on either side to move into. We could bounce it to a fifth track, but for now we will keep it all on one track. To this end we are going to use the razor blade to make some room. Move the playhead about forty frames ahead of the beginning of this second ring. We want to make it about a 15-frame hole, because it does not seem like we have to move the ring far. Make a cut in the track with the razor blade. Go fifteen frames down the road — to the right — and make another cut (see Figure 8.7). Delete the trim (see Figure 8.8).

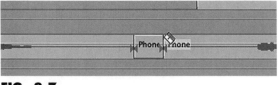

FIG. 8.7

Now, do the same after the second ring (see Figure 8.9). With gaps before and after the ring we can now slide it back and forth. You can either click on it and drag it or the preferred method is to move it on the keyboard as described in Chapter IV. The comma key (,) moves the clip left and the period key (.) moves it right. This is an

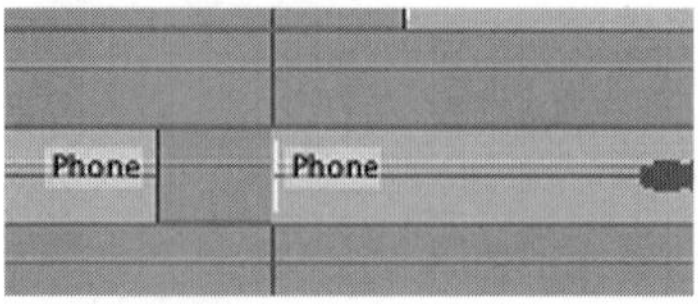

FIG. 8.8

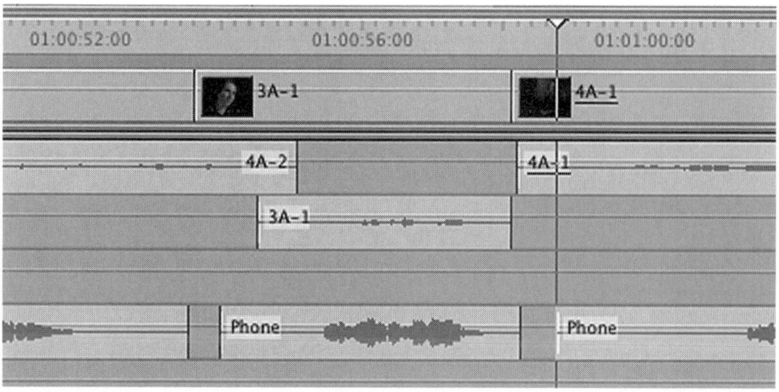

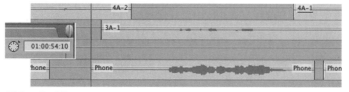

FIG. 8.9

FIG. 8.10

extremely handy function for many different applications. We can move it and listen to it and then try something else. We finally decide we want the ring to start at TL-TC/00:55:25 with the clip starting at TL-TC/00:55:10 (see Figure 8.10) — an eleven-frame move.

We make a similar decision with the final two rings. We want to move both of them forward, potentially slightly different amounts. There is

FIG. 8.11

free real estate right before the first ring, so we just use kybd: comma and kybd: period to move the clip. The ring starts at TL-TC/01:13:14 (see Figure 8.11). We move it forward and find that we like it starting at

TL-TC/01:12:13, a full second before (see Figure 8.12). Can we cheat it this much? I think so. The position of the last ring seems okay so I think we will just leave it.

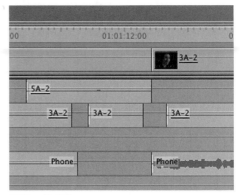

FIG. 8.12

VOLUME CONTROL

Controlling the volume of clips is a constant concern. You will obviously be doing a lot of this, so following are a few simple examples. There are a number of ways to control volume. FCP 4 has a brand new mixer in the menus at Tools>Mixer. This will be covered in Chapter XIII, although you should take a look at that material before investing extensive time following the procedures described here. Other than FCP's mixer, the most commonly used approach is a standard Timeline function. Go to the bottom band of the Timeline and find the Clip Overlay symbol: (**A**) . Click on it and a horizontal red line will appear across all the audio clips the entire length of the Timeline. Put the pointer right on the red line and the arrow changes to the vertical drag symbol (**B**) . With this, you can drag the volume up or down as desired. As you drag, a small box will display the decibel (dB) change. A dB is a rather complicated measurement, although in most recording and playback applications it represents the change in volume from a norm, which hopefully is a perfect recording.

Full volume on this telephone ring is a little loud so we are going to want to do some general changing. Now, click on the red line in the first set of rings and drag it to −12 db (see Figure 8.13). With default sizes, it may be difficult to drag to that exacting a standard, so choose a bigger Track Height at (**C**) for tighter discriminations. The volume change will only affect the parameters of the audio clip on which you are dragging. As a starting point, drag to −12 dB on all the separate phone clips. Save changes.

FIG. 8.13

Equally important, you may want to change the volume on just a portion of the clip. This can range from just making something a little louder or quieter to a full fade-out or fade-up of the sound. Whatever your goal, shifting volumes is reasonably easy to do. Again, this is cheating in terms of the phone rings but, if you make subtle changes, most viewers will buy in. Moreover, if the sound is intrusive or dialogue is buried because no change was added, the result can really call attention to itself. Select the Pen Tool (**D**) from the Tool Palette. Next you want to determine the parameter — the boundaries — of the sound you want to lower or increase. In this case we want to make the phone sound a little quieter in certain places.

We determine that we want the fourth phone ring to be a little lower so we need to fade slightly between the third and fourth ring. Put a Pen tool mark — a keyframe — at TL-TC/40:24 and another at TL-TC/42:26. Drag the audio after the second pen mark down to −20 dB (see Figure 8.14).

The ring here is much less intrusive, but the shift from the previous ring draws attention to itself. If we bring it down a little as well, we get a more consistent sound.

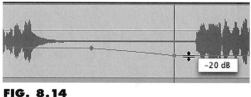

FIG. 8.14

Now, we want to fade down between the second and third rings, so let's put a pen mark at 34:12 and one at 36:20. Position the drag symbol below the third ring and drag it down to −15 dB (see Figure 8.15). The sound kind of stairsteps — cascades — down. The next set of rings now come

FIG. 8.15

in too loud, so we should drag all the subsequent ones down to −20 as well, although you can experiment with changes. We might want to increase volume later to make it sound more insistent.

Volume control will be discussed a little more in Chapter XIII, but these general principles can be applied to any clip, be it dialogue effects, narration, music, or whatever. There are also some effects that can be executed at Effects>Audio Transitions. Here you can do slight cross fades between single-strand sound clips. Click on an audio cut and the (**E**) symbol will appear. Now you can choose between a 0 dB and +3 dB cross fade. Listen to these and see how they work. For me, they tend to be too schematic but try them on your own.

REPLACING DIALOGUE

It is not at all uncommon to want to grab lines that had better readings or higher sound quality from other takes. Moreover, dialogue frequently is replaced with studio recordings, called **Automated Dialogue Replacement** (ADR), that are done to shore up poorly scripted scenes, improve poorly conceived performances, or replace recordings that were done in impossible sound conditions.

I liked readings of a line Fritz has early in the script, "Somebody will be with you shortly," more in later setups than in earlier setups. He is over-the-shoulder in the take we decided to use and, as is sometimes the case, you save the hard work on the performance for the on-camera times. It is a very simple matter to take the preferred reading and lay it into position, particularly as in this instance when it is off-camera.

FIG. 8.16

The first step is to find the piece of dialogue we want to use. We opened from the original audio takes in the Audio Bin, both to focus on the audio and so we did not have to deal with the picture. We listened to all the takes of 4A and decided number 4 was the one we wanted. We found the beginning of Fritz's line and hit Mark In. The waveform showed a slight bump before we hear Fritz (see Figure 8.16), but we went with the sound of his voice because we can always restore this part if needed.

Mark In at TC/19:00:24 in the Viewer. We want to save as much ambience as possible at the end (we will address the beginning momentarily) so we stop just before the next audio and Mark Out at TC/19:03:17.

Our next job is to line up this new piece correctly, using the original line as our guide. Find the beginning of Fritz's line in 2A-4 in the Timeline. Frritz's line appears to start at TL-TC/00:21:06. Mark In on the Canvas. Let's set the destination at Track 3 (A3) to put the replacement line on our extra dialogue track. Overwrite edit. Once the clip is in position, we are going to use non-destructive editing to add a little to the front so we can see what we are doing (see Figure 8.17).

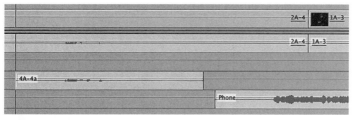

FIG. 8.17

Select the maximum Track Height to get a good look at this. Now we will listen to this and see how well it "choruses" — that is, if the two lines sound as if they are occurring simultaneously. Play. One sounds behind the other. It is almost impossible to get it right the first time. Highlight the replacement line and move it with the period or the comma keys to try different combinations. The lines may have slightly different pacing but we want to find the best match. If they are too far off, we may need to find a different reading or actually trim within the replacement line. Here we find if we move to the right one frame, we get a pretty good match (see Figure 8.18).

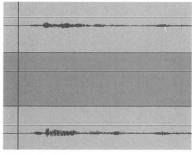

FIG. 8.18

Now we have to cut out the old line. The rule here is: Put the maximum in, take the minimum out. We want to save as much ambience as possible from the original sync take. We have already dragged 4A-4 to

FIG. 8.19

maximum length. Now eliminate the old line. You will have to mute audio track 3, the button on the far right of the track, to hear what needs to happen to A1. 2A-4 is a sync track — linked — so you will have to Option/Razor Blade the line. The original line runs from roughly TL-TC/00:20:04 to TL-TC/00:22:13. Cut it and delete it (see Figure 8.19), and you have great handles.

COMPLETING AB ROLLING

In the commercial world, you do not have to worry your pretty head about A and B rolling the sound. Unless you actually are the someone else doing it, and it's a pretty good gig, someone else does it. But if we have done single-strand cutting we need to AB Roll before we head to a professional mix or before we do it ourselves.

We have already established the need for bouncing tracks and now is the time to complete the process, whether you did some of it during editing or not. In this we are just going to move every other track down to the second audio track. In some instances, it may be judicious to move things to a third track, so we will do that when the time comes. During this process, we will also create the handles that were discussed in Chapter VI.

Bouncing tracks is easy. Simply press the Shift key and drag the audio for 2A-4 to the desired track. If the video wants to move as well, lock the track. The Shift key keeps the audio piece from traveling horizontally while you drag. If you do not use the Shift key, the audio will probably drift right or left. An "out of sync" indicator — a small box on the clip — will tell you how far out you have gone and you can easily drag it back. Using Shift saves you the trouble.

Creating handles is not quite as straightforward, but still fairly easy. The first cut — the transition between 1A-4 and 2A-4 — is a good example.

Move the audio for 2A-4 to the second track (see Figure 8.20). With the Option key depressed, move the arrow to the end of the audio on 1A-4. When the arrow turns into the drag symbol, drag the audio a few seconds longer (see Figure 8.21). You will be able to see if there is any activity on the track from the waveform and/or by listening to it. We have dragged the audio out into the man's first line. Find the beginning of the line and trim off everything unnecessary, saving only whatever clean ambience you can (see Figure 8.22). Do the same at the end and beginning of 2A-4. Remember to use the Option key when you do all dragging and trimming (see Figure 8.23).

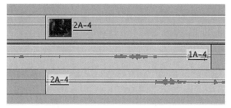

FIG. 8.20

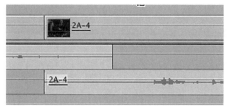

FIG. 8.21

FIG. 8.22

FIG. 8.23

EFFECTS AND MUSIC

We have supplied a light ambience track that can be dropped in against the picture. It can be found in the SFX Bin in the Restaurant Ambience clip. Drop it in before the beginning of the visuals. We will wait to determine exact positioning for when we have some music in place. We will want this to be very low, so experiment with volume levels, but again we will wait for music to finalize.

What music would be appropriate for this? We will let you decide, but importing music is reasonably easy. In these limited circumstances, copyright should not be an issue. Be aware, however, that for your own wonderful project, securing permission is standard operating procedure. This may involve anything from getting turned down to paying licensing fees but, if you intend to show your project to anyone, permission is required.

Insert the chosen CD in your CPU. The CD will appear on the desktop and each track will be represented by a file when opened, generally an AIFF one although other approaches may occasionally be used. You can copy the chosen track with iTunes or simply drag it to a folder or the hard drive. Be sure to copy the song to the hard drive before importing. If you import from the CD, FCP will always need the CD. One irritation of this method is that the tracks are numbered and do not have song titles with them, but rename as needed, and then launch FCP. Go to File> Import>Files and find the song's file on the desktop or wherever you put it. The song will appear as a clip in the Browser and it is an easy matter to insert it in the Timeline. You will have to create a new track for it, as described in Chapter IV. Once in the Timeline, you can move it around and see what you think is best. You can start the music at the beginning or create a fade-up at some point. Experiment and see what kind of positions work. Once you have the music in position, you can shift the ambience around, change volume, and create a relationship that works with both the picture and music.

We have supplied a professionally mixed track — the creation of which will be discussed in Chapter XVI — with this cut of the picture. It can be found in the *Waiting Tables* Media folder, titled *WT* Project Stereo Mix. Take a look and listen and see how it compares with what you have done.

STARTING YOUR OWN PROJECT

The tutorial has presumably provided a good starting point for getting in and understanding some of the basics of Final Cut Pro 4. It contains a number of possibilities ranging from the most basic cuts to fairly advanced, yet still straightforward, editing. Now it's time for you to get involved in your own projects, and once you do, getting started correctly is of paramount importance. This is where FCP, and all NLE editing, can get tricky. If you have not set up correctly, you can run into crippling problems down the road.

FORMATS

Format choice is critical — both in terms of production and mastering. It will have a huge impact on the end game of your project and not understanding choices can make some big roadblocks loom in your path. So what follows is the situation in terms of which video formats are available. Film formats will be discussed in Chapter XIV.

To start, you have a number of global choices. The first choice is between analog and digital. While we will elaborate on this, this is essentially a no-brainer. Forget VHS and its siblings and get access to a digital camera. There are plenty of ways to waste your time, but you are truly wasting your time with VHS or any of the other competing analog formats, most of which are truly obsolete. You will produce nothing saleable on anything but the most top-end analog camera — BetaSP. And if you can afford to shoot with it, you can afford to shoot digital.

DV (Digital Video) refers to a class of digital formats that were devised to work with new standards. It includes Mini-DV, DVCAM, and DVCPRO with a fourth Digital S trying to be adopted. Some people are already asking: Is DV dead? With Panasonic's new HDTV camcorder, there is a very real possibility that some form of HDTV will supplant DV. This is a normal progression. HDTV is a digital format, so the basic thrust of gear and systems, like FCP, will remain the same. It will simply be a new format.

The next question is a little more tricky, deciding between interlace and progressive scan video. Both formats have been described elsewhere, but NTSC has been the standard for years. 99% of the consumer television sets in the United States are NTSC and this format will be with us for a long time. However, the FCC has mandated that all broadcast convert to **High Definition Television (HDTV)**. It will be a while yet, but it is undoubtedly on the horizon. Actually, HDTV can be many different things, including either interlace or progressive. More on this later.

The next questions have to do with how the image is recorded. Both analog and digital cameras have different "schemes" for how to deal with the massive amounts of information inherent in the video signals. To make intelligent choices in terms of formats, you first have to understand **compression**. Compression is the video world's imperfect way of dealing with the difficult issue of how all the data is processed and recorded to tape. This can get quite technical, but we will try to present the concepts in lay terms. Even the simplest VHS image is very complex and formats just go up from there. The bigger the image pixel-wise, the more challenging storage and retrieval of each frame becomes. To facilitate the rapid display of information, most formats compress the image so it is less complex. The hardware actually "throws away" duplicate information in order to reduce the demands on transmission. The typical example is a blue sky — the repeating blue information being discarded. Some formats, like Mini-DV, compress very dramatically. Higher-end gear uses less compression, but almost anything you use in the field is going to have at least some compression. There are only a few formats that do not compress at all, and they are mostly studio mastering formats — the kind of thing George Lucas is playing around with on his *Star Wars* episodes. Film, by the way, does not compress.

Once we get into this, the difference between **composite** and **component** video sheds some light on how video signals differ. These have to do with the way the video signal is divided and transported in order for transmission to occur. The video signal is composed of both the **luminance** and **chrominance** elements of the image. Luminance refers to the general brightness of the image, the ability to show detail from light to dark areas. Chrominance refers to the color quality, the saturation of the image. Many picture color schemes break the image down to the primary colors of light — red, green, blue (RGB). Composite video and film are good examples. Others break it down to the subtractive colors of light —cyan, yellow, magenta (CYM). Still others, including component video, combine percentage of luminance and chrominance.

Most of the television and video recording gear that you have contact with on a daily basis is composite. All elements of composite video, which is only analog, are contained in the same interleaved signal, with the monitor separating the signal into four parts for display, one each for red, green and blue, and the fourth for sync. The drawback is that all four are combined into that one signal — meaning that they have to cram the information into a small overlapping space. The upside is that the signal is not as large and complex, and can be broadcast with minimal complications.

Component, which can be either analog or digital, splits the signal differently, separating the picture information into two or more separate components. The most common separates the picture into three signals, one for general luminance characteristics (Y) and one that carries most of the red information (R-Y) and one that carries most of the blue (B-Y) — the green encoded in these last two. The Y value is calculated by using small percentages of each of RGB. The other two, B-Y and R-Y, are color difference signals. When all three are combined, they create the full color image. Referred to as Y, B-Y, B-R, the individual signals are electronically "sampled", with a complete sampling producing such a complex signal that both recording and broadcast become challenges — an issue related to bandwidth. Thus, different **sampling rates** are used to create a manageable signal. Luminance requires full sampling, because it is the general light-to-dark character of the image. B-Y and R-Y can be sampled at lower resolutions to create this more manageable signal.

The representation of sampling rates is expressed as a standard ratio. Mini-DV, as well as many other formats, samples at 4:1:1. It samples luminance four times for every one time it samples both R-Y and B-Y. High-end formats like HDCAM, of which Sony's CineAlta 24p camera is perhaps the best known, sample at 4:2:2. One brand-new HDCAM samples at 4:4:4. If there was something directly correlating in film, it would be considered to sample at 4:4:4. Sampling rates, by the way, are 13.5 million samples per second for luminance. Doing the math will supply the rest.

Sampling and compression frequently get confused. Sampling is a very exact ratio of video elements — reducing color resolution through a consistently applied formula while maintaining all of the picture's luminance characteristics. Compression eliminates redundant luminance and chrominance information in a way that is not exactly random, but varies from image to image depending on blue sky, green forest, or Red Riding Hood's red coat. Mini-DV uses a compression rate of 5:1. It records one-fifth of the information.

The 4:1:1 color space has proved to be very robust for consumer and pro-sumer applications, but is generally deemed not detailed enough for high-end image applications. Compositing and other extensive image manipulations require 4:2:2 or better — one more thing to think about when choosing formats. This all may seem to be of the more-than-you-need-to-know category, but once we get into color correction and a few other issues, some basics are required.

ANALOG FORMATS

The biggest thing to keep in mind about analog formats is, with one notable exception, to avoid them at all costs. Well, you can't really avoid them, but keep their role in the process to a minimum, primarily going that route for distribution and viewing purposes. VHS, Super VHS, Hi8, and all the rest do not have the image quality, and particularly not the sustainable image quality, to be useful players in a modern production process. Consumers lived with VHS for the first twenty years of home video recording and viewing, and it was a necessary stage. Consumer digital formats have already paved a new road. Indeed, there is now a camera format that writes to DVD. It has a USB 2 connection that is virtually as fast as FireWire. Stay away from anything that is plain USB.

There are many problems with analog video, a significant one being generational loss. Every time you copy from one videotape to another, you lose a **generation**. Generations were, and still are, the unavoidable reality — one wants to call it the bane — of all things analog. Simply, when you make a copy of anything analog, it deteriorates slightly — the amount depending on the medium. Film holds up okay for a while, although contrast and grain increase with every copy. Many times when you are seeing an older film, you are seeing prints that are many generations from the original, which is why many look so bad. Seen in their original pristine form, when available, many of the pioneering films are stunning visual experiences. Audio can go quite a few generations and hold up well, as it had to in the old conventional film edit. Analog video deteriorates very rapidly, and was often not that good to begin with. A third-generation copy of a VHS tape can be so blocky and indistinct that it is almost unwatchable.

The bottom line, of course, is simply image quality. Most analog formats, again with notable exceptions, just do not produce an image that looks good and generally cannot be broadcast to high standards. A few analog mediums bear discussion simply because you will still find them in use.

BetaSP (Superior Performance) by Sony is the only analog format being used extensively in any kind of professional situation. It is still used by television stations and some transfer houses. It is an excellent medium, with almost digital-like image quality. It holds up to generational loss much better than consumer grades. It is, however, still an analog medium and subject to the limitations of that form — with generational loss being an issue.

It is very doubtful, however, that you are going to be shooting on BetaSP, because the cameras are very expensive and usually only maintained within a professional production facility. Indeed, BetaSP is high enough up in the production hierarchy that the average individual and the small producer will not have access to it. Access is often going to be as a studio deck that a post-production facility would use when mastering your tapes. And if you are in that situation, that studio is probably going to have digital equipment anyway. As good as BetaSP is, humble old Mini-DV has both a better signal-to-noise ratio and luminance bandwidth.

1 inch is a reel-to-reel medium formerly used extensively in broadcasting and is actually still a factor as well. It was not a shooting medium, unless you count program feeds in highly sophisticated studio situations. It is generally a mastering medium that was used prior to the acceptance of digital formats. HDTV, in particular, has largely pushed it aside. It is still used in circumstances where companies have not fully switched over to digital — a situation that presumably will be rectified over the next few years.

3/4″— U-Matic video was the professional medium of 20–25 years ago. Coming in a large 8″ x 5″x 1 1/2″ cassette, the format was the production medium of choice for television stations, cable access centers, and production companies through the mid-1980s. For some reason, unknown to any but the most hidebound advertising flacks, it was a staple as a playback unit for years and years in agencies, casting companies, and the like — staying around long after its useful life was over. The incredible efficiency of DVDs, CDs, and even Mini-DV tapes has really ended this reign of terror. However, you may find units still in use, particularly internationally, where digital has not yet made the same kind of inroads.

VHS has been the consumer standard for many years for both video cameras and retail rental and sales. It has largely been supplanted over the last few years by Mini-DV and DVD respectively. VHS is a clunky 4″ x 7″ x 1″ with a half-inch-wide tape. Enough said.

SVHS was the "industrial" version of VHS, being designed for small production companies that wanted a step up from the limited quality of standard VHS. It received pretty wide use for a few years so old tapes in the format will show up.

There are a bunch of others, including 8mm, Hi8, and Betamax. Many of them are still around and being sold, but Mini-DV cameras have come down in price to the extent that there is no reason not to go digital.

DIGITAL FORMATS

All the listed formats are digital videotape that play and record digital videotape in a hardshell cassette.

When we start talking about digital video, naming rights need to be clearly understood. The confusion is in that there are a number of digital formats, but when we are talking about DV, with capital letters, we are talking about something very specific. DV is a family of digital formats specifically designed to interface with computer programs like FCP. Even within this there can be confusion. What you see referred to as DV in older texts should now be referred to as Mini-DV to be specific. It was designed to be an amateur standard, something that would put this amazing new technology to use. But Sony and Panasonic could not help but introduce competing advanced gear (DVCAM and DVCPRO respectively) creating what, including Mini-DV, we might call the **DV25 Family**. All of these sample at 4:1:1, hence the "25" in the name — chrominance samples are made at one-quarter of luminance. What distinguishes the advanced gear is higher tape speed that allows for a wider track that yields, among other things, fewer dropouts and thus greater consistency. Panasonic has gone a step further and introduced a 4:2:2 format, starting the DV50 family. JVC has weighed in here as well, although the tape size is different. The DV family consists of:

Mini-DV was the industry consumer standard agreed upon in the early 1990s. Using a very small tape (see Figure 9.1), cameras range from the good-sized Sony DX1000 to some miniature versions. Many of the basics have been discussed elsewhere, but it is a

FIG. 9.1

robust system that can be used in semi-professional and even some professional situations.

DVCAM is Sony's improvement on Mini-DV. It can use either a standard Mini-DV cassette or a larger cassette (see Figure 9.1). A deck like the Sony DSR-11 pictured in Chapter I can take the large tape and has a notched slot for the Mini-DV size. Students and independents often use this as a mastering medium to get slightly more stability than Mini-DV.

DVCPRO and **DVCPRO50** are Panasonic's improvement on the Mini-DV format. It can also use either Mini-DV cassettes, a mid-size version, or a larger cassette. The latter two are specific to DVCPRO. As stated, Panasonic has upped the ante with DVCPRO50 which samples at 4:2:2.

Digital S is JVC's "sort-of" contribution to this group. It also compresses at 4:2:2. It is "sort of" because it uses the old half-inch tape configuration and comes in a souped-up VHS shell. At this point, Final Cut Pro does not have a preset for this format although a third party may provide the necessary interface.

Again these are all the DV formats, DV being distinguished from digital video. The rest of the digital formats are:

Digital Beta — Always called DigiBeta, this is the standard for much professional mastering and television news (ENG). It is a half-inch-wide tape that comes in a variety of cassette sizes and running times. If you shoot film, many telecine facilities master to DigiBeta and it is the required submission format for most grants or screenings (NEA, PBS, et cetera).

BetacamSX is a very heavily compressed format that Sony has a tried to established as a lower-end alternative to DigiBeta.

The D series is a loosely grouped set of formats, coming from many different manufacturers and with many different tape standards. At this point, there is D1 through D9, although there is, for mysterious reasons, no D8. Some are just other standards under a different name. D7 is DVCPRO and D9 is Digital S. D1 was introduced in 1986 and for many years was the only completely uncompressed video format. As such, it has been a very popular mastering format providing excellent results in many circumstances. D5 is another uncompressed format that is getting a lot of use. Produced by Panasonic, the format is commonly adapted to HDTV.

HDTV is somewhat misunderstood because it includes many different standards. You can have interlaced (i) HDTV and progressive (p) HDTV. You can have1080i and 1080p HDTV and 24p HDTV, as well as 720i and 720p. Frame rates can run from 60, 30, 29.97, 25, 24, and finally 23.98. For the consumer, the choices have become bewildering. HDTV players should be able to play most of these, although finding a consumer television that will display 24p can be costly. As suggested, HDTV will grow in popularity and may one day supplant DV. JVC has a new consumer-priced HDTV camcorder that will undoubtedly have an impact on the shape of things. HDTV has a much higher data rate than DV and is only supportable in FCP with third-party hardware.

24p is a relatively new 24-frame video standard. 24 just refers to the frame rate and can come in HDTV or standard video varieties. 24-frame video has been around for a while, but the recent trend started with Sony's CineAlta HDCAM camera. This is a 24-frame HDTV format. For non-HDTV, Panasonic has a relatively new 24p Mini-DV camcorder. 24p HDTV has become the new universal mastering format. It has gained widespread adoption because every episodic television show is then already set up to transfer to any standard from the original 24-frame source — either 24p or film. It easily translates to 29.97, the 25 frames of PAL and SECAM, the 24 frames of film, and just about anything else.

HARDWARE AND SOFTWARE

Final Cut Pro can run perfectly well with a monitor, a CPU, and some kind of deck or camera. There are, of course, many add-ons that will aid and improve its performance. Many of these have to do with either storage or FCP's Real-Time capabilities. That said, the newest generation of G5 desktops now claim to execute almost all FCP functions in real time. However, not everyone has one yet.

There are many third-party cards and other hardware for Final Cut Pro. In addition, media can be exported out of FCP into a number of other programs for alteration. OMF audio applications notwithstanding, FCP material can be exported out to Adobe Photoshop, Adobe After Effects, Lightworks, Combustion, Shake, and a host of high-level specialty programs. The next section will detail the path to moving material out and back in again.

By itself, FCP only supports capture from DV formats and an audio capture card is handy for bringing sound in from almost any source. In their absence, transferring audio from your recorded source to CD and then importing it into FCP provides an excellent route. A good versatile CD burner is helpful. Audio can be recorded directly into FCP from a microphone, so if you anticipate this, find a mic or miking system that will reproduce the kinds of audio (voice, effects, et cetera) you will be recording.

Get yourself a good external hard drive. Back-up and storage are critical. For DV work, it should be a FireWire drive with a good gig capacity (120 is a generally affordable level). Spinning rates of a minimum of 7200rpm are required. Beyond DV, more sophisticated solutions are required. RAID arrays are built up of multiple drives functioning as a single drive, which can support the large throughput of data required by high-end formats like HDTV.

The most popular sideboard gear includes Real-Time Cards, High Definition Cards, and breakout boxes that connect to your computer with a single FireWire cable. The Matrox RTMac is one popular card for processing Real-Time effects. The new external FireWire boxes facilitate capture and playback of uncompressed audio and video in multiple formats. Again, unadorned FCP only supports DV (plus a few multimedia formats).

Get a good NTSC monitor to check color accuracy. Another issue is speakers and clean sound. Get yourself a good set of speakers and appropriate amplification. The amplifiers in a typical Mac computer are adequate but not electrifying. Quality audio cutting demands that you get a sound chain that will show all warts and blemishes. You want to get a clean audio source and the audio cards in Macs can be improved upon. Again, the latest G5s have a pretty good amount of power in this regard.

Eventually you will want to get either a Mini-DV or DVCAM deck. If you make your camera do double duty, it will eventually wear out. Cameras work fine in a desktop setup, but a deck is designed for VTR functions and a camera is designed for shooting. Eventually you should have dedicated gear.

PRESETS AND PREFERENCES

Most everyone is familiar with the concepts of presets and preferences and the way they access many different options. These are the software choices you make before embarking on or, at least in terms of preferences, during a project. A lot of people know where they are and essentially what they do, but have never touched them. For simple projects in FCP, you should be able to continue in this vein. However, embarking on more complex and ambitious projects will require that you need to indicate what format you will be using, understand dropframe time code issues, know sample rates for audio, and a host of other things. Many of the attendant choices can be altered as needed during editing, but some things have to be chosen from the start.

If you are anything like me, when something is not working I just barge in and try things like a bull in a china shop. In many instances, you can really create a mess if you tinker around too much. Again, if you just want to use FCP for playing around with some standard video footage, things are very simple. You can use the defaults and never worry your pretty head about anything. But if your project is complicated — and matchback is at the top of the "complicated" pyramid — your task is more difficult.

There are just a few places where preferences are found. Most of the critical choices are found in the software menu — the Final Cut Pro menu (see Figure 9.2) — under Easy Setup..., Audio/Video Settings..., User Preferences..., and System Settings.... The other key place to make choices is in the Sequence menu at Settings. The four in the FCP menu are all choices made when you initiate a project. Once you have started editing, you can only make adjustments in a few of these

FIG. 9.2

items. Sequence>Settings, which has many of the same choices as User Preferences, is for when you need to change things during the editing process. Easy Setup is for getting in and doing simple editing, usually in DV. Beyond Easy Setup, most global (preset) choices are found under Audio/Video Settings, and most individual choices (preferences) are found under User Preferences or System Settings. These latter two provide all the information about clips, Timelines, Sequences, and the like that you will need to know during your edit. A few other important functions can be found in the general menus and they will be covered after the main items.

One of the major things about all these tabs is that you need to monitor them so things are not set incorrectly. If other people are using your computer and FCP in particular, things can get changed around without your knowledge. Sometimes you can do it yourself without being aware. If you are anything like me, when something does not work, I go hunting — search and destroy on a few particular occasions. When I was first learning FCP, I would try to find what in the menus or tabs controls some recalcitrant function. I usually found a solution. Sometimes, not so much any more, I made a horrible mess. Become familiar with where things should be set and how things function, in order to ensure that you or someone else has not left a little ambush-waiting-to-happen.

My most recent almost-fiasco was when I was working with some clients and we could not get FCP to recognize an external video device in order to capture. The FireWire was connected and the EVD was on, but FCP just would not recognize it. The cure-all solution; Restart. Nothing. As I pondered and my audience waited, it quickly occurred to me that one reason that FCP would not recognize an NTSC device is the NTSC part. If someone had switched to a different standard in Audio/Video Settings, FCP would be looking for a different device. Sure enough, someone had left it at DV 23.98 and selecting DV-NTSC at Easy Setup solved the problem without too much time lost.

EASY SETUP

For general editing, Easy Setup is the most commonly used starting point. It simply lists the four most typical choices (see Figure 9.3), two for most common video standards and two for image resolution. Custom Setup self-selects if you choose other formats in the Audio/Video Settings window. The overriding choice you see here is the one between PAL and NTSC (G). Again, NTSC is the standard for the USA, Mexico, Canada, Japan and quite a few countries in the Western hemi-

FIG. 9.3

sphere. FCP is designed for international use and the PAL format is used extensively throughout the world. FCP cannot be used for the third somewhat limited standard, SECAM. Beyond that, it is then simply a choice between standard resolution DV and lower Real-Time presentations (Online/ Offline). OfflineRT, whether NTSC or PAL, is a lower-resolution format that is less taxing on the computer's processor and allows for easier playback of complex effects. Be aware that if you choose Offline, you will have to return to higher-resolution footage to complete a high-quality show (see pages 214-9). FCP defaults to the most common approach for consumers and prosumers in the United States, DV-NTSC.

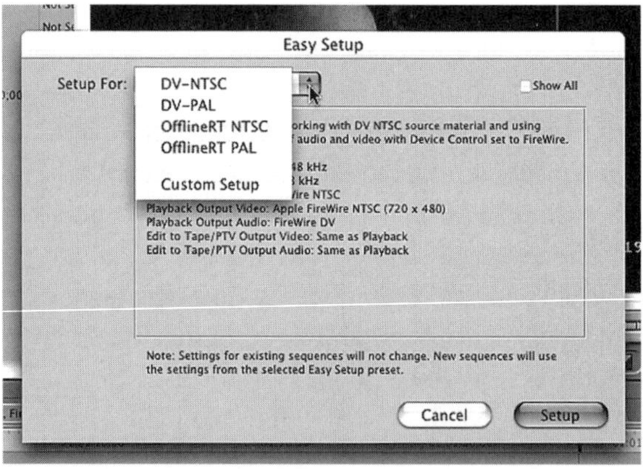

Past Easy Setup, you have to search the program's inner workings for more sophisticated choices. That is, if you are working with any format other than the most standard and straightforward DV options, you will need to go further into the menus. The number of choices therein can be almost bewildering, with different formats, frame rates and dropframe issues added to the mix.

AUDIO/VIDEO SETTINGS

Audio/Video Settings is where you will find the global choices. Here, you choose all the presets which designate the type of format you are using and the resolution of playback and capture, as well as check video and audio playback configurations. In essence, this simply gives the choice of the frame rates and systems with which you will be working. When chosen, it will set all defaults to a standard way of working. As you become more experienced, you may want to fiddle with some of the defaults, but these choices position you well for the work.

The Audio/Video Settings window opens with five tabs, the first of which summa-

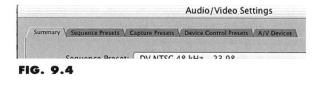

FIG. 9.4

rizes the contents of the other four (see Figure 9.4). You can actually make most of your choices from this tab with a pop-up–style menu available on each summary point. Take a look at these. Each of the tabs represents a specific aspect of the FCP's interface with DV.

Using the summary tabs, we can see what the options are for each one of the presets (see Figure 9.5). Starting with Sequence Preset: Click on the down arrow to the right (see Figure 9.6) The top choice, DV-NTSC 48 kHz, is the Easy Setup default. It includes Mini-DV, DVCAM, and DVCPRO, all running at 29.97 with 48 kHz being the audio sampling rate. Frame rates of 24 and 23.98 will be covered in Chapter 15 and "Anamorphic" refers to a rather esoteric image squeezing process that allows for wide screen. The same choices are replicated for PAL, with the first indicating PAL's standard 25-frame running rate and only handling Mini-DV and DVCAM. DVCPRO50 has a different compression scheme and requires separate handling, as does regular DVCPRO in PAL. The Offline Real-Time choices replicate the format choices above them but at a lower resolution. The Uncompressed choices are for editing high-end uncompressed video. This video cannot be captured normally, but can be brought in through external hardware or downloaded from other sources.

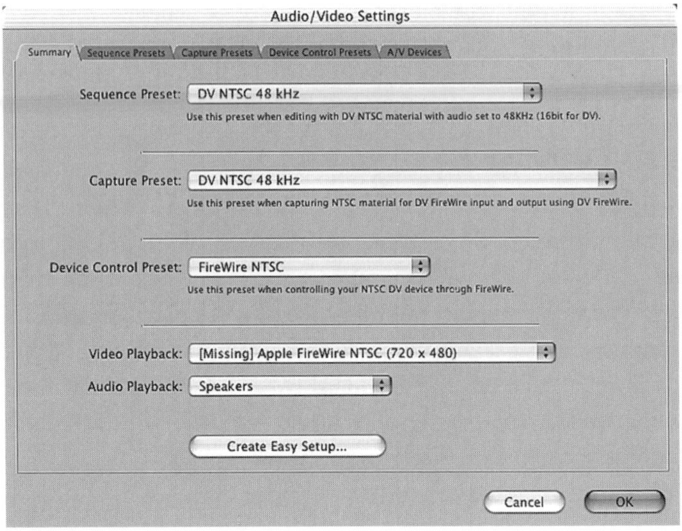
Audio/Video Settings
Summary
Sequence Presets
Capture Presets
Device Control Presets
A/V Devices
Sequence Preset:
DV NTSC 48 kHz
Use this preset when editing with DV NTSC material with audio set to 48KHz (16bit for DV).
Capture Preset:
DV NTSC 48 kHz
Use this preset when capturing NTSC material for DV FireWire input and output using DV FireWire.
Device Control Preset:
FireWire NTSC
Use this preset when controlling your NTSC DV device through FireWire.
Video Playback:
[Missing] Apple FireWire NTSC (720 x 480)
Audio Playback:
Speakers
Create Easy Setup...
Cancel
OK

FIG. 9.5

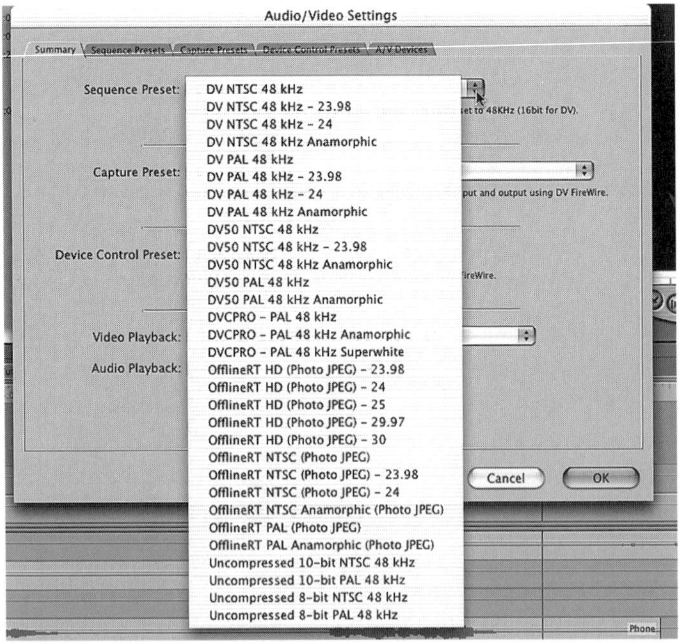
Audio/Video Settings
Summary
Sequence Presets
Capture Presets
Device Control Presets
A/V Devices
Sequence Preset:
Capture Preset:
Device Control Preset:
Video Playback:
Audio Playback:
DV NTSC 48 kHz
DV NTSC 48 kHz - 23.98
DV NTSC 48 kHz - 24
DV NTSC 48 kHz Anamorphic
DV PAL 48 kHz
DV PAL 48 kHz - 23.98
DV PAL 48 kHz - 24
DV PAL 48 kHz Anamorphic
DV50 NTSC 48 kHz
DV50 NTSC 48 kHz - 23.98
DV50 NTSC 48 kHz Anamorphic
DV50 PAL 48 kHz
DV50 PAL 48 kHz Anamorphic
DVCPRO - PAL 48 kHz
DVCPRO - PAL 48 kHz Anamorphic
DVCPRO - PAL 48 kHz Superwhite
OfflineRT HD (Photo JPEG) - 23.98
OfflineRT HD (Photo JPEG) - 24
OfflineRT HD (Photo JPEG) - 25
OfflineRT HD (Photo JPEG) - 29.97
OfflineRT HD (Photo JPEG) - 30
OfflineRT NTSC (Photo JPEG)
OfflineRT NTSC (Photo JPEG) - 23.98
OfflineRT NTSC (Photo JPEG) - 24
OfflineRT NTSC Anamorphic (Photo JPEG)
OfflineRT PAL (Photo JPEG)
OfflineRT PAL Anamorphic (Photo JPEG)
Uncompressed 10-bit NTSC 48 kHz
Uncompressed 10-bit PAL 48 kHz
Uncompressed 8-bit NTSC 48 kHz
Uncompressed 8-bit PAL 48 kHz
Cancel
OK
Phone

FIG. 9.6

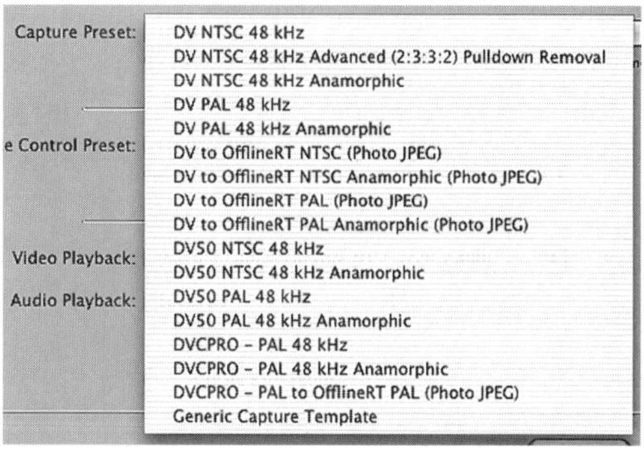
Capture Preset:
e Control Preset:
Video Playback:
Audio Playback:
DV NTSC 48 kHz
DV NTSC 48 kHz Advanced (2:3:3:2) Pulldown Removal
DV NTSC 48 kHz Anamorphic
DV PAL 48 kHz
DV PAL 48 kHz Anamorphic
DV to OfflineRT NTSC (Photo JPEG)
DV to OfflineRT NTSC Anamorphic (Photo JPEG)
DV to OfflineRT PAL (Photo JPEG)
DV to OfflineRT PAL Anamorphic (Photo JPEG)
DV50 NTSC 48 kHz
DV50 NTSC 48 kHz Anamorphic
DV50 PAL 48 kHz
DV50 PAL 48 kHz Anamorphic
DVCPRO - PAL 48 kHz
DVCPRO - PAL 48 kHz Anamorphic
DVCPRO - PAL to OfflineRT PAL (Photo JPEG)
Generic Capture Template

FIG. 9.7

Capture Preset has a similar, although shorter list (see Figure 9.7). It simply designates what source the media is going to be captured from. Unless you are doing something very complex, it should match the Sequence Preset. It only duplicates the top half of the previous list, because resolution will be dictated by the previous choice.

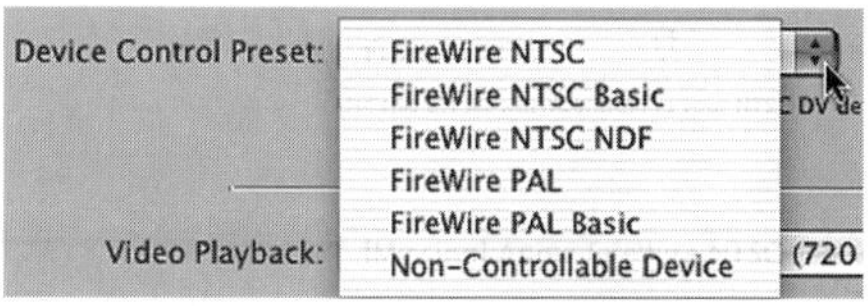
Device Control Preset:
Video Playback:
FireWire NTSC
FireWire NTSC Basic
FireWire NTSC NDF
FireWire PAL
FireWire PAL Basic
Non-Controllable Device
(720

FIG. 9.8

The Device Control Preset simply indicates the type of connection between external video device (see Figure 9.8), usually FireWire, and computer. It defaults to FireWire NTSC, which is the most common choice in NTSC countries. The only complicating factor here is whether to use dropframe or nondropframe (NDF) — the third choice.

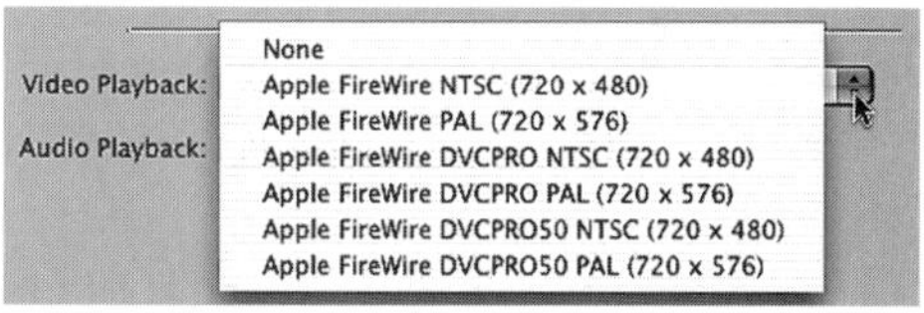
Video Playback:
Audio Playback:
None
Apple FireWire NTSC (720 x 480)
Apple FireWire PAL (720 x 576)
Apple FireWire DVCPRO NTSC (720 x 480)
Apple FireWire DVCPRO PAL (720 x 576)
Apple FireWire DVCPRO50 NTSC (720 x 480)
Apple FireWire DVCPRO50 PAL (720 x 576)

FIG. 9.9

Video Playback states whether the external video device has been located by FCP and what it is (see Figure 9.9). If you do not have an EVD switched on, it will come up as "None." All NTSC-DV25 formats will come up as the second on the list, NTSC-720x480. This is not really switchable in that FCP recognizes the EVD and will display what it is.

Audio Playback:
Speakers
FireWire DV
FireWire DV (DV50)
Create Easy Setup...

FIG. 9.10

Audio Playback is similar. It lists where your audio should be playing back (see Figure 9.10). With no EVD on, it should playback through the computer's speakers. If you have a third-party audio amplification system, it should be displayed and chosen here. With an

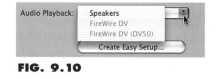

EVD on, the audio will go to it and FireWire DV will be highlighted. If the EVD is a camera, audio will play through the camera's speaker, as humble as it might be. If the EVD is a deck, you will have to rig up a speaker or send it to a monitor that will play sound. External Video in the View menu interfaces with this.

A few other choices can be found on the individual tabs. These will be covered where necessary.

USER PREFERENCES

User Preferences is where many important decisions are made. Again, this is where choices are made when a project is initiated, although a few items are switchable. Many of these same items are duplicated in Sequence>Settings and if something has to be changed during editing, you often go there. User Preference opens to five tabs (see Figure 9.11). Probably the most important are

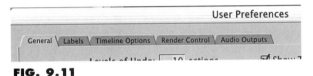

FIG. 9.11

the General and Timeline Options tabs. It would be impossible to go through every choice here, so we will just hit some highlights — the commonly used options. Following are a few of the choices displayed in the General tab (see Figure 9.12). Levels of Undo can be increased and decreased in the top box. Below that, the number of recent clips that are displayed in the pop-up menu on the Viewer can be changed. Below that, the number of frames trimmed in the Trim Edit Window can be changed. Half-way down, the length of titles and other pieces created in FCP can be changed at Still/Freeze Duration. We will leave Dupe Detection for the film folks and Autosave Vault is self-explanatory.

On the right hand side, the most important concept is the issue of dropped frames — one preference section that is changeable in midstream. When FCP runs across a frame or group of frames that have flawed information or, particularly, overtax the computer's capabilities, frames will be dropped. You can enable or disable warnings that will stop playback and make you aware of the problem. Enabling warnings can be very helpful in estimating playback problems; however, when you just need to get a program out to tape, it can be a real hindrance. I had one show that had to be to someone for approval the next day and trying to

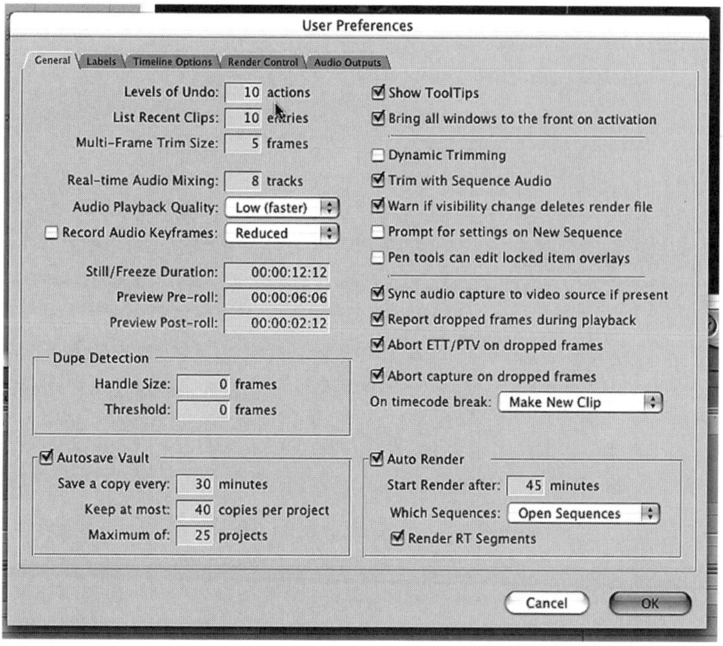

User Preferences

General \ Labels \ Timeline Options \ Render Control \ Audio Outputs \

Levels of Undo: 10 actions ☑ Show ToolTips
List Recent Clips: 10 entries ☑ Bring all windows to the front on activation
Multi-Frame Trim Size: 5 frames ☐ Dynamic Trimming
Real-time Audio Mixing: 8 tracks ☑ Trim with Sequence Audio
Audio Playback Quality: Low (faster) ☑ Warn if visibility change deletes render file
☐ Record Audio Keyframes: Reduced ☐ Prompt for settings on New Sequence
☐ Pen tools can edit locked item overlays
Still/Freeze Duration: 00:00:12:12
Preview Pre-roll: 00:00:06:06 ☑ Sync audio capture to video source if present
Preview Post-roll: 00:00:02:12 ☑ Report dropped frames during playback
☑ Abort ETT/PTV on dropped frames
Dupe Detection
Handle Size: 0 frames ☑ Abort capture on dropped frames
Threshold: 0 frames On timecode break: Make New Clip

☑ Autosave Vault ☑ Auto Render
Save a copy every: 30 minutes Start Render after: 45 minutes
Keep at most: 40 copies per project Which Sequences: Open Sequences
Maximum of: 25 projects ☑ Render RT Segments

Cancel   OK

FIG. 9.12

get it out to tape was constantly being interrupted by dropped frames. I finally came in and found the "Report dropped frames on playback" and turned it off. I was able to get the show out to tape and address the problem later. Below that, you generally want to abort capture on dropped frames because they will cause problems down the road. A few other items will be addressed where pertinent.

The Labels tab is used only for giving new names to labels (see Figure 9.13). The top orange one will be highlighted when you choose the tab and you can simply type in the

User Preferences

General \ Labels \ Timeline Options \ Render Control \ Audio Outputs \

Good Take
Best Take
Alternate Shots
Interviews
B Roll

FIG. 9.13

description you want. Labeling itself is applied by Control clicking on a clip and going to Label at the bottom of the contextual menu. Then choose a color in the submenu. The label you typed in will show up in Item Properties and the hidden part of the Browser.

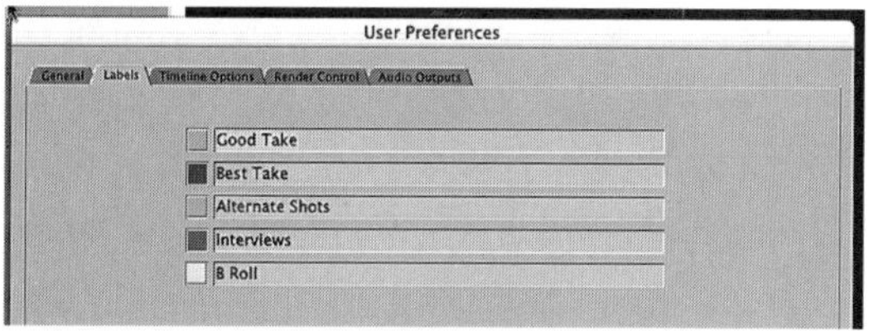

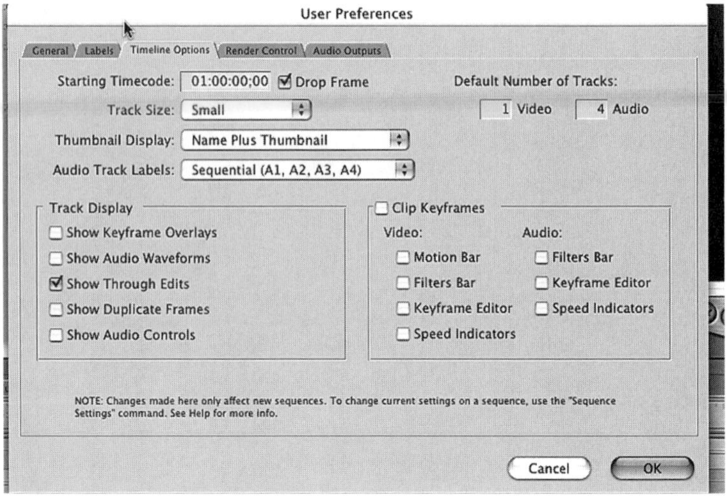

FIG. 9.14

Timeline Options (see Figure 9.14) gives access to some critical choices in how the Timeline is set up and operates. It is virtually duplicated in Sequence>Settings, where it is more frequently accessed, because you often want to toggle back and forth during the editing process. Some of its functions can be accessed elsewhere. The Starting Time code window sets where program time code begins in the Ruler. Programs are usually started at one hour — FCP defaults to that — but editors frequently like to have some room in front of that for leaders and working space. We started *WT* at 00:59:58:00 for these reasons. Choosing DV-NTSC in Easy Setup defaults to dropframe video (G) requiring a change to nondropframe for projects that need an accurate time code count — *WT* was edited NDF. Track size can be changed here or on the Timeline and the next option allows you to choose the way clips are identified. Everything else applies in specific situations and you will use them as need dictates. The only one used constantly is the Show Audio Waveforms, which displays the waveform in the actual clip in the Timeline — a very useful function.

Render Control (see Figure 9.15) sets the level of Real-Time functions. Both frame rates and image resolution can be changed to make render images more playable. The top three checked boxes control what aspects of the image will have their percentages changed. If you change frame rates, FCP drops frames from the clip to make things more

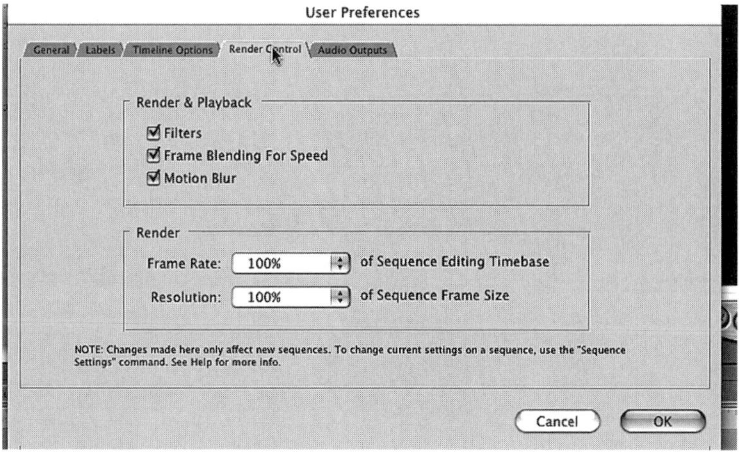

FIG. 9.15

playable. It should probably be changed by no more than 20% or the result will not give much of a representation of the image. Resolution can be changed dramatically.

Audio Outputs (see Figure 9.16) is pretty straightforward. There is only one default choice. To output any other way would require third-party hardware and/or software. It would be chosen here if installed.

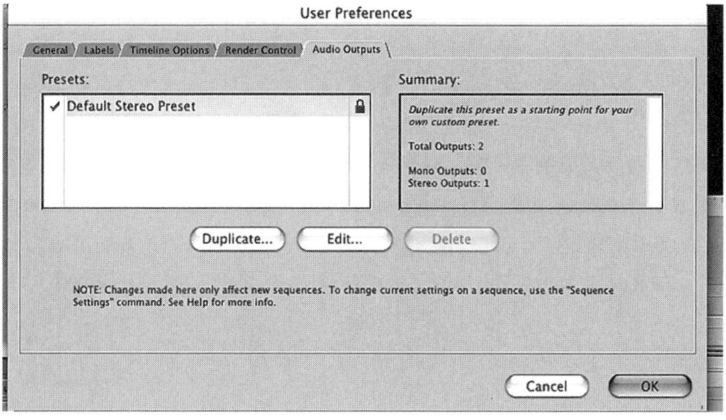

FIG. 9.16

SYSTEM SETTINGS

There are five tabs for System Settings (see Figure 9.17). These, again, affect the day-to-day operations of FCP. They differ from User Preferences in that they control how FCP relates to and interfaces with other software, the general setup of your computer, and, in particular, OS X.

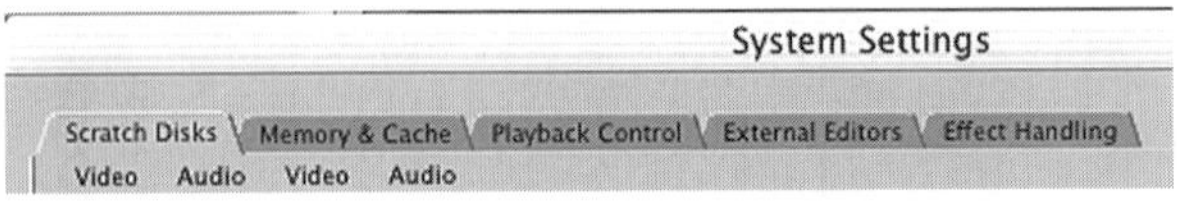

FIG. 9.17

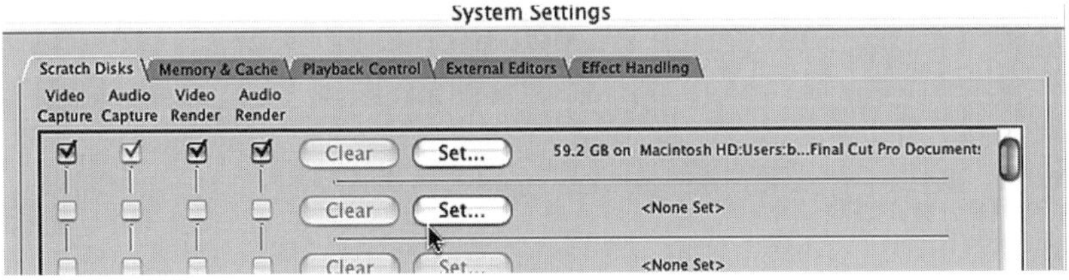

FIG. 9.18

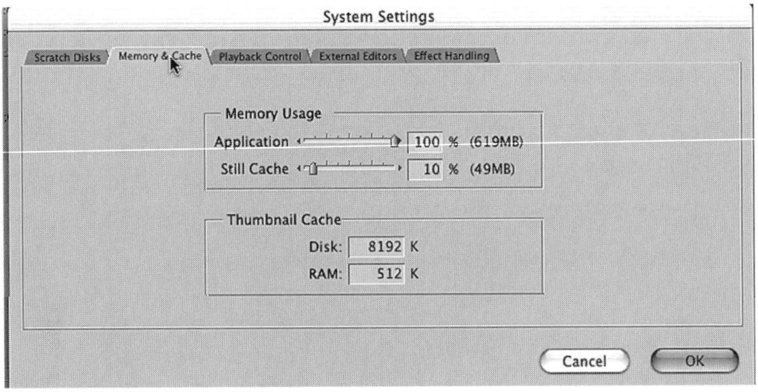

FIG. 9.19

System Settings opens to the Scratch Disks tab (see Figure 9.18). Herein is one of the more critical choices you will make. This is where you determine where all the media that you capture and create for any project is stored. Keeping stored media organized and keeping the path to it clear and untroubled plays a significant role in being successful with FCP. This can be set globally here at the beginning or, more commonly, is set when you go to capture your clips. Details of using this tab will be covered in the next chapter on capture.

Memory & Cache (see Figure 9.19) is for devoting different amounts of RAM to Final Cut Pro than would normally be assigned to it by OS X.

OS X is probably smarter than you are, and certainly smarter than I am, at assigning memory. Use at your own risk.

Playback Control (see Figure 9.20) is mostly about Real-Time functions. The top two options are generally the most frequently used. Pulldown

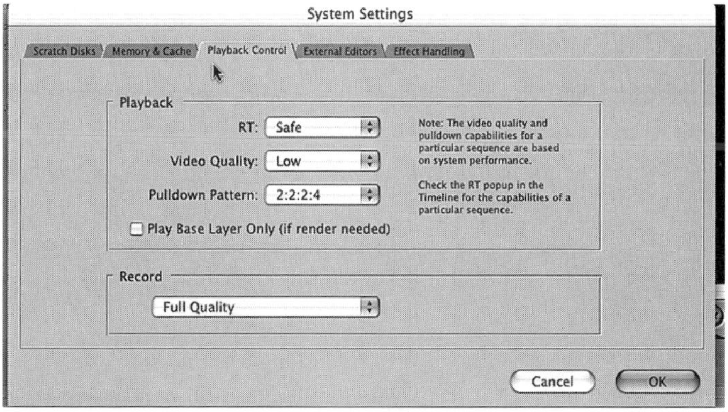

FIG. 9.20

pattern is a complex issue. It refers strictly to projects edited at 24 or 23.98 frames per second. Frames have to be eliminated when you do your original conversion from 29.97 video to 24 or 23.98. To play on an NTSC monitor, fields have to be reinserted and this is where this function comes in. It analyzes your computer's processor and inserts the most appropriate pulldown pattern for the speed of your machine.

External Editor (see Figure 9.21) is for opening material in other applications — it allows you to process FCP media through other software. A good example is if you have a still frame of an image that you want to

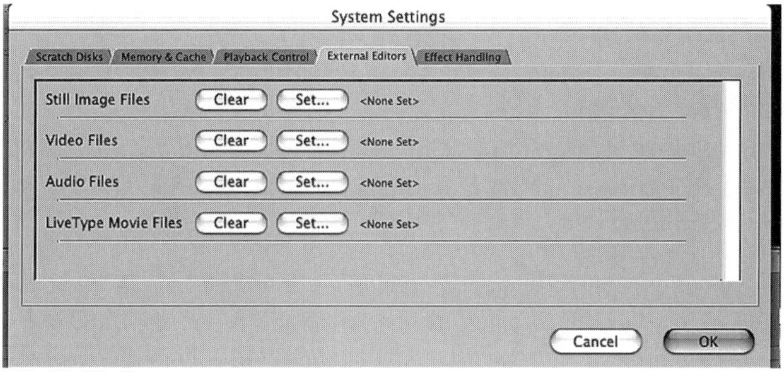

FIG. 9.21

manipulate. You can open it through an application like Adobe Photoshop and manipulate the media there. When you click on set, the Choose a File window will appear. We would find Adobe Photoshop in our Applications Folder and open it. Now anytime you click on a still image, it will launch Photoshop. Manipulate the image as desired, hit save in the supporting software, and it will update the image in Final Cut. Audio programs, compositing programs, and a variety of others can be used.

Effect Handling (see Figure 9.22) is similar to the previous tab except that it allows you to process FCP media through third-party hardware. A good example would be allowing you to process through Real-Time hardware

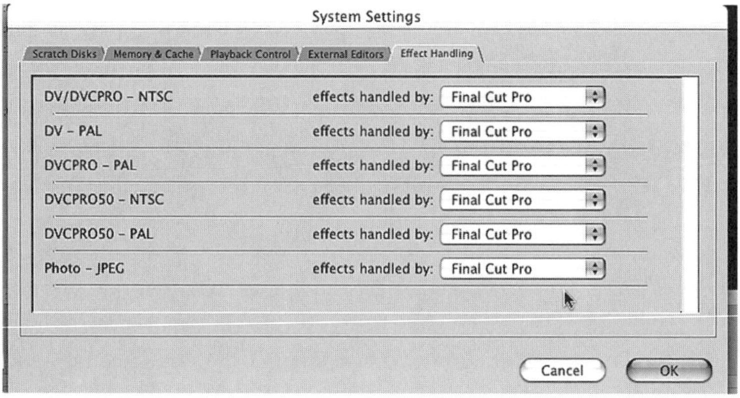

FIG. 9.22

to handle complicated effects. Matrox RTmac and Cinewave are particularly frequent choices for handling many effects. If you chose None in the dropdown menus, effects will not play back at all — one possible use would be if effects were overtaxing your computer and you wanted an unhindered playback.

SEQUENCE>SETTINGS

This is the most significant place in the menus to make choices, and thus for making changes, during the editing process. The five tabs duplicate many of the choices in User Preferences.

The General tab (see Figure 9.23) gives the more global changes. These are all things that are transferred over from the preset tabs and there is not much here that you are likely to change. However, if something is going wrong, this is a quick place to check the way things are set up.

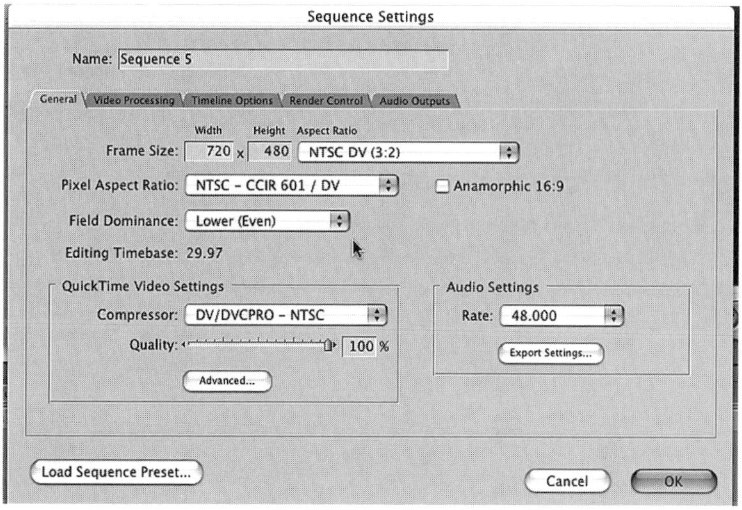

FIG. 9.23

The Video Processing tab (see Figure 9.24) controls whether you render in 8-bit YUV or RGB, with YUV being the default. The only reason to change is if you had an interface that did not support YUV. Below that, FCP defaults to Superwhite, a quality of white above normal broadcast tolerances. Consumer video cameras frequently can record at this Superwhite level, so FCP is set up to expect that. It is common practice for the colorist to be very careful to keep all levels within broadcast tolerances in a telecine transfer (G), as was done with *Waiting Tables*. There are specific measuring tools that ensure this. These will be discussed in Chapter XIII.

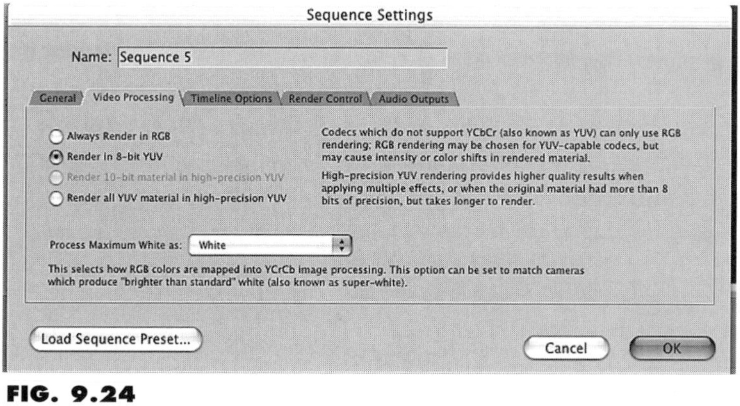

FIG. 9.24

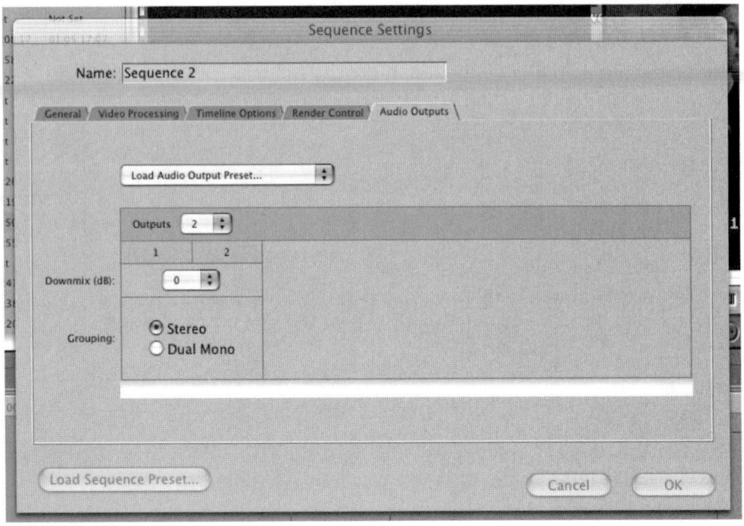

FIG. 9.25

The Timeline Options tab is almost an exact duplicate of the one in User Preferences, only missing the track defaults. The Track Display items get the most frequent use, again particularly Show Audio Waveforms. Render Quality is an exact duplicate of the User Preferences tab.

Audio Outputs (see Figure 9.25) is a little different. Here you can apply uniform modifications to your audio. There is use for this but frequently what you are applying is good for some audio and not good for other. Generally stay with presets unless you know what you are doing.

MENU PREFERENCES

The two items at the bottom of the Edit menu — Item Properties and Project Properties — offer important information about the clips and how metadata is being tracked. When you select Item Properties, a submenu will give three options (see Figure 9.26). Format is the most commonly used and when selected, the other two will be in the background.

FIG. 9.26

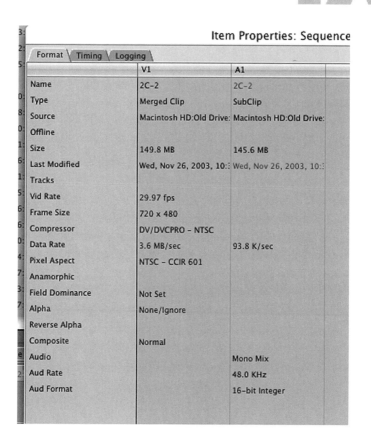

Item Properties: Sequence		
Format \ **Timing** \ **Logging**		
	V1	A1
Name	2C-2	2C-2
Type	Merged Clip	SubClip
Source	Macintosh HD:Old Drive:	Macintosh HD:Old Drive:
Offline		
Size	149.8 MB	145.6 MB
Last Modified	Wed, Nov 26, 2003, 10::	Wed, Nov 26, 2003, 10::
Tracks		
Vid Rate	29.97 fps	
Frame Size	720 x 480	
Compressor	DV/DVCPRO – NTSC	
Data Rate	3.6 MB/sec	93.8 K/sec
Pixel Aspect	NTSC – CCIR 601	
Anamorphic		
Field Dominance	Not Set	
Alpha	None/Ignore	
Reverse Alpha		
Composite	Normal	
Audio		Mono Mix
Aud Rate		48.0 KHz
Aud Format		16-bit Integer

FIG. 9.27

Selecting Format gives you quick access to all the information about clips and audio (see Figure 9.27). When you start working with different frame rates and CD sampling rates versus FCP's defaults, a quick check of things is often in order. Particularly when you are shuffling between different projects and different Timelines, these items can answer any questions if you are coming up with any conflicts. Conflicts can produce many problems, but usually the result is clips mysteriously going offline or suddenly getting something, usually red, appearing in the render bar. Timing just gives the In and Out points, time code numbers, and a few other things. Logging gives the data and descriptions you have entered, usually during capture.

FIG. 9.28

The last item on the View menu, External Video, indicates whether an external video device is active (see Figure 9.28). If no EVD is active, all items here are not available. Having the EVD on affects sound playback. Check here if you cannot get sound.

At first, getting all the preferences and presets set correctly can look somewhat like wandering through a maze. For now, you probably can just go with Easy Setup, but eventually you are going to want to — have to — know what is occurring in the deep recesses of FCP — in these tabs. Start getting familiar with the inner workings of FCP and you will be able to head off a lot of problems.

THE CAPTURE PROCESS

apture, and its attendant requirements, is a time-consuming step that has to occur before you can start editing. It is the primary way of getting your media — your video and audio — into the computer and Final Cut Pro. Certain types of media can be imported, but capturing is most common. Occasionally, you will see the capture process referred to as **digitizing**, but digitizing is only necessary when the source that you are starting with is an analog tape, say a VHS tape or any other conventional tape format. Digitizing an analog source can either be accomplished by transferring the material to a digital video tape recorder (VTR) or camera or by employing specific hardware. Sony makes a commonly used product, which can digitize the signal as it goes into the computer. If your source is already digital — be it from Mini-DV, DVCAM, DVCPRO, or whatever — it simply needs to be captured.

There are a number of ways of bringing media into the computer, but the most common is to use the previously described external video device — either a digital camera or digital VTR designed specifically for the purpose — to playback the material you want to input into your computer. Connected to the CPU with FireWire, the camera or VTR essentially becomes a computer peripheral with all the playback functions (Play, Pause, Rewind, et cetera) taken over in the appropriate windows in the software. This is referred to as **deck control**, in which FCP is controlling everything the playback unit does. The typical home desktop situation will employ the camera as the external video device for maximum efficiency — you do not have to buy both a camera and a VTR. Newer computers come "media ready," but some computers may require a **media card** to input from the interlaced video of an NTSC source to the progressive scan of the computer.

Every segment of media you capture through the conventional FCP approach is converted into a Quicktime file. This is the case whether you are capturing video, audio, or the two together. To create any other type of file requires third-party hardware and software designed for the purpose, although different types of files can be imported into the Browser. Again, these Quicktime files can be quite big, with every four and one-half minutes of video requiring about a gigabyte of storage. All newly created files will be sent to a Capture Scratch folder, the creation and location of which will be described in the next section.

LOG AND CAPTURE

If you are originating on video, most of the time you will be capturing audio and video together. In that case, what is presented in this section will suffice for initial capture. If your job is more complicated, which eventually it will be and as it was for *Waiting Tables*, the following sections will cover some of the complexities of bringing in picture and sound separately.

In most NLE programs, capture is integrated with some logging function and FCP combines these two in its "Log and Capture" window. This is a two-part process. First we log the shots, thus creating the information that drives capture. Logging is simply creating names and identifying the location of your media. Once clips are logged, they can actually be captured into the computer. For the amateur, logging may appear to be a cumbersome step, but as your projects become more complex it becomes a critical part of the process. In professional situations, logging is so important to the downstream management of a project that a very sophisticated semi-science/growth industry has arisen around it.

FIG. 10.1

As stated, most NLE systems are now using FireWire and the Final Cut Pro interface is constructed around that connection. Illustrations herein use a Sony VX1000, a common high-end Mini-DV camera (see Figure 10.1). If you are using a deck, all basic procedures apply. Set the camera up next to your computer and make sure the FireWire is attached from the "DV In/Out" port on the camera to the connection in the back of the computer.

194

If you are not actually starting to edit your own footage, you should initiate a new project just to follow some of the steps. With no applications open, go to File>New Folder. Rename this Untitled Folder, New Project Folder. Then:

Step #1 — Turn on the camera. The switch is usually on the back and there is a choice between turning on the camera's shooting function or its VTR function. When capturing, it should be set to VTR (see Figure 10.2). The camera must be on when you start, as FCP must initialize the EVD in order to capture.

FIG. 10.2

Step #2 — Launch FCP. This time the "External Video" dialogue box will not appear because you have the camera connected and switched on. If this dialogue box does appear, check all connections and try again. If you forgot to turn the camera on, simply turn it on and click Check Again. To follow along, go to File>Save Project As. In the Save window, type in "New Project" (or whatever you are doing) and send it to the folder you just created (see Figure 10.3).

FIG. 10.3

Step #3 — Insert the source tape into the camera.

G. 10.5

Find the "EJECT" button on the camera and open the tape compartment (see Figure 10.4). When the carriage opens, insert the Mini-DV tape (see Figure 10.5). Press the mechanism closed and, after the camera has finished feeding the tape, close the lid. When you close the carriage, a warning box will appear telling you that you have a

FIG. 10.4

new tape in and that you should enter a reel number in the logging area of the L & C window (see next step). Type 1 in the indicated space. If your project has more than one reel, be very careful to number and label each reel. Depending upon how complicated your approach is, certain functions of FCP as well as proprietary software may require these reels later on and scrupulous numbering and record keeping is a must. This logging area is also important for keeping track of other pertinent information.

Step #4 — Go to the File menu in FCP. Scroll down to and open Log and Capture (See Figure 10.6).

The Log and Capture (L & C) window opens with a screen that says "Preview Disabled." This is where the

FIG. 10.6

media from your source tape will play. All the controls identified in previous chapters are present (see Figure 10.7). You will notice that in the middle of the bottom left side it says "VTR OK." This is an indication that FCP is communicating with the camera. If it says "No Connection," you need to close FCP, check connections, and re-launch.

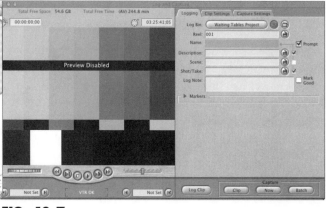

FIG. 10.7

Step #5 — Make sure all settings are correct for the media you want to capture.

There are three important tabs on the right side of the L & C window (see Figure 10.8). The window opens to the Logging tab which will be discussed forthwith. Underneath that are the Clip Settings and Capture Settings tabs. First, click on Clip Settings. Here you will choose what media you are capturing. The upper functions are for image control and only work with third-party capture hardware. Right below this, however, you will see the critical choices — **Capture:** and **Audio Format:**, both with attendant pop-up menus. With Capture:, there are three choices:

1. capturing audio by itself
2. capturing video by itself
3. capturing video and audio together

FIG. 10.8

The third option — Aud + Vid — would generally be for material that originated on video, because picture and sound are recorded together on the tape. When film is being shot, however, sound and picture are recorded separately on location. Thus, capturing each individually is the usual option (see sidebar). Once captured individually, sound and picture must then be synced up just as in a conventional film approach.

Most post-production facilities offer the service of syncing up the location audio during the telecine process, and if you choose this rather expensive but time-saving option, you may be capturing audio and video together even if you shot film. The commercial world has the audio synced up during telecine.

No matter what your sync-up situation, the "Only" capture functions are used extensively for MOS footage and non-production sound such as music, effects, and narration. The Audio Format: menu has all the choices for inputting sound. These will be covered later in this chapter.

Select what media you want captured. We captured image first for *Waiting Tables*, so we chose "Video Only." If you shot video, you will want "Aud + Vid." Either way, the process proceeds in the same fashion.

Next, click on the "Capture Settings" tab (see Figure 10.9). This is where we determine the destination — the final resting place — for everything we are going to capture, whether audio or video. The **Device Control:** and **Capture/Input:** selections are presets that have already been cho-

FIG. 10.9

FIG. 10.10

FIG. 10.11

sen in the FCP menu at Easy Setup or Audio/Video Setting. The important piece here is the **Scratch Disks** button. Note that next to this is an indication of how much free space your computer has available for media. Keep track of this and remember that video takes up a lot of space.

Click on Scratch Disks and its tab will appear (see Figure 10.10). Again, we have seen this tab before in Preferences in the FCP menu. We can set destination either here or there, but this seems a more natural part of the flow. To keep your piece organized, you probably want to keep all elements together in one folder, in this instance the New Project Folder we just created. When you click the Set button to the right of the top row of check boxes, the Choose a Folder window will appear (see Figure 10.11). Then you have to follow the path to

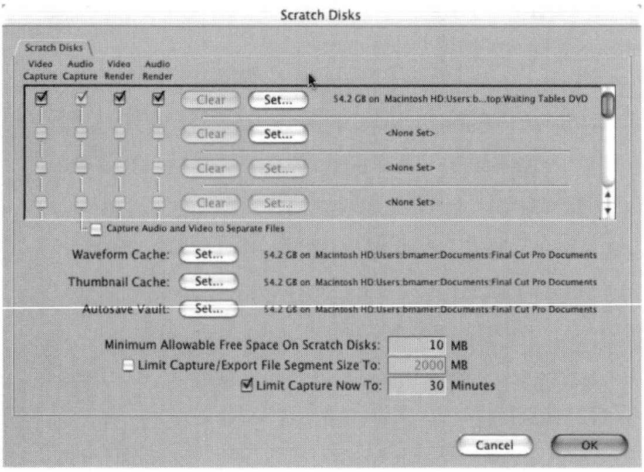

where you want the media to end up — choose the Desktop and find the New Project Folder. Double-click on this. The screen will return to the Scratch Disks window and the new path will be listed to the right in the top row of Scratch Disks. Click OK. When finished, you should be aware that a number of new folders have been automatically created. The four check boxes on the Scratch Disks window are marked Video and Audio Capture and Video and Audio Render. The Audio Capture box is not available because a

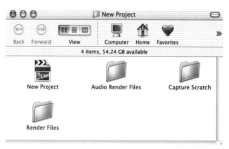

FIG. 10.12

third-party audio capture card is required to create non-Quicktime audio files. With the other three boxes checked, folders for each one are created in the folder you selected in the Scratch Disks window (see Figure 10.12). If you open the New Project folder, you will see Capture Scratch, Render Files, and Audio Render Files folders. All newly captured material will be sent to the Capture Scratch folder. Make sure you have set these two tabs correctly or complications will occur down the road.

Step #6 — Mark the "in" and "out" points of the shot you want to capture.

For any project of even modest complexity, each shot should be captured separately, rather than in sequences or in groups. Press play in the Log and Capture window. To capture an individual take, simply scrub to the first frame of the desired shot, click the In marker, and then scrub to the last frame of the shot and click the Out marker. With *Waiting Tables*, we started with Scene 1A, Take 1 (not included on DVD), found the **flash frame** — the first frame of a shot that, because the camera is getting up to speed, is a little brighter (see Figure 10.13) — and marked In

FIG. 10.13

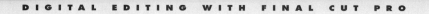

FIG. 10.14

at TC/01:00:07:25. We went to the end and marked an Out at TC/01:00:50:24 (see Figure 10.14). It is generally a good idea to just capture the entire shot rather than attempt to be discriminating and just capture the part of the shot you think you are going to use. First, your ideas may change about what you need as the editing progresses, and second, there is a general unwritten rule in the editing room to not mix editorial stages. Mixing functions will draw already tedious start-up procedures out to unbearable lengths.

LOGGING

Organization of materials is of paramount importance. Staying organized in a conventional film edit was, and still is, extremely important with a specific editing crew member, the **Assistant Editor**, devoted to logging, storing, and retrieving shots as the editor worked with them. If anything, organization is even more important in an NLE edit. With film there are pieces to refer to and search for. With NLE all you have is a bunch of icons and what is written down. Computers can be a great void if material gets lost. If logging text is flawed or incomplete, you will find yourself spending more time searching than editing.

Step #7 — Once you have marked the in and out points, click the Log Clip button (**A**) on the right bottom side of the L & C window.

A dialogue box will appear (see Figure 10.15) where you can identify the clip and register any pertinent information. The numbering system created for use on the slates which identifies both the scene (the shot) being executed and the take number is generally used. We can also type in any comments about the quality of the take — NG, Select, and so on. Click OK. We would then log some more clips.

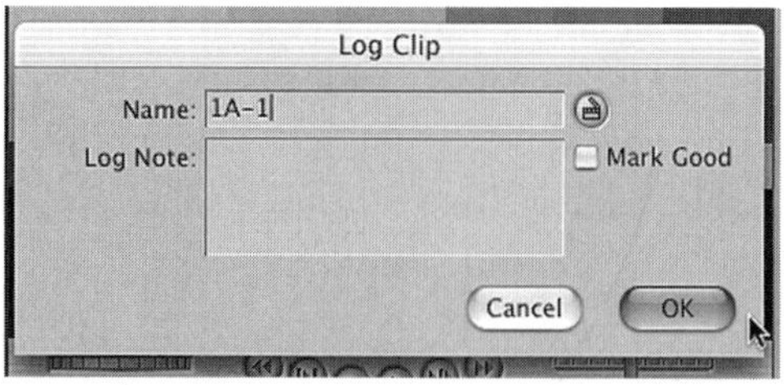

Log Clip

Name: 1A-1

Log Note:

☐ Mark Good

Cancel   OK

FIG. 10.15

The term "scene" can be confusing because there are different sequential scene numbers in a script and each setup is identified as a scene. Although we did not do this for the tutorial, I like to create an acronym for the production (*Waiting Tables* would be WT) as well as use a script scene number. This would precede clip scene and take numbers to always identify to which project the clips belong. If you are working on more than one project, just using numbers leaves the opportunity for duplication, a potential that can lead to confusing both the editor and the computer. In our example, we might call this clip WT, 1A-3. If we later capture the audio separately, we might call it WT, 1A-3a (a for audio).

FIG. 10.16

Once a clip is logged, an icon with a diagonal red line through it will appear in the Browser (see Figure 10.16). This means that the clip has been identified and logged, but not yet actually captured. Video clips will be represented as a small film frame and audio as a small speaker. Clips with the red line are considered **offline**.

In addition, it is highly recommended that you keep a written log of all shots and their rough content. If convenient, this can be done on or in conjunction with the Camera Reports (see Chapter 2). All documenting that occurs now may save extensive time later, when memory of the details of this early stage can become sketchy. Every clip in the production should have a unique name and a paper trail. However, that unique name should be part of a well-designed system. When I first started with FCP, when I was at a loss for a name, I would occasionally come up with what at the time seemed like a logical title for a clip. What was logical one day, however, may completely escape you the next day or, more likely, a month down the road. Then that poor logically named clip is lost somewhere in hyperspace. Or you look at some oddball clip name and for the life of you, you cannot remember what the content is. So you have to open a mess of clips to find what you are looking for. And when you cannot find it, you start to wonder if it was there in the first place. If you are punchy from a day's editing, hyperspace can start to feel like the Twilight Zone.

CAPTURING

Step #8 — Log as many clips as you want and when done, click on the Batch button (see Figure 10.17).

FIG. 10.17

There are three different methods of capturing, all essentially duplicated in most other NLE software. The choices are Clip, Now, and Batch. Clip is for capturing clips one at a time; Now is for capturing material on the fly; Batch is for capturing a number of previously logged clips. Choosing Now, of course, precludes previous logging and is for capturing a bunch of material quickly. It is also good for finessing in material that does not have appropriate time code. Batch is for when you have logged a number of clips and want to bring them all in in one process; clearly the preferred method with the editor logging quite a few clips and then allowing the hardware to do the rest.

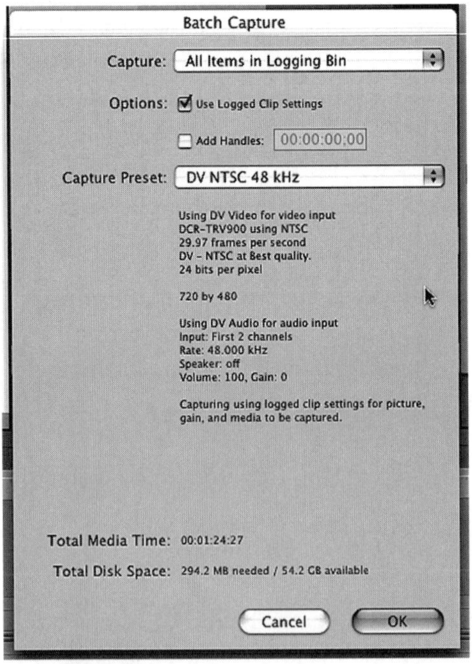

Once you have a number of clips logged, hit Batch capture. The software will ask for verification (see Figure 10. 18). Before you click OK, check the top Capture: menu. FCP defaults to Selected Items in the Logging Bin, which will only capture clips you have highlighted. When you capture for

Batch Capture

Capture: All Items in Logging Bin

Options: ☑ Use Logged Clip Settings

☐ Add Handles: 00:00:00;00

Capture Preset: DV NTSC 48 kHz

Using DV Video for video input
DCR-TRV900 using NTSC
29.97 frames per second
DV – NTSC at Best quality.
24 bits per pixel

720 by 480

Using DV Audio for audio input
Input: First 2 channels
Rate: 48.000 kHz
Speaker: off
Volume: 100, Gain: 0

Capturing using logged clip settings for picture, gain, and media to be captured.

Total Media Time: 00:01:24;27

Total Disk Space: 294.2 MB needed / 54.2 GB available

Cancel   OK

FIG. 10.18

the first time on a new project, be sure it is set to All Items in Logging Bin in order to get everything you have logged. After your first capture, select Offline Items in Logging Bin (see Figure 10.19), which did not appear before.

FIG. 10.19

Then click OK and another box will appear (see Figure 10.20). This simply tells you how many clips will be captured. Click OK and the capture process will start. The software will instruct the camera to back up and cue at the first shot logged. That shot will then be captured and the camera will cue up for the second clip. And so on.

FIG. 10.20

The logging window (see Figure 10.21) will play the clip as it is being captured. This playback always looks very blocky, but do not become overly concerned. Your captured clip will play back normally. When capturing is finished, another box will appear that simply states that the capture is done and what has occurred (see Figure 10.22).

FIG. 10.21

When capture is complete, the red line through the clips in the Bin will disappear and the clip symbols will be represented normally (see Figure 10.23).

FIG. 10.23

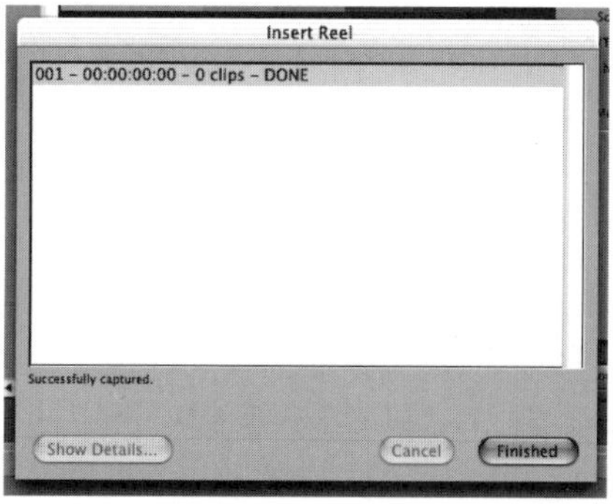

FIG. 10.22

As with everything, be sure to save frequently. Save after every batch capture. Capturing is a pain, but losing a significant amount of material means you have to go back and do it all over again. Once you have everything in the computer, editing can proceed. Of course you may have to do some syncing up, but otherwise you are set to go.

AUDIO CAPTURE

The capture of sound, whether recorded synchronous with picture or not, is often executed separately. Again, if you originated on video and recorded audio on the videotape, the previous description of capture will be adequate for initial efforts; just use the Aud + Vid in the Clip Settings tab (see the end of this section for audio settings). However, the sound on set is frequently recorded separately and, more to the point, there are many sound effects and music pieces and the like that will eventually have to be brought in as well.

Audio capture can be done a number of different ways. The most typical is to simply capture it as you did the picture. In this instance, we would record the audio directly onto a (probably) Mini-DV camera or deck, or transfer the audio from our original audiotapes to Mini-DV. This latter can be done by setting up from the analog audio outs on the playback unit to the input on a Mini-DV camera or deck. Most decks and cameras are set up to digitize the analog signal. Different cameras have different styles of input, usually executed with a cord supplied with the camera. The most common approach is to have three RCA plugs on one end — one each for video, left channel audio, and right channel audio — going to a single Mini plug on the camera end, which has the tip dedicated to video and a band on the shaft for each track of audio. Just hook up the audio plugs on the playback deck and make the transfer. With the audio on Mini-DV, a conventional capture can proceed, but be sure to check the different options for bringing it in found later in this section. The only drawback to this is that if the audio is digital, it loses a generation in the analog transfer. More on this briefly.

Past these straightforward issues, there are essentially two important variables in audio concerning capture. There are, however, many variables within both of these initial global choices. The first distinction is whether the audio is production sound — that is, sync audio recorded on location, or wild sound — music, effects, narration, or dub audio recorded away from the camera rolling. The second distinction is whether it is analog or digital, with the many different recording formats coming into play from there.

If the production sound was recorded on a separate recorder (double system), as it always is with film and occasionally is with video, we have to find a way to get it into the computer and it must be brought in so the sound can be synchronized to picture (see sidebar). If the audio was recorded on

> For people going the double system route, be aware that there is one other significant issue called pulldown regarding capturing or importing audio that can be synced up to picture that will be covered in Chapter XIV.

a sync analog recorder, a common option being the old-fashioned but rugged Nagra sync sound recorder, then it must be digitized and recorded to a medium from which we can capture. If the production sound is digital, typically recorded on a DAT (all digital recorders are by definition sync recorders), then we are just faced with the second part of this equation — getting it into FCP. With analog, one option is the aforementioned transfer to a Mini-DV tape. Set up your playback unit for sync playback (talk to a tech), transfer to Mini-DV, and then proceed with a standard capture. In terms of digital, unless you have the new G5s with digital audio input, FCP will not capture from a DAT or any digital recorder, unless there is a third-party card or FireWire ASB breakout box. To bypass all this, we could transfer each production tape to an aif file, given the right software and hardware. We could do this from an analog tape as well, again given the right tools. Dump it onto a CD for backup and/or transfer, remembering FCP samples at 48K. This is what we did with *Waiting Tables* and we then used FCP's Import function to bring it all in. With wild sound, the sound will require the same handling prior to capture, but sync is not an issue.

If doing a standard capture, once we have the audio in an acceptable form, the Clip Settings tab provides options for how you bring audio in (see Figure 10.24). The choices here are:

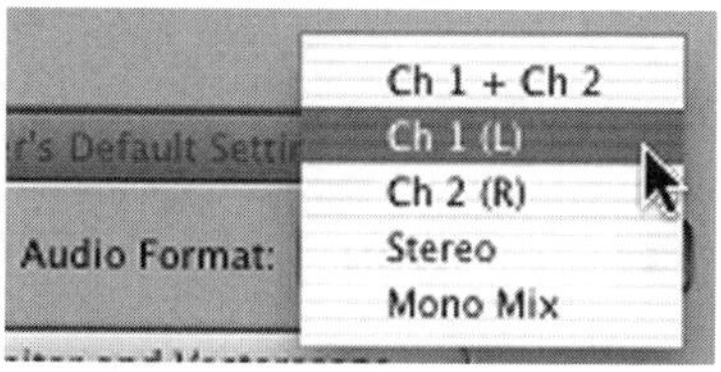

FIG. 10.24

- Channel 1 and 2 (Ch 1 + Ch 2) brings the two tracks in as separate tracks. They can be linked and unlinked and moved separately.

- Ch 1 (L) brings in the left channel of your source only; this has to do with where the audio is on your location sound. *WT* was recorded on the left channel.

- Ch 2 (R) brings in right (Right) only;

- Stereo brings in the two tracks linked. They are unlinkable.

- Mono Mix takes left and right tracks from original recordings and mixes them onto a mono track.

SUBCLIPS

The only issue with audio if you bring it in as a file is how to handle such a long piece of information. We took the entire twenty-plus minutes of audio for *Waiting Tables* and imported it as a single file. We could take the entire audio clip into the Timeline and sync picture to it in there. Then we call that a rough footage sequence and pull takes out as needed — we would have to cut them out with the razor blade. We then take them to a separate sequence with the rough cut. The two drawbacks to this are that there are limitations to what you can do to clips opened from the Timeline and the clips have the entire 20+ minutes of sound represented, making working space in the Viewer's scrubber bar cramped.

For these and other reasons, we wanted to have the synced clips available in the Browser, so we decided to subclip — divide — the audio into individual takes. After importing it and creating its own bin (Audio Bin), we opened the long clip, WaitingTables48KL.aif, from the Browser. We

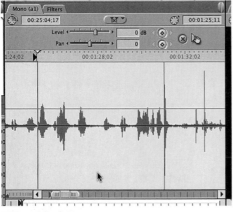

start at the beginning. Find where scene 1A-1 starts — right before we hear the sound person say "speed." Mark an In (see Figure 10.25). Roll to the end of the take, just after the director says "cut." Mark an Out. Go to the Modify menu and scroll to the first item — Make Subclip (see Figure 10.26). It will not be available in the menu until you mark an In and Out. After having done this, an

FIG. 10.25

audio icon labeled WaitingTables48KL.aifSubclip will appear in the Browser with the label highlighted. Simply type in scene and take number — 1A-1a. (I put the *a* after it to indicate audio.) Do this for every individual take. It seems like it will take a while but you get in a rhythm and it does not take too much longer than the actual tape and much shorter than capturing from Mini-DV.

SYNCING UP

The tutorial example is from a film shoot, which means sound and picture were recorded separately and thus have to be matched, or synced, up. As stated, telecine studios can sync up for you for a price — an approach that is quite common in the industry. For us average citizens who have to do manual syncing, we just have one more step to go through before we can actually start cutting. As with so many things in NLE editing, there are many ways to go about this even within an individual software program. This is our preferred method. You have the raw materials available in the Audio Bin and Pix Bin, so you can have at it too. We will start with 1A-3. You should open a new sequence for this as well.

Step #1 — Open 1A-3 from the Pix Bin in the Browser. Scrub through it until you find the frame where the slate hits — where the two bars come together. Use the left/right arrow keys to move back-and-forth until you find the exact frame. You will be able to see where the slate is starting to come down and the exact frame where it hits (see Figure 10.27-29).

Step #2 — With the playhead resting on this frame, click on or otherwise set "Mark In," and use the "Overwrite" function to bring the clip into the Timeline (see Figure 10.30).

FIG. 10.26

FIG. 10.27

FIG. 10.28

FIG. 10.29

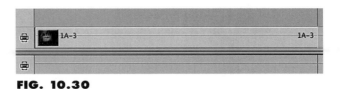

FIG. 10.30

Step #3 — With the clip in the Timeline, the playhead automatically goes to the last frame. Bring the playhead back to the head of the shot by hitting the "up" arrow on the keyboard.

Step #4 — Open the corresponding sound take, which we subclipped in the last section, in the Viewer. Search through the waveform for the hit

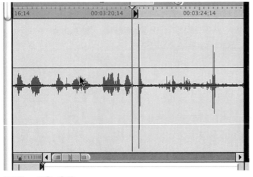

FIG. 10.31

FIG. 10.32

FIG. 10.33

of the slate. The audio hit of the slate should show a major deviation from the center of the wave-form, so you can both hear it and see its visual representation (see Figure 10.31). We left the playhead a little ahead of the slate in the Figure so you could see the wave-form. Place the playhead on the first frame — the attack — of the audio slate, click on "Mark In," and use the "Overwrite" function again. Both pic-ture and sound are now sitting "in sync" in the Timeline (see Figure 10.32).

It may be the film editor in me, where all the pieces are the same length, but I also like to square off the end of the take with the razor blade (see Figure 10.33).

LINKING

Linking has been discussed in other contexts previously and is the next step here. While picture and sound are in sync as they sit in the Timeline, any attempt to move them will pull them out of sync because the relationship has not been finalized. They must be linked.

Step #5 — Click on and highlight the audio and then Command>click on the picture. This "associates" the clips and is one way to group any number of elements together. However, this "association" is just temporary because when we click outside these clips, the group highlighting goes away. To complete the actual linking process, press Command>L or find Link under the Modify menu. Underlines now appear beneath the written video and audio names (see Figure 10.34) indicating that sound and picture are now locked in sync. This relationship is now "permanent," the quotation marks indicating that there are ways to undo the relationship — hit Command>L or unlink everything at Linked Selection on the Timeline.

FIG. 10.34

Step #6 — Before moving ahead, we want to visually check to make sure the slate is right. This can be difficult to evaluate with the synced clip starting at the hit of the slate. Use the function that allows you to extend the material ahead of the slate. You will have to drag the clips away from the head of the Timeline to get some room. Put the arrow right at the head of the just-synced shot. When the drag symbol, the vertical double lines with arrows, appears, click on it and drag the beginning of the shot forward to the beginning of the clip. Run it forward and backward a few times to make sure it is right. Single frame if necessary. You can un-link and use the period and comma keys to move frames. You can go crazy with this if you do too much of it, but check for errors that really jump out at you.

Step #7 — It is recommended that the newly synced shot be dragged back into a new bin so the synced version is available to you from the

Browser. Again, some things are not available to you when a clip is opened from the Timeline. Go to File>New>Bin and name the new bin "Sync Bin." Just drag the new clip with its linked audio straight to this new bin. I would leave the clip name the same, so connection with the Quicktime file, and eventually Cinema Tools if used, remains consistent.

WORKFLOW

Our purpose here is to give an overview of workflows and their general attributes. Specifics will be provided in later chapters.

The concept of workflow can be applied to any part of the production process. To put it simply, a productive workflow is the sequence of events to complete a specific project in the least amount of time, while spending as little money as possible. Workflow is efficiency. The more complicated you make your workflow, the less smoothly it will assist you in completing a task. Keep It Simple.

Organizing a project for efficient execution begins, unfortunately, with paperwork and planning. There is a tendency to jump right in and start capturing, editing, and throwing in effects. One must take care of some housekeeping first. It is one of the things that is very difficult for teachers to communicate to students. In the old analog days, a student project may just have been a bunch of tapes or rolls of film tossed in a box or a backpack — a sight that would make any Hollywood professional shiver. I had one student who carried all her materials around in an old suitcase. For a while, the department took on the character of a bus station.

With NLE you do not have the physical volume of material that you have with a film edit. Here you have a much more insidious enemy. It is the hyperspace of any computer. Things can literally get lost in the ozone. If you forget what you have named something or where you have put it, you may have a difficult time finding it again. To short-circuit the impending chaos it is important to set up all of the bins in your Browser in a fashion that makes sense. It is industry practice to create a separate bin for audio, video, music, sound effects, graphics, and sequences (or cuts).

Each stage of any workflow relies on the one before it. It assumes that one task must be completed before another can begin. An example of this would be to finish offline editing before you move on to the online edit. If you have to go back and forth between the two you end up wasting time and money, and the quality of the final product often suffers as well. We have all heard the stories of Hollywood films that went into production while the screenplay was still in the process of being re-written. What usually results is a film that feels patched together and comes in way over budget.

FILE MANAGEMENT

Setting your scratch disk to the same location is imperative if you expect to move media from one system to another. It is common practice for an assistant or apprentice editor to capture footage on a separate system and then transfer that footage to the editing workstation by FireWire drive or video server. This keeps editors busy on the edit instead of waiting through the capture process.

FCP is exact in its link to source media. The smallest change in location or name of the original file can disconnect media from the project. I was absent-mindedly tapping on keys to wake up my computer one day and accidentally renamed the WT folder. Suddenly everything needed to be reconnected. If you were to change a file name in the bin, say because you had duplicated it elsewhere, the actual name on the Quicktime file does not change. This will then cause problems when looking for the original file.

Two documents were created during production, the camera report and the lined script; both are included as pdf files inside the *Waiting Tables Documents* folder on the DVD. The editor begins a project by reading these documents and cataloging the associated media. For larger projects like a feature film, some editors will also create a scene list referencing the tape or camera rolls that contain the material for that scene. By placing these in a notebook, the editor is armed for the battle ahead.

STORAGE AND RUNTIME LIMITATIONS

Workflow must be planned before production starts. Camera selection is just as important as who will do graphics creation and compositing. How will sound be recorded, single or double system? How will media storage be handled, and who will perform the final color correction? Will multiple editors be working on the same project and need access to the same media? You also need to consider how you will back up your final project for archival purposes. Storage is also a consideration for your online house. What capabilities and limitations must be considered regarding the post house? During the production of the feature film *Vernie* (Jason Wallace, producer, 2003) we had an exceedingly low budget and the post house we used could only allocate enough Hi-Def storage capacity to hold 30 minutes of 24p video at a time. This meant the project had to be divided up into thirds. Knowing this ahead of time allowed us to design our workflow around this limitation, therefore keeping everyone on the sound side of things happy.

If finishing a 35mm film edit, you have to consider that the final film will be divided into 20-minute reels for projection. Keeping this in mind during your edit keeps your film from being cut arbitrarily mid-scene by the people putting together the final pieces. Except for the absolutely independent maker (who risks being overwhelmed), everything you do is going to pass through someone else's hands.

EDIT DECISION LISTS

We have danced around the edges of the Edit Decision List (EDL) so far, but it is a central player in any workflow. The EDL is based on the beginning and ending time code numbers that are created for clips during editing. If we begin a clip at frame TC-01:02:24:05 and end it TC-01:02:33:13, as the first clip in *WT* does, that information is stored in a file along with all the other beginning and ending numbers. FCP, and most NLEs, can then generate a text file that can be printed or exported to other environments, where it can drive the rebuilding of an edit with original or otherwise upstream media. The EDL also points to where each recorded clip is in the Timeline, that is, the first clip in Sequence, Fine Cut starts at TL-TC/01:00:00:00 and all others have Timeline start points as well. EDLs will play ever-increasing roles as your work gets more sophisticated.

THE BIG FOUR

You have basically four workflows to consider when initiating a project. They range from the most common to the least: shooting on video and finishing on video, shooting on film and finishing on video, shooting on film and finishing on film, and finally, shooting on video and finishing on film. Finishing on video includes broadcast, Internet, cd/dvd, and so on.

The following workflows describe what works best for generic projects. Comparing them will give you a good idea of how things differ between film and video projects. Similarly, projects with either high graphic content or extensive image manipulation will require a unique workflow to handle its specific needs. This is even more important now that **Computer Generated Imagery (CGI)** is commonplace in most commercial production. We will begin with the simplest "DV-Only" production, through a video offline/online situation, moving on to 24p High-Definition, and finally to the most complicated workflow, cutting the negative for a film finish.

SHOOT ON VIDEO, EDIT ON VIDEO, FINISH ON VIDEO

The simplest workflow exists for DV-Only productions. Shoot on a DV camera, use that same camera to capture your video into the computer, edit, create all of the effects and add color correction, and complete the final sound mix. All without leaving Final Cut Pro. The original DV camera becomes the mastering deck as well. The efficiency and low cost of this system makes it very appealing to independent producers and mom-and-pop shops.

A step up from DV-Only is the workflow for a video offline/online edit. Shoot with a camera that is part of a high-end system with much higher resolution than DV. DigiBeta or High-Definition are shot and then down-converted to DV with matching time code and window burns (G). The edit is performed within FCP with compositing and graphics created at a lower resolution. An EDL is then exported so that the original tapes can be used to recreate the cut at a high resolution. Audio is exported and mixed professionally at another location and graphics and composites must be recreated on higher end systems. In this situation, FCP basically becomes a design tool to make all of the major decisions in a low-cost environment.

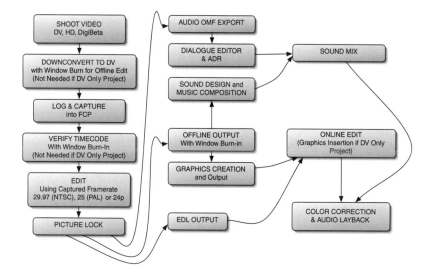

SHOOT ON FILM, EDIT ON VIDEO, FINISH ON VIDEO

Most episodic television is still shot on film, then finished and broadcast on video. The workflow is practically the same, with one difference — transferring the film to video through the telecine process. Audio is recorded double system, so sound is synched to video at telecine or later. From this point on, many producers would handle the project with the same workflow as a project shot on video. However, there is an increasing trend — one that we subscribe to — that even though it may never go back to film, it makes much more sense to remove the pulldown and edit at 24 fps. First, removing those extra frames means less media to store and manipulate, and second, setting up a Cinema Tools database takes very little time and leaves you the option to go back to cut the negative if the urge ever strikes you (see Chapter XIV for details on this). It is now so easy to cut at 24 that it just makes sense to do it that way. Indeed, many of the episodic programs that do originate on video are shooting on 24p and posting HDTV at 24.

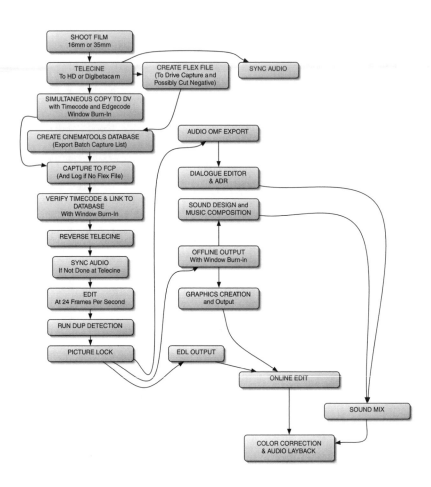

It should be noted that 24-frame progressive video acquisition is making inroads on the use of film in broadcast arenas. Use of these formats eliminates several steps before the edit takes place, specifically developing the negative, telecine, and syncing the sound. It also allows the director and director of photography to see their dailies immediately.

While it is not finished in Final Cut Pro, ABC-TV's *NYPD Blue* (Steven Bochco Productions) provides a typical example of the workflow of a high-end tape-to-tape finish. The show is filmed on the Fox lot in Century City, just west of Beverly Hills. It is shot on 35mm film and they continue to use the four perf approach, because it leaves open the option of conforming the negative (see Chapter XIV for an explanation of this rather arcane complication). *NYPD Blue* has always conformed the negative for archival reasons, but the efficacy of a negative conform is becoming more and more debatable. The afterlife of a show can be handled in a number of ways. Conforming can be done anytime down the road and, probably more importantly, retransfers from the original negative can be used to rebuild a show if the digital copies start to deteriorate. Shows that are using three perf appear to be counting on this last option or are saving money until some measure of success makes an afterlife appear to be a possibility.

The negative is processed at FotoKem labs in Burbank and then sent to *NYPD Blues'* post-production facility, Westwind Media, also in Burbank. The film is telecined to D5, one of the high-end, completely uncompressed formats that can be adapted for HDTV. From this D5 master, DVCAM clones are made that are then sent to the editorial team back on the Fox lot. There are three editorial teams, working under a supervising editor, that work on the show, each assigned seven or eight episodes a year. Depending on how quickly they need to be turned around for broadcast, they get anywhere from three weeks, a rushed period for an hour-long format, to six weeks to complete their part of the work.

Typically, the film that is shot during a day is processed in the evening. At Westwind, the takes the director has chosen are telecined overnight and the DVCAM clones are back to the editing rooms by morning. All production sound is synced during telecine. The assistant editor will spend the morning capturing this previous day's footage with the aid of flex files (see Chapters XIV and XV). The assistant editor has a significant amount of paperwork and computer work to do, making sure all time code and keynumber information is encoded correctly, checking over lined scripts, and organizing the material on hard drives. The show is shot with two cameras, so there is effort devoted to coordinating the cameras with a single audio track and laying them out for efficient access by the editor. After completing this work, the clips are organized on a server-style drive that makes it available on an editor's workstation. Then the hard work of editing begins.

In the short edit timeline (three weeks), the editorial staff will have to have a cut of a show ready for a "Director's Cut" screening at the week-and-a-half mark. The producer, director, and any other pertinent staff will take a look at the rough cut of the show with the editorial staff. After discussion and notes, the editorial staff will start streamlining the episode, working toward the broadcast length of around 43 minutes. Another screening occurs and then the editorial staff has roughly one week to bring the show to picture lock.

As suggested, the editor works almost entirely with the production sound — the tracks recorded during filming. He or she generally uses some stock background sounds and a scratch music track to give the scenes fullness for the screenings. Once picture lock is called, the edit is turned over to the previously mentioned finishing crew. The assistant editor strips out all the "for position only" sound, leaving just the production tracks and then the EDLs are emailed back to Westwind Media. The EDL's are imported into Smoke, an assembly program from Discreet that uses the EDLs to drive the rebuilding of the edited program from the D5 masters. It is mostly a process in which studio personnel feed the system individual tapes as they are requested by the software.

All subsequent work will be done to or against this master and once the show is entirely rebuilt, all other work can commence. The dialogue editor and the sound effects editor start plying their estimable trade with the tracks. ADR people are called in if necessary and actors are brought back in if lines have to be replaced for technical reasons or added. Foley artists start creating all the layers of background sound — phones, sirens, footsteps, background chatter, doors opening and closing, et cetera. All the sound effects and the like are created from scratch for every episode. It would be tempting to use library effects, but these effects, if used exclusively over a period of time, give episodes a sameness that can work against a show. Once all tracks are built, the episode goes into the mixing studio where all levels and effects are finalized.

The almost finished show is brought into the DaVinci 2K, a software and hardware environment commonly used in post-production, for color correction — the online finish. Many shows used to go back to retransferring from the film negative for this finish, but finishing from the tape masters has advanced to the point where only a few, if any, shows still go the film route. Tape-to-tape has become the norm. Fire, another common post-production image manipulation program, is then used for titling and "dirt-spotting" — a process of going through and repairing the inevitable small scratches and dirt spots that occur when you shoot film. Not all shows go through this stage, but the show's producers set very high standards for the physical quality of the show. Once all finishing processes are concluded, the D5 version is down-converted to a 720p HDTV version and a standard video version that are ready to be delivered to ABC for broadcast.

SHOOT ON FILM, EDIT ON VIDEO, FINISH ON FILM

The most complicated workflow results anytime one format is used to edit another format. This is doubly true when the format is physically different as well. The ability to get back to film after a video edit is entirely based on being able to keep track of the relationship between film frames and video frames. To get film into a video-based edit system and still be able to track its frames requires a database. The information is created at

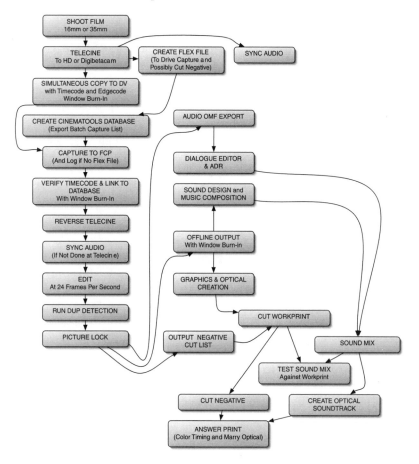

the telecine process or after the video is captured into FCP. This data becomes part of the metadata that FCP tracks. This database is then used to cut the film negative for prints. The difference in frame rates between film and video used to only allow accuracy within 2 frames at each edit. This was a mess until the ability to edit video at 24 frames per second made this discrepancy a thing of the past. This will be a primary subject in the concluding three chapters of this text.

SHOOT ON VIDEO, EDIT ON VIDEO, FINISH ON FILM

The approach here is to do a complete video finish and then have that tape converted — photographed, as it were — to film. This might seem like an odd idea at first, but it became a very powerful way for independent filmmakers to get their film produced cheaply with the option of having theatrical distribution. As covered elsewhere, it has always been a facet of high-end production with that being the route of George Lucas's last *Star Wars* saga. Indeed, one of the key uses of video-to-film transfer is to incorporate an aesthetic inherent in video itself — for filmmakers who want to translate the look, feel, and flexibility of video shooting to the big screen. Video could be shot on DV, or any other video format, then edited without concern or need to track film elements. The

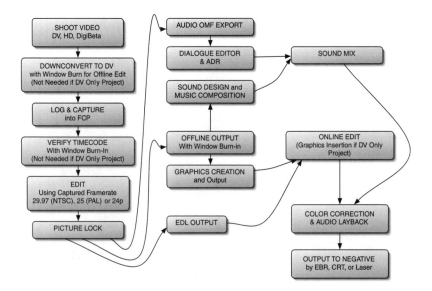

workflow here is the same as video acquisition and finish with the addition of another step. This step is performed by competing technologies: Cathode Ray Tube (CRT) recording or Electron Beam Recording (EBR). CRT is the low-budg approach with EBR being both very expensive and dramatically higher quality. These systems will remove additional video frames in NTSC while doing their best to maintain smooth motion before recording the images to the film negative. This explains why, for a time, filmmakers planning this workflow frequently shot PAL video. PAL is recorded at 25 fps, making an easier transfer to the 24-frame film format. Much of this work now goes to 24p.

FRAME RATE BLESSINGS OR BLUES

One complication of editing media acquired at 24 fps, whether film or video, is that many producers have been forced for economic reasons to transfer the media at some point to 29.97. Editing 24-frame acquired material at 30 fps (with 3:2 pulldown inserted, see page 279) works fine for a videotape finish, but if you intend to go back to cut the original negative it makes more sense to cut in a 24-frame Timeline vs. a 30-frame Timeline. Now that FCP supports true 24 and 23.98 editing, through Reverse Telecine in Cinema Tools, there is no reason to deal with the inaccuracies that plague 24 fps projects cut at 30 frames per second. More on this in Chapter XIV.

For the production of *Vernie* we shot 24p high-definition video. Actually, we shot 23.98 which basically built in the .1% slowdown that would be necessary to transfer 24-frame material to 29.97 fps during the transfer process. I knew that maintaining this speed—29.97—throughout the entire production process would streamline our audio edit. We couldn't afford Cinema Tools, which was a separate program at the time, so I made the decision to edit at 29.97 and have our online facility convert our EDL to 23.98 fps for the HD online.

While our HD online was being performed, we exported our OMF file and delivered it to the audio editor for sound design. We gave the sound team a DV copy that was printed to video directly from our offline Timeline so that they could get started. When we finished our online, I brought a copy to the sound people. They laid it next to their audio and we began to watch it. Everything looked great for the first ten minutes or so but soon we began to notice that some shots were out of sync with their dialogue. This was bizarre because it was not consistent; some were dead on in sync. Long story short, this is exactly what happens when you edit 24-frame material at 29.97 and then finish it at 24 fps. The plus or minus two frame discrepancy is additive and you never know where it will show up.

Our solution was to go into every shot and find some sound to check audio sync, whether it was a bilabial (m, b, or p) in someone speaking, or a pen hitting a desk, nudging sound a frame or two this way or that. After a while you begin to question the sync of every shot. Trust me, hindsight is 20/20 and the Cinema Tools investment would have been worth it. The moral of the story is if you shoot 24 frames and plan to finish at 24 frames, make sure you edit 24 frames. Period.

BACKUP

Accidentally deleting a file, or losing or damaging a tape does not happen very often, but when it does it is a disaster. If your project was shot on a high-end video format your smartest course of action would be to make a DV copy of your camera original for offline editing and then lock your original tapes safely away.

If you shot DV, you will actually be performing an online edit and therefore will not require a window burn copy, but I do strongly suggest a digital **clone** be made of your DV camera original as a precaution. Video decks are not perfect and you can almost guarantee a damaged tape during crunch time. Simple transfers — say, from one camera to another — will not do, because the time code is not included. The identification of a transfer as a clone indicates time code information has been transferred as well.

At the end of every session, make sure to make a backup copy of your project file in a separate physical location from your original. Zip disks, CD-Rs and FireWire drives are perfect for this. If you do a window burn during telecine, be sure to have them do a clean copy at the same time. You may, and will if you are doing a video finish, want to rebuild your show with this clean copy from an EDL.

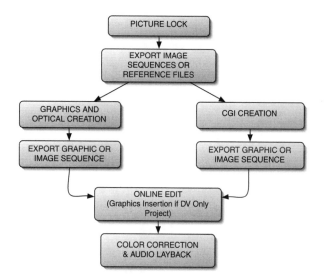

GRAPHICS AND COMPOSITING WORKFLOW

As soon as you have picture lock, compositing and graphics creation can begin. FCP is a very able compositor, but it is also great at building mockups and setting the timing of graphics that will be created in other programs. In the world of 3D animation it is common for hand-drawn sketches to be scanned in and inserted into the Timeline as a placeholder for the graphics to come. Dedicated workstations are great for creating titles/overlays, CGI (including 3D animation and character creation), and compositing. Remember, anytime you will be working with another person or company, find out what they need instead of assuming.

TITLES/OVERLAYS

Titling is actually a form of compositing, but it is best left in its own category of Overlays because titles don't usually interact with the footage that has been shot, it simply lies over the top of it. In order to create and position a title or graphic overlay, most workstations only need a single

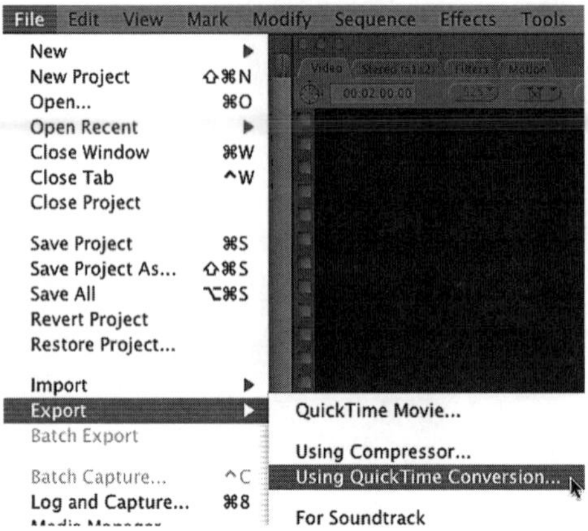
File Edit View Mark Modify Sequence Effects Tools
New
New Project ⇧⌘N
Open... ⌘O
Open Recent
Close Window ⌘W
Close Tab ^W
Close Project
Save Project ⌘S
Save Project As... ⇧⌘S
Save All ⌥⌘S
Revert Project
Restore Project...
Import
Export
Batch Export
Batch Capture... ^C
Log and Capture... ⌘8
QuickTime Movie...
Using Compressor...
Using QuickTime Conversion...
For Soundtrack

FIG. 11.1

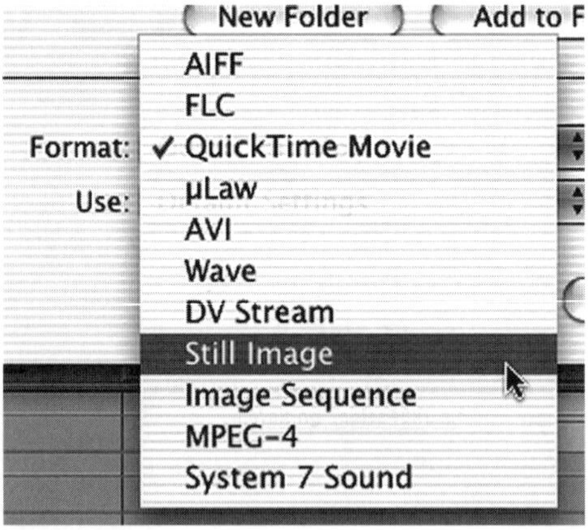
New Folder
Add to F
Format:
Use:
AIFF
FLC
✓ QuickTime Movie
µLaw
AVI
Wave
DV Stream
Still Image
Image Sequence
MPEG-4
System 7 Sound

FIG. 11.2

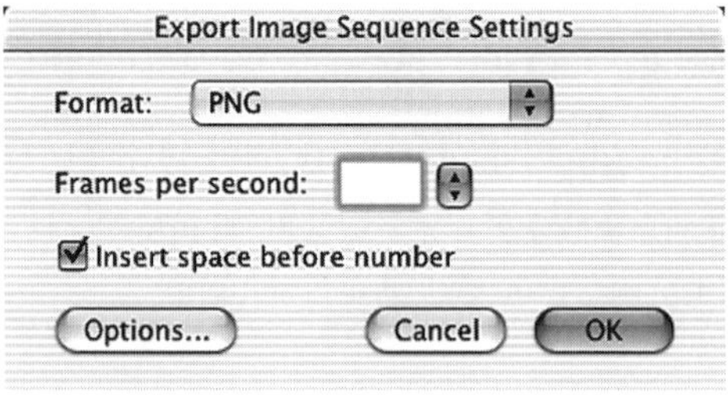
Export Image Sequence Settings
Format: PNG
Frames per second:
Insert space before number
Options...
Cancel
OK

FIG. 11.3

frame of the clip that will lie underneath. The only course of action here is to export a still frame from the clip in the Timeline that requires an overlay. To do this, park the playhead on the frame in the Timeline and choose File>Export >Using Quicktime Conversion (see Figure 11.1). Click the Format drop down menu (see Figure 11.2) from the ensuing Save Window. Slide down and select Still Image. Click the Options button next to Format and choose your format on the Export Image Sequence Settings box (see Figure 11.3). Pick a format that will work for your graphic artist — most programs will work with an uncompressed TGA (Targa) or TIFF image (see Figure 11.4). If you need scrolling credits over black, only timing from first frame to last must be considered.

The final title or graphic can be exported as a still, or a series of stills if the graphic is animated like the high-speed graphic transitions you see on the news. This series of stills are numbered sequentially in a single folder. Before you import this series of stills into FCP, you must go to Final Cut Pro>User Preferences, and change the "Still/Freeze Duration"

FIG. 11.4

to one frame (00:00:00:01). Import the folder that contains the numbered image sequence and open the folder in the Browser. Create a new sequence and name it according to the animation. Select all of the images at once and drag them into the new Timeline. Now click the tab on your original sequence to activate it and drag the sequence that contains your animation into the Timeline as an overlay. This sequence will act just like a clip so you can add filters, transitions, and color correction to your heart's content. Quicktime Pro, if you own a license, can combine these images into a single clip for you, making the media management in FCP less of a burden.

CGI

CGI is anything that is created in a computer. Technically titles could fall into this category, but we are referring to 3D forms, whether they be static objects like architecture or machinery, or animated objects like life forms, liquid, or morphs. Morphs refer to changing one object into another, say a person into an animal, or a car into a boat. Morphs are sometimes created with a live action image.

Titling and overlays only needed a still image as a reference, but CGI and Compositing need a sequence of images to use as a reference. To create an Image Sequence in FCP, set an In and Out point in the Timeline. File->Export>Using Quicktime Conversion, then select Image Sequence from the format box. Again, you have to select your format and give it a name. Then click Save. This image sequence can then be opened as a reference by your graphic artist in their workstation. When completed, the CGI artist will export an image sequence for use directly in FCP, or for compositing.

COMPOSITING

Combining live action elements with other live action elements or computer-generated elements so that they appear to interact with each other as though they were shot together is the essence of compositing. This type of precision requires the cleanest images so it is best to shoot your project uncompressed and in Progressive Scan mode. If it is a 29.97 show and you know certain shots will be composited, at a minimum shoot those particular shots at 30p. Progressive scan gives a much cleaner image to work with when compared to an interlaced image, especially when there is movement in the frame.

Also try to avoid any format that is highly compressed like DV. Compression works for playback, but introduces artifacts that undermine a compositor's efforts to build a clean composition. Compositing is the most difficult part of a project to yield realistic results, so do not skimp on this. A poorly composited sequence will guarantee a high cheese factor — a technical term — for your audience.

While these last parts get into some high-end intricacies, the major work-flow issue for the novice is organizing your clips and your capture scratch so there is always a clear path between the two. Get familiar with scratch disks, be aware of issues when transferring from one workstation to another, and just know where things are. If the project is going to pass through anyone else's hands, be sure to be in constant communication so you know exactly what they need from you. Keeping it simple, communication, and organization are the keys. As suggested, a lot of people just plow in. This may work for initial efforts but is a recipe for disaster as your projects get larger. The more you understand where things should be, the more untroubled the editorial process will be.

SPECIAL EFFECTS

mage manipulation, compositing, and associated topics are all subjects that require extended discussion. The goal of this text is to cover film-style cutting and how to employ matchback, but a brief introduction to these kinds of special effects is in order. The important thing to be clear on is that when finishing on film is the goal, most of the effects we will discuss in this chapter — effects easily applied in FCP — either can only be executed to film at some effort and expense or, in some cases, cannot effectively be executed at all. This does not mean many effects are not done in films. It simply means that what can be accomplished in FCP with a quick menu choice and a little render time, takes planning and then farming the effect out to the appropriate personnel to execute. And then "standing back and writing big checks" as a friend of mine once joked. Of course in this day and age, you can always finish an effect on video and then transfer it over to film, but this as well can create complications and, again, expense.

When we talk about creating effects in terms of film, we start talking about **opticals**. Creating a film optical is the process of applying an effect to something already shot. With film, this requires going to an **optical printer**, a piece of lab equipment that is essentially a camera loaded with raw stock pointing into a projector, both of which are operated frame-by-frame — re-photographing existing footage. To create a wipe or a freeze frame or anything similar, the effect has to be planned out and shot animation-style — one frame at a time. Labs create effects like this all the time, although they do it less and less as digital becomes more viable. They are set up for it and it is not a huge deal. But opticals are not cheap and the costs can start to add up. In many cases, duplicating some of the simplest video effects can prove anywhere from cost-prohibitive to impossible.

And the truly hard effects — forget it. When the Terminator walks through a gate, you ain't going to make that happen on an optical printer. Here, however, we get back again into that messy realm. You can take your video with your swell video effect and have it transferred to film. It can then be cut into your edited workprint (see glossary) like anything else. The problem is that it is going to look different from the surrounding footage. You can do this to the whole sequence or project, but the cash register is going to take a long time to stop ringing.

So FCP provides many ways to manipulate or otherwise distort the image. In a video context, you can have at it to your heart's content. This is fine, but you should always have a reason. Too often, extensive image manipulation seems unmotivated, simply done to spice up essentially uninteresting footage.

IMAGE MANIPULATION

THE VIDEO FILTERS MENU

FCP has a wide variety of filters and effects that can be applied to the image. Most of them are found in the menus at Effects>Video Filters (see Figure 12.1). The same menu can be accessed in the Effects tab in the Brower — Video Filters. Each one of the options under Video Filters (VF) allows access to further submenus that have numerous choices. These submenus allow you an almost Adobe Photoshop-like ability to apply many different possibilities to the image. There are over eighty total choices, although there are some compositing functions thrown into the mix. These choices again range from the commonly used to the almost silly.

Effects can be applied to shots opened from the Browser, but they generally do not play very well and must be rendered in the Timeline anyway. It is

FIG. 12.1

generally best to open the clip from the Timeline — double click on it and it will appear in the Viewer. Go to the VF menu and choose your effect. The render bar will appear above the shot in the Timeline. In the Viewer, click on the Filters tab and it will now be dedicated to the effect you have chosen. Drag the Effects tab over the Canvas (or Browser), so you can work in it while you see what is being applied in the Viewer. Every Effects tab will be a little different, depending on what the effect's parameters are. Each effect will have a default setting and then the tab will allow you to modify — often just increase — the effect. As an example, the first item on the menu, the Gaussian Blur (see Figure 12.2), will slightly blur the image and then the slider on the Effects tab is used to increase it. In this instance, the Radius slider controls how soft the image is (see Figure 12.3). The smallest effect is on the left and in this example, the effect is about a third of the total possible. If the slider is taken all the way to the right, it will increase the effect to almost complete abstraction.

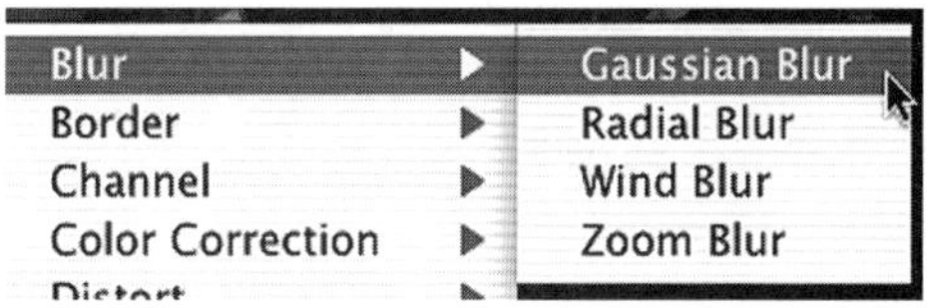

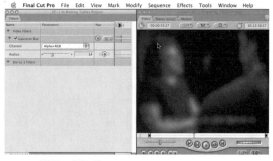

FIG. 12.2

FIG. 12.3

Some of the things in the Visual Effects menu are rarely used or are used only if you are doing specific jobs, like compositing. Others come into play quite frequently. Color Correction and Image Control are probably the most commonly used, and color correction will be one of the key topics of the next chapter. Again with this, a laundry list of what each choice will do would be endless. Get some free time and have at it.

THE WIREFRAME

The Wireframe is the tool used to create and plot out any kind of movement or distortion of the frame. It is an X-shaped overlay frame that superimposes on top of the image (see Figure 12.4). We can grab the

FIG. 12.4

corners and resize the image — make it smaller or larger. With the Wireframe up, we can click anywhere in the image and drag it to different parts of the frame. Among many other things, this allows us to do split screens and combined screens. We can also grab the corners and rotate the image. In conjunction with the motion tab, we can also plot out movement of a frame. We can do this by grabbing the frame and moving it, or we can control the Wireframe's movement by typing in points in its travel. More on this later.

To access the Wireframe, go up to the View menu and scroll down to Image & Wireframe, which allows us to see both the clip and the Wireframe at the same time. The Wireframe can be brought up by itself just below. To play around with this, let's bring up Judy's MOS shot from

FIG. 12.5

the Browser (3B-1). To start, we need to re-size the desired clip in the Viewer. This is an important step in that it allows us to manipulate the parameters of the shot from outside its edges. Go to the Zoom pop-up menu and scroll down to 25%. This makes for a smaller image with a wide gray border (see Figure 12.5).

Go to any corner and, as the pointer lands on it, the crosshairs (+) will appear. Click on the corner and drag the image smaller (see Figure 12.6). You can also drag it larger. As the pointer approaches, the rotate symbol (**A**) may appear for a brief second; you can experiment with this as well.

Now click in the smaller image we have created and drag it down to the bottom left hand corner (see Figure 12.7). You have undoubtedly noticed that the checkerboard has appeared in the open areas, indicating that we will be able to see lower video levels through this. Just for argument's sake, set an In point at TC:15:15:05 and an Out point at TC:15:16:24. Set an In point at TL-TC:01:01:28:05 in the Timeline and do a Superimpose edit (see Figure 12.8). This is only the beginning.

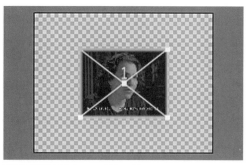

FIG. 12.6

This function is for making whole frame changes; as you will notice, it is the entire image that gets bigger or smaller. While making it bigger changes the contents of the frame, to be more selective about the con-tents see the Crop tool in the next section. Theoretically, the

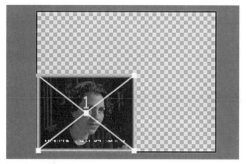

FIG. 12.7

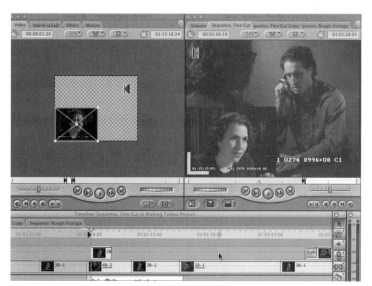

FIG. 12.8

previously described function also allows us to crop an image to eliminate unwanted elements. We can make it bigger and lose things around the edges. If the sound boom dipped into frame at some point or the DP accidentally got a little bit of a light stand, we could change the framing to get rid of it. The unfortunate by-product — and it can be a deal-killer — is that the cropped image will have a different pixel count and the image will look anything from slightly to radically different than your other footage.

CROP/DISTORT TOOLS

On the Tool Palette are two previously undiscussed tools — Crop and Distort. These are both used in conjunction with the Wireframe. The Crop tool allows us to shift and resize the image, while maintaining its four-corner dimensions. It differs from the resizing described in the previous section in that the contents of the image stay the same size, just the borders are shifted, thus excluding parts of the original frame. The Distort tool allows us to reshape the image, making the four corners variable

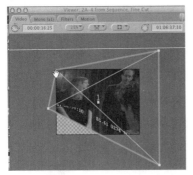

thus creating essentially funhouse mirror–style distortions. Follow all the steps in the previous section. Select one of the tools and go to the corner of the Wireframe. Click and reshape the image as desired. In conjunction with the command key, the four sides get smaller or larger in unison when using the Crop tool. Each corner can be manipulated separately with the Distort tool (see Figure 12.9).

FIG. 12.9

SLOW MOTION/FAST MOTION

Creating motion effects is quite common. This is taking the footage shot in real time and either slowing it down or speeding it up. In film, motion effects are generally created in the camera. Running at different frame rates produce these effects, with faster rates producing slow motion and slower rates producing fast motion. Some video cameras can run at different rates, but they are the more expensive and produce varying results.

In video, motion effects are typically introduced in post-production. You can digitally change the speed of a clip. Unfortunately, it frequently looks like you have digitally changed the speed of the clip. The movement can look artificial and "electronic." Still, some very nice things can be done. Speed effects can be applied to clips when opened either from the Timeline or the Browser. It is generally preferable either to duplicate a clip in the Browser and then apply the change to the copy or to open from the Timeline. If just opened from the Browser, whatever change is applied to a clip is semi-permanent — the clip will always have that motion effect and can only be seen in its original form by changing the speed back again. If changed from the Timeline, the new changed clip can be dragged to the Browser for storage. Motion effects cannot be applied to sync clips unless the audio and video have exactly the same beginning and ending points.

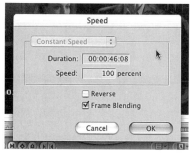

You access speed changes in the menus at Modify>Speed. The Speed window will appear and you simply type in the percentage change you want (see Figure 12.10). It works in a way that is

FIG. 12.10

not particularly intuitive. Slow motion requires lower percentages and fast motion higher. 50% doubles the length of the clip and 25% makes it four times longer. 200% makes it twice as fast. And so on. Be aware that motion effects give the computer's processor a real workout and can take a long time to render.

Creating motion effects brings up that whole discussion about when to use film. The two biggest users of film in the United States, the government and NFL Films, continue to use film precisely because of its greater ability to create quality motion effects. At one point, there was a rumor going around that NFL Films was going digital. But NFL Films rarely shoots at 24 frames and the motion effects still require film. In fact, they have recently opened a new headquarters with a state-of-the-art film processing lab in the heart of the building. NASA shoots its lift-offs and landings from many perspectives to be able to analyze any of the stress factors associated with the terrific pressures involved. Film, here, is the clear medium of choice.

FREEZE FRAMES

A freeze frame is simply where the action freezes in mid-movement. In film, freeze frames are a bother. The optical printer would have to be involved, with the intended shot being duplicated camera-frame for pro-jector-frame up until the desired image and then multiple frames made of this one. Generations are again an issue. A number of films have made great use of this effect. The last shot of Francois Truffaut's *The 400 Blows* (1959) has a great freeze as Antoine Doinel looks back at the land as he runs along a beach. The last shot of George Roy Hills' *Butch Cassidy and the Sundance Kid* (1969) has the freeze on the duo as they go out to face insurmountable odds. Even documentaries use them well, with *Gimme Shelter* (1970) by Albert and David Maysles and Charlotte Zwerin having a freeze on Mick Jagger after he has viewed the footage of the murder at the Altamount concert. You can see that we have kind of a last shot theme going on here. They still can be highly effective.

In FCP, you have to identify the frame that you want to freeze. Again it is best to do this in the Timeline. Park the playhead at the desired frame. In the menus go to Modify>Make Freeze Frame (kybd: Shift>N). Ten sec-onds of the frame will appear in the Viewer. It is a simple matter now to just time out how much you want and edit it into the Timeline. The play-head should be exactly where you want this new piece to go. It will probably need to be rendered. You can make the default amount created longer in User Preferences>Timeline Options>Still/Freeze Duration, but you must do it when you initiate the project. Barring that, you can edit the clip into the Timeline, drag it longer, and render that as well.

THE MOTION TAB

The Motion tab is found in the background of the Viewer and allows you to put many elements in FCP in motion. It is particularly useful for titles, graphics, and animation, and can play a significant role in compositing and CGI. Almost anything in FCP can be animated. You can animate color correction, you can animate effects like reverb to audio — almost any-thing you do in a tab in the Viewer has the motion control Timeline hidden to the right. When you click on the Motion tab, you will see many controls similar to what we saw in the titling section. It also has a mini-Timeline that is initially hidden on the right. There are many intricate

steps to creating motion and the first few times you try it, you undoubtedly will make some sequencing mistakes. But, have Undo handy, or quit
without saving changes, if things get out of hand. Be persistent.

We will just do some simple things with titles, so create a title as we did
in Chapter VII. Do the following in Sequence, Fine Cut.

1. On the Viewer, go to the Generator pop-up menu and go to
   Text>Text.
2. Click on the Controls tab in the Viewer.
3. Highlight **Sample Text** and type in END in caps.
4. Find a point just before Fritz says "Babe." Mark an In on the Canvas
   and do a Superimpose edit.
5. Trim this new title down so it ends just after the image fades out.

Many machines will indicate that this new title clip in V2 will need to be
rendered — the red line — but we will wait for that. Now to create some
movement.

1. Double-click in the new title to open it in the Canvas, select Image +
   Wireframe from one of the View menus, and choose 25% from the
   Zoom menu.
2. Click on the Motion tab in the Viewer.
3. We are going to need to make the Motion tab larger so we can see the
   Timeline part of the tab. Click in the top bar and drag the tab to the
   left over the Browser. Then click in the thumb set and stretch it to the
   right, leaving the Canvas visible.
4. You will see the motion Timeline with the area of the title clip in
   white. If this area is small, just zoom in on it, because you will want
   some real estate (see Figure 12.11).

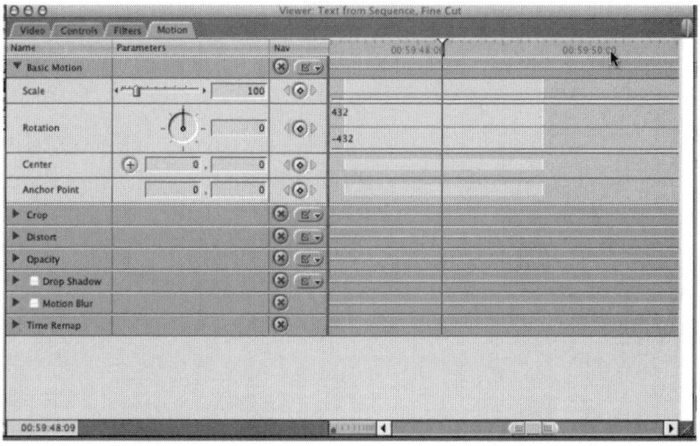

We will be working with the top three controls. Scale, Rotation, and Center refer to the shape and position of the title — they actually move the entire frame, but to simplify things we

FIG. 12.11

will refer to this in terms of title. All creation of movement is done in conjunction with the Wireframe. We can either type in points in the boxes in the control panels or just drag the Wireframe, with our movements being reflected numerically in the boxes. Scale controls the size of the title. Rotation controls the orientation — the angle — of the title. Center controls the East/West/North/South positioning of the title. There are many other options below that.

The object here is to plot out points in the shape and position of the title on the motion tab's Timeline. FCP plots out all the in-between frames and will "animate" the elements in the way you have dictated. Keyframes are used to plot out these points in the movement over time. In its simplest manifestation, we could start the title in the center, which it defaults to, and move it off to the right. We would put the playhead at the beginning of the title by either moving it in the tab or in the Timeline — they move in tandem. Click the keyframe button (**B**) on the tab and a keyframe is laid at the beginning of the clip in the motion tab. Hit the down arrow key to go to the end of the clip. Click the + in Center panel and in the Canvas drag the Wireframe off to the right — the numbers will change in the boxes as you do. Click keyframe again and you have plotted the title movement off-frame right (see Figure 12.12). Render it if you want to see it in real time.

FIG. 12.12

Again using a straightforward example, our intent here is to put another title with End on it over Fritz's last shot. For no better reason than to show you how it is done, we are going to have the title start off-frame, rotate to the left, move into the center of the frame, get bigger, and fade-out.

The starting point is to create the initial position of the title. We want it off frame and at a 90 degree angle.

1. Be sure the playhead is still parked at the beginning of the clip. Go to Center and click on the +. Click on the Wireframe in the Canvas and drag it off to the right, then click on keyframe in the Center Panel.

Move up to Rotation.
Click on keyframe
and type 90 into the
box. Click anywhere
in the panel and the
effect will apply —
the Wireframe will

FIG. 12.13

rotate 90 degrees (see Figure 12.13). We are not going to change from
the default Scale of the title here so simply click the panel's keyframe.

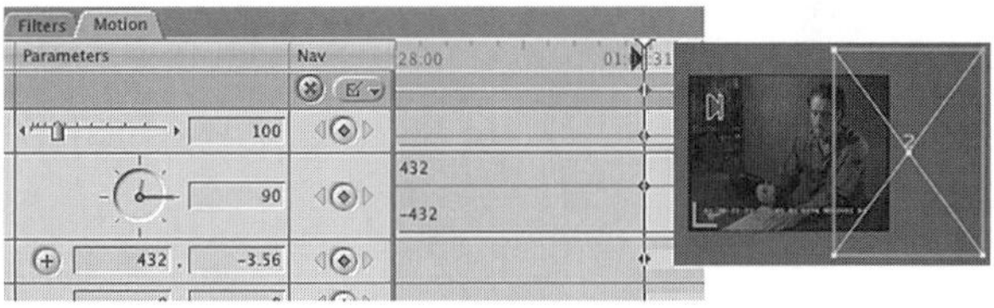

Now we want to plot the ending point. We will go in reverse order here.

2. Park the playhead at the end of the clip. Go to scale and type in 300.
   Click the keyframe bottom and then click somewhere in the panel.

3. Go to rotation and type in zero, which will level it. Click keyframe and
   then click in the panel to apply.

4. Go to Center and click in the +. Click on the Wireframe in the Canvas
   and drag it back to
   the center of the
   frame. Click on the
   keyframe. This is
   the end position
   (see Figure 12.14).

FIG. 12.14

5. Go to the Effects tab and drag a
   fade-out over to the end of the title
   in the Timeline.

6. Single frame through the overlapped
   pieces and get a sense of what it
   looks like (see Figure 12.15).

In looking at this, I decided on two
changes. I realize that the effect will
fade out before it is finished and I want
a steeper angle as the title enters the

FIG. 12.15

frame. I decide I want the effect to tilt more to the right. We can use the
first two methods to change position or we can also just drag at the
keyframe, which may be the easiest way once you have some points
inserted. I click on the first rotation keyframe and simply drag it up, the
amount of change being displayed in a box (see Figure 12.16). Next, we
want to change the end point, but I decide on just the Rotation and

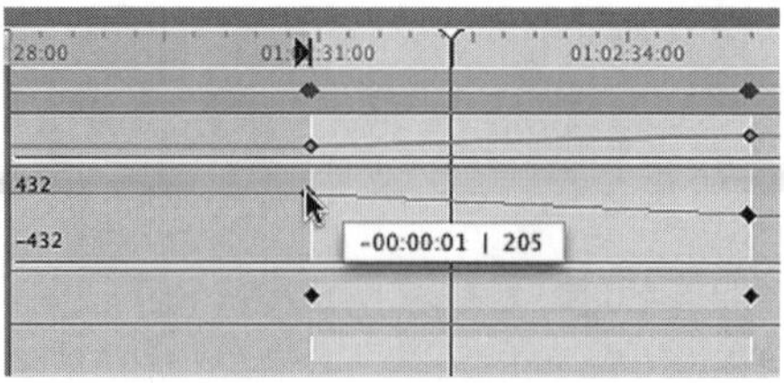

FIG. 12.16

Center, letting the title continue to get larger. I decide to end things at TL-TC/2:34:01 so I park the playhead there and move the final values to there, typing them in, using the Wireframe, or dragging. This is our final (see Figure 12.17). Render and play.

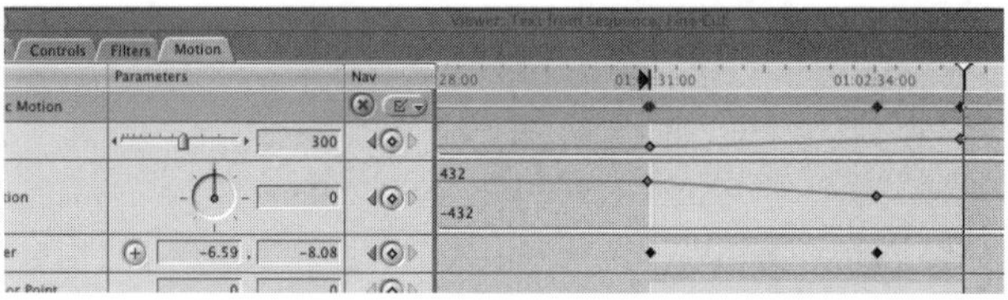

FIG. 12.17

COMPOSITING

As suggested, compositing is a close cousin to superimposition, although layering may be a better term. In its simplest form, it is a great way to throw animated titles over image. In its most complicated form, it can layer and interrelate immensely complex imagery on the order of things seen in *The Lord of the Rings* trilogy, the *Matrix* series and a host of other recent offerings.

Creating dense and layered images is usually a matter of very careful planning on the set. It involves employing blue screen mattes or, more frequently these days, green screen mattes. These are used to "block out" certain areas of the image, which we will then lay other image over. Then the ability to build things digitally becomes paramount.

Again, the material for *Waiting Tables* does not really lend itself to any particular compositing. We include one example that suggests some of the power of compositing and gives a pretty good overview of Final Cut Pro's ability to create a wide variety of effects. The wall behind Fritz is by no means uniform but it is the only thing that has any consistent color and exposure elements. In a standard situation, a green or blue matte would cover the desired area. It is critical, and also very challenging, that the matte be lit evenly. If exposure is uneven, color will render differently. The goal is to isolate one color on the spectrum and uniformly eliminate it so something else can be laid in.

Open Fritz'z second-to-last shot in the Viewer. Compositing functions are found under the previously mentioned Modify>Composite Mode (see pages 149-50) or, more usefully, under Effects>Video Filters. Key and Matte are the two big ones in this latter menu and we are going to key out a specific color so Key>Color Key (see Figure 12.18). You will notice the Blue and Green Screen Option above. The Color Key controls open in the Filters Tab. Click on it and drag it over the Browser. Click on the Video tab so we see the clip (see Figure 12.19).

FIG. 12.18

We want to sample a color that we are then going to isolate. To do this we use the eyedropper in the color panel (see Figure 12.20).

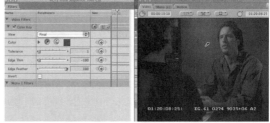

FIG. 12.19

FIG. 12.20

Take the eyedropper and put it at a place that makes sense — we are

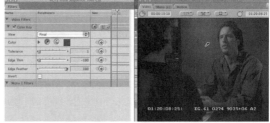

FIG. 12.21

trying to pick a point halfway between the lightest and darkest shades (see Figure 12.21).

With the eyedropper we have chosen the color of one pixel that we can key out. Whatever is at that same color will also be keyed out. In a blue or green screen, the object is to be able to key everything at that one color out. Here, there is a very narrow limit to what is exactly the same shade. To broaden this, we need to include pixels with similar color qualities. The Tolerance slider brings in an increasing amount of information with adjacent chrominance characteristics. As we slide it to the right, more and more of the checkerboard will start to appear (see Figure 12.22). Eventually we will start to spill over into Fritz's face. However, both Edge Thin and, particularly, Edge Feather will reduce the impact of information at the edge of the color's tolerance. Between these three, we can maximize the area on the wall through which lower levels will be visible. We can put this clip on V2 and anything below will show through the transparent checkerboard areas. We threw an outdoors scene on V1 and got the following result (see Figure 12.24).

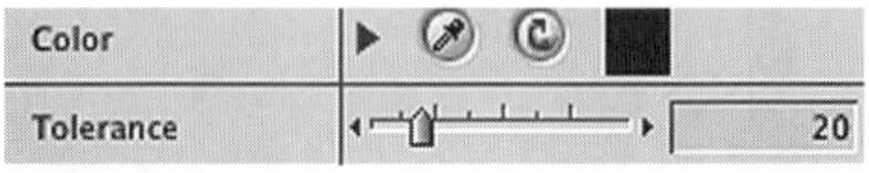

FIG. 12.22

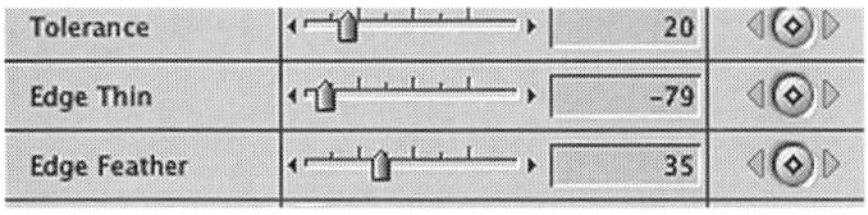

FIG. 12.23

FIG. 12.24

FIG. 12.25

One very useful feature is accessed right above the colors panel. It defaults to Final which displays the final image in the Canvas, but if you click on it, a drop-down menu appears. Slide down to Source, Matte, Final and the Viewer and Canvas break into quadrants that display all the elements of your composite (see Figure 12.25, Folio page 6). As with so many other things, you could animate this effect as well in the Timeline hidden to the right side.

This example underscores the limitations of working with a source area that is not uniformly lighted. If you notice, we pick up a little of the color in Fritz's hands and even can pick out a little of the detail in the hidden shot. Color should be consistent in order to effectively key an area out. The crop tool can be used to isolate areas, so there are a few other options.

Clearly, the film world is in love with compositing. You can now do things that were undreamed of before. The whole *Lord of the Rings* trilogy would be unthinkable without this incredible technology. As popular as it is, I have potential students who want to learn compositing before they learn how to make a film. Get the basics down before you put your man on the moon.

FINISHING IN FINAL CUT PRO

Essentially three things have to happen to finish a piece from FCP. First you need to mix down all the audio to finished tracks (you don't have to but you should). Then you probably want to do anything from some very modest to extensive color correction (again, you don't have to but you should). Then you have to output it to tape or DVD (this you do have to do, unless you have made it just for your own viewing pleasure).

AUDIO

The audio will generally require extensive work before the best possible track can be achieved. FCP not only has a very useful mixer, which is new to version 4, but there are extensive signal processing capabilities that allow us to change and clean up our tracks.

THE MIXER

The mixer is found at Tools>Mixer in the menus (see Figure 13.1). This allows you to go through and set and eventually finalize all levels, as well as assists you in analyzing the consistency and character of the tracks. When you open the mixer, it will display the number of tracks you have built for FCP. At this point, we were employing six tracks to facilitate some of the things we were doing. A1 is on the first channel and all tracks have a fader assigned to them as well as meters to monitor the volume of the sound. These latter function in the same way as the general audio meter. Above that are sliders for panning from left to right channels and the familiar mute/solo buttons. The top buttons on the right are a

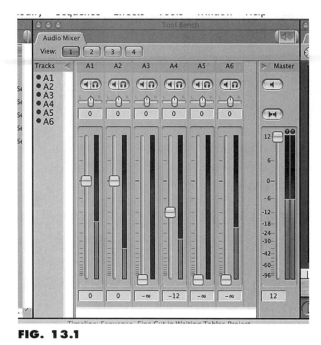

FIG. 13.1

Master mute and a Downmix button, a function that puts broad volume control on everything. The master meter is below these.

When you open the Mixer, the faders will be up on the tracks that are being used wherever the play-head is parked and they will indicate the volume levels at that point. At the point represented in the figure, there is an overlap on the two dialogue tracks with the phone on the fourth fader. The numerical level in dBs is displayed on a scale on the master as well as a number in a window at the bottom of each fader. 0 means that we have not done anything to that clip's audio, either here or with the clip overlays. The –12 on the phone means that we dragged the clip overlay line to that level, harking back to something we did in Chapter VIII. Minus infinity, a strange concept, means that there is no audio at that point or we have dragged it to the bottom. If you hit play, the fader levels will shift, as if by an unseen hand, to the levels we set in the Timeline.

One of the nicest features on the mixer is the ability to shift volume from here in real time. To do this, we use the **Record Audio Keyframes (A)** function in the upper right hand corner of the window. Click on it and it will turn green. In that mode, FCP will record whatever fader shifts you make as a track plays in real time. When you stop, the red clip overlay line will show the variations and keyframes will be inserted wherever you shifted the fader.

As an example, the volume of Fritz's line had caught our sound guy a little off-guard at the beginning of 4B-2 at TL-TC/1:27:25. We want to cushion it

FIG. 13.2

a little bit, but I want the ambience to match with the previous clip (we will deal with the gap momentarily). I want to dip the volume just as he is starting to speak and then bring it back for the rest of the delivery. I executed a quick few dB fade down and then fade back up in real time and made the change (see Figure 13.2).

USING HANDLES

How and why to create handles was covered in chapters V and VIII. Now is the time to put them to use. Again, we create them to cushion or finesse the sound from clip to clip. The goal is to make the sound consistent from one clip to the next. Again, in a professional situation, there is a member of the editorial team whose sole job is this — the dialogue editor. Open Sequence, Fine Cut. The cut between 1A-4 and 2A-4 was our previous example and can serve here as well. The big arbiter here is your ear, but essentially we want to just create a cross fade on the overlapped part. To do this, we put a keyframe in 1A-4 where the overlap with 2A-4 starts and one at the end. Click on this last keyframe and drag it all the way to the bottom. Put a keyframe in 2A-4 at the beginning of the clip and then where the overlap with 1A-4 ends. Drag the first keyframe to the bottom (see Figure 13.3). The key is to listen to this and check consistency with your hopefully sensitized ears. This is where having good speakers is particularly critical. If it sounds consistent, you should be good although this is where having professionally trained ears is best. Mixing equalization into this may produce an even better match.

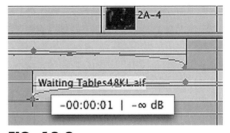

FIG. 13.3

FILLING AMBIENCE HOLES

Gaps in ambience are quite common. Directors occasionally speak during takes (though obviously never over an actor's line readings), editors extend actor's pauses, and excessive unwanted ambience may require trimming close to lines. Before investing extensive time filling them, be sure you have thought out future track plans. If the film is going to have music or some loud underlying effect, it may cover any problems. However, you still want the track to be reasonably consistent, so you should address all problems. Keep in mind that the sound mixer record-ed an ambience track — labeled as Room Tone in the Audio Bin. We open this clip from the Browser, Mark In and Out on a small section of it, and Overwrite edit it on A3 across from the gap (see Figure 13.4). A3 is a dia-logue track so we will later move the ambience piece elsewhere.

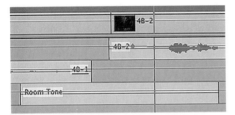

FIG. 13.4

We listen to this and it is quickly evident that this ambience does not match. There was a refrigera-tor or something on during these takes that renders the room tone unsuitable. This is not uncom-mon when recording on location where you cannot control every-thing. So what do we do? First, Undo. The simple solution is to find a quiet section of one of the actual takes and "steal" some ambience. There is in fact a quiet section in the preceding take in the Timeline. Re-open just the audio section from the Audio Bin (4A-1a) in the Browser. Find the quiet part and cut it out. Overwrite edit again. This is much better although the exit out of the ambience is audible. Do a quick fade-out and you are set to go (see Figure 13.5). Every cut in the piece may require the kind of attention described here and in the previous section.

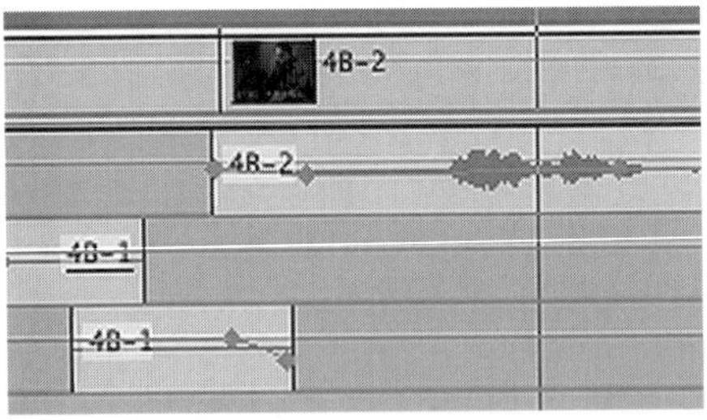

FIG. 13.5

SIGNAL PROCESSING

Signal processing is an umbrella term for a wide variety of audio manip-ulations, ranging from using **equalization** for changing the character of sound or eliminating unwanted elements to altering the sound for expressive effect with reverb, echo, and the like. The biggest arena is equalization. An equalizer — FCP has a number of them — is used to manipulate the volume at a chosen frequency. At a professional mix, a truly skilled mixer will be able to bring tremendous resources to bear on cleaning up and sweetening your tracks. There are arguments as to whether you can "improve" sound, but you can certainly make positive changes, increase consistency, and get rid of problematic ambience. Almost all audio, even if virtually perfectly recorded, gets some processing at a professional mix.

The range of sound is represented by frequencies in **Hertz** (Hz). Low frequencies are low sounds — everything from about 50 to 200 Hz. Middle C is 260 Hz. High sounds can range up around 2500 Hz, give or take a few hundred. An equalizer can isolate at specific frequencies and can raise or lower the volume at that specific frequency. The highest-end equalizers can isolate at many points along the range — called bands — and thus make very tight discriminations in eliminating or increasing specific elements.

There are quite a few sound manipulation tools in FCP at Effects>Audio Filters (AF). Handled in the same way as the Video Filters, the Audio Filters are divided into Apple and Final Cut Pro filters, the former imported from Quicktime and the latter designed specifically for FCP. Each has a wide variety of possibilities (see Figure 13.6) although those looking for a conventional multiple-band equalizer will be disappointed. There is a three-band equalizer, but its discriminations are so broad as to be almost useless. The Apple and Final Cut Pro menus give you a kind of laundry list approach to signal processing. If you can't make something do what you want, you can certainly find something else that

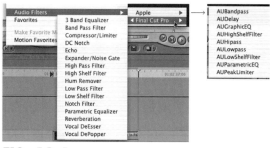

FIG. 13.6

will. All the functions are spread through options that control low, mid, and high frequencies.

We could try to eliminate the refrigerator motor sound from the audio in 4B-1. If we can get it, we can apply it to the other pieces that are similarly affected. Double-click on the audio for 4B-1. I have found the Parametric Equalizer in the Final Cut Pro menu to be a particularly good tool. Select it. It will come up in the Filters menu in the Viewer. Click on the tab and drag it over the Browser. The waveform in the Viewer will have the red clip overlay line on it. This can also be raised in the Viewer and we want the effect to be as loud as it can be so we can make changes. Drag the red

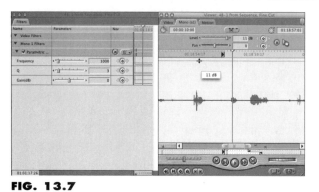

FIG. 13.7

line to the top of the window (see Figure 13.7). The parametric equalizer opens to sounds at 1000 Hz and defaults to 3 Q and 0 gain. Q widens or narrows the affected frequencies and Gain is volume level (13.7). We can use the Frequency slider to select the Hz at which we want to equalize. This kind of sound — a refrigerator hum — is usually somewhere around 200 Hz, so set accordingly. Then, experiment — effects apply as you make changes. The trick is to eliminate sounds without drastically changing the quality of the voices. I can certainly get rid of that hum, but the voices may sound completely different from surrounding takes. This is again where an experienced mixer can be an invaluable resource.

I find that if I set Q to 7 and Gain to −19, I get rid of most of the hum and the voices still sound good (see Figure 13.8). I am left with a certain nervousness, though, that I have overdone it. It sounds okay to my ear, which is the final arbiter, but there are better, more experienced ears out there than mine. As Ayn Rand is often quoted, "Taste is subjective, but great taste is not." I know many people who could tell immediately if the sound changes were problematic. The major question is how it will sound in other venues, a theater, a cheap, tinny TV speaker, et cetera. Experience is the key here.

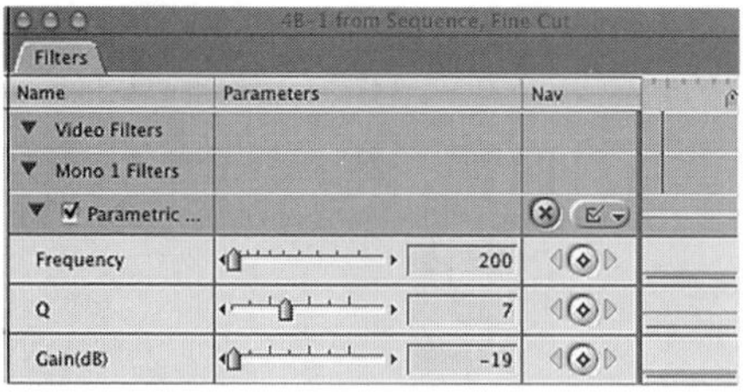

FIG. 13.8

Filters accumulate. If we select Parametric Equalizer again, a new panel will appear and we can select a different frequency to equalize. So experiment with all the different possibilities. Remember, there is a Timeline to the right of all these tabs and all effects can be plotted out in time.

FINAL MIX

There is not actually a final mix like there used to be in the old days. You have created all the information for the soundtrack while cutting handles, doing volume control, and plotting out equalization. Now it just needs to be written to a file. Your Timeline will always play the tracks, but you should write this final file. Time always does funny things to media. Create this final file and you can always go back to it. Keep a version with the original tracks and you can always change that, and then go back and re-write the file.

You can create this file at File>Export>Audio to AIFF (see Figure 13.9). The Save window will come up and you can name it and give it a destination.

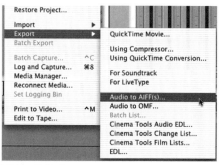

To apply it to your piece, I would duplicate the sequence from which you made the AIFF file. Strip all the audio off this

FIG. 13.9

new sequence — the Track Forward Tool is handy for this. Import the new file you just made and Overwrite it in the audio tracks. Line it up with your picture (see Chapter XVI for creating start marks).

THE COLORIST

The rationale for color correction is simply that individual clips can benefit from adjustments in their color and/or exposure. A number of functions in FCP provide extensive control over the picture we have already shot. This control can occur at many different stages in post-production although, generally, the most significant manipulation is usually saved for the final stages.

There are essentially three reasons to color correct. One is to correct a problem that occurred during shooting. Another, and this is probably most common, is to just give a shot that something "extra," bring a dimension to the image that you simply could not achieve during shooting. The last is to manipulate the image to create a "look" that is desired by the production team. Sometimes the first creates the need for one or the other of the last two. Mistakes when originating on video can range from forgetting to white balance, to misreading a small LED screen, to just having elements that you cannot control in shooting. Originating on film is a little more tricky. Elements require more control and mistakes often do not show until the processed film arrives back from the lab. An experienced DP should not make big errors, but a little sweetening can often add a new dimension to even the best-shot image. Be aware, however, that excessive manipulation can destroy an image's integrity as well.

We should not plan on color control as a cover-up for bad shooting, while still understanding that we do have some level of post-production control. Too frequently on a set, you overhear someone saying that they will have something "fixed" in telecine or color correction or somewhere else down the line. There is a certain air of defeatism to this attitude that suggests we have just not prepared ourselves well and exerted enough control to get the image that we want. When a colorist has to make extensive repairs to an image, it limits what other qualities he or she may be able to bring to it. Still, given limited budgets and tight time constraints, there are things that are unavoidable and you can come to depend on some level of assistance at this stage. Depend but don't become dependent.

From very near its beginnings, film has had a wide range of post-production exposure and, eventually, color controls. In the early days of video recording, there were very limited controls over the image. The early video world had very crude gain controls — allowing only the lightening and darkening of the analog image. In the mid-1970s, we started to see more sophisticated control over both color and brightness, but only within the highest end of the market, with what was called a Time Base Corrector. Correction in an analog environment was particularly difficult because of generation loss. The development of digital equipment was able to turn the modest advances in analog correction into a very sophisticated science. As capabilities grew, the role of the person running the gear evolved from being a technician who knew the dials to a skilled artisan who became called the **video colorist**.

Being a good video colorist requires both an extensive knowledge of the technical parameters of analog and digital video and a great eye for the beauty and character of color — the aesthetic nature of color. One with only the former skills can only set up and calibrate equipment — an ability by no means to be underrated. A person without the latter skills cannot guarantee that your final product is going to look as good as it can and, in particular, be visually consistent. The technology for color correction has developed to the extent that you can walk in with a product looking one way and make it look completely different.

In the most common approach, color correction is about achieving natural color — normal skin tones, appropriate sky coloration, believable fabric colors, uncolored shadow areas, and the like. However, recent trends have been to use color correction to create a highly manipulated and expressive image. The commercial world formerly ran almost exclusively on reproducing a standard representation of the real world. Now commercials have become as, if not more, expressionistic than the most atmospheric dramatic pieces.

With all this potential for control, the beginner should venture forth with the knowledge that this is another one of those "just because you can do it does not mean you can do it" things. You can make a terrible mess of things. The goal in most pieces is to create a consistent visual style — correction that finds continuity between images. Just like sound, color and exposure will come in all over the map if you are careless. You can get each shot in a sequence looking great individually — or sell yourself on the idea that they look great — and then find that they look like they were not just shot in different spaces but on different planets. To further complicate matters, excessive or uninformed color correction can take you out of the norms for a broadcast-quality signal.

Achieving quality and consistent color correction requires understanding some of the issues discussed in Chapter IX: compression, sampling, composite vs. component, and the like. To get an initial grasp on the parameters on control, a return to **luminance** and **chrominance** is the starting point. Again, luminance is brightness and by extension detail and chrominance is color. On a color corrector, chrominance is manipulated either partially or completely by **hue** and **saturation** controls. Hue is the actual color and saturation is the amount — the volume or percentage —

of the color of any given shade: 100% of red is red, 25% of red is pink, 50% green and 50% red is yellow, and so on.

THE VIDEO SCOPES

The major tools a colorist uses to analyze the video signal and maintain consistency are the **waveform monitor** (which monitors luminance) and the **vectorscope** (which monitors chrominance). These were both newly supplied with FCP 3 and refined with FCP 4, advancing the software's color control capabilities dramatically over a short period. A primary purpose of these two is to allow you to keep the signal within a broadcast safe range. They are also equally important for maintaining consistent tonality and color from shot to shot. These are available in the

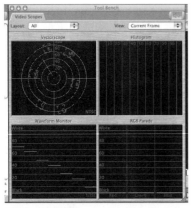

FIG. 13.10

menus at Tools>Video Scopes. Open it and the Video Scopes tab will appear with the **Histogram** and the **RGB Parade** on the right (see Figure 13.10). The Histogram and the Parade monitor are also valuable, being alternative displays of luminance and chrominance respectively. On the right, there is a pop-up menu that determines what the monitors are analyzing, the image in the Viewer or the Canvas. Set it to Viewer for our examples. The left hand pop-up menu allows you to choose

what scope configuration you have up on the tab. The scopes are analyzing the image where the playhead is parked.

The waveform monitor gives a visual representation of the progression of light to dark elements in the image. Measured in IRE (Institute of Radio Engineers), it grades the blacks at the bottom and the whites at the top. 7.5 IRE is considered true black in the US, although other countries often use a different black standard. The top of the scale is white. All these scopes read the image left to right.

The standard approach is to get good rich blacks and good rich whites. As you correct, the scope will interpret the quality of your black and white elements, as well as everything in between. If you brighten the image, you may move everything out of the blacks, thus never achieving a true black. The same applies with white in shifting darker. This is not necessarily a bad thing; given that for expressive reasons you may want to have a slight fog level in your blacks or some shift in your white. Maintaining consistency and keeping within broadcast tolerances is the issue. If you raise the black level of a clip, you should do the same to the other clips to remain consistent within a scene.

The vectorscope measures hue and color saturation. The little peg coming up at about ten o'clock from the middle is often called the "flesh tone line." Hue adjusts the information around this line. For standard representation of Caucasian flesh tones, all information should be consistent along the line or just slightly to one side or the other. In this diverse age, one would think some other approaches would have come to the fore.

The RGB Parade is a kind of waveform monitor that gives us separate representations of each primary color. If we take the MS shot of Fritz (4C), we see that shot is very heavily weighted to the red, but they are the darker reds (see Figure 13.11).

On the waveform monitor, the black of Judy's shirt is very heavily represented on the left. As we travel right, we see the brighter elements of the image shooting up a little in the middle with the spike of Fritz's face just to the right. There are really no white elements in the frame so we see nothing anywhere at the top. The RGB Parade is very helpful. As

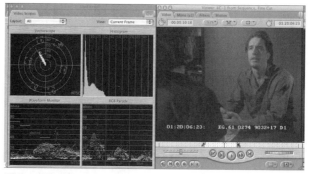

FIG. 13.11

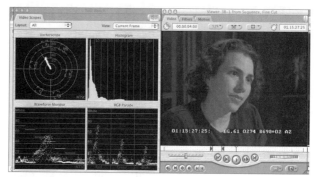

FIG. 13.12

we look at it, we will see that the image is very dominated by reds — reds to the darker end. The green is a little more present, because there are some yellow aspects to the shot. There is very minimal blue in the shot.

Judy's close-up is of interest as well (see Figure 13.12). On the waveform monitor again, the black of Judy's shirt is very heavily represented on the left, with it also showing up on the right as well along with some dark background elements. The image is more dominated by flesh tones because she is brighter and it is a close-up. We see the peak in the middle although there are still no white elements in the image. In the RGB Parade, we see the same dominance of red but it is a much lighter red. The same occurs with green and blue.

COLOR CORRECTION

There are two main color correction tools, both found at Effects>Video Filters>Color Correction: the Color Corrector and Color Corrector 3-way. These can both also be found in the Effects tab in the Browser (there is another useful corrector at Quicktime>). The Color Corrector is used for general changes (see Figure 13.13). It just has two color wheels (see page 129 for a discussion of color wheels), one for Balance and one for Hue. The sliders at the bottom control saturation. The bottom one controls overall saturation and the other three control luminance at their stated tones. The other elements are also found on the next corrector and will be covered there. The discriminations on the Color Corrector are fairly shallow, although a simple tool is often just the right thing for a simple job.

FIG. 13.13

The other is the Color Corrector 3-Way, which is a much more sophisticated instrument (see Figure 13.14). The Color Corrector 3-way allows control of tonality at all colors and shades. As with the first one, the slider on the bottom controls overall saturation — it can take the image from black-and-white to deeply saturated. The sliders under each color wheel allow you to control luminance in the high-tones (the whites and light grays), the mid-tones (medium gray and adjacent shades) and the blacks

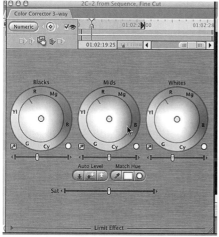

FIG. 13.14

and dark grays respectively. Each wheel allows you to control color in that tone range.

As with everything like this, the Color Corrector 3-way opens as a tab in the background of the Viewer. Drag the tab over to cover the Browser, so you can see it and the Viewer at the same time. To look at what the wheels can do, park the playhead on a clip and open it in the Viewer. A render bar will appear above the clip in the Timeline, the shade as always dependent on your processor. Just for argument's sake, let's open the Video Scopes and drag them over the Canvas.

The sliders are reasonably self-explanatory and just require experimentation. The white circle in the center of each color wheel is called the color indicator. It defaults to white in the center and can be dragged toward the desired color, with the image reflecting the change. Be aware that it drags very slowly. If you drag while depressing Command, it will speed it up a little. The white circle to the lower right of each wheel will jump the color indicator back to the center, while eliminating the change(s) in the image. Pressing the Shift key while dragging will make the color indicator's drag trajectory straight toward the outside or inside of the circle.

Most colorists suggest you get the luminance correct first and then work on the color. Keeping blacks at the right place on the waveform monitor (7.5 IRE) is an important goal to keep in mind when correcting for a realistic image. It can be instructive to take an image "out-of-whack" to see how its properties change in these regards. What happens if we take the just-used close-up of Judy and simply slide the luminance fader up a little for the blacks — the fader under the left-hand wheel (see Figure 13.15, Folio page 7)? You will see the blacks of her shirt as well as everything in the background move up into the grays. Look what it has done to the Video Scopes particularly in comparison with Figure 13.11. The black levels have all moved up into the 40% level and nowhere in the image are we achieving a true black. If we slide the blacks down, we will do what is called "crushing" the blacks — moving too much out of the black range.

255

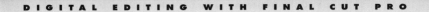

FIG. 13.15

FIG. 13.16

Color shifts do the same (see Figure 13.16, Folio page 7). If we drag the mids toward the blue in Fritz's shot, we reduce the red component and increase the blue on both the waveform monitor and the RGB Parade. Notice the effect on the information around the flesh tone line.

The typical workflow is to do moderate correction early in initial transfers and then save the extensive work for when you can see the shots side-by-side in their final order. A typical workflow for an episodic TV show would be to do a high-resolution transfer from the film, with as much color correction as makes sense. Transfer would be to DigiBeta or, as is becoming the norm, to an HDTV format (D5 is typical). Low-resolution transfer tapes are turned over to the editors for cutting. When finished, EDLs from the low-res edit rebuild the show from the original transfers and then extensive color correction is applied.

Again, a render bar will appear above the shot in the Timeline when you open a clip with the Color Corrector 3-way. It is frequently red and color correction requires a lot of real estate for the render files. Management of this can be a big issue as it uses up free space very rapidly. Be aware that if you max out a computer, it makes Final Cut Pro very unstable. The program may start dropping frames and develop a host of playback problems.

One of the first major projects that I did in FCP was a documentary on the installation of a new president at a local college. The man was African American and, as is so often the case, the already atrocious lighting did a particularly inadequate job on him, particularly given the automatic exposure choice of the video cameras used by inexperienced camera operators. We had three different camera angles on him and he was on camera for over twenty minutes. In this instance, I was going to be cutting from the three angles and mixing in audience cutaways as well. If I corrected late in the process, I would have had to go in and correct every short piece in the final edit. I corrected all three shots in their entirety before the edit and saved a lot of work. Keep in mind that all this needed to be rendered so I had both the time and storage space of 60 minutes of rendered footage to contend with.

By the same token, however, you may not want to dedicate the extra space on the hard drive for color correcting material you will not use.

One other nice feature of both color correctors is that the changes can be applied to other shots either upstream or downstream. This feature is in the upper lefthand corner (see Figure 13.17) in the Copy Filters Control.

FIG. 13.17

On the left, you can copy and apply the color correction information from a clip two ahead of the clip you presently have open in the Viewer — great for simple shot/reverse shot shooting. The next is copy to the clip one ahead. The middle one allows you to drag the filter information to any clip in the Timeline. The next allows you to copy the information to the clip in the Timeline just after the one you are working on in the Viewer and the final jumps two after.

Above this are some other useful features (see Figure 13.18). The square with the X allows you to toggle back and forth between what you have applied and the original, presum-

FIG. 13.18

ably uncorrected image. Numeric will open panels that have recorded what filter values you have created for a specific clip. Hit Visual on this tab and it opens the Color Corrector 3-way that you created for the clip. One critical aspect of color correction is keeping track of what corrections have been applied, both in terms of applying the change to other shots and knowing what you have done in case you want to do some more.

The color corrector 3-way tab also has a number of white balance and automatic balance features. The eyedropper is used to balance for white. These are set to norms that may or may not be right for your shot. Still, they can be very handy in some instances.

REMEMBER:

The playhead must be in the clip!	GET THE LUMINANCE FIRST.
Hue is in the Wheels.	Be careful with color. You can sell
Luminance is in the three sliders.	yourself a bill of goods and really
Saturation is down below.	overdo it.

BLACK AND WHITE

This is not really a finishing thing but it fits in with color correction issues. Removing the color from a shot is a goal one hears with some frequency. There are a number of ways of doing this. One is with the desaturate sliders in color correction. The quick way is at Effects>Video Filters>Image Control>Desaturate. It will probably need to be rendered. It is a good idea to duplicate the clip from which you want to remove the color, so you have easy access to a color version if you need it down the road.

PRINT TO VIDEO

Outputting to video is relatively straightforward, although there can be pitfalls. I have found that just making sure your EVD is on before launching FCP, hitting record on it, and hitting play in FCP gives a good transfer. The more usual approach is to use Print to Video in the File menu. This gives you access to leaders and a number of other things that will streamline your show. Select Print to Video and its own window will come up (see Figure 13.19). You can put on color bars and a countdown leader, as well as create a text slate where you can put down particulars of production company, producer, et cetera.

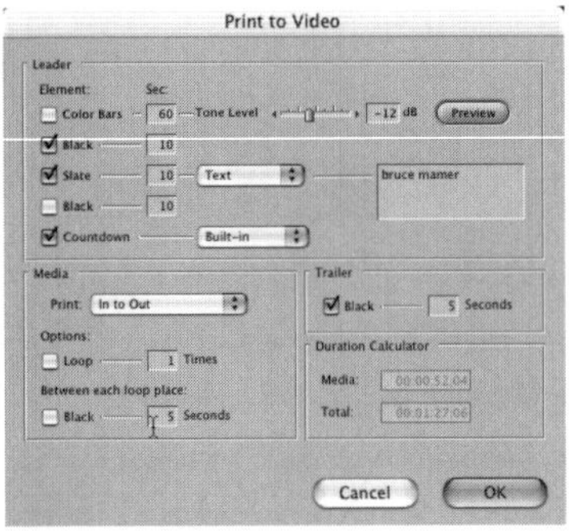

FIG. 13.19

Possibly the most significant thing is that Print to Video will also "focus" all your computer's and FCP's resources on playing back your show. In a complex show, how much this adds to presentation will always be a matter of speculation.

Dropping frames is one of your main enemies. Having everything properly rendered is equally important. Play your show with some frequency to see if any playback problems are developing. Obviously, getting a good quality product out is one of the foremost goals. Track any problems you are having and address them to the best of your ability — having credible outside advice is critical.

FILM MATCHBACK

F ilm matchback is the process of shooting on motion picture film, transferring to video, editing in an NLE environment, and then returning to your motion picture film negative. Most frequently, this is done in order to create a final product — a film print — which can be projected in a theater. Cinema Tools is FCP's matchback program. It used to be sold as an additional product with earlier versions but, with the introduction of FCP 4, it is now sold as a bundled part of the general package. There are a number of other NLE programs that have a matchback component, most notably Avid Film Composer which has been an industry standard for years. Cinema Tools is new enough that it has not yet gained the wide acceptance of Film Composer, but at a fraction of the cost it may catch up soon. Express DV, Avid's new pricepoint competitor to FCP, has a matchback component that will ratchet the competition up a notch.

The process of matchback depends on establishing a precise relationship between your video edit and the film that you shot on location. You must be able to find the exact pieces of film that correspond to the video clips you have edited into your Timeline. While this may not at first appear to be that challenging an issue, it requires fastidious preparation and pinpoint execution. You would think that you could just go back and find the appropriate frames but, within the great crush of thousands of frames, it is from very difficult to impossible to distinguish one frame from another. A two-hour film contains approximately 160,000 individual frames. Try sorting through that dustbin. Without the capability to identify exact frames, the whole thing would become an absolute train wreck. Fortunately, Final Cut Pro has Cinema Tools.

FIG. 14.1

As we have seen, any Timeline edit will produce an EDL consisting of time code numbers representing the beginning and ending frames of every clip. Those time code numbers must be translated into information that facilitates cutting the film negative. The bottom line is that when you use a shot in your video edit, you need to return to your film, find exactly the same beginning and ending frames, and pull the entire exact shot. If you make a mistake and pull even a slightly different piece, it will not correspond to the piece of sound you have used. Worse yet, and this would be a cataclysmic mistake, if the piece you pull is longer or shorter it will throw the entire project out of sync.

Time code produces what we have referred to as a "permanent address" for every frame in video. In order to interrelate video with film, we clearly require a permanent address for every frame of film. This is provided by a system of latent numbers that are called either edge numbers or key numbers. Embedded by the manufacturer and made visible when processed, these are a set of ascending numbers that are positioned along the edge of the film. In 16mm they occur every 20 frames — every six inches (see Figure 14.1). In 35mm they occur ever 16 frames (every foot). On the film, there are actually three sets of numbers and letters. The first set, EG61 (see Figure 14.2), refers to batch numbers and dates produced. The small dot above the E means this is the zero frame, the one from which we do all counting. The second set refers to rolls within a batch and the third set is the ascending numbers. The last four numbers here are 8706. 20 frames down the road will be 8707, and so forth. The numbers are also bar-coded on the film by the manufacturer. This is for the

FIG. 14.2

telecine to read in order to create transfer and matchback information.

In sum, your video edit must produce the information to go back and cut your negative. There must be communication between the time code that has driven your video edit and the edge numbers. Reconciling the two, again, is not at all simple. The chief bad actors here are frame rate conversions and synchronization of sound. Film is shot at 24 frames a second and video is shot at 30 (actually 29.97). If you shoot on film and transfer to video, a conversion is required between the two different frame rates. The solution is to introduce what is called 3:2 pulldown (see next section for complete details). This entails the production of extra video frames that do not correspond to actual film frames — a necessary solution that leads to predictable problems. In addition, both the difference between the fractional video rate of 29.97 and the whole number rate of film and the necessity to be so precise in pulling pieces make synchronization of sound and image an issue of equal magnitude.

Assuming there are readers with no experience in the process, you would be poorly advised to try this completely on your own. If you make any missteps in transferring and inputting information, and there are many complex steps, you may have to go back and start over when you find your mistake. Or, worst-case scenario, you may miss your mistake and cut your negative incorrectly. Calamity, thy name is a botched negative cut. At any cost, enlist someone who knows what they are doing.

Major recommendation: MAKE A SHORT FILM. Do a conventional film edit on it; cut on a flatbed editing table; cut mag stock; go all the way through the process; finish it on film. You must understand the film process to understand matchback. Any attempt you make at matchback without a clear understanding of how a conventional film edit works is doomed to failure. As I write these chapters, I feel a slight twinge of guilt (very slight, mind you), in that you will not learn matchback simply from reading this book. You must learn it from practice, with which this book can be an invaluable aid (that is where the guilt goes away). If you were to try to do something as ambitious as a feature without attempting some small "dry runs," you will spend more money fixing your mistakes than shooting some tests will cost. Do a scene like *WT*, make matchback work with it, and then shoot your bigger project.

WHY FILM?

Shooting on film is the domain of feature films, episodic television programs, music videos, and commercials (see sidebar #1). Pretty much everything else is shot on video. Clearly, there are video incursions into the four categories. A significant number of features have been successfully shot on video. Some episodic TV has gone to 24p (see sidebar #2). MTV, bless them for this at least, will not accept anything that does not originate on film except from a few established artists. But the majority of commercial projects are still shot on film, for reasons of image quality, projectability (if we can coin a term), archival storage, and simple "if it ain't broke don't fix it."

> **Specialty uses persist as well. NASA shoots millions of feet of film a year and NFL Films is not far behind.**

Matchback really only pertains to the worlds of feature films and, to a substantially lesser degree, episodic television. Music videos and commercials only require a video as the final product (see sidebar). The only place that film prints are required is if you want to project in a theater (feature or festival films) or if you need it for archival or duplication purposes. Many episodic television shows keep track of the matchback information, mostly for archival (that is, syndication) purposes. Recognizing the possibility that they might need film prints somewhere down the road, they are just hedging their bets by keeping their options open.

> While this information may have limited application, the September 2003 issue of *The Hollywood Reporter* stated that of the 96 new "scripted" episodic TV programs, 60 originated on film and 36 originated on video. Interestingly, of the 36 that originated on video, 35 were comedies and one was a drama. Film origination was used for 48 dramas and 12 comedies. The "reality" programs are all, of course, shot on video.

Once we get into matchback, we bring up the whole question (debate?) of whether to originate on film or not. While this discussion may be beyond the scope of this text, there are a number of points that should be made.

Why would we want to shoot on film? Well, the clearest reason is because we want to end up on film — that is, have a motion picture print that we can project in a theater. The truth is that your neighborhood movie theater, for the time being and at least the moderately foreseeable future, is still projecting motion picture film on a reflecting screen. The bottom line is that if you want to wind up on film, you probably want to shoot on film. If you post solely on video, what is your final product when you are done? A video. A video is great if you are headed for a cable or network showing, but if you want to show in a theater, you have a potentially insurmountable problem.

One wild card in all this is that you can create a film print from videotape. But, unless you are George Lucas or Lars von Trier, going into a project with this as a vague goal in mind is tantamount to artistic and economic suicide. An indifferent transfer of a feature from video to film is about $35,000, and prices escalate dramatically to attain quality. And unless you had a top DP, your picture may (will) look dreadful. Now a few films have survived lesser visuals to be moderately successful; *Chuck and Buck* and *Full Frontal* come to mind. And one, *The Blair Witch Project*, was a huge success. But the list about stops there. We can whine and cry about audiences being conditioned to the slick Hollywood look, but reality is reality. You cannot buck the fact that films without strong visuals, or at least credible visuals, face an uphill battle at best.

To go into a project with the ill-defined notion that you are going to interest someone in transferring your video to film borders on the nutty (of course, sometimes a little nuttiness is a prerequisite for a vision). You are not going to interest anyone in seeing your video because nobody saw your video in the first place, because it is not on film. With extremely limited exceptions, distributors only pick up films because they have somewhere excited an audience. The chances of you exciting an audience with a videotape in hand is limited. Not that it has not happened, but Robert Rodriguez did it with *El Mariachi* (1992), but he had film originals to go back to.

Image quality is the other issue. The bottom line is that for a whole lot of applications, digital video is simply not there yet. I cannot tell you how many times I have seen THE comparison — two monitors, side-by side, showing the identical shots, one originating on film and the other originating on the latest high-end video camera. I can usually barely tell the difference — it can be quite difficult. Both look great. But the comparison is on video monitors. The question is: What does it look like on the screen?

If you have a lot of resources, you can make digital video look almost like film transferred to video. But if it takes so many resources, why not shoot on film? Price, you say. But it is the resources that are most expensive. The bottom line is video simply does not have the warmth and depth of film. Of course someone will ask: What if my project does not really need warmth and depth? This is the real question. Effects-heavy movies like *Star Wars — Attack of the Clones*, action films like Robert Rodriguez' *Once Upon a Time in Mexico*, or any of the *Terminator* films have enough of a fantasy element that the image can survive if not benefit from the look of material originating on video. But, if aesthetically your project needs the look of film, film is the answer. Simply stated, one is not the other. One is not better than the other. They each have their applications and when you take into account both image quality and projection, if you need to originate and/or end on film, matchback is probably in your future.

"If it ain't broke" and archival issues are critical as well. To the former, the systems and equipment to shoot and handle 35mm in production and post-production have been in place and been refined for over one hundred years. All the support systems you could ever want are designed for it and are largely bulletproof — it simply works with minimal failure. 16mm is getting more use, but the systems of camera support, et cetera, are not as developed and widely available as they are in 35mm. On the other hand, Digital Video still has some question marks. The cameras are in place and working, but formats change or become obsolete very rapidly and the unstable nature of the electronic signal (dropout, degradation over time, signal path problems) can be problematic. When you have a roll of film in your hands, you have something that it will take either a fool or an act of God to destroy. The gremlins of the computer world can work their magic on a video project, unassisted. As to archival, the afterlife of media has become a significant profit center for production companies. As one producer said, "These are our assets and we must protect our product." Film is still the archival medium of choice, being that we can stick it in a climate-controlled vault and know that it will still be there in twenty or thirty years. Digital archiving will become more prevalent, but for now it is mostly film.

THE MATCHBACK PROCESS

One critical point first. Matchback must be anticipated from the very start of a project. You cannot shoot on film, post in NLE, and then decide on a whim that you want to do matchback after the editing is finished. The information must be encoded in your first film-to-video transfers, the databases must be created before editing is started, and they must be maintained throughout the editorial process. If you were to edit without using Cinema Tools and later decide you wanted to do matchback after you have a finished product, you would have to retransfer and essentially reconstruct the entire edit of the film. Basically you would have to start over from scratch. EDLs help, but it is still a lot of work and expense.

So, why do we need this dedicated piece of software? When you enter the shadowy world of film matchback, life gets very complicated. Again, it is mismatched frame rates and different sound speeds that can make life miserable. If you are a person who does not like to work to exacting standards, you may want to find someone who understands the process and "write big checks" to them. Don't find someone who says they understand it or who can "get hold of" someone who does. Find the person who understands it and can demonstrate that they have done it before — walked through the process step-by-step on preferably more than one occasion.

When you are working with film, you are working with the bright, shiny world of whole numbers, and even, as opposed to odd, whole numbers to boot. Many numbers are multiples and divisors of 24, the fps rate in film. When you move into the world of video, you are moving into the murky, shadowy world of fractions, and not even rational fractions. Video does not actually run at 29.97, it runs at 29.97002617…. It is not only not a rational number, it is what is called (hold your breath) a non-repeating, non-terminating decimal. If your final product is on video, you may not need to worry too much about these unending fractions. Unless your video gets into the precise timings of network broadcast, when you get into the ugly world of dropframe and nondropframe (G).

It seems like it should be simple. You transfer your film to video and capture it into your computer. You do all your editing until you have the project exactly the way you want it. At that point, all you need to do is figure out where your cuts are, go back to the film and make the same cut on film. Were life only that easy. Clearly, the industry has learned to work within this world, if not effortlessly then at least with a system that remains reasonably bulletproof. If you are an independent, you have to execute without that extended support system.

One of the worst mistakes is to embark on a project without sorting out all the options and understanding all the processes when you start. Matchback requires as extensive a knowledge of the film process as the video. To achieve some perspective on this, we need to step back and give some background on the nature of both film and video.

THE FILM PROCESS

The conventional film edit is, to a certain degree, a thing of the past. There are a few brave and stalwart holdouts who still cut their features on film, but the rest of the world has moved on to NLE. And matchback if necessary. Still, understanding how film and its attendant sound is cut is required if the matchback process is going to work. And indeed, if you want to originate and end up on film, there is still a very strong argument for cutting on film. But we won't go there.

Motion picture film is a succession of still images arranged vertically on a strip of celluloid, with sprocket holes arrayed down the edges. When these still images are projected in succession, they give the illusion of movement. For replication of natural movement, film is shot at 24 frames per second (fps). Slow motion is created by shooting more frames per second and fast motion by shooting fewer. The standard running speed on all projectors is 24 fps. The sprocket holes are what are employed to mechanically drive the film through both camera and projector. The sprocket holes are also employed as the defining measuring stick of footage, frames, and, by extension, time. Sound and picture are handled as separate entities in a conventional film edit, and correlating the lengths of each media is the key to maintaining sync between the two. In essence, the sprocket holes are to film as time code is to video. Well, not exactly, but you get the idea.

The actual film that runs through the camera while shooting is called the **original** (see sidebar). It is a precious commodity as it holds the key to all subsequent versions of the work. After shooting, the original is processed and then used to create a **workprint**, a frame-for-frame duplicate copy made by sandwiching the original with an unexposed roll of film and running it through a printer. All work of the editing room is done with these workprints. The original is treated as the fragile vessel it is. It is handled with great care and never projected or viewed in any other manner. It is certainly not cut, at least in initial stages, or otherwise handled. It exists almost solely as a printing medium and/or for transfer to video.

Most people are aware that film can be shot in either **negative**, in which all light areas are dark on the film and vice versa, or **reversal**, where what you see is what you get. Most commercial projects are shot on negative film, whether color or black and white. Reversal film has many shortcomings, the most problematic of which is that it does not print as well. With feature films opening in anywhere from a dozen to thousands of theaters nationally, having high-quality prints is critical.

With a few exceptions, telecine transfers are made directly from the negative with the image "reversed" in the electronics. Obviously with negative, a print or video transfer is necessary. The negative, by itself, is not a viewable entity. With negative being the industry standard, you tend to hear the word negative and original used synonymously. We will use the term negative but be aware that whatever passed through the camera on location, whether negative or reversal, is the original.

For a while, it was thought that transfer to video would eliminate the need for expensive workprints. Transfer from your negative to video, edit in NLE, produce a film cut list from your EDL, cut your negative and make a film print. But the feature world at least has found otherwise. The camera crews found that they needed the workprint to check their work, to get a clear handle on focus, lighting, and a host of other issues. The workprint was also needed for test screenings. It is hard to test screen from a video monitor. As we shall see, the people who cut the negative are also greatly aided by having a cut workprint as their guide. We strongly recommend that you make a workprint if you are going the matchback route. This will become clear, but the workprint exists as a way of checking if everything you are doing in NLE is working correctly. Without it, you can head into creating your final print with some fatally flawed information that will necessitate extensive and costly revisions.

FORMATS

There are two formats that remain in common use — 35mm and 16mm. 16mm has a variant called Super 16, which uses the image area differently to capture more information on the film. Many have heard of Super 8, an older amateur medium that gets occasional professional use, particularly in transfer to video. However, it cannot be employed if matchback is desired (no edge numbers).

35mm is an inch and three-eighths wide. It has a row of sprocket holes on each side and there are four sprocket holes per frame (although there is also a three hole process in increasing use). 35mm is the standard for most commercial production. It is also very expensive; about $50 a minute, bought, processed, and workprinted. Swap the last item out with video transfer and the price is about the same. Or do both and your costs just escalate.

16mm is about 3/4 of an inch wide and has one sprocket hole per frame. It can be bought either with sprocket holes on one side (**single perf** or **one row**) or on both sides (**double perf** or **two row**). Either can be used for general shooting, but single perf has to be used for Super 16. Costs are about $25 a minute, bought, processed, and workprinted. Neither the 35 or 16mm dollar figures include finishing costs.

Super 16 is used solely when the intent is to blow up to 35mm or transfer to HDTV, although its precise purpose is now somewhat up in the air. For years, the standard line was that if you are going to blow up to 35mm for theatrical release, shoot on Super 16. The reasoning was that 16mm had quite a bit of grain, a concept similar to pixels, and having the greater information of Super 16 reduced the graininess inherent in the blow-up process. But in the last few years, Kodak has produced 16mm film stocks that have drastically reduced grain. One school of thought says shoot on regular 16mm because the grain is not an issue and, if the situation warrants, you can always make a 16mm print of the film. A 16mm print can always be the source for blow-ups or transfers to NTSC or PAL. One more thing to sort out.

CUTTING SOUND AND IMAGE

In a conventional film edit, all sound is transferred to and edited on magnetic film stock, called **mag stock** or just **mag**. Mag stock has the same magnetic coating as a conventional audiotape, and is a sprocketed medium of the same size and dimension as the film stock (see Figure 14.3). It is cut with splicers just like the picture — all picture and sound is cut and spliced together with a **tape splicer** in this stage (see Figure 14.4). Mag stock is not widely used any longer, although it plays a significant role in the way the standard Hollywood feature is approaching matchback. Employing it in certain stages of your matchback project may also be advisable. More later.

FIG. 14.3

As stated, sound and picture are recorded separately during filming. The camera obviously records the picture. The sound must be recorded on a digital recorder or a conventional recorder that can be speed-controlled. Synchronization of sound and picture is the issue. Camera and recorder need to run at controllable speeds

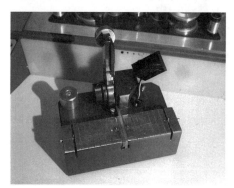

FIG. 14.4

because if speeds vary, as they do on analog consumer and non-specifically designed equipment, there is no way that the two media can run together at the same speed. Thus, they would not have the ability to be synced. By definition, digital recorders — often a DAT is employed on location — are speed controlled because of the nature of the medium. The norm for the analog decades before was the Nagra quarter-inch sound recorder, a versatile and still perfectly usable machine as well. Recording picture and sound separately at first appears cumbersome, but is actually quite flexible and produces generally higher-quality sound. There are sound-on-film processes, but their use in the editing room is awkward (read impossible). So you record on DAT or conventional tape on location, and then transfer to mag stock for your editing.

With sound and image recorded separately, the dailies need to go through a process called **syncing up**. This is the process wherein the editor, actually an apprentice editor, goes through and manually matches up the two media — the workprint and the mag stock. The ubiquitous slate is the tool used to accomplish this. The editor finds the precise visual frame where the slate bars come together — the white stripes are very helpful in this. Then he or she finds the exact frame in the audio where the hit of the slate — the attack — is found. The two are then matched up. While many aspects of the conventional film edit have become rarities, this is, for rather arcane reasons, one of the few parts of the process that remain essentially intact.

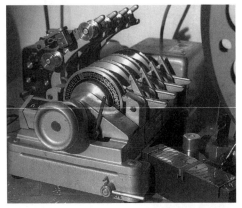

FIG. 14.5

A **synchronizer** (see Figure 14.5) is employed to match sound and picture and run them at the same rate. The synchronizer has interlocked drums (four in this example) with sprocket teeth around the outer edge. Each drum has a locking mechanism that clamps the film against the drum and sprocket teeth. Syncing up is described in detail in other texts, but essentially the picture frame with the hit of the slate is locked into the second drum (see Figure 14.5). The audio hit is locked directly across from the picture hit. The shot can now be fed through the synchronizer "in sync." We create matched starting points for each piece, usually hole punches in leaders before it. If you have picture that is, for example, 12 feet, 18 frames long, the sound for it will be exactly the same length — at least in the sync up and first assembly stages. As we do our overlaps and the like, lengths may change, but the sync that is established by these initial relationships is maintained throughout the editorial process. The shots are synced sequentially on the large rolls of workprint.

The full complexities of the process are not possible to flesh out in this limited space, but this is the way sync is maintained in the conventional film edit — by being rolled frame-by-frame through the synchronizer or a more advanced tool. For those of you who have seen flatbed film editing tables, they are just more sophisticated versions of the synchronizer — a cruder and more difficult instrument. However, because of its precision, the synchronizer is still justifiably used for syncing up.

As described in Chapter II, the apprentice will pull the selects and cut them into the first assembly. At that point, you have two big rolls, one of picture and one of mag stock (more if a longer film). There are a variety of ways to proceed, but in the conventional film edit, you start to add and layer sound by cutting more rolls of sound, called **mixtracks**. If we wanted music, we would record it onto mag stock and build it onto another roll. Matched starting points and the sprocket holes control all sync. If we want the music to start a minute into the film, we would cut a minute of slug — sound fill that can be junk picture or leader — before it. Effects are handled the same way. Obviously picture cutting is going on simultaneously, but a large part of the editing process is cutting multiple mixtracks, creating a full and rich soundtrack by layering speech, music, and effects. When you are done, a typical film would have dozens of separate mixtracks. A typical beginning student film would have a much smaller number.

FINISHING

So all cutting is done with workprints, and sound is cut on separate pieces of mag stock, with multiple rolls being created. It should be emphasized that this is a very offline process. Your workprint is getting a little dog-eared and you can only look at the whole thing with sound on an editing table (unless you want to pay a lot of money). The whole thing is not put together on one medium until the very end. This is another plus for the NLE world, where you get a clean-looking product with all the sound throughout your edit. It is, however, on video.

When the editorial team has the film exactly the way they want it, with every shot in place and at exactly the length desired and the sound is all layered with every piece creating just the perfect effect, we are ready to finish the film. There are three major finishing processes to creating a final film print. They are: 1) mixing the audio down to one track; 2) cutting the film negative; and 3) marrying the two together on a final piece of film — the **answer print** — the lab's best initial shot at printing the film. The first two of these three, mixing and negative cutting, create the elements — the rolls of picture and sound — required to create the answer print. The sequence of the first two processes is up to you, with varying philosophies on whether to mix or cut neg first.

MIX

In the audio mixing session, the goal is to produce *the* finished audio for the show. The final product is the already described **master mix**. Previously, it was on one uncut piece of mag stock (again, more than one roll if a feature or otherwise longer film).

While you can theoretically mix in FCP by yourself, in the old days you had to take your project to a large audio post-production facility. The mixing studio itself contained a bank (or banks) of mag stock playback machines all interlocked to a projector that projected the **edited workprint (EWP)**. All individual mixtracks were threaded up and set to their start points, as was the EWP. While different start marks are used by different people throughout the process, synchronization of rolls is what the familiar countdown leader was, and still is, mostly about. All the mixtracks are played back through a mixer used to set volume levels. Mixing boards also had, and of course still have, modest to extensive equalization capabilities and the sound was set up so it could be patched out to other signal processing equipment if more manipulation was necessary. With the editor(s) present, the mixing crew would work through the film in short stretches, setting audio levels, doing fade-outs and fade-ups, and doing such signal processing as required. The mixed show was output to a mag stock recorder, with the master mix recorded on an uncut virgin piece of mag stock.

Today, mixing studios remain about the same except all sound is handled digitally, even if you cut on the old, analog mag stock medium (the mixtracks would be dropped off before the mix and digitized). Either way, with the tracks stored digitally, the mix proceeds as before. A professional mix is a very expensive process with smaller studios charging around $200 an hour and the big guns charging $700-$800 and more. While expensive, we repeat our recommendations that you take it to the pros. The gain should be an intelligible and even sound track. People squawk a lot about nice visuals, but a bad soundtrack is as quick a viewer turn-off as you will ever find.

The fundamental principle of the master mix, recorded on the sprocket-ed mag stock, is that it is exactly the same length as the EWP. From the start marks at the head to any tail markings, the synchronization between the master mix and the EWP is dependent upon a frame-for-frame match between the two media. When you are done with the mix, you will have two rolls of film — the EWP and master mix — of the exact same size. All those multiple mixtracks that you have labored over so intensively have served their purpose and can be put out to pasture.

From the master mix, your lab will create an **optical master** — a print-ing component that is the source for the sound in the final print. Sound in theatrical projection, with a few specialized exceptions, is photograph-ic. The optical master is a clear piece of film with one thin stripe down the side opposite the sprocket holes. On close inspection, the stripe has a series of diamond-shaped patterns that are the photographic record of the sound. Again, the optical master will be used to print the sound onto the answer print. Keep in mind that the optical master is generally made directly from the master mix recorded on the sprocketed mag stock.

NEGATIVE CUTTING

Once the mix is done, the edited workprint and all the uncut negative are sent to the **negative cutter** — a person who "conforms" the original to what was done in the EWP. The neg cutter uses the edge numbers as his or her "guideposts" in finding and cutting the shots out of the original. The neg cutter will count from the first and last edge numbers of every individual shot in the EWP and reproduce the cuts in the origi-nal. The synchronizer is the tool used to make sure the workprint and original are matching frame-by-frame. A special **cement splicer** is used, employing a slight over-lap of a frame that is bonded to the next piece of film (see Figure 14.6).

FIG. 14.6

Negative cutting is a process that must be done to the most exacting standards, with maintenance of an uncompromised original and careful handling being the highest priorities. The neg cutter must be scrupulous in the recording and matching of the edge numbers on the shots and cuts must be executed only after all elements have been checked thoroughly. If, heaven forbid, the neg is cut in the wrong place, an endless number of problems occur. Once something is cut, it cannot be restored to its original form because frames are ruined in creating the overlap of the cement splicing (more on that later). Thus, a slight jump in the action is unavoidable if you put a shot back together. If you move the cut and use a different piece of the shot, the sound will not be in sync. If you go back and get another take, you will have to replace the sound as well, requiring a remix of all or a substantial part of the film (a reason why some producers have the negative cut before the audio mix).

In addition, there are simple issues of making sure the fragile film is not damaged. If dirt gets embedded in the emulsion, for example, that flaw will stay with the film for its entire life span. The neg cutter works in a **clean room**, a specially designed space that is as dust- and dirt-free an environment as possible. The rooms are designed to be cleaned easily and often have cleaning filters in the air passage ducts. The neg cutter handles the film with white cotton gloves and makes sure the film comes in contact with as few surfaces as possible. Obviously, if the neg is in any way mishandled — scratched, broken, smudged — the entire project can be compromised.

Before proceeding to conforming the negative, the EWP must be marked to communicate all your intentions to both the neg cutter and the lab that will make the answer print. To do this, you use either a white or yellow grease pencil (China marker) and literally mark all cuts and draw all effects right on the workprint — the only effects executable in this stage again being fades, dissolves, and supers. When you are done, every splice in your workprint should have a mark on it. You should check all complex effects with your negative cutter, but following are the common markings:

- All actual cuts should be marked with a C.
- All unintentional cuts, that is, points where you cut, changed your mind, and re-spliced pieces back together again, should be marked with the = symbol. Be sure to check these for continuous edge numbers.

- All fade-ups are marked with a sideways triangle going from small to large.
- All fade-outs are marked with a sideways triangle going the opposite direction.
- All dissolves drop the fade-up symbol on top of the fade-out symbol for an overlapped effect.
- Check with your neg cutter for marking supers.

So the neg cutter goes through and "re-builds" the entire film from the beginning to end. In 16mm, the original is actually cut into two rolls, called A & B rolls. This is done to facilitate optical effects (fades, dissolves, and superimpositions) and to mask the overlap that is required in cement splicing. 35mm is cut into a single roll, with all the fades and dissolves executed as optical during post-production. The overlap of cement splicing is hidden in the theatrical widescreen mask used in standard projection.

THE ANSWER PRINT

On to a final product. As stated, the rerecording mixers and the negative cutter produce the elements required to create a final film print. When they have done their work, you send the result of their efforts to the lab of your choice. In 16mm, you will generally send the lab four elements: the master mix (or optical master if you have had it converted elsewhere); the A roll; the B roll: and the EWP (they need this last because it indicates all effects). You could potentially have more than A & B rolls, if you are doing complex visual effects.

Once at the lab, your original is subject to intense scrutiny. Just as you can do with the color corrector in FCP, the original is analyzed for color and exposure. The light that exposes your film in the printer is broken down into the three primary colors of light, giving you separate control over the red, green, and blue components of your image. Called the **printer lights**, these also allow you to control exposure. The **timer**, the person who grades the film, will assign a value for each color for every shot in the film.

They will also program in all printer effects, at least in 16mm. As suggested, you can create dissolves, fades, and superimpositions in the final print in 16mm. And that is it. All other effects, freeze framers, wipes, and the like, have to be created as **opticals** by a lab or optical house during the editing process and cut into the EWP.

CRITICAL CONCERNS

Before moving on we need to cover two critical issues: lost frames and video effects.

The issue of lost frames is hard for people to get their hands around. A cement splice works on the principle of overlapping a little piece of a frame onto the frame you are cutting it to. In our example of film on the first page of this chapter, the last frame showing of the shot is 8706 plus one frame. The overlap is created out of 8706 plus two frames, with that frame being ruined in the splicing process. Actually, for handling purposes, the neg cutter takes half of 8706 plus three frames, destroying that frame as well. The bottom line: the neg cutter requires a frame and a half at the beginning and end of all shots. This one-and-a-half frames — effectively two frames although this gets complicated — that are ruined have corresponding frames, both in the workprint and in the video transfer. If you use those frames anywhere else in your program, the neg cutter will not be able to conform your film. You must "trim out" — make sure they are not used — the two frames on either end of all your shots. This does not mean that you decide on the piece you want, drop it into the show, and then trim two frames off the beginning and the end. It means that you decide what piece you want to use and make sure that the two frames on either end are left in unused outtakes.

In a lot of instances, this happens naturally. Shots with slates at the beginning and where the director calls cut at the end automatically have frames to spare. Where it is frequently an issue is when you are cutting in MOS inserts or cutting non-sync footage, such as in an experimental film or a music video. In essence, it comes into play when you want to use a given shot more than once. You want to use one piece of a shot here in the program and you want to use the next consecutive piece somewhere else. If you have used a clip up to a certain point and want to use the next consecutive piece, you simply have to trim out the frame-and-a-half for the tail of the first and the frame-and-a-half at the head of the next shot. Trim out three frames and set them aside — physically with film, digitally with NLE. This is a tricky issue and there will be an example on page 311.

When you create an EDL for the negative cutter, Cinema Tools will print a warning covering this issue. Before you declare picture lock, run CT and check for conflicts. If you were to export the audio in an OMF application and later have problems in your EDL, you would have to do quite a bit of repair to solve the problems created. This also can cause issues with fades, dissolves, and supers, so check all effects carefully.

In terms of video effects, they must also be carefully tracked. Be aware that if you create effects in FCP, they may not (read will not) exist in the film. All kinds of effects are available in FCP — irises, page peels, et cetera — and are as easy as drag, drop, and render. The render part is the key. Remember that whenever you render something, you are creating something new — and that something new may not, more likely does not, exist in your original film footage. Keep in mind that the only effects that the lab can create in an answer print are fades, dissolves, and superimpositions.

Color correction is the same. If you do color correction in FCP, you may not be able to reproduce the changes exactly in your answer print. You can make a shot look absolutely breathtaking in FCP, but the lab may not be able to duplicate the effect. Similarly, you might "save" a flawed shot — one with color or exposure problems — and find the lab cannot do similar magic. Conversely, you may be able to do some things to film that are not achievable in FCP. These are all issues of both communication and the tolerances of printing film stock. Some things you can do in video which you cannot do in film and some things you can do in film which you cannot do in video. A young DP of my acquaintance was missing some exposures on a film and a friend in the telecine suite thought she was doing him a favor by correcting his mistakes and not letting on. The proverbial chickens came home to roost in the answer print — a very expensive place to start making corrections, particularly in this case when the premiere was just a few days down the road. If you are going back to film, you may not want to do any corrections at all.

One last note: This should be obvious but you cannot use clips more than once in the Timeline if you intend to matchback to film. A clip represents one piece of film. If a clip is used, that piece of film is then cut into the AB rolls. The AB rolls are run continuously as they are printed, so you cannot re-use, that is, re-print, individual pieces of film. If you want to re-use shots, they must be duplicated on an optical printer or, if multiple uses can be foreseen, multiple takes should be done during shooting to avoid generation problems.

THE VIDEOTAPE

Video can be recorded in a number of manners. It can be stored in the old analog way on a magnetic tape. It can be stored digitally, again on a conventional magnetic medium. Or it can be stored on the hard drive of a computer. With the exception of new HDTV and a few other applications, everything in the United States — whether digital or analog — is recorded in NTSC. NTSC comes in for a lot of heat, but it is a robust system that led the world to modern broadcast recording. NTSC does have difficulty communicating with other formats, which can make it somewhat unwieldy.

As suggested earlier, in NTSC video the information is stored in frames on the videotape. Each frame is composed of two fields arranged diagonally on the tape (see page 20). Each field is composed of alternating vertical lines of information. Each field is presented sequentially and interlaced to create a complete composite image.

In the beginning, video ran at a true 30 fps. While there is extensive lore about why this happened, when color arrived, tape speed had to be slowed down to avoid unwanted artifacts. It was slowed down 0.1 percent (.001) to 29.97. Now this does not appear to be much, but it has a discernable impact, particularly in longer shows. The major problem comes with synchronization with sound when we go either from or back to film — the audio requiring either **pulldown** or **pullup**. More on this after some other issues are discussed.

THE TRANSFER INTERFACE

The first step after shooting is telecine (G), the transfer of your processed film to video. Here you have two completely different formats, with completely different rates and completely different tracking systems. How do we begin to integrate them?

Messily.

The first problem is how to reconcile the frame rate of film with the frame rate of video. I am tempted to say we are about to get into higher-level math, but this is probably somewhere in the eighth grade.

3:2 PULLDOWN

In order to get from the 24 frames of film to the 30 frames of video, we need to create more video frames. The problem is that these two numbers are not divisible in a non-fractional form. We cannot multiple 24 by anything to get 30 without creating fractional frames. However, once we remember that every video frame is composed of two separate fields, we realize there are some numbers with which we can work — there are actually 60 pieces of information per second. Now, how can we produce 60 fields out of 24 frames? Divide them and you get two and one-half, again a fraction. But if you print each frame twice, you get forty-eight with a remainder of twelve. How do we make up that extra twelve? If we print half of the frames to two fields (12 x 2 = 24) and the other half to three fields (12 x 3 = 36), we have our sixty (24 + 36). Thus 3:2 pulldown. The standard telecine prints one film frame to two fields and then the next film frame to three fields. And so on. It looks like this (see Figure 14.7):

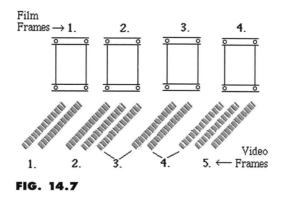

FIG. 14.7

As you can see, we are taking four film frames and turning them into five video frames, and thus 24 film to 30 video.

Each one of these transferred film frames has a slightly different relationship to the video frame. Again, this does not seem hugely important, but is critically important to matchback — important enough that each type of frame is designated with an identifying letter (see Figure 14.8).

The first video frame, called the A frame, is the only one that corresponds to one film frame (and this is highly significant). It is two fields long and starts on the first field of a video frame. The second film frame is transferred to three fields, and is identified as the B frame. It starts on the first

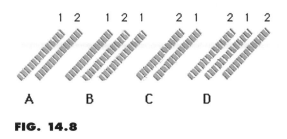

FIG. 14.8

field of the second video frame, but extends halfway into the third video frame. The third film frame — the C frame — is transferred again to two fields, but it begins on a second field and extends into the first field of the fourth video frame. The D frame starts on the second field of the fourth video frame and completes the fifth video frame. Within this structure, we are creating a lot of half frames and oddball frames. Again, only one corresponds exactly to a film frame — the A frame.

In converting from four to five frames, we have, in essence, created a phantom frame — a frame that has no relationship to any film frame. If the editor cuts on this frame, the matchback information will be flawed. And actually, the problem is more complex than this. If we cut on a half video frame, it has both a different time and frame relationship to the film. Even the much vaunted A frame does not truly correspond. It represents a 30th of a second as opposed to the 24th of film. These time differences are marginal, but again slight discrepancies can emerge.

One way to solve these discrepancies was to indicate for the editor which frames were the bad boys. Appearing right after the edge number in the window burn, the frames would be identified by their letters and the bad actors would be underlined. With the telecine turning four film frames into five video frames, one had to be listed twice: the D frame. The firstt video frame (A) is a good frame. The second video (B) frame is a good frame because it starts on a first field. The third video frame (C) is bad because, even though it is two fields, it mixes the third and fourth video frames. The fourth video frame (D1) is bad because it also mixes film frames. The fifth frame (D2) is good because the fourth film frame lands on the two discrete first and second fields of the fifth video frame. Some NLE programs left it up to the editor not to cut on a bad field, others produced a warning when you tried.

280

Well, this is obviously problematic. Within this 3:2 system, there is all kind of potential for minor discrepancies. Those discrepancies will show up in the synchronization of sound and picture. And when we say minor, we mean minor. For every shot you use, you have chosen one piece of picture and one piece of sound to be in sync. For the sound to remain in sync, you have to pull the right piece of picture. If there are slight discrepancies in the picture pulled, there will be slight discrepancies in sync. Sync that is slightly off may not be very noticeable to the average viewer, but it is a matter of what can be tolerated. Problems may not look too bad when the presentation is on the small screen. But when the image is thrown across a huge screen in a big theater — magnified 150,000 to 300,00 times — it may be less acceptable. And the small screen is getting bigger and bigger.

PULLUP AND PULLDOWN

So cutting at 29.97 causes some problems. There is another significant problem. The numbers suggest a conversion from a real 24 fps to a real 30 fps but, when the film is telecined, it is also being slowed down to 29.97. As suggested, the transferred film you see is 0.1% slower than film run at a true 24 frames per second. This does not make any visible difference, but it does create problems with the sound, which again was recorded separately on location. Sound is running at its real-time rate. If just used in FCP without modification, sound will actually start to drift out of sync. Across a short take, this is probably unnoticeable. But across a show? The film will drift out by 1.8 frames per minute, which will be a noticeable offset. It will drift out by 18 frames (just over half a second) over a ten-minute show, a catastrophic problem. This is an issue at the take level, but a huge issue at the show level.

Because your takes are relatively short, and the sound will be broken up individually to match each take (see pages 206-7), you could probably get away with not addressing this when you sync up. But you should anyway. It is best to develop good habits and your longest takes may show some drift anyway. This is a good reason to bring the sound in as a whole file as we did with WT, but either way, speed is very easily changed. Start by opening the desired clip from the Browser. Go to Modify: Speed. The Speed dialogue box will open (see Figure 14.9) and type 99.9 into the window. Hit OK and the change will apply. Your sound is now matched,

FIG. 14.9

speed-wise at least, to your picture. That is pulldown.

This is all relatively easy and not usually disastrous if you are inattentive to detail. Going the other direction, however, requires that you and other people involved in post-production know what is at issue. When we are matching back to film, the cut film will play at the real-time rate. All the sound you have cut in FCP will thus be 0.1% slower than the film. If you have a 30-minute show, it would be off by 54 frames — almost two seconds — by the end. The solution is relatively simple, as long as you and other people know what needs to be done. The audio has to be speeded up by 0.1% — this is pullup — before or when the optical master is made. This can theoretically be done in the speed window again — type in 100.1%. However, more frequently, a post-production facility will be finishing the audio. In this case, and they should be very familiar with this issue, they have to do the pullup. You just have to be sure to tell them.

REVERSE TELECINE

Many editors worked this way — cutting 29.97, creating negative cut lists and thus accepting slight slippage — but it was not viable for anyone working to exacting standards, like those in the feature world. So what are some solutions? Cutting in 24-frame video is the answer. That is, to take the 30-frame video of NTSC and convert it back to 24 frames. The video goes through a "reverse telecine" process that subtracts the extra fields created in 3:2 pulldown. A feature of Cinema Tools as well as available in other NLE programs, the Reverse Telecine function essentially undoes 3:2 pulldown. It goes through and truly gives you a one-to-one relationship between what you are doing on the video and what you will eventually be doing with the film. As suggested, Cinema Tools is a data tracking program and Reverse Telecine is the only aspect that may be considered to "do something" to the visual material.

This eliminates any sloppiness in matching 29.97 cut lists to 24-frame film and theoretically eliminates the need for pullup and pulldown. There is one drawback, however, and that is that 24-frame video does not generally play well to NTSC monitors. All your computer screens can handle it, but if you want to make a tape or just screen it on any old monitor, the FireWire will not be able to render a consistent picture. Making tapes and playing the show for test viewers and interested parties is of critical importance. For this reason, a number of editors cut at **23.98** — the 0.1% slowdown from 24 — which matches the slowdown from 30 to 29.97. This plays both to computer and NTSC monitors. This solves the problem, but reintroduces pullup/pulldown issues. In this, it is just important that all post-production personnel are aware of the requirements.

Specifics of how to execute Reverse Telecine and how it operates will be covered in Chapter XV.

HOW THE FEATURE WORLD IS DOING MATCHBACK

Of course there is no one single way matchback applies in features but there is a fairly standard approach. We bring it up here because you should know it and it is slightly different from the process we are going to follow. It integrates a substantial amount of film technology, mostly because you need material to screen for audiences and because the bulletproof aspects of the film edit provide security against calamity.

The biggest difference between the Hollywood approach and the more standard commercial approach, which is the way we did it on *WT* (see below), is how the project is initiated. Our first step with *WT*, as well as with most short projects, was to transfer to video from the negative and then do our sync up in FCP. The feature world, however, transfers to video from the synced workprint. They make a workprint, transfer all the sound to mag stock, and do a conventional sync up. Once they are done, they have the two rolls — one of workprint, the other of synced mag stock. Then they will do a scratch transfer — scratch in that it is only intended for the edit room. This can be done in a telecine suite that has an interlocked mag stock playback unit (not all do) or there is equipment specifically designed for the job. KEM, one of the top manufacturers of post-production film equipment, has created modified flatbed editing tables that can make this kind of transfer. Called the Cine Maestro, they have taken a four-plate — denoting one picture and one sound transport — and outfitted it with a transfer chain.

In the transfer process, time code and edge numbers can then be interrelated. However, rather than using the edge numbers, most features use a set of created ink numbers that are far more convenient. The synced workprint and attendant mag stock are sent to a post-production facility that machine prints a similar 8-digit combination of letters and numbers on both rolls. Spread across two frames on the edges, if the picture started at AAAA 0001, the corresponding sound roll would start at exactly AAAA 0001 as well. Conventional film edits have used these numbers for years, so they are very familiar to apprentice and assistant editors. They have been useful for maintaining sync and, moreover, for organizing the massive amount of footage shot on a feature. But we will leave that for the film textbooks.

The edit is then conducted in NLE. When finished, a cut list is produced through Cinema Tools using the inked-in edge numbers. Rather than cutting the neg, however, the editorial staff conforms the previously uncut workprint to this list. The workprint can then be checked against the audio for accuracy and test screenings can occur. One option is to transfer the audio mixdown back to mag stock and project the film "double system" — a mag stock playback machine and a film projector interlocked to play picture and audio in sync. Even more common, the sound can be transferred to a DAT and the DAT can be interlocked with a film projector. The mag stock that was used in the sync up has no further role in the process.

When it finally becomes time to make prints, the negative cutter then has both the list of numbers and the actual workprint in front of them. Having the workprint is the ultimate test of accuracy — the final chamber in the bulletproof film edit. Printed lists are hard to work from and if there are any mistakes, there is no way the negative cutter would know before major damage occurred. A negative cutter's reputation rests on his or her ability to put the negative together cleanly and without making mistakes. But every one of us, no matter what we think, is to varying degrees shy of perfection. Mistakes happen. Any person, when presented with just a massive list of numbers, is going to make at least some mistakes. The workprint provides negative cutters with an unerring reference as to what the negative should look like. The editor on one feature I was tangentially involved with said the conformed negative that was made from just a printed list came back with 27 mistakes.

OUR APPROACH WITH *WT*

With *Waiting Tables*, we went ahead and also made a workprint at the time of processing. However, unlike the previous approach, we patiently set the workprint aside as the FCP edit of the piece was being done. We transferred the negative to video and did our sync up with the sound in FCP. Given local facilities, transferring from sync workprint would have added an unnecessary level of expense and complexity and would not leave us with a video that could be considered as a final product. After all the editing and OMF work (see pages 300-9), we printed out a cut list of edge numbers for the neg cutter using the database created in Cinema Tools. Then our path re-converged with the feature world's. Rather than taking it directly to the neg cutter, we took the list back to the workprint and then conformed the workprint to what we had done in FCP, in essence creating an EWP. We took the master mix that had been created in Pro Tools and had a local lab—CineSound—create a conventional mag stock version of it. This is the point for the independent where mag stock is again a useful entity. When we made the mag stock version, we asked the lab to pullup the sound — speed it up 0.1% — so it would match picture. If we forgot to do this, we would most assuredly be out of sync. We took the master mix on mag and the EWP, threw it on a conventional flatbed editing table, and just made sure the sound and picture relationship was correct. The opportunities for drift or mistakes are just too great for you not to check. Given limited resources, this is the only way you can be absolutely 100% sure that your audio and picture are in sync — it is your insurance. The feature world can slave a DAT to the projector with the EWP to check, but that may not be possible for the typical indie.

When all our checking was done, we sent the EWP and the uncut original to the negative cutter. AB rolls were created, the master mix was converted to an optical master, and an answer print was struck. The whole final process will be followed in detail in Chapter XVI.

Before starting this process, you need to take into account that every frame in the workprint will appear in your final film. If you have frames that you do not want in your final film, they better not be in your EWP. And conversely, if you have frames that you want in your final film, they better be in your EWP. Everything represented in your workprint must have a corresponding piece of original. This is where a lot of people get tripped up, particularly in the NLE age. They find some great piece of film or video and try to work it into their edit. If you want to go back to film, you need a corresponding original. Many wonderful films have been made out of "found footage," a la *Atomic Café* (1982), but you need to have something to put in your AB rolls in order to use it.

CINEMA TOOLS

Again, Cinema Tools is a database. Except for one very significant function, "Reverse Telecine," it plays no active role in the editing process. It simply keeps track of the information needed to matchback from the video you edited to the film that you actually shot on location. The bottom line is that Cinema Tools (CT) creates a permanent relationship between the time code of your video clips and the key numbers of the film. This is not a relationship between the clips in your Browser, but a relationship between the actual files in your Capture Scratch.

Keep in mind as we go through this that we are completely starting the editing process over from scratch — from the very beginning. We are going to have to capture our clips into the Browser, sync up sound, cut the picture, and build our audio. What we have done in previous chapters in our 29.97 edit is pertinent only in that we know how the piece should cut. If our intent is to cut entirely in a 24-frame environment in order to have a frame-for-frame matchback to film, then we must do this from the start so we do not have problems with both the edge numbers and our audio down the road. When we say 24, 23.98 frames per second needs to be included in the discussion. More on that briefly.

The first thing obviously is to capture your shots from video. Keep in mind that, although we are going to cut at 24 (or 23.98), we are going to do initial capture at 29.97 and will Reverse Telecine to 24. Whether capture is done by flex files or manual logging, it is recommended here that you try to do all the capture work at one time. If you spread it out over a period of time, the potential for flaws and missed material becomes exponentially higher. This might not be feasible on bigger projects where new footage is coming in on a daily basis, but managing initial smaller ones can shed light on more ambitious undertakings.

FLEX FILES

Be sure you understand all the capture information in Chapter X before delving into this material.

All hail the flex file. The flex file, also called a **telecine log**, is created during the telecine session. Essentially, it is encoded information that is used both to drive capture and create the database for Cinema Tools. It makes your life significantly easier. With the exception of 24p video, it only pertains when you shoot on film and transfer to video and is particularly pertinent when you have the intention of returning to the film negative. It is not an absolute necessity but it does a lot of heavy lifting and life can be significantly more strenuous without it.

The flex file is created by the colorist, or more likely an assistant, during the telecine process. As the colorist is making scene-to-scene corrections, he or she simply types in or encodes the beginning and ending time code numbers of every take which, of course, is the information you need for log and capture. They define a take as from flash-to-flash. All scene and take numbers are taken from the slates and/or the camera reports. When the time code numbers are entered, the key numbers are also logged as well. It is a mechanical process, but must be done correctly or there will be problems.

A flex file does all the messy work that you would normally have to do by hand during the capture process, logging beginning and ending time code for all the shots. It also is used to interrelate time code and edge numbers. With the one significant exception, Cinema Tools itself is just data management software. It continually updates the relationship between your Quicktime files and the film's key numbers. You can manually enter all this information if you do not get a flex file, but the flex file saves you a lot of steps.

Most telecine facilities in major urban areas are set up to create flex files, but you might find them to be a piece of exotica in smaller markets. Their creation only flourishes in areas where a significant amount of matchback is being done, mainly where a large number of features are being shot and finished — L.A., New York, Chicago, et cetera. No matter where you are, make sure your colorist knows what a flex file is and is going to execute it correctly. Occasionally a telecine house will create a flex file for the entire roll of film, logging in the first legible number of a (generally) 400' roll and the last one. The notion, I guess, is that the entire roll will be captured and then the editor will break it down into subclips as desired. However, to do the whole Cinema Tools process most efficiently, data should be created for every take.

THE PROCESS

Step one with the flex file and Cinema Tools is to use the data to drive original capture. The beauty of the flex file is that you do not have to go through all your footage, still-framing flash frames and logging time code numbers. It has all been done for you and you can enter the database and walk away while FCP captures all your footage. With the tutorial, you will be able to follow along with this process although, because the footage is already in files on your computer, capture is completed. The visual tutorial will fill in the blanks. Again, keep in mind that we are starting from scratch.

FIG. 15.1

Launch Cinema Tools (**A**). When you open CT for the first time, a dialogue box titled "Open Database" will appear (see Figure 15.1). I, of course, dutifully tried to figure this one out for an inordinate period of time, thinking that it required some action on my part. You have not created a database yet so there is nothing to open. Hit "Cancel." We need to create a new one — go to Database>New Database in the menus (see Figure 15.2).

FIG. 15.2

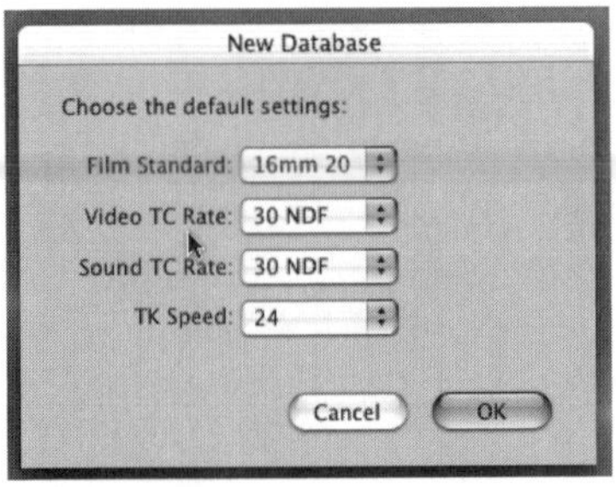

FIG. 15.3

FIG. 15.4

FIG. 15.5

Next it will ask you to identify the properties of the database (see Figure 15.3). The choices for the first item are 16mm20, which indicates 16mm and an edge number every 20 frames. The other choice is 35mm4perf, the latter part indicating 4 perforations — the standard. 3 perf is generally not used in matchback applications and is not supported (a recent upgrade has fixed this on the telecine). The next two indicate video frame rates and dropframe or nondropframe. The last is frames per second, generally 24 in the United States. Hit OK. For the tutorial, use the selections indicated in the illustration.

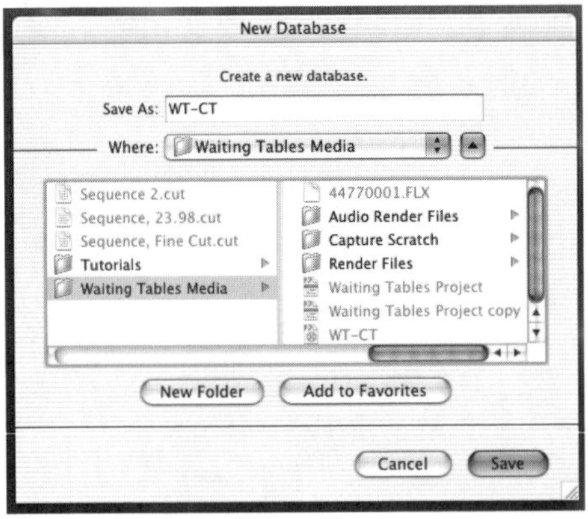

The next dialogue box, called New Database (see Figure 15.4), asks you to name and find a destination for the Database. Call it WT-CT (for Cinema Tools) and put it on the desktop.

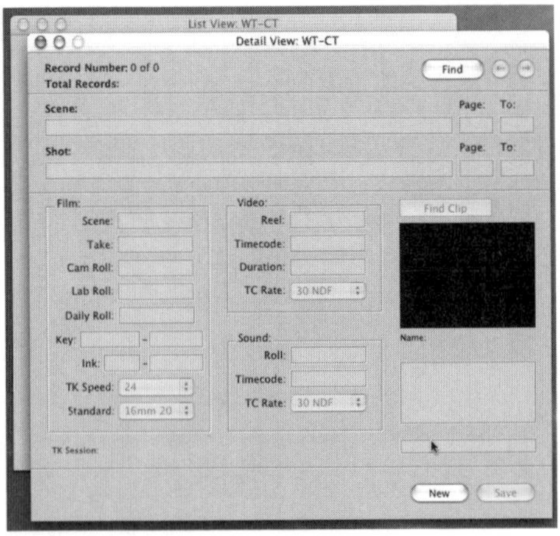

When you click Save, two windows will come up. The front window is titled Detail View: WT-CT (see Figure 15.5) and the background window is List View: WT-CT (see Figure 15.6). Detail View will not be important for now so click on List View.

Then the next step is to import your flex file into CT. Flex files are usually delivered on floppies so, given the drives in most modern computers, you need to get it into your CPU. Not recently, I was stuck in L.A. with a flex file on a floppy and no floppy drive. It did not take me long to track down the necessary hardware, but if I had had the foresight to just ask the lab to attach the flex file to an email, I would have been up and going much more quickly. It is a very small piece of information. The flex file for WT was 16 kilobytes. The flex file, here identified by the lab as 44770001.FLX, is in the Waiting Tables Media folder.

FIG. 15.6

In the menus, go to File> Import>Telecine Log (see Figure 15.7).

FIG. 15.7

The "Import a Telecine Log File" window will appear (see Figure 15.8) asking you to identify the flex file you want to import. Find it in Waiting Tables Media, select it, and click Choose. A dialogue box will appear that, in our *WT* example, states that 32 files will be imported (see Figure 15.9).

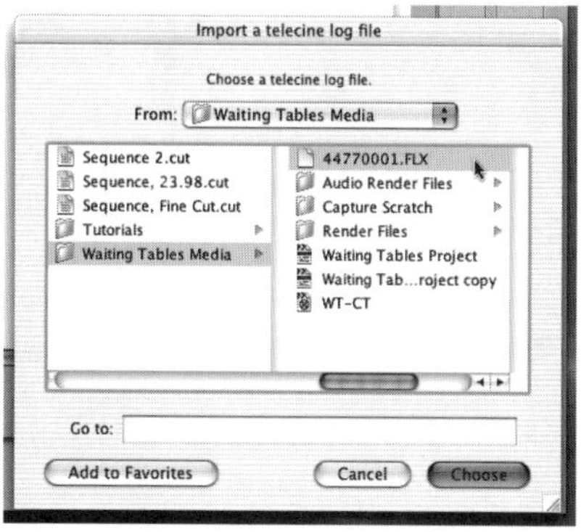

Click OK and all the logging information will appear in List

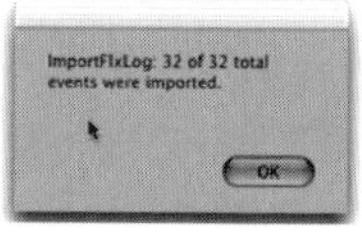

FIG. 15.8

FIG. 15.9

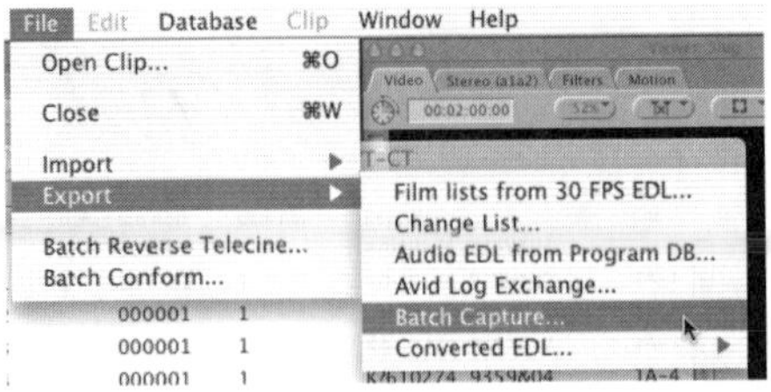

FIG. 15.11

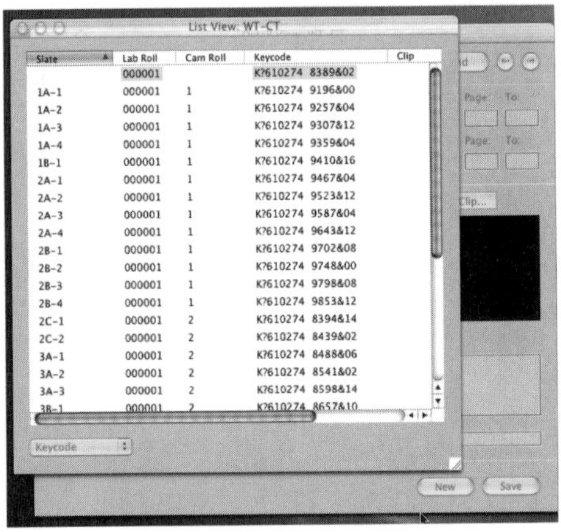

FIG. 15.10

FIG. 15.12

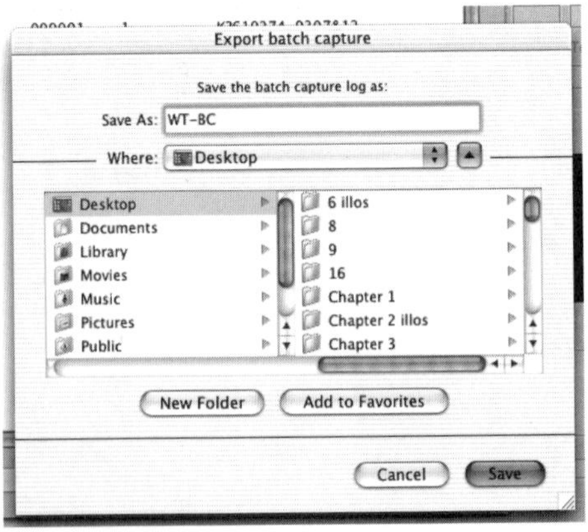

FIG. 15.13

View: WT-CT (see Figure 15.10). Now, go to File>Export> Batch Capture (see Figure 15.11).

A window will appear titled "Export Batch Capture," giving you the choice between FCP video and FCP audio (see Figure 15.12). Select FCP video and click OK.

The final window, also "Export Batch Capture," asks again for a title and destination, WT-BC — or batch list — and then let's send it to the desktop just so we do not lose it (see Figure 15.13). Having created a Batch Capture file (**B**), we are ready to start the capture process. Go to the program menu and click Hide Cinema Tools (Command: H). Just hide it, do not close it. We will be using it again relatively soon.

Before launching FCP, make sure that your external video device, whether camera or deck, is switched on and make sure the tape from the telecine session is inserted. Open FCP. Go to File>New Project. Go to File>Save Project As and title this WT, 23.98. Open "Log and Capture." Before importing the capture data, you want to set media destination and select the type of media to be captured. On the right side of the Log and

Capture window, go to Clip Settings and choose Vid Only. Next go to **Capture Settings** and set your Scratch disks. Check pages 198-9 if you need to review setting scratch disks.

Go to File>Import>Batch List at 29.97 fps (see Figure 15.14).

FIG. 15.14

The Choose a File window will appear (see Figure 15.15). In Choose a File, go to the desktop, select WT-BC and click Choose.

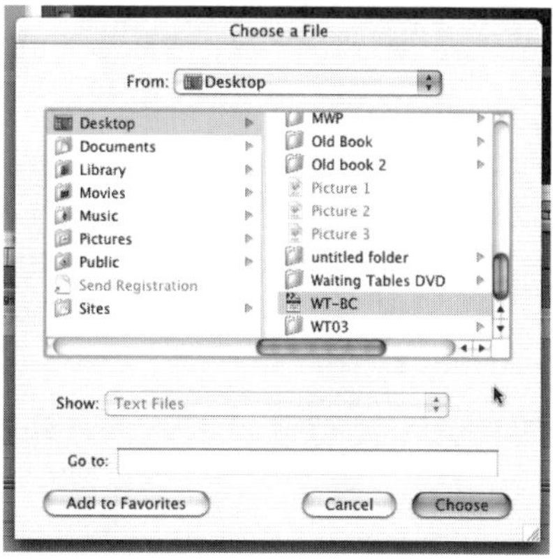

All the files will now appear in the Browser, with the red line through them, indicating they are offline (see Figure 15.16), that is, they have not yet been captured. Go to **Batch** capture and start the process detailed on pages 202-4. Once the process starts, you can walk away and relax until the entire project is captured. Again, the tutorial material will not capture because it is already in the computer, but you can continue to follow along with this discussion.

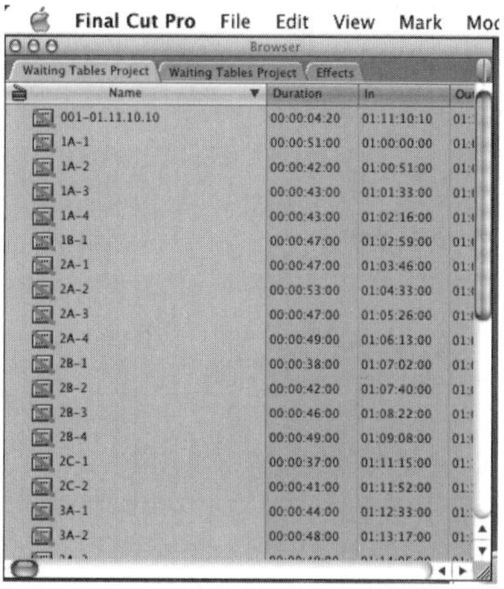

VERY IMPORTANT: Before you go do any editing, re-open Cinema Tools and in the menus go to Database>Connect Clips (see Figure 5.17). Follow the Find a Clip path to Waiting Tables DVD>Capture Scratch> Waiting Tables Project and

FIG. 15.15

FIG. 15.16

choose the first clip in the window. It may ask you to choose more than one. Keep choosing clip files until CT gets the idea and connects the whole database. IF YOU START EDITING WITHOUT DOING THIS, CT WILL NOT RECORD YOUR CUTS ACCURATELY.

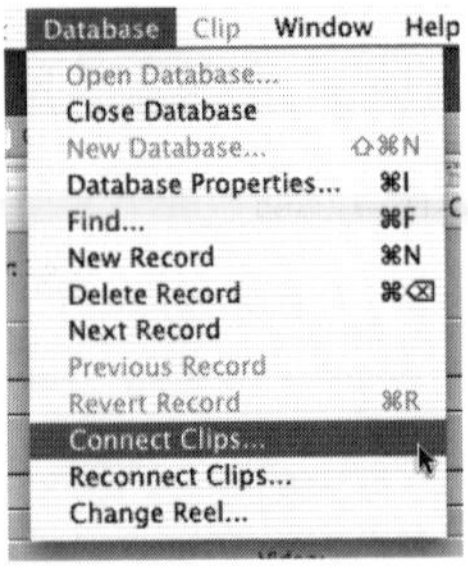

USING CINEMA TOOLS
WITHOUT A FLEX FILE

FIG. 15.17

The flex file is a wonderful thing, but occasionally you find yourself in a place where you cannot get one. In that case, you have to enter everything by hand. You have to start with a conventional capture, going through the tape, finding and logging all the time code numbers manually, and doing batch capture. Remember here that we are once again starting over from scratch. We will be renaming everything again.

Once everything is captured and saved, make sure the Browser with the clips you want to export into Cinema Tools is open and active. In our example, double click on the Sync Bin. Go to File: Export: Batch List. FCP will give you a save window. Name it WT-BL, for Waiting Tables-Batch List and send it to the Desktop (**C**). Close FCP.

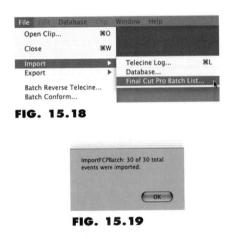

FIG. 15.18

FIG. 15.19

Go through the same process as in the previous section, starting from paragraph four where it says: Open Cinema Tools. The only difference is that when you go to File: Import, you will choose Final Cut Pro Batch List instead of Telecine Log (see Figure 15.18).

CT will ask you where you want to save it: Desktop. It will tell you how many clips are coming in (see Figure 15.19) — the number here will be slightly different than the one in the tutorial.

All the takes will appear in the **List View: WT-CT** dialogue box (see Figure 15.20). Double click on the first one.

A window **Detail View: WT-CT** will come forward from the background (see Figure 15.21). On the right you will see a box that says Connect Clip. Click on this and the Find a Clip window will appear. The first time this window appears, you will have to put some effort into locating the clip in the computer. Find Waiting Tables DVD and then find Capture Scratch. In Capture Scratch there will be a Waiting Tables Project folder and then the files. Find 1A-3. Double click on 1A-3 or click on it and select Choose on the lower right. When you click on Connect Clip for the next take, Cinema Tools will/ should find its way here.

Titled by the clip name, a large window with the first frame of the clip displayed will come up (see Figure 15.22). Here is where we connect the file for the clip with the database. The first thing to do is use the left/right arrow to find an A frame. The frames are identified in the window burn to the right of the key numbers. THIS IS CRUCIAL. Cinema Tools must log onto

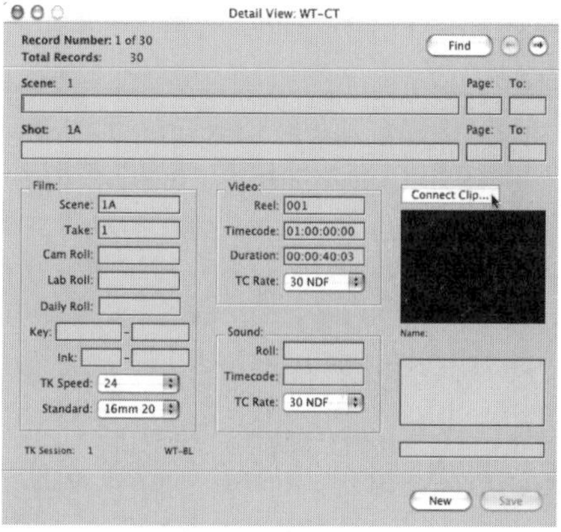

FIG. 15.20

FIG. 15.21

FIG. 15.22

an A frame to track information correctly. The A frame is the only frame where there is a one-to-one relationship between a video frame and a motion picture film frame. All the others begin on a half field or are three fields long. IGNORE THIS AT CERTAIN PERIL. The entire database information will be flawed if you choose any other type of frame.

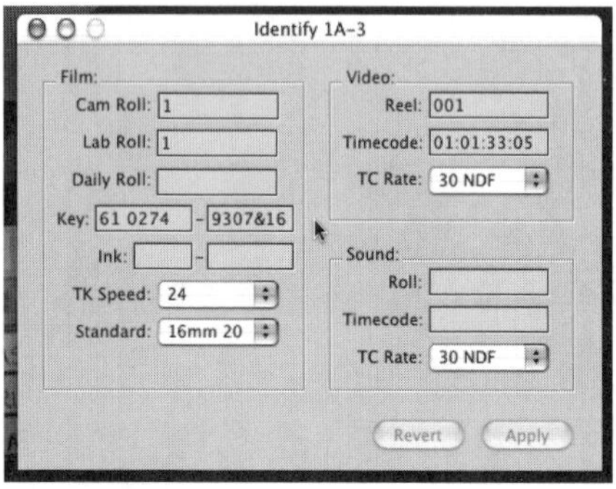

FIG. 15.23

Toggle back and forth on the clip with the left/right arrow buttons until you find an A frame and hit Identify from the right-hand buttons. A smaller window titled with the clip name will appear (see Figure 15.23). There will be four fields (skip Daily Roll for now) that are empty on the upper left: Camera Roll, Lab Roll, Keycode, and Keynum. You will see a place for the previously mentioned ink numbers right below this. In larger projects, these first two will be very important and the information will be needed from the camera and lab reports. In this small project with just two rolls, we can label the first two of these with a number one. The keycode is the identifying number from the roll (in this case 61 0274) and will remain a constant until we go to Camera Roll 2. The next one is the actual edge number and, of course, is the critical one. In our example, we would type in 9307&16. Click Apply and move on.

Except, just to be safe, we want to do one more thing. Recognizing the fact of human error (it is a fact, not a possibility), it is exceptionally easy to occasionally misread or type in a wrong number. Double-check everything. Click on the slider on the bottom of the clip window in CT and

FIG. 15.24

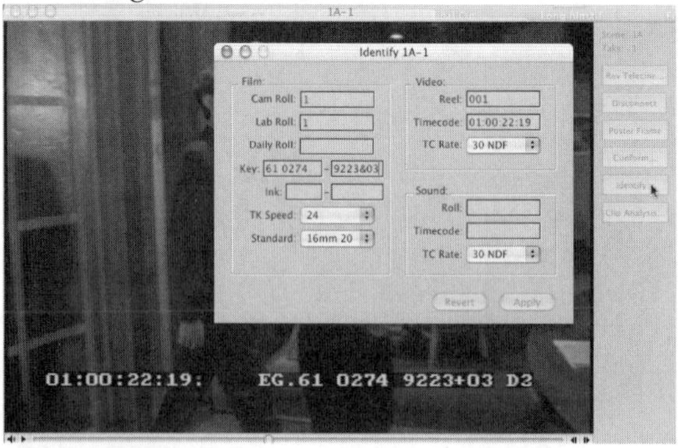

move a little way into the shot. It does not make any difference how far you go but find an edge number that is nice and clear. Click Identify and check to make sure that the edge number on the shot matches the edge number in the identify box (see Figure 15.24). Occasionally you will find slight discrepancies, but move a frame and it will probably line up correctly.

Go through and do this with every clip. It is painstaking but once done, you are good to go. Now Cinema Tools is tracking the relationship between all your edge numbers and the time code.

REVERSE TELECINE

Again, what Reverse Telecine does is to make the 29.97 video into 24-frame video (or you can choose 23.98). It "undoes" the work of 3:2 pulldown by going through all the captured footage — all the Quicktime files — duplicating them while removing that third field for every other transferred frame that was created in telecine. In so doing, it recreates an exact relation frame-for-frame with the film. We go from five video frames for every four film frames to a one-to-one relationship. When we are cutting video in a 24-frame environment, we can thus have an exact relationship with our film frames. Be aware that we are creating entirely new Quicktime files for every clip. We will need almost as much storage as the original capture, although the elimination of that third field makes the files somewhat smaller.

With the CT database open, go to File>Batch Reverse Telecine. The Batch Reverse Telecine window will appear, asking you to find the Capture Scratch Folder that you want to reverse. Go into the Waiting Tables DVD folder, and find and open the Capture Scratch folder. Click on the first file (1A-3) and click OK. After determining one more option, CT will reverse this file and then all the other files in the folder.

TO 23.98 OR TO 24

The next window is important (see Figure 15.25). The choice we faced earlier was whether to cut our piece at 29.97, 24, or 23.98. 29.97 has the drawbacks listed in the previous chapter, but your life will be a little easier. The world is 29.97, at least in our limited sphere, and the slight slippage in sync may be worth the simplicity found staying in that environment. But the "slight slippage in sync" is unacceptable in many realms,

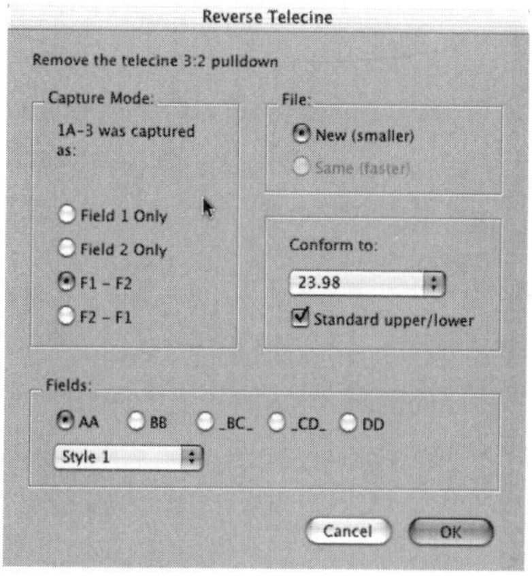

FIG. 15.25

particularly that of features. In this instance we want to use the Reverse Telecine function in Cinema Tools so we can work in a 24-frame environment — the only environment where there is a true one-to-one relationship between film and video frames. Except there is one further complication.

Then the choice is 23.98 or 24 — the options are in the middle-right under Conform to: in the window in Figure 15.25. 23.98 is simply 24-frame video with the 0.1% slowdown of NTSC video applied. The only reason to use 23.98 instead of 24, and it is a big reason, is for playback quality. Your computer can play 24 frame video fine — actually your computer needs to be adapted to play 29.97. But 24 will not play out well to NTSC. The FireWire cannot render the signal to 29.97 compatibility, or can at best render it poorly, depending on the power of your machine. If you want to show it to clients, friends, or test audiences, you can only play your show on your potentially inadequate computer screen. If you have an HD monitor, you are also okay. But as long as the majority of monitors are NTSC, and they are the vast majority, playback will be an issue. If you want to make tapes to send to people for whatever purposes, you have problems with 24.

The only downside of choosing 23.98 is that pulldown and pullup become part of the scenario again. Our audio, unless transferred to Mini-DV, must be pulled down before we sync up (see pages 207-8) and the final product — the final mix — will have to be pulled up to match the answer print.

When the Reverse Telecine process occurs, three new folders will be created in the Capture Scratch file, titled respectively Originals, Reverse, and Skipped (see Figure 15.26). The first is just the original 29.97 files, unless you unchecked Save Originals on the previous window, in which case this folder will not be created. The Reverse folder is your new 23.98 files. Occasionally, Reverse Telecine will skip files for no particular reason other than a slight oddity in the progression from file to file. These can usually be rectified by an individual reverse found on the Details window.

FIG. 15.26

So we have the entire project at 23.98 and our database is in place. We would choose a 23.98 Preset on the Sequence Preset tab in Audio/Video Settings on the Final Cut Pro menu. Now the edit begins and, once finished, we are ready, with the help of Cinema Tools, to create a film print.

FINISHING — BEYOND FCP

As suggested, it is perfectly possible to finish your piece in Final Cut Pro and have a very good product. FCP is a very robust program and you can achieve perfectly adequate results in that environment. However, if finishing on film or for broadcast — or for simply getting the highest quality possible — what you have done in FCP is frequently exported or translated into other environments to create the highest-quality presentation possible. This is standard operating procedure in the commercial world.

The process of matchback — exporting negative cut lists to create a final film print — has already been detailed, but we will walk through the process here. The other two major export processes that are common are finishing the audio in proprietary software (OMF) and doing an online edit with EDLs, going back to your original video transfers for color correction and optimum image quality (see sidebar). The audio export can be done whether you are finishing on film or video. The online edit would be a high-end video finish, whether you originated on film or video. If you originated on film, you could do both a film finish and a high-end video finish if you had the budget and there was a clear purpose. However, your goal is usually one or the other, so justifying the high expense of doing both would require a lot of thought. Both the audio and video finishes are reasonably uncomplicated and bulletproof operations although you, the maker, need to be properly prepared.

The tutorial was entirely cut, we should say recut, at 23.98. Our 29.97 edit was only valuable in that we had already made some of the hard editorial decisions. So we proceeded to take this 23.98 edit, finish the audio, and finish on film.

As suggested in Chapter XI, it was recently common to return to the film negative for a high-end video finish — a film-to-tape finish. The appropriate film takes would be re-telecined at high resolution and the show re-built with EDLs. This should be counted as an option as well, although tape-to-tape finish has become prevalent in most larger markets.

OPEN MEDIA FRAMEWORK

An OMF audio export takes all the sound tracks you have built in your Timeline, on no matter how many tracks, and makes it into a transportable file. It draws from your capture scratch audio files, whether they be aif or Quicktime files or part of linked clip files or whatever. The process of creating the file will take the parts of audio you have used and lay them out on a timeline that can be opened by other software. Audio does not require nearly as much storage space as video, but an OMF file can be moderately sizable. A typical ten-minute piece would yield around a 150 to 200 megabyte file (see sidebar).

If you are doing matchback, be sure to run Cinema Tools to alert for multiple usages before going to the OMF stage. Any usage problems will affect your audio (see page 311).

The starting point for an OMF audio export is to find a post-production studio or individual — the software, while not cheap, could be used in a sophisticated desktop configuration — that is set up to import OMF and do the work. This should be relatively easy to find in most major urban centers. We will go through the questions you need to ask as the discussion progresses. While there are a number of programs you can import into, Pro Tools is one of the most commonly used finishing environments. A typical setup would have Pro Tools on the computer, with a high quality monitor and an excellent speaker system. A post-production facility will usually have an extensive sound effects and music library as well. A catalog of available effects and music would be computerized and the media would either be in files on the computer or available on CDs.

The situation we face in this kind of session has evolved dramatically since the ice age of mixing on mag stock. The major difference is that with mag stock, you had to show up at the mix with all your sound in place and cut to the correct length. In a digital mix, at least for short pieces, you can show up with your base tracks, and then effects and music can be done in the session. This is probably not as good an idea for longer forms, but an awful lot can be done quickly in the session. In the old days, you had to find all the sound, record and/or organize it, transfer it all to mag stock, and then build all the mixtracks on the flatbed editing table. There was modest opportunity to add an effect here or there during the mix and there were scratch mixes and pre-mixes, but if you did not have the majority of work done, you simply did not initiate the final mixdown. Now, you can be building audio tracks as you are creating the information for mixing.

You still need to cut all your base audio tracks in FCP. As suggested, in a professional situation, the editor will work with production sound, maybe a few key effects, and possibly some scratch music — many editors will dissuade this last one because you simply cannot know how the edit fits unless you have the final music. As an individual working on your own project, how much complex sound you build is dependent on how specific your perception is of the character and unique quality of your sound design. If the sound effects you envision are easily obtainable off libraries, the job you do may be pretty bare bones. If you envision much more unique sound and need to execute it yourself, you may be doing extensive recording and track building before exporting your audio.

The simple physical act of mixing has changed as well. In a mag stock mix, if you had an audio fade-out, the rerecording mixer had to slide down the fader in real time as the audio was being committed to tape. Every change had to be done manually, with the rerecording mixers of old looking like a graceful octopus with their hands all over the mixer, shoving faders and twisting dials. Now all movements on the audio — volume changes and signal processing (equalization, reverb, et cetera) — are programmed into the software and are executed identically on every pass. The mixing board, whether a physical one or one from the digital realm existing on a monitor, shifts the faders as if by an unseen phantom hand. If we decide we do not like something — a volume change or whatever — you simply re-program. The session person programs in all shifts and signal processing as the mix is refined and built.

As the situation has changed, so have the titles. The person running the mix in the old days was called the rerecording mixer, a title that indicated that this was a process of rerecording — of laying down to tape — sound that had already been edited into position. The laying-down-to-tape metaphor does not work quite so well in the digital world. What do we call this new person who builds and programs the final audio? Post-production Audio Supervisor suggests they were involved in the editing from the beginning (which they may have been). Effects Editor suggests less than they actually do. Well, no one has quite come up with it yet. They are essentially the session supervisor, so we will call them something approximate to this. This "session person" works primarily on the keyboard, with the CPU not only having the software but also having access to the extensive lists of effects. In the session for *Waiting Tables*, there was a big old mixing board taking up a lot of space on the desk, but like the six-shooters in *The Wild Bunch*, it never got drawn from its holster.

MAKING START MARKS

On *Waiting Tables*, we chose to work with Darin Heinis of Aaron Stokes Music & Sound in Minneapolis because we have a longstanding relationship and respect his work. Darin works with Pro Tools 5.1.3, a typical environment to work with in post-production audio. What he required of us was the OMF file, made from the audio we had already done in Final Cut Pro, transferred to a CD. We also needed the visuals on a separate tape. The OMF files are just composed of audio and we obviously need to be watching the cut picture to make our final decisions.

We transferred the video for *WT* to Mini-DV and then it was brought in separately at the session and played through a function of Pro Tools. Before doing this, we needed to create some kind of start marks so we could sync sound and picture at the session. There are a number of ways of doing this. Check with the studio for what they need. A typical way of doing this is to use the old-fashioned film countdown leader. Countdown leaders are available in the Extras folder on the Final Cut Pro Installation disc. The "2" on the countdown is a single frame, and, as is standard, FCP's countdown leaders have a corresponding single-frame beep tone right across from it. This has been the traditional way of lining up picture and audio in the film world for years.

There are other ways of doing this. In this instance, we just put a couple of frames of random picture a few seconds in front of the first shot. Then we cut a few frames of a constant tone, like the telephone sound, exactly corresponding and the same length on the audio. Check with your post-production studio to see what their standard is.

CREATING THE OMF FILE

FIG. 16.1

FIG. 16.2

Once we have our start marks, we can begin. To make an OMF file:

1. Make sure the Timeline is active. In the menus, go to File>Export>Audio to OMF (see Figure 16.1).

2. The Audio Export dialogue box will appear (see Figure 16.2). Sample Rate for FCP is always 48 kHz and Sample Size is almost always 16-bit. This is something you may want to bring up with your intended session person. The Handle Length box is critical and brings up a previous extended discussion about overlapping audio in order to finesse sound transitions. We recommended that you create handles as you go but, either way, you are going to want to give the session person something with which to work. Recognizing the importance of this, FCP's designers added the ability to give the mixer extra real estate with which to work (as do all NLE programs with OMF). FCP defaults to one-second handles but two seconds was requested as a better safety. The OMF file then draws the audio you have used plus an extra two seconds on either end. Obviously these handles can go back into unwanted material, but the handles do not appear in the opened OMF file. The OMF file opens with just the pieces you have used, but the handles are available in the same non-destructive way it works in FCP. They are there for the session person to draw from if needed. They can drag the clip longer and, from the waveforms or just listening, see what is available to them. Many times the handles provide what is needed. If not, another solution needs to be found. More on that later.

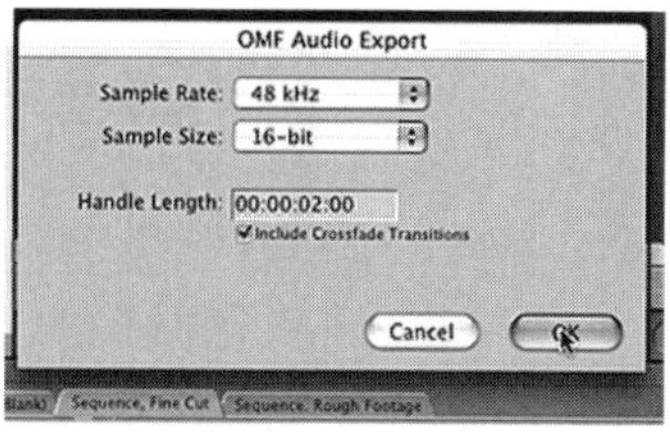

FIG. 16.3

FIG. 16.4

3. FCP will then ask you to name the new file and select a destination (see Figure 16.3). It defaults to the sequence name plus .omf. It is your choice. Having a poor memory for where I send stuff, I always choose the Desktop as destination.

4. FCP will create the file (see Figure 16.4). It will appear on the desktop and can be copied to a CD or whatever media is requested (see Figure 16.5).

Sequence 2.omf

FIG. 16.5

THE SESSION

An OMF file does not open automatically in the import software. In this instance, we used a third-party product, DigiTranslator, and that converted the OMF information to the Pro Tools format. When the piece is appropriately translated it will open with all the tracks arranged horizontally as in FCP. The picture is then brought in and positioned — the studio must have the software and hardware to do this. You are then set to go. The picture comes in as thumbnails across the top of the Pro Tools window and plays in real time through the monitor (see Figure 16.6). The OMF file eliminates any volume and equalization controls you have created, leaving all such decisions to be finalized in the mix.

From here, all the building and the refinement can occur. In this instance, the session person becomes the dialogue editor, effects editor, and music editor. While the order you address things is up to individual choice, Darin began with the dialogue. If you have good speakers on your desktop, you can hear that there are slight differences between the ambience in some of the takes. We did not have permission to turn off all the coolers and refrigerators in the restaurant (a dangerous idea in many instances), so occasionally we hear a slight hum in the background. The goal is to even out the ambience and fill in gaps, and make the dialogue as rich and dynamic as possible.

As suggested, the general approach is to use the handles to finesse each transition and make it sound as smooth as possible. We knew that restaurant sound effects and music would undoubtedly cover up many

FIG. 16.6

flaws, but we still want to create as consistent a track as possible. We then worked on each individual transition in the audio. If you had not A- and B-rolled the audio while cutting, the session supervisor would do so now.

Emulating some of the things we did in evening out our FCP tracks, cross fades were introduced at most dialogue breaks. The transition from "Do you think they are in a hurry?" to "Nah, you've got a few minutes" looked like this on the Pro Tools screen (see Figure 16.7). The diagonal lines are the fade-outs done on the ambience after the individual lines. We can hear the dialogue but the waveforms also indicate beginnings and ends. Once applied, these fade-outs will automatically execute every time the piece is played.

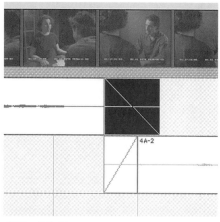

FIG. 16.7

Figure 16.8 shows the way the cut between 3A-2 ("How many letters?") and 5A-2 looked in FCP followed by how the translation in Pro Tools looked.

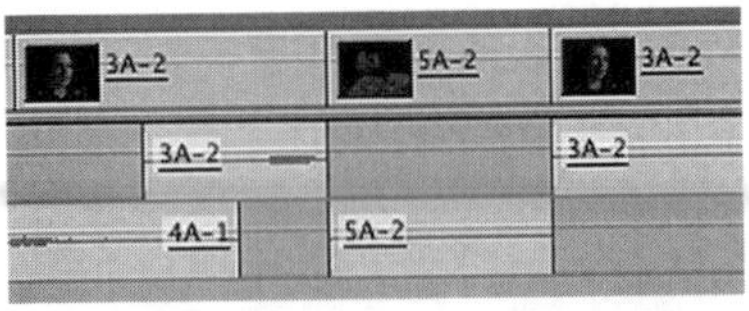

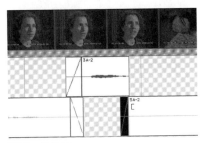

FIG. 16.8

We A- and B-rolled in FCP but did not build a handle here, knowing how fast our session supervisor could do it (see Figure 16.9).

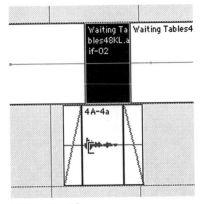

FIG. 16.9

The replaced line was particularly instructive. Some kind of ambient hum was a big presence in the original take, 2A-4. We tried ramping down on the 2A-4 and ramping up on the replacement take, 4A-4, but the absence of the hum in the latter was problematic in that there was a noticeably different quality in the transition. So Darin "stole" a little ambience from another quiet part of the take and "crunched" it into the hole (see Figure 16.10). When you do it this way, there is a possibility there might be slight ambience differences at the cut, owing to differing record levels in the location tracks. We might hear a harsh audio transition when the piece is just laid in the middle. If that were the case, it would have to be taken to another track, expanded, and ramped — finessed — to sound consistent. However, this sounded fine and we knew music and ambience would cover anything we were missing. The black is the "crunched-in" audio ambience.

FIG. 16.10

The phone was next. The recording of the phone was imperfect — there is excess sound of some movement and a slight hum — so we experimented with some library phone sounds. My decision was that I liked the original phone, so we went to work correcting its flaws. As I should have, I had left all the ambience just in case it was needed. Darin listened to the sound and decided to eliminate as much of the ambience as possible in order to eliminate the hum, which is covered up by the actual sound. So he cut as close to the front of the sound as possible and then did a

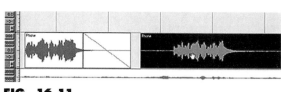

quick fade-out at the end in order to keep the reverberation but not the hum (see Figure 16.11).

FIG. 16.11

EFFECTS

It is typical in a short form like *WT* or particularly in commercials to work entirely from available library effects. There is neither the time nor the budget nor, in all frankness, the interest in doing an extensive original effects campaign. Commercials are not meant for posterity so the effects found in libraries are usually more than adequate. Commercials have a "shelf-life" that is very short and do not need audio that will sound dynamic ten years down the road. On a feature, which has much riding on the distinctive and rich character of the sound, there may be extensive work on recording original and unique sound effects. Another factor is that a commercial is destined for the generally tinny sound of a small TV speaker in a potentially noisy home environment, whereas a feature is going to be on a quality system in the hopefully acoustically perfect theatrical setting, the paper-thin walls of the multiplexes notwithstanding. Unless you are going for something very distinctive in the audio, you will probably go the easy route.

The effects libraries are generally cataloged on the computer's hard drive. In this instance, we typed in "restaurant" to see what kind of general ambience we could find. In the effects you will find anything from very general ambience to very specific clinks of plates or glasses to silverware, et cetera. We scrolled through the multitude of effects and came across some that might fit our purpose (see Figure 16.12).

3010	Restaurant,light	Lunch-dishes,vent hum,traffic in BG
3010	Restaurant,light	Lunch-dishes
3010	Restaurant,med.	Lunch-dishes
3010	Restaurant,heavy	Lunch-dishes,large room
3010	Restaurant,heavy	Dinner-general rumble,dishes ver. # 1
3010	Restaurant,heavy	Dinner-general rumble,dishes ver. # 2

FIG. 16.12

It is supposed to be a slow time in this particular restaurant, so I definitely wanted a very light ambience as a bed below the dialogue. As I listened to the options, even the lightest one was a little busy for my taste. I knew it could be finessed by shifting volume, but was unsure if it could be cleared out as much as I wanted. I knew we also were going to use very quiet music with which the ambience could be blended and, in some instances, covered. The recorded effect was not quite the length of the scene, so we laid it in from the start and then duplicated a little for the end. Darin rode the volume level through it in real time to attempt to get just the right levels in the appropriate places. We then adjusted from there as necessary. Indeed, we were able to tone it down to the extent that it worked perfectly (see the trajectory of his volume control in Figure 16.13, Folio page 8). I also knew I wanted an occasional clink of plates and silverware, so we did a search on that as well. We found some likely prospects and went through and placed them.

The last thing was the music. Phil Aaron of Aaron Stokes very generously allowed us to use one of his jazz pieces. We tried starting it in a variety of different places — before the titles, as the picture started, and a few others — and eventually decided it should start during the main titles. The digital world is a strange world because at that point, we were done. You do not have to execute the mix, it simply is. The mix was then saved as an aif file, which we will be able to easily import into FCP (see Figure 16.14). Figure 16.15 is a representation of the final track layout.

WaitingTablesFINAL.aif

FIG. 16.14

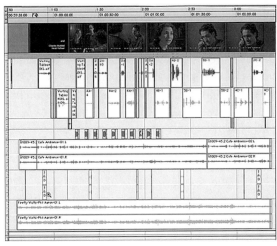

FIG. 16.15

The last step is to bring the new audio back into FCP, syncing it up against the edited show. The mix was given to us on a CD which we loaded into the computer. The file was transferred to the desktop. Then in the menus we went to File>Import>Files. In the Choose a File window, we find the mix and import it into the Browser. At this point, we are going to line it up in the Timeline, but we generally want to line it up free of all the previously built tracks. Given the occasional need to return to original tracks, we do not want to eliminate the base tracks yet, so we will simply duplicate the sequence (click on the sequence in the Browser and go to File>Duplicate). Then we deleted all the old audio in this new sequence — locked the picture and with the aid of (**A**), just deleted each track. We could also use (**A**) to copy the visual and paste it into a new sequence. Then:

1. Park the playhead at the beginning on the first start mark frame.

2. Open the mix in the Viewer and find the beginning frame of tone.

3. Hit Mark In on the Viewer.

4. Do an Overwrite edit.

You can see the video final of the project at WT Project Stereo Mix in the Waiting Tables Media Folder.

CUTTING THE WORKPRINT AND NEGATIVE

If a film finish is the order of business, the next step is to go back to the workprint and conform it to what we have done in the 23.98 FCP edit (not supplied). Again, this is completely for insurance. You will have a negative cut list and you could theoretically just go and cut the negative. The dangers in this have been described, but the workprint is the way features and most sensible people are going. Actually, conforming the workprint is a relatively simple, although time-consuming process. It does, however, require a high level of concentration and scrupulous attention to detail. Where it can get messy is if there are any complications.

The first step is to create the printed list of edge numbers. In the menus go to File>Export>Cinema Tools Film List (see Figure 16.16).

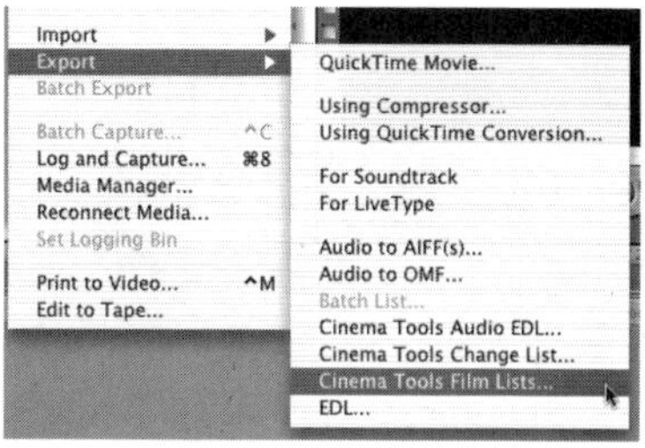

FIG. 16.16

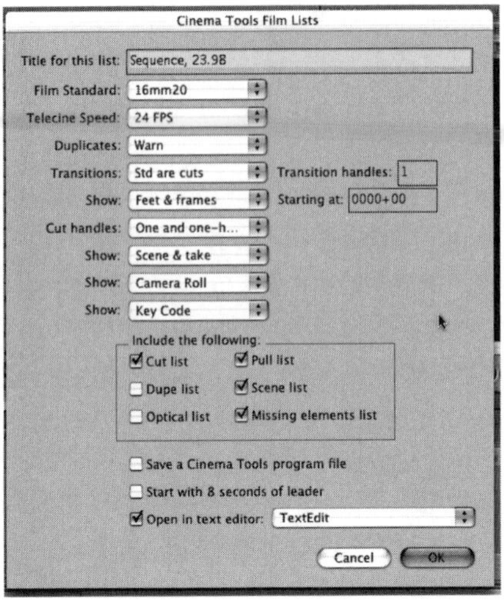

FIG. 16.17

The Cinema Tools Film List window will appear offering a myriad of options (see Figure 16.17).

Most of the defaults on this are adequate for a simple show like *WT*. **Duplicates:** should be left in Warn because it lets you know if you have used any video footage more than once. This would make the negative unconformable if there were any double usages. This includes **Cut handles:**, because, as stated in Chapter XIV, the negative cutter requires a frame and a half of unused negative on every cut. This should be left at one and one-half — the industry standard — unless otherwise instructed by the neg cutter.

So we hit OK and Cinema Tools creates our list. The cut list is included in its entirety on the Waiting Tables DVD in Waiting Tables Documents at WT Negative Cut List.pdf. Here is a small sample of what it looks like (the first two items are the leader and the titles, which were done later). Look at the columns to see what is included. The **In Frame** and **Out Frame** columns list the actual edge numbers.

The cut list in construction order:

Shot	Footage	Length	Keycode	In Frame	Out Frame	Roll	Scene	Take
001	0000+00	0004+32	<missing>		<missing>			
002	0004+32	0008+14	Slug		leader			
003	0013+06	0005+24	K?610274	9369&00	9380&03	1	1A	4
004	0018+30	0010+05	K?610274	9655&06	9675&10	1	2A	4
005	0028+35	0003+17	K?610274	9343&04	9350&00	1	1A	3
006	0032+12	0002+03	K?610274	8909&07	8913&09	2	4A	4
007	0034+15	0001+06	K?610274	9444&03	9446&08	1	1B	1
008	0035+21	0005+08	K?610274	9566&10	9576&17	1	2A	2
009	0040+29	0004+28	K?610274	8833&05	8842&12	2	4A	2

The first time I ran the cut list for *WT*, I found that I had indeed made one stupid mistake (see Figure 16.18). The tightest cut I had

Check for double usages:

Warning: 1 frame(s) re-used from   K?610274-9987&02 to   K?610274-9987&02.
The first usage occurs in program "Sequence 2" with Scene 5A Take 2 at 01:01:27:02.
The second usage occurs in program "Sequence 2" with Scene 5A Take 2 at 01:01:29:15.
The cut list shots are 13 and 15.

FIG. 16.18

was between the first use of 5A-2 and the second use of 5A-2 — it is in this kind of double usage that you will run into the most problems. I had ended the first take at edge number 9987+00 and started the second take at 9987+03. Three frames, right — one and a half per take. If I had taken a minute to think about it, I would have realized my error. This only leaves two frames for the conformist — 9987+01 and 02. This is easy enough to correct as long as I catch the mistake now. We have to trim a frame from the end of the first usage or the beginning of the second. We do this and rerun Cinema Tools.

This is why we recommend you run Cinema Tools Film List before you mix because we cannot just trim that one frame out if our audio is finished. That would leave the picture a frame shorter and everything from that point on would be that one frame out of sync. In this instance, we actually have a very simple solution. We simply trim out the one frame and then make Judy's shot between the 5As one frame longer. This is a very simple usage problem to rectify, but others may not yield themselves to such simple solutions.

Now to conform the workprint. You can do this on a flatbed editing table or with rewinds and a synchronizer. I chose to do it on a table (see Figure 16.19). You start with the uncut workprint, a core to put the assembled new cut on, and the printed list. We build the show from the beginning and

FIG. 16.19

search through the workprint for the shots. Having a camera report is very handy, to quickly know where to find things. In the Figure, the workprint is in the middle and the built show is the roll in the upper right hand corner. Everything is done with a tape splicer. The only real issue is how to count the frames. We will use the very last cut from image to image in the scene as an example. It looks like this in the cut list with the pertinent numbers highlighted:

				In Frame	Out Frame			
028	0096+27	0005+21	K?610274	8472&01	8483&01	2	2C	2
029	0102+08	0003+06	K?610274	9048&18	9055&03	2	4C	1

This is what the cut looks like (see Figure 16.20). The first shot ends at edge number 8403+01, on the right of the Figure, and the second shot begins at 9048+18, on the left of the Figure. Again, the frame with dot on it — above the E in EG1 — is the zero frame

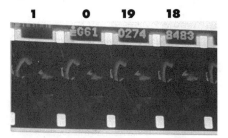

FIG. 16.20

So the counting goes for the first shot: EG61 is zero and the next frame to the left is one. We include the frame that has the number — 8483+01 (see Figure 16.21). Note: There is no number 20 — the zero frame counts as it.

FIG. 16.21

And for the second shot: EG61 is zero and the next frame to the right is nineteen and then eighteen. Cut to the right of this frame (See Figure 16.22). The actual frame with the ascending number is an 18 frame.

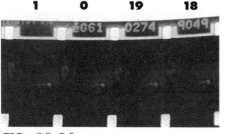

FIG. 16.22

So, assemble the workprint and find a good negative cutter. Leaders will have to be put on and so on. Consult with them about appropriate setup. Mark the workprint as directed in Chapter 14 and, with audio in hand, you are set. If you go this route, we have been recommending as forcefully as possible that you have a lab make a mag stock transfer from the aif file created in the process described in the last section. The lab will have to do the pullup on it for it to be right. Line up the visual and audio on an editing table and make 100% sure they are in sync.

The negative cutter makes the A and B rolls, the lab converts the mag stock master, or whatever source it comes from, to an optical master and you are ready for the lab to take the elements — along with EWP — and make a final print. The lab will color correct and check exposure and create the best looking answer print possible.

THE ONLINE EDIT

The process of onlining is going back to your original tapes or high-resolution telecine transfers and rebuilding the show from them. This process can be done — is done — whether you originated on film or on video. In the film path, if you are a somewhat typical independent, you transferred your film to a high-end tape format, frequently DigiBeta. From there you made Mini-DV or DVCAM clones so you could capture into FCP. In the video path, you created clones from your original tapes to save wear and tear on your originals and because, as in the previous example, Mini-DV or DVCAM was the preferred capture source.

From your FCP edit, you create an EDL. With the Timeline activem, the EDL function is found under File>Export. The EDL and all your original tapes are taken to an online editing facility. These can be very expensive environments, with typical post-production studios charging $700 per hour and up. At this stage, we can do extensive color correction and whatever other sweetening and effects desired. You are using your originals to make a high-quality version of your edited piece, with the EDL's listing of the beginning and ending time code numbers of every clip being used to rebuild your show.

We did not online *Waiting Tables*, so we do not have much graphic material on it, but the process is pretty straightforward. To a certain extent, it is highly anti-climactic. You just sit back and watch it all happen, although you have strong opinions about color correction and you express them clearly. If you have a talented and responsive colorist, they will take what you say and execute and bring a little to the table as well.

In all these paths, the creation of high-quality audio and picture are the heavily pursued goals. FCP can produce an excellent finished product whether you complete it entirely in that environment or take it to a higher level. As suggested, it is not always easy but a polished finished work is the end result for those willing to go through the many steps.

CONCLUSION

As with everything in the computer world, much has changed from the time we started writing this book to its conclusion. The two major strides forward are the advanced power of the MacIntosh G5 and the continued acceptance of Final Cut Pro within the industry. Apple boasts that the latest upgrades of FCP 4 have broken through the Real-Time barrier by fully taking advantage of the power of the new G5 computer. Again, one of the big knocks against FCP has been that it is slow, the amount of time devoted to rendering being one of the chief drawbacks. While there has been some grousing that the new G5s, which crank at incredible rates and need advanced cooling systems to keep them from overheating, are slightly overstating their case, this is a highly significant advance. If this is not a full step, it is very clearly a huge step in overcoming a major obstacle to widespread industry acceptance. Whatever distance, if any, is yet to be traversed will undoubtedly be covered.

To the latter concern, word comes that NBC's *Scrubs* has become the first episodic television program to execute postproduction primarily with FCP. Los Angeles has been an Avid town since the painful evolution away from film editing. But the quality and pricepoint of FCP are starting to make people take notice. There are rumblings in the rumor mill of other shows converting over as well. In addition, the Cohen Brothers edited their last film, *Intolerable Cruelty* (2003), entirely in FCP. The great editor of *Apocalypse Now*, Walter Murch, recently completed *Cold Mountain* (Anthony Minghella, 2003) in Final Cut Pro. Outside of L.A., production companies and television stations are starting to adopt it as well.

One of the major concerns expressed in current trade literature is that Final Cut Pro is an "off-the-shelf" product by a company that has many other product lines as well. FCP's major competitors are dedicated systems coming from companies whose lifeblood is supporting their one series of products. Another common theme is that FCP 3, while an excellent product, could not do all the things needed to be a player in the commercial world. Sound cutting, among other things, was not fine enough and stable enough to hold up. But FCP 4, particularly in conjunction with Cinema Tools and other add-ons, is proving robust enough to prove itself in the marketplace. And a $1000 off-the-shelf product that can hold up to much spendier systems is going to receive high-level consideration. FCP's support, stability, and efficiency have all proved to be viable for commercial work. Indeed, much will have changed between this writing and when this book makes it to the shelves of the local bookstore. Final Cut Pro still does not do some things well. (Interfacing multiple cameras is one example.) But it does many things exceedingly well and rapid improvement continues.

But what does this all have to do with the many independents and beginners who will read this book? Again, one major theme here has been that, unless you are that rare lone-gun iconoclast, you want to involve more and more people in your projects. You cannot possibly do every craft position well. As you involve more people, your approach must, by force, become increasingly professional. You cannot communicate to sound people, titling people, or anyone else unless you have moved the project forward in a way with which other people can work.

Again, Final Cut Pro is not a wonder product. It will not do the work for you. It is a great product at a great price. As you learn more about its potential, you will understand more of the possibilities at your fingertips. Final Cut Pro, or any editing product, will not make you a great editor. I have seen great editing done with a pair of scissors. I have seen horrible editing done on the most expensive NLE systems. But if you challenge yourself, you will only get better.

A NOTE ON FINAL CUT PRO HD

As this book goes to press, Apple has just announced a free upgrade from FCP 4 to FCP HD. This is essentially FCP 4 upgraded to interface over FireWire with the new generation of Panasonic HD cameras. Everything in this book is current, except that you can now work with HD in a native FCP environment without third party hardware. Choices will be found in the menus under Final Cut Pro>Audio/Video Settings in the Sequence Settings tab.

GLOSSARY

A and B roll sound — Bouncing consecutive audio clips from one track to another, providing the opportunity to make the sound consistent.

active window — The window that has last been used. You have to be aware of where you are so that you understand which functions are available and how your actions affect FCP's performance.

ADR — Short for Automated Dialogue Replacement, it is a method of creating new dialogue or replacing dialogue that is deemed unsuitable for either technical or aesthetic reasons.

ambience (presence or **room tone)** — Every space where you shoot will have a specific audio character, even when things are silent. The sound crew will always roll a minute or two of silence to patch in holes in the audio tracks in editing.

base tracks — The tracks that FCP opens to by default, one picture track and four audio tracks.

boom operator — The person who holds the boom with the microphone, used to record the sound from a scene.

camera report — A log of the day's shooting, invaluable in keeping track of production activity but indispensable in the editing room.

capture — The process of bringing media (all your shots and audio) into the computer.

Capture Scratch — A folder where the Quicktime files created from audio and/or video are captured and stored.

CGI — Short for Computer Generated Images, these are usually graphics and/or animation that are created in the computer.

chrominance — The color elements of an image. This is often distinguished from the brightness elements of the image — the luminance.

clip overlays — Horizontal lines running across the length of the clips in the Timeline. The red ones on audio control volume, the black ones on video control visibility.

colorist — See video colorist

color wheel — A circle representing all the shades of color. There are a number of access points to color wheels in FCP.

command key — The command key is next to the Space bar and its use in conjunction with other keys, gives access to many of key operational functions of FCP: Quitting, Saving, et cetera.

component video — Separates brightness and color into separate signals for a higher quality image than composite video. The resulting signal is higher quality but requires extensive bandwidth that can make broadcast problematic.

composite video — Combines all the video information (color and brightness) into a single electrical signal. The signal is relatively simple and can be broadcast easily, but quality can be compromised by difficulties in separation.

compositing — The layering of images generally to create sophisticated special effects.

compression — The discarding of duplicate visual information to facilitate the storage and retrieval of large amounts of information.

CYM —The three subtractive colors of light: cyan, magenta, yellow.

deck control — Refers to an NLE program's ability to control the functions — to drive — an external video playback and recording device through a FireWire or similar connection.

destination control — A button on the left of the Timeline that, when chosen, selects the destination of audio or video that is being edited into the Timeline.

dialogue editor — A member of the editorial team whose main job is to work with the dialogue tracks to make them as even and consistent as possible.

Digital Video (DV) — With caps, denotes a family of digital video formats that interface with the computer with a FireWire connection. Mini-DV, DVCAM, and DVCPro are the three standards.

digital video — With small letters, denotes all video standards that encode a digital signal.

edited workprint (ewp) — The edited version of film made with the workprint version of the film footage shot on location.

edge numbers — Sequentially ascending numbers that are printed into a film stock by the manufacturer. These are critical in going back to the original to make a film print, whether editing film or NLE.

equalization — A term denoting the electronic manipulation of audio at chosen frequencies, in order to lessen or enhance certain elements of the recorded signal. Critical in creating an even and consistent as well as dynamic sound track

external video device — The deck or camera that is connected by FireWire to a nonlinear editing system.

fields — In NTSC, the frame is divided into two fields, each having alternating horizontal lines of information that, when presented sequentially, comprise the image.

files — In terms of FCP, these are Quicktime capture scratch files, assorted types of audio files, or data files that are being imported into or exported out of FCP.

final audio mixdown — When all audio tracks are built exactly as you want, the audio will be mixed down to a final version. In NLE, with all volume and equalization programmed in, this has been simplified to just creating a file.

FireWire — A high-volume transfer mechanism to move media into or between computers.

first assembly or **string out** — The layout of unedited footage in the order of intended use. This was the standard approach in conventional film editing. While unnecessary in a video edit, it can still be very useful to lay the clips out sequentially.

flash frame — When the camera is started, the first and last frames are overexposed because the camera is going slower while getting up to speed. These are used by many postproduction personnel to find and identify the beginning and ends of shots.

flex file — A data file created during telecine. Composed of the beginning and ending time code numbers of every shot, it is used to both drive capture and create a CinemaTools' database.

frames — Discrete still images that, when presented sequentially, provide the illusion of movement.

frames per second (fps) — Film runs at 24 fps in the United States. Different video standards running at a variety of rate, the most common of which is NTSC which runs at 29.97.

freeze frame — The repeated printing of one image within the general flow of a shot. These are used to freeze action.

generations — Successive copies of an analog source.

handles — Overlapping quiet periods of sync taken to finesse the audio transitions from take to take.

HDTV (High Definition Television) — A broad umbrella standard for a newer class of high-resolution digital video.

headroom — The room above a person's head in a composition or the room above 0 on an audio recorder's VU meter.

head — The beginning of a sequence or a roll of film.

ink numbers — A set of inked-in numbers that are applied to picture and accompanying sound in a conventional film edit. Used for maintaining sync and organizing footage. Also invaluable in the matchback process on high-end productions.

interlace — Refers to the NTSC approach to image presentation, where two fields of alternating lines of video information are presented sequentially to comprise the image.

incoming — Refers to the second shot as you execute a cut from one shot to another.

keycode — Kodak's official name for edge numbers.

keyframes — Applied by the pen tool, Add Keyframe buttons, and a few other sources, keyframes plot out the movement in audio and video effects.

key numbers — The set of six letters and numbers that precede the ascending edge numbers. Used to identify rolls and batch numbers.

lined script — A version of script that indicates with vertical lines what shots and takes cover what part of the script.

linking—Concerns the way you connect audio and video clips in the Timeline and elsewhere.

luminance — The brightness elements of an image — often as distinguished from the color elements — the chrominance.

mag stock — The same dimension and construction as the film stock, mag stock is coated with same magnetic recording medium as a conventional tape. It is the standard medium for editing sound in a conventional film edit.

markers — These are available in the Viewer or Canvas and can be applied to mark a place in the video or audio so you can match things to it or find specific points later.

Mini-DV — The consumer standard that was devised by major manufacturers in the early 1990s. It has proved robust enough to be used in semi-professional and professional applications.

mixtracks — The name for the multiple rolls of mag stock that compose the sound for a project in a conventional film edit.

MOS (Mit out Sound) — Clips shot on location where accompanying sound was not recorded. Sound can be eliminated from sync takes and they can then be treated as MOS pieces.

negative — An image with opposite or reversed color and brightness elements. Almost all commercial originating on film is shot on negative because of wider latitude, tighter grain structure, and better printing results.

negative cutter — Also called a conformist, this person conforms the original film to all the decisions made in the film workprint or in an NLE edit.

non-destructive editing — A feature of all but the most consumer NLEs. It is where elements of a trimmed clip can be restored in the Timeline.

NLE — An umbrella term for computer editing systems — the acronym for digital non-linear editing.

NTSC — The broadcast standard for the United States, Japan, Canada, and a number of other countries. Most video in these countries — broadcast, VHS, DVDs, camcorders — record and play the NTSC signal, although a new standard is starting to press — **progressive video** or **HDTV**. More on that later. The other most widely-adopted international standard is **PAL** (Phase Alternating Line). **SECAM** (Sequential Couleur Avec Memoire) is another lesser-used standard, adopted in France, Iraq, and a few other countries.

offline — Editing in a less expensive environment in order to have decisions made before going into an online environment. Clips that are logged but not captured are also considered offline.

online — Finishing editing in an expensive environment that allows many different resources to be brought to bear. Clips that are logged and subsequently captured are considered online. Any media that is available is considered online.

Open Media Framework (OMF) — A cross-platform audio export standard that allows you to work on audio cut in FCP in other software.

Option key — Located to the right of the Command key and allows access to many key functions.

opticals — Visual effects in a motion picture.

original — In film or video, this is the actual film or tape that passed through the camera during shooting. Care for and preservation of the original is critical to creating finished versions of a project.

outgoing — Refers to the first shot as you execute a cut from one shot to another.

PAL (Phase Alternating Line) — A video standard used in the United Kingdom, many European countries, and quite a few other countries around the world.

picture lock — The point where the editorial team declares picture cutting finished. The project is then turned over to a variety of sound editors.

playhead — The vertical line with the yellow triangle on top that indicates where playback is in a show or clip.

production sound — The sound recorded on location or on the set during shooting.

progressive video — A newer video standard that stores each frame of video as a single piece of information to be displayed fully on the monitor. All computers display progressive video.

Real-Time — This is an umbrella term for FCP's ability to playback media created in FCP in real time. This is dependent on the power of your computer and how you set certain playback functions.

rendering — Rendering is the creation of new media based on a change in a clip (add an effect, add titles, do color correction, et cetera) or the creation of something new (like a title).

resolution — The number of pixels per inch in any image.

reversal — A film stock that produces a positive image. Reversal is not used extensively professionally.

reverse telecine — The process of rendering footage from 29.97 to 24 frame or 23.98 video. This process literally undoes the work of 3:2 pulldown.

saturation — The volume of color in an image. Desaturating an image makes it black and white.

script supervisor — The crew member who, among other things, is responsible for keeping track of continuity.

scrubbing — Moving slowly or quickly with the playhead through audio or video.

SECAM — A third video standard that is used in a number of countries.

single-strand cutting — In film or NLE, an editing approach that leaves sync track on one track in the Timeline.

sound mixer — The head of the sound crew. He or she runs the recorder, sets levels and dictates mic positions.

source control — The button on the left of the Timeline that is used to designate the destination of audio or video being brought in from the Viewer or Browser.

synchronizer — A piece of film equipment — generally with four interlocked drums — that locks picture and/or audio together so it is fed through in sync.

synchronous sound — Sound that accompanies picture where voice or any sound occur together. While audio and video are often recorded together, you will increasingly see them as separate entities.

sync takes — Shots where audio was recorded during filming. On film shoots, audio is recorded on a separate recorder, With video, audio is most frequently recorded on the videotape, but can also be done separately.

RGB — The additive colors of light: red, green, and blue.

tail — The end of a sequence or a roll of film.

telecine — A high-end machine where transfer from film to video occurs.

three point editing — The choosing of three in and out points, wherein the fourth point is supplied by the program.

time code — The rolling clock that provides a "permanent address" for all video frames. Embedded in one of a videotape's tracks, it reads in hours; minutes; seconds; and frames.

transitions — An umbrella term for the many devices like fades dissolves and wipes that can get you from one place or time to another.

window burns — These are generally rolling time code and edge numbers that are burned into the image in the lower part of the frame. They play an important, although not indispensable, roll in matchback to film. Many video projects will just have time code burned in because it helps with general organization.

Wireframe — An X shaped frame found in the View menu with which you plot out movements of titles and other images.

workprint — A frame for frame duplicate print made from the original film.

vertical editing — A term denoting that the video on the highest track take precedence over lower tracks. To see things in lower levels, you must manipulate the visibility or transparency of upper level video.

video colorist — The person in a telecine or color correction suite who can manipulate the exposure and/or color of a shot.

visibility — Indicates the settings for a clip that allows one to "see through" the visuals to lower layers of video. Used in superimposing, compositing, and a number of other functions.

zoom tools — There are many tools to change the size and shape of elements in the Timeline, Viewer, or Canvas.

INDEX

A
AB rolling
    completing, 164–165, 317
Action Safe Frame, 134
Active windows, 31, 102, 317
Additive Dissolve, 146
Adobe Reader, 14
Adobe Systems, 3
ADR (Automated Dialogue Replacement), 317
Advanced editing, 121–128
    overlapping cuts, 121–122
    track configurations, 123–128
Ambience, 115, 317
    filling holes in, 245–246
Analog formats, 170–172
    BetaSP, 171
    1 inch, 171–172
    SVHS, 172
    3/4", 172
    VHS, 172
Answer print, 272, 275
Apple, 3
Application, 167–192
    formats, 167–175
    hardware and software, 175–176
    presets and preferences, 176–192
Arrange function, 38
Arrow key, 16
Aspect, 135
Assistant Editor, 200
Atomic Café, 276
Audio, 243–249
    adding sound effects, 155–157
    approach to, 114–118
    building in Final Cut Pro, 154–166
    completing AB rolling, 164–165
    effects and music, 165–166

    filling ambience holes, 245–246
    final mix, 249
    the mixer, 243–245
    replacing dialogue, 162–164
    repositioning sound effects, 157–160
    signal processing, 246–249
    using handles, 245
    volume control, 160–162
Audio capture, 204–207
    subclips, 206–207
Audio Controls, 81
Audio design, 153–166
Audio meters, 90–92
Audio/video settings, 33, 179–182
Auto Kerning, 135
Auto Select control, 81
Automated Dialogue Replacement (ADR), 162
Avid Technologies, 3

B
Backup, 222–223
Base tracks, 79, 317
Batch capture, 293
BetacamSX, 174
BetaSP formats, 171
Bins, 65–66
Black and white, 258
The Blair Witch Project, 263
Boom operator, 115, 317
Bouncing tracks, 118–120
Browser window, 11–12
Butch Cassidy and the Sundance Kid, 234

C
Cable puller, 115
Camera

logic of, 45
Camera reports, 13, 53, 56–57, 317
Canvas window, 11, 74–78
    Fit to Fill, 76, 78
    Insert, 76, 78
    Overwrite, 76, 78
    Replace, 76, 78
    Superimpose, 76, 78
Capture process, 4, 33, 193–210, 317
    audio capture, 204–207
    linking, 209–210
    log and capture, 194–204
    syncing up, 207–208
Capture Scratch, 199, 317
Capture Settings, 197–198, 293
Cement splicer, 273
CGI (Computer Generated Images), 214,
    225, 317
Chrominance, 169, 251, 317
Chuck and Buck, 263
Cinema tools (CT), 14, 287–298
    flex files, 288–298
Clean room, 274
Clip Keyframes, 81
Clip overlays, 81–82, 317
Clips, 11
    finalizing, 24–25
    linked, 23
Clone, 222
Close Gap function, 96
Close-Ups (CU), 105
Cold Mountain, 315
Color correction, 30, 254–258
    black and white, 258
Color Wheel, 133, 318
Colorist, 249–254, 317
    video, 250, 252–254
Command key, 15, 318
Commercial productions, 27
Common effects, 141–147
    drag, drop, and render, 142–147
Component video, 168–169, 318
Composite mode, 149–150
Composite video, 168–169, 318
Compositing, 26–27, 221–222, 238–241,
    318
Compression, 20, 168, 318
Computer Generated Imagery. *See* CGI
Concerns
    critical, 276–277
Conformist, 320
Contextual menus, 62

Continuity, 112
Crawl, 137
Crop tool, 90, 232
Cross Dissolve, 144–145
CT. *See* Cinema tools
CU. *See* Close-Ups
Cut points
    anticipating, 105
Cutting
    on action, 105
    advanced, 121–128
    sound and image, 269–271
    the workprint and negative, 309–313
CYM (cyan, magenta, yellow), 133, 169,
    318

D
D series format, 174
Deck control, 9, 193, 318
Desktop, 59–84
    the audio meters, 90–92
    three (or four) ways to do everything,
        59–62
    the tool palette, 85–90
    tricks, 92–102
    the windows, 62–84
Destination control, 80, 318
DF. *See* Dropframe time code
Dialogue editor, 117
Digital Beta, 174
Digital cameras, 9
Digital formats, 172–175
    BetacamSX, 174
    D series, 174
    Digital S, 173–174
    DVCAM, 173
    DVCPRO/DVCPRO50, 173
    HDTV, 174
    Mini-DV, 20, 173, 320, xv
    24p, 174–175
Digital interface, 9–10
Digital Video (DV), 167, 172–174, 318, xv
Digital VTR, 9, 193
Digitizing, 193
Dip to Color Dissolve, 146
Disbelief
    willing suspension of, 41
Dissolve, 141
Distort tool, 90
Dither Dissolve, 146
Double perf film, 268
Drawing clips up, 96–97

Dropframe (DF) time code, 18, 26
DV Revolution, 47
DVCAM, 9–10, 173, 217
DVCPRO/DVCPRO50, 173

E
ECU. *See* Edit Control Unit
Edge numbers, 260, 273, 284, 287–295, 318
Edit Control Unit (ECU), 42–43
Edit decision lists (EDLs), 28, 213, 309–312
Edit menu, 34
Edit Select tool, 86
Edit to Tape, 34
EditDroid, 2
Edited workprint (EWP), 272, 318
Editing, 103–120
    advanced, 121–128
    approach to audio, 114–118
    bouncing tracks, 118–120
    MOS inserts, 112–114
    saving, 120
    straight cuts, 104–112
Editor, 45–48
    Assistant, 200
    video, 46–48
EDLs. *See* Edit decision lists
Effects, 307–309
    and music, 165–166
Effects menu, 37
El Mariachi, 263
End key, 16
Equalization, 246, 318
EVD. *See* External video device
EWP. *See* Edited workprint
Export function, 33, 292, 294, 309, 313
External video device (EVD), 9, 11

F
Fade, 141, 274–277
Fade In Fade Out Dissolve, 144
Fast motion, 232–233
FBS. *See* Full Body Shots
Fields, 19–20, 278–280, 318
File management, 212
File menu, 33–34
Files, 21, 318
Film matchback, 259–286
    the film process, 266–271
    finishing, 271–277

the matchback process, 265–266
shooting on film, 262–265
the transfer interface, 278–286
the videotape, 278
Film process, 28, 266–271
    cutting sound and image, 269–271
    formats, 268
    length recommendation, 261–262
Final audio mixdown, 30, 319
Final Cut Pro, 315–316
    building audio in, 154–166
    editing process in, 59–62
    finishing in, 243–258
    launching, 10–13
    menu, 33
    specific issues, 31–32
Final mix, 249
Fine cut, 40, 44–45
Finishing, 243–258, 271–277, 299–314
    the answer print, 275
    audio, 243–249
    color correction, 254–258
    the colorist, 249–254
    critical concerns, 276–277
    mix, 272–273
    negative cutting, 273–275, 309–313
    the online edit, 313–314
    Open Media Framework, 300–309
    print to video, 258
    workprint cutting, 309–313
FireWire connection, 9–10, 319
First assembly, 41, 319
Fit
    to Fill, 76, 78
    to window, 102
Fixing sync, 97–98
Flash frame, 199, 319
Flex files, 288–298, 319
    to 23.98 or to 24, 297–298
    the process, 289–294
    reverse telecine, 297
    using cinema tools without, 294–297
Flying Spot Scanner, 21
Formats, 20–21, 167–175, 268
    BetacamSX, 174
    D series, 174
    Digital Beta, 174
    Digital S, 173–174
    DVCAM, 173
    DVCPRO/DVCPRO50, 173
    HDTV, 174

Mini-DV, 20, 173, 320, xv
24p, 174–175
The 400 Blows, 234
fps. *See* Frames per second
Frame rate, 221–222
Frames, 19–20, 319
Frames per second (fps), 19, 319
Freeze frame, 234, 319
Full Body Shots (FBS), 105
Full Frontal, 19, 263
Full Metal Jacket, 41, 121
Function keys, 15–16

G
Generations, 170–171, 319
Gimme Shelter, 234
Graffiti Bridge, 3
Graphics
    CGI, 225
    and compositing workflow, 223–226
    titles/overlays, 223–225

H
Hand tool, 90
Handles, 116, 164–165, 249, 319
    using, 245
Hardware, 175–176
HDTV (High Definition Television), 168,
    174, 319
Head, 29, 319
Headroom, 91, 319
Help menu, 38
High-res, 28
Highlighting, 23
Hill, George Roy, 234
Hiss, 91
Histogram, 252
Home key, 16
Hue, 251
Huston, John, 51

I
IEEE 1394, 9
Image manipulation, 228–234
    crop/distort tools, 232
    freeze frames, 234
    slow motion/fast motion, 232–233
    the video filters menu, 228–229
    the wireframe, 229–232
Import function, 33, 291–294, 309
In points, 29, 43
Incoming, 29, 319

Independent productions, 27
Ink numbers, 319
Insert, 76, 78
Interlace, 319
Intolerable Cruelty, 315

K
Key numbers, 319
Keyboard, 99
    layout, 37
    shortcuts, 15
Keycode, 319
Keyframes, 70, 319
Kubrick, Stanley, 40, 121

L
La Bute, Neal, 121
LBNB. *See* Low budge/no budge
    productions
Leading, 135
Lined script, 53–56, 320
Linking, 23–24, 102, 209–210, 320
    clips, 23
Living in Oblivion, 115
Locking, 102
Logging, 33, 200–202
Long Shots (LS), 105
The Lord of the Rings trilogy, 238, 241
Low budge/no budge (LBNB)
    productions, 27
Low-res, 28–29
LS. *See* Long Shots
Lucas, George, 2
Luminance, 169, 251, 320

M
Macromedia, 3
Mag stock, 269, 320
The Maltese Falcon, 51
Mark Clip, 71
Mark menu, 35
Markers, 70, 320
Marking Controls, 70
Master mix, 272
Master scene technique, 105
Match Cut, 105
Match Frame, 71
Matchback process, 26, 265–266
    in the feature world, 283–285
Matrix series, 238
Maysles, Albert and David, 234
Media

reconnecting, 14, 33–34, 100–101
Media cards, 193
Medium shots (MS), 105
Menu preferences, 190–192
Menus
    contextual, 62
    pop-up, 62
    software, 32–42
Mini-DV, 20, 173, 320, xv
Mini TOC, 17–18
Mix, 272–273
Mixer, 243–245
    rerecording, 30
Mixtracks, 271, 320
Modify menu, 36
MOS (Mit Out Sound), 28, 320
    inserts, 112–114
Motion tab, 234–238
Moving around
    in the timeline and clips, 92–93
MS. See Medium shots
Murch, Walter, 51

N
National Television Systems Committee.
    See NTSC
NDF. See Nondropframe time code
Negative cutter, 273, 320
Negative cutting, 273–275
Negatives, 267, 320
Nesting, 97
NLE. See Nonlinear editing
Noise floor, 91
Non-Additive Dissolve, 146
Non-destructive editing, 30, 320
Nondropframe (NDF) time code, 18, 26
Nonlinear editing (NLE), 3, 42–45, 286,
    320
NTSC (National Television Systems
    Committee), 19, 168, 320
    monitor, 11
Numeric keypad, 16
NYPD Blue, 48, 61, 216–217

O
Offline files, 14, 29, 201, 320
Once Upon a Time in Mexico, 264
1 inch formats, 171–172
One row film, 268
Online edit, 313–314
Online files, 29, 320

Open Media Framework (OMF), 153,
    300–309, 320
    creating the OMF file, 303–304
    effects, 307–309
    making start marks, 302–303
    the session, 304–307
Optical master, 273
Opticals, 227, 275, 321
    printer, 227
Option key, 23, 102, 321
Origin option, 134
Original, 267, 321
OS X, 15
OTS. See Over-the-Shoulder Shot
Out points, 29, 43
Outgoing, 29, 321
Outline, 138
Over-the-Shoulder Shot (OTS), 105
Overlapping cuts, 121–122
Overlays
    titles, 223–225
Overwrite, 76, 78

P
PAL (Phase Alternating Line), 19, 320–321
    monitor, 11
Paperwork, 53–57
    camera reports, 56–57
    the lined script, 54–56
Pen Delete, 90
Pen Smooth, 90
Pen tool, 90
Phase Alternating Line. See PAL
Picture lock, 117, 321
Playhead, 64, 321
Pop-up menus, 62
Preferences, 176–192
    menu, 190–192
    user, 182–185
Premiere (Adobe), 3
Presence, 115, 317
Presets, 176–192
    audio/video settings, 179–182
    easy setup, 178–179
    sequence>settings, 188–190
    system settings, 186–188
Prince, 3
Print to Video, 34, 258
Printer lights, 275
Production sound, 115, 321
Program time code, 18, 148

Progressive video, 320–321
Pullup and pulldown, 278, 281–282

Q
Quicktime, 13

R
Rae, Freya, 51, 54
Razor Blade tool, 89
Reading the script, 50–51
Real-time (RT), 24–26, 139, 321
Reconnecting media, 14, 33–34, 100–101
Reference issues, 28–30
Rendering, 24–25, 139–141, 321
Replace, 76, 78
Replacing dialogue, 162–164
Repositioning sound effects, 157–160
Resolution, 28–29, 321
Reversal, 267, 321
Reverse telecine, 282–283, 297, 321
RGB Parade, 252
RGB (red/green/blue), 30, 133, 322
Ripple Delete key, 96
Ripple Dissolve, 146
Ripple tool, 86–88
Rodriguez, Robert, 263–264
Roll tool, 86–88
Room tone, 115, 317
Rough cut, 40–42
Rough footage, 51
RT. *See* Real-time
Runtime limitations, 212–213

S
Sampling rates, 169
Saturation, 251, 321
Saving, 102, 120
Scratch Disks button, 198
Script
    reading, 50–51
Script supervisor, 53, 321
Scrolling Text, 138
Scrub Video tool, 90
Scrubber bar, 63
Scrubbing, 64, 321
Scrubs, 315
SECAM (Sequential Couleur Avec
    Memoire), 320–321
Select Track, 96–97
Selection tool, 85–86
Selects, 41

Sequence menu, 36
Sequence timeline, 65
Sequence>settings, 188–190
Services, 33
Session, 304–307
Settings..., 36
Setup
    easy, 178–179
The Shape of Things, 121–122
Shoot on film, 262–265
Shoot on film, edit on video
    finish on film, 219–220
    finish on video, 215–219
Shoot on video, edit on video
    finish on film, 220–221
    finish on video, 214–215
"Shooting for the edit," 105
Shots, 11
The Show, 32
Signal processing, 246–249
Single perf film, 268
Single-strand cutting, 114, 321
Slide tool, 86–88
Slip tool, 86–88
Slow motion, 232–233
Snapping, 31
Soderbergh, Steven, 19
Software, 175–176
Software menus, 32–42
    Edit menu, 34
    Effects menu, 3
    File menu, 33–34
    Final Cut Pro menu, 33
    Help menu, 38
    Mark menu, 35
    Modify menu, 36
    Sequence menu, 36
    Tools menu, 37
    View menu, 34–35
    Window menu, 38
Solo, 81
Sound effects
    adding, 155–157
    repositioning, 157–160
Sound mixer, 115, 321
Source control, 80, 321
Special effects, 227–241
    compositing, 238–241
    image manipulation, 228–234
    the motion tab, 234–238
Stages, 39–45

Start marks
    making, 302–303
Storage limitations, 212–213
Straight cuts, 104–112
String out, 41, 319
Subclips, 206–207
Superimposition/layering video, 76, 78,
    147–152
    composite mode, 149–150
    supering titles, 150–152
Supering titles, 150–152
SVHS formats, 172
Sync takes, 322
Synchronization, 2
    fixing, 97–98
Synchronizer, 270, 322
Synchronous sound, 22–23, 322
Syncing up, 22, 207–208, 270
System preferences, 33
System settings, 186–188

T
Tail, 29, 322
Tape splicer, 269
Telecine log, 288
Telecines, 21–22, 215–216, 261, 322
Terminator films, 264
Three point editing, 322
3/4" formats, 172
3:2 pulldown, 279–281
Thumb tabs, 82
Time code, 18–19, 322
    dropframe, 18
    nondropframe, 18
    program, 18
    traveling with, 93
Timecode..., 36
Timeline window, 11–13, 78–84
Timemap tool, 86–88
Timer, 275
Title Safe Frame, 134
Titles
    creating, 129–138
    overlays, 223–225
Tool palette, 85–90
Tools
    menu, 37
    missing, 102
Track Height, 82
Track Locks, 81
Track Select tool, 86

Track Visibility controls, 79
Tracks, 4, 135
    configurations, 123–128
    creating new, 98–99
Tracks, working on linked, 23
Transfer interface, 278–286
    how the feature world is doing
    matchback, 283–285
    our approach with *Waiting Tables*,
    285–286
    pullup and pulldown, 281–282
    reverse telecine, 282–283
    3:2 pulldown, 279–281
Transitions, 32, 322
Transport Controls, 68, 71
Tricks, 92–102
    creating new tracks, 98–99
    drawing clips up, 96–97
    fit to window, wireframe, and
    missing tools, 102
    fixing sync, 97–98
    keyboard, 99
    moving around in the timeline and
    clips, 92–93
    reconnecting media, 100–101
    trimming clips, 93–96
Trim Edit window, 94–95
Trimming clips, 93–96
Truffaut, Francois, 234
Tutorial, 48–53
    copying, 13–14
    notes on, 52–53
    reading the script, 50–51
    rough footage, 51
24p format, 174–175
Two row film, 268
Typewriter, 138

U
Undo, 31–32
Use Subpixels, 135
User preferences, 33, 182–185

V
Vectorscope, 252
Vernie, 213, 221
Vertical editing, 147, 322
VHS formats, 172
Video colorist, 250, 322
Video editor, 46–48
Video filters menu, 228–229

Video scopes, 252–254
Videotape, 28, 278. *See also* Audio/video
  settings
View menu, 34–35
Viewers, 66–74
Visibility, 135, 322
Volume control, 160–162
VTR
  digital, 9

W
Waiting Tables, 4, 238, 285–286
Waveforms, 67, 153
  monitoring, 252
The Wild Bunch, 302
Window burns, 26, 322
Window menu, 38
Windows, 15, 62–84
  active, 31, 102, 317
  the Browser, 64–66
  the Canvas, 74–78
  fit to, 102
  the Timeline, 78–84
  the Viewer, 66–74
Wireframe, 102, 229–232, 322
Workflow, 211–226

backup, 222–223
the big four, 214–221
edit decision lists, 213
file management, 212
frame rate blessings or blues, 221–222
graphics and compositing workflow,
  223–226
shoot on film, edit on video, finish
  on film, 219–220
shoot on film, edit on video, finish
  on video, 215–219
shoot on video, edit on video, finish
  on film, 220–221
shoot on video, edit on video, finish
  on video, 214–215
storage and runtime limitations,
  212–213
Working methods, 42–44
Working style, 59–62
Workprint, 267, 322

Z
Zoom Control, 82
Zoom Slider, 82
Zoom tools, 89–90, 322

ABOUT THE AUTHORS

BRUCE MAMER

Bruce Mamer currently teaches film production full-time after many years of freelance experience in features, independents, commercials, and documentaries. He has worked in numerous capacities in the industry, from directing social service and independent films to working on lighting and camera crews to doing extensive location and studio sound work. He received his Master's degree in film history and criticism from Southern Illinois University–Carbondale in 1978 and is presently at Minneapolis College in Minneapolis, MN, teaching all levels of film production. He is also the author of a major textbook on film production.

JASON WALLACE

Author Jason Wallace is an award-winning film and video producer/director/editor who lectures and consults on current trends in film production technology. He has produced, directed, and edited an extensive list of short films and video projects throughout his eleven years in the industry. In 2000, Wallace was co-producer and editor on the 35mm feature film *Mulligan* while his own narrative short film *Escape Attempt* was broadcast nationally on the Independent Film Channel. Most recently he produced and edited the 24p feature film *Vernie* that is currently seeking distribution. He also teaches editing with Final Cut Pro through Minneapolis College's Continuing Education Program. As a guest lecturer and panelist, he is frequently asked to discuss the process of low-budget film and video production. He lives and works in Minneapolis.

MICHAEL WIESE PRODUCTIONS
www.mwp.com

We are delighted that you have found, and are enjoying, our books.

Since 1981, we've been all about providing filmmakers with the very best information on the craft of filmmaking: from screenwriting to funding, from directing to camera, acting, editing, distribution, and new media.

It is our goal to inspire and empower a generation (or two) of filmmakers and videomakers like yourself. But we want to go beyond providing you with just the basics. We want to shake you and inspire you to reach for your dreams and go beyond what's been done before. Most films that come out each year waste our time and enslave our imaginations. We want to give you the confidence to create from your authentic center, to bring something from your own experience that will truly inspire others and bring humanity to its full potential — avoiding those urges to manufacture derivative work in order to be accepted.

Movies, television, the Internet, and new media all have incredible power to transform. As you prepare your next project, know that it is in your hands to choose to create something magnificent and enduring for generations to come.

This is not an impossible goal, because you've got a little help. Our authors are some of the most creative mentors in the business, willing to share their hard-earned insights with you. Their books will point you in the right direction but, ultimately, it's up to you to seek that authentic something on which to spend your precious time.

We applaud your efforts and are here to support you. Let us hear from you.

Sincerely,

Michael Wiese

Filmmaker, Publisher

THE EYE IS QUICKER
Film Editing: Making A Good Film Better

Richard D. Pepperman

Did you ever want to know how to apply simple and practical work techniques to all that film editing theory? Here is an authentic "how-to" guide — adaptable to all tools and technologies — to make you a better editor of film or video. This is the most comprehensive book on the principles, methods, and strategies vital to the creative art of film editing.

Pepperman's vibrant approach uses dozens of terrific sequences from a wide array of films to teach you how editing can make a good film better. He defines what is constant in all great work and gives you all the tips you need to achieve your own greatness.

The Eye is Quicker is indispensable for screenwriters, directors, and, of course, film and video editors.

"The qualities that have made Richard so inspiring and beloved a teacher — passion, curiosity, humor, and humility — make this book as alive and enticing as a class or conversation with him. *The Eye Is Quicker* will benefit future generations of film editors. It is a very good read for film lovers, and a rich mine for practitioners in the other arts."
— Jennifer Dunning, *New York Times*

"Pepperman brings decades of experience as an editor and teacher to lessons supported by example and illustration. Here is a voice that is caring and supportive. To read *The Eye Is Quicker* is to attend a master class."
— Vincent LoBrutto, Author, *Stanley Kubrick: A Biography*

Richard D. Pepperman is a teacher and thesis advisor at The School Of Visual Arts, where he has been honored with the Distinguished Artist-Teacher Award.

$27.95 | 350 pages | Order # 116RLS | ISBN: 0-941188-84-1

FILM DIRECTING: SHOT BY SHOT
Visualizing from
Concept to Screen

Steven D. Katz

Over 160,000 Sold! International best-seller!

Film Directing: Shot by Shot — with its famous blue cover — is the best-known book on directing and a favorite of professional directors as an on-set quick reference guide.

This international bestseller is a complete catalog of visual techniques and their stylistic implications, enabling working filmmakers to expand their knowledge.

Contains in-depth information on shot composition, staging sequences, visualization tools, framing and composition techniques, camera movement, blocking tracking shots, script analysis, and much more.

Includes over 750 storyboards and illustrations, with never-before-published storyboards from Steven Spielberg's *Empire of the Sun*, Orson Welles' *Citizen Kane*, and Alfred Hitchcock's *The Birds*.

"(To become a director) you have to teach yourself what makes movies good and what makes them bad. John Singleton has been my mentor... he's the one who told me what movies to watch and to read *Shot by Shot*."
— Ice Cube, *New York Times*

"A generous number of photos and superb illustrations accompany each concept, many of the graphics being from Katz' own pen... *Film Directing: Shot by Shot* is a feast for the eyes."
— *Videomaker Magazine*

Steven D. Katz is also the author of *Film Directing: Cinematic Motion*.

$27.95 | 366 pages | Order # 7RLS | ISBN: 0-941188-10-8

URS | 1.800.833.5738 | www.mwp.com

DIRECTING FEATURE FILMS
The Creative Collaboration between Directors, Writers, and Actors

Mark Travis

The director is the guide, the inspiration, the focus that can shepherd hundreds of artists through the most chaotic, complex collaboration imaginable. But how does one person draw all these individuals together to realize a single vision?

Directing Feature Films takes you through the entire creative process of filmmaking — from concept to completion. You will learn how to really read a script, find its core, determine your vision, and effectively communicate with writers, actors, designers, cinematographers, editors, composers, and all the members of your creative team to ensure that vision reaches the screen.

$26.95 | 402 pages | Order # 96RLS | ISBN: 0-94118-43-4

FROM WORD TO IMAGE
Storyboarding and the Filmmaking Process

Marcie Begleiter

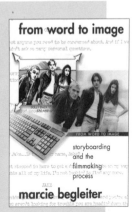

Whether you're a director, screenwriter, producer, editor, or storyboard artist, the ability to tell stories with images is essential to your craft. In this remarkable book, Marcie Begleiter offers the tools to help both word- and image-oriented artists learn how to develop and sharpen their visual storytelling skills via storyboarding.

Readers are taken on a step-by-step journey into the previsualization process, including breaking down the script, using overhead diagrams to block out shots, and creating usable drawings for film frames that collaborators can easily understand. Also includes discussions of compositional strategies, perspective, and figure notation as well as practical information on getting gigs, working on location, collaborating with other crew members, and much more.

$26.95 | 224 pages | Order # 45RLS | ISBN: 0-941188-28-0

ORDER FORM

ORDER THESE PRODUCTS, PLEASE CALL 24 HOURS - 7 DAYS A WEEK
IT CARD ORDERS 1-800-833-5738 OR FAX YOUR ORDER (818) 986-3408
OR MAIL THIS ORDER FORM TO:

MICHAEL WIESE PRODUCTIONS
11288 VENTURA BLVD., # 621
STUDIO CITY, CA 91604
E-MAIL: MWPSALES@MWP.COM
WEB SITE: WWW.MWP.COM

WRITE OR FAX FOR A FREE CATALOG

PLEASE SEND ME THE FOLLOWING BOOKS:

TITLE	ORDER NUMBER (#RLS _____)	AMOUNT
	SHIPPING	
	CALIFORNIA TAX (8.00%)	
	TOTAL ENCLOSED	

SHIPPING:
ALL ORDERS MUST BE PREPAID, UPS GROUND SERVICE ONE ITEM - $3.95
EACH ADDITIONAL ITEM ADD $2.00
EXPRESS - 3 BUSINESS DAYS ADD $12.00 PER ORDER
OVERSEAS
SURFACE - $15.00 EACH ITEM   AIRMAIL - $30.00 EACH ITEM

PLEASE MAKE CHECK OR MONEY ORDER PAYABLE TO:

MICHAEL WIESE PRODUCTIONS

(CHECK ONE) ____ MASTERCARD ____VISA ____AMEX

CREDIT CARD NUMBER _____

EXPIRATION DATE _____

CARDHOLDER'S NAME _____

CARDHOLDER'S SIGNATURE _____

SHIP TO:

NAME _____

ADDRESS _____

CITY _____ STATE _____ ZIP _____

COUNTRY _____ TELEPHONE _____

ORDER ONLINE FOR THE LOWEST PRICES

24 HOURS | 1.800.833.5738 | www.mwp.com